THE FIRST MESSIAH

THE
FIRST
MESSIAH

INVESTIGATING THE SAVIOR
BEFORE JESUS

MICHAEL O. WISE

HarperSanFrancisco
A Division of HarperCollins*Publishers*

HarperCollins books may be purchased for educational, business, or sales promotional use. For information please write: Special Markets Department, HarperCollins Publishers, Inc., 10 East 53rd Street, New York, NY 10022.

HarperCollins Web Site: http://www.harpercollins.com

HarperCollins,® 👑,® and HarperSanFrancisco™
are trademarks of HarperCollins Publishers, Inc.

FIRST EDITION

Library of Congress Cataloging-in-Publication Data
Wise, Michael Owen 1954–
The first messiah : investigating the savior before Jesus / Michael O. Wise. — 1st ed.
p. cm.
Includes bibliographical references.
ISBN 0-06-069645-1 (hardcover)
ISBN 0–06–069646-X (pbk.)
1. Thanksgiving Psalms—Criticism, interpretation, etc.   2. Teacher of Righteousness.
3. Messiah—Judaism—History of doctrines.   I. Title.
BM488.T5W57   1999
296.3´36—dc21   98-30670

99 00 01 02 03 RRD(H)❖ 10 9 8 7 6 5 4 3 2 1

FOR CATHY, MY WIFE

without whom this book would have been

neither conceived nor born

CONTENTS

ACKNOWLEDGMENTS

I have been thinking about many of the ideas in this book for years. Yet the work drew its particular impetus from an informal graduate seminar on the ancient Jewish writing called *Thanksgiving Hymns* (also known by its Hebrew name, *Hodayot*) held in the summer and fall of 1995. This was a small seminar, indeed; it comprised just two people.

Each week Michael Douglas and I would meet in the main library of the University of Chicago to discuss a new hymn, its interrelationships with other ancient literature, and modern pathways to interpretation. We read widely in the relevant sociological and anthropological scholarship, wrestling with and debating the semantics of ancient Hebrew in the light of Second Temple history and the comparative study of millenarian movements.

Our understanding of the hymns fed off the dynamic of these seminar meetings, to the point that neither of us can any longer say precisely who thought what first. In any case, we came to a basic agreement on a new historical and social model for understanding the *Thanksgiving Hymns,* and though we arched in different directions after ignition and lift-off, these meetings launched both Douglas's dissertation and the present volume. The seminar also pushed us to write together a detailed commentary on the text. That book will address a variety of technical issues that lie outside the present purview. I want to signal my profound indebtedness to Dr. Douglas, and at the same time simply to say, "Thank you, my friend, for all your help and stimulation in the quest for understanding."

I have also benefited enormously from lengthy give-and-take with Professor James Tabor of the University of North Carolina at Charlotte, our discussions ranging across the topics of ancient Jewish biblical interpretation, millennial hopes, modern sectarianism, and Jesus. Professor Tabor has probably known and talked with more messianic claimants than any man or woman alive. He was unfailingly generous with his help, guiding me to obscure bibliography familiar (almost only) to him, and prodding me to think thoughts that would otherwise never have occurred to me. To him I say, "Thanks, Jim."

Many other colleagues have offered helpful suggestions, criticisms, or encouragement along the way, but particular thanks must go to Professor

Norman Golb of the University of Chicago, Professor Douglas Penney of Wheaton College, and to a number of my colleagues at Northwestern College: Dr. Charles Aling, Dr. Clyde Billington, Dr. Ardel Caneday, Dr. Douglas Huffman, Dr. David K. Johnson, Mr. Mark Muska, Mr. Randy Nelson, and Dr. John Sailhamer. The administration of the college has likewise done much to encourage my scholarship, and I am deeply appreciative.

This book has benefited in a special way from the kindness and giftedness of women in my family. My mother, Ms. Imogen Wise, is probably the most widely read person I have ever met; she examined each chapter as critically as a mother can be expected to do, and also offered suggestions for analogies and illustrations whenever I would call and ask for help with an idea. My sister, Ms. Victoria Truesdale, is the person everyone always thought would become the writer in the family. (Strange that it turned out to be me, the would-be professional baseball player who spent his adolescence devouring the *Baseball Encyclopedia* rather than great literature. But I do know how many batters Walter Johnson struck out in 1911.) Vicki generously put her literary training and her talent at my disposal in improving my work. Thank you, Vicki; thank you, Mom.

My wife, Cathy, was the most help of all. She discussed with me the concept of the book and how to present it. She was right there with me each step of the way, from beginning to end, talking over my ideas, helping me to formulate them more clearly, to express them more precisely. She read and critiqued every chapter; typically, I would be defensive at first, but finally muster the intelligence to see that she was right in most of her criticisms. Cathy was especially helpful in red-flagging my occasional slips into academic prose or overly technical writing. And she was always ready to offer encouragement when that was needed, but never falsely, and always in love. All of these things were over and above the sacrifices she made in allowing me to work—to write and rewrite, prepare lectures and teach— while she kept our home together. Words haven't the power to express my thanks, Cathy, and I won't ask them to try. Let us meet on that higher plane of the soul, and there let me tell you what ears cannot hear.

The writer's adage has it that a man needs but one wife and one editor. My editor, Mr. Mark Chimsky, has shown me the wisdom of that saying, and improved every page of this book while proving to be that rare person: a friend in time of trouble. Thank you, Mark. Mark's assistant, Mr. Eric Hunt, has also been unflaggingly helpful in facilitating communications and keeping track of details.

September 1998, St. Paul, Minnesota

CHAPTER 1

OF MESSIAHS
AND MYTH-DREAMS

All men dream: but not equally. Those who dream by night in the
dusty recesses of their minds wake in the day to find that it was van-
ity: but the dreamers of the day are dangerous men, for they may act
their dream with open eyes, to make it possible.

> T. E. Lawrence, the suppressed introductory chapter for *The
> Seven Pillars of Wisdom*

I know that everything you are, you are through me, and everything
I am, I am through you alone!

> Adolf Hitler, to the people of Germany

IN THE MID–1960s a group of Pacific Islanders living on New Hanover,
Papua New Guinea, raised one thousand dollars to buy President Lyndon
Johnson. Their plan was to present him with this sum—a fortune in their
eyes—and so induce him to come be their leader.[1]

"How strange!" we may think, intending to relegate the matter to life's
curiosity file, or perhaps to submit this fact to the *Guinness Book of World
Records,* as representing simultaneously the highest and the lowest valuation ever placed on an American president. That these islanders might
somehow constitute a piece of the puzzle for understanding Jesus would
never cross our minds. And yet they do.

Moreover, the thinking of these islanders backlights another figure, a man whose very existence was long ago forgotten, a man who, all unrecognized, has had a profound impact on European—and hence Western—civilization. I speak of a Jerusalem priest who died a century before Jesus confronted Pilate, a man whose ideas of God, and of what God was about to do, impelled the Jews of his day toward conflict, brother against brother. I speak of a man whose beliefs about himself were to change his world, a world into which Jesus of Nazareth would one day be born, and so change the course of history. I speak of a man only now rediscovered.

I speak of the first messiah.

The islanders of New Guinea; the earliest followers of Jesus; the movement founded by the first messiah—these were all species of what social anthropologists call "crisis cults." What precisely does this provocative phrase mean? A measure of the answer lies in the jungles of the South Pacific.

CARGO CULT

Imagine yourself born black on a tropical island seven hundred and fifty miles northeast of Australia. Although in your midtwenties, you have never been more than a few miles from the village of your birth. Your family and everyone you know subsists by hunting and cultivating large gardens on the outskirts of the village. For generations this has been the way of life, an existence laboriously hewn out with stone tools—but someday things will change. You have been taught that your dead ancestors and those of everyone else in the village will return, ghostly spirits in great ships, bringing gifts and ushering in an era of utopian plenty.

Imagine further your excitement when one blaze-blue afternoon a ship appears silhouetted on the horizon, different in design and far larger than anything your people have ever built. You squint against the moist salt wind in your face, eyes tearing, straining to see. Sails billowing full, the ship veers in toward shore. As it draws near, you are stunned to make out light-skinned figures scurrying back and forth on the deck, readying the ship for port. The ancestors!

When the ship has come to ground, you and all the village crowd about the strange white newcomers and admire the treasures they have brought with them. Here is a workmanship and a wealth beyond all that the legends have described. Yet soon develops a puzzling problem.

These light-skinned people and their actions correspond to your beliefs about what the dawn of the millennium will bring in every way—except one: they refuse to hand over the fabulous cargo. Instead, they keep it for themselves. What can it mean? Who are they? Are they really the ancestors after all? You and many others begin to suspect not. Now the issue becomes how to get the goods that the spirits intended for you but that these greedy interlopers have somehow intercepted.

This scenario or one much like it played out repeatedly in the middle of the nineteenth century. It gave rise to a type of crisis cult known as "cargo cult."[2] These movements first arose as early as 1885 in Fiji, soon after Europeans began arriving in Melanesia in force, and they continue to this day. The islanders who sought to buy Lyndon Johnson belonged to such a group. Thousands of people dropped all normal activities to await Johnson's appearance on a mountaintop, expecting him to rule over them and bestow upon them the vast wealth of the United States.

Participants in a cargo cult engage in various exotic rites in order to entice the spirits to grant them Western manufactured goods, from axes to aspirins. They construct large, thatched houses called "aeroplanes" or "ships" to receive the goods. In elaborate ceremonies they dance and whirl, chant and shake, sometimes foaming at the mouth. They may copulate promiscuously in ritual. Europeans have been threatened, even attacked, for it is obvious that they know how to tap the spiritual source of the cargo, yet they continue to deny the islanders a share in the secret.

The fact that Europeans possess these goods is a source of baffled resentment and chagrin for the Melanesians. Long years of observing the foreigners have convinced them that the whites are not half the people the islanders themselves are. All they seem to do is sit and fan themselves while issuing commands. It is the islanders who do all the work. Why then should these whites, useless for every practical task, have been given the secret of the cargo? And to make matters worse, the interlopers are invincible in battle.

In 1937 in the Madang district of New Guinea, a man called Mambu led one of the best documented of these cargo movements. Mambu was a native of Apingam and had been baptized a Roman Catholic (along with the cargo, white people brought missionaries). One December morning of that year, after a period as a contract laborer in Rabaul on the coast, Mambu returned home and was discovered at 5 A.M. in the local church. There he had carried out all the preparations for the service that was to begin an hour later, although these preparations were the duties of the missionary and his assistants. Mambu was severely rebuked by the missionary.

A week or so later, Mambu was passing the church when the bell began to peal for the evening prayers. One was supposed to stand and pray, but instead Mambu knelt. These were the first intimations that the islander had begun to construct a new doctrine.

Soon thereafter word reached the mission that Mambu was at the fore of a burgeoning new movement in the hinterland. His doctrine was a mélange of traditional native beliefs and Christianity, but it was distinctly antiwhite and antigovernment. Since the whites had discriminated against the islanders and had deceived them, he argued, it was no longer necessary to obey them or to submit to the government.

He revealed the secret that the ancestors lived inside a volcano on an island off the coast, Manum Island. There they produced all sorts of goods for their descendants—mirrors, flashlights, dye, loincloths, even houses— but as soon as the cargo reached Rabaul the whites confiscated it. Since Mambu had just come from that town and could claim to have observed this interdiction, to many islanders his arguments seemed plausible. Mambu further revealed that to prevent this thievery the ancestors now planned to convey the goods themselves in a large ship. As further guarantee against white interference, they would avoid all established ports. Instead, part of the coast would miraculously cleave and spread wide, forming a new harbor for the ship. Garden work would then become a thing of the past, as the cargo included rich supplies of rice and beef; Mambu and his followers could settle into a life of ease.

Mambu urged the acolytes to cease paying taxes to the government and likewise to stop working for the whites. Let them pay their taxes instead to Mambu, who now styled himself the "Black King." The whites could clean the roads and carry their own burdens. The Catholics, too, were exploiting the people, Mambu explained, and the best response was simply to have nothing more to do with them. The islanders should boycott the mission stations and schools.

If the people neglected to obey any of Mambu's new tenets, he warned, the coming of the cargo would be delayed. Any islander choosing not to join him would be shut out of the millennium. Those who persisted in attending white churches would burn along with those buildings.

Beyond teaching these doctrines, the islander king initiated a series of new rituals for the people. Foremost was his baptismal rite. New followers were brought to government rest houses built along the roads. They would enter the houses in pairs, a man and a woman. Mambu would cut off the woman's grass skirt and the man's loincloth, then sprinkle their genitals with water. Next, European-made skirts and loincloths were substituted for the native versions, which Mambu disparaged in pidgin as "nogud." Wearing the traditional clothing, he explained, was hindering the return of the ancestors.

Mambu piled the used native clothing into two heaps divided by gender, digging a grave next to each heap. Standing with a crucifix first in one grave, then the other, Mambu would make the sign of the cross over the crucifix and over that grave's heap of clothing. Then he would jump out of the grave, the clothes were piled in, and dirt was shoveled in on top. This ritual served as a dramatic symbol of the islander claim to European goods and power.

For about two months Mambu's movement steadily gained steam, until nearly all the villages of the Madang region came under its sway. Everywhere one looked were natives wearing European dress. The people built a special house for Mambu and several temples where his cultic rites could be performed. He laid claim to special powers, including invulnerability, and he received ceremonial greetings and farewells wherever he went. Continually, Mambu urged his followers to be faithful to the new religious rites and obligations. The ancestors must not be delayed. As an earnest of the food soon to come, he doled out small amounts of miracle food: rice and fish, sent by the ancestors.

By this time government authorities were beginning to realize the potential seriousness of the rebellious new movement. Also, the mission was increasingly unhappy over the very effective boycott that Mambu had organized. Police were sent to the region, and in March 1938 they arrested Mambu. He received a six-month prison term in Madang, then was sent into permanent exile.

His followers were at first unshaken. They claimed that their king had merely gone elsewhere to preach his gospel. He would return. Another wave of cultic activity broke out in May of that year. But by late June of

1938, everything had quieted down and the Europeans believed that matters were back to normal, Mambu forgotten.

They were wrong.

SOON AFTER World War II, a new and much more dynamic cargo cult movement sprang up in the Madang district. The leader this time was a man named Yali. This movement invoked some of Mambu's doctrines and specifically looked back to him. Indeed, without Yali ever requesting it, people addressed him as the Black King, Mambu's old title.

Yali was a war hero who had returned from service to immense popularity back home on the Rai Coast, just south of Mambu's erstwhile sphere of influence. Minor cargo cult leaders seized upon his popularity to advance their own agenda. They proclaimed that Yali, known to have visited Australia, had in reality been killed during the war and had visited Australia only in the spirit. After that, they said, he journeyed to heaven and saw God. God promised him that the cargo would soon arrive, after which Yali returned to earth as a spirit. It was this spirit, not the old Yali of the flesh, who now walked among them.

Evangelists of this new doctrine spread the message over a wide area. Believers massed themselves in large villages, where native Lutheran missionaries who now embraced the new teaching baptized them.

At first Yali repudiated the cargo cult leaders and publicly attacked the ideas being promulgated in his name. He was himself a Christian. Yet a series of events led him to become disillusioned with this faith. He began in 1946 to speak out against the missions, blaming them for continuing the indentured labor system. Yali told the people to insist on getting paid for their work. In 1947, growing alarmed with his activities, government officials summoned Yali to Port Moresby, the capital of Papua New Guinea. While there, he told officials that he did not believe in cargo cult ideas. During this same visit, however, something happened that made him do an about-face.

A native showed him a book he had obtained on evolution. "This, not Christianity, is what the whites really believe," he told Yali. Yali was thunderstruck. If this was the secret European belief, then their ideas were not far from the ancestral religion of his own people. Both believed in human descent from animals! Enraged at the deceit being perpetrated by the whites, Yali turned much more violently against the mission and returned to the religion of his ancestors. When cult leaders led by a visionary new prophet named Gurek approached him in 1948, he welcomed their advances.

Under Yali the cargo cult jettisoned the Christian elements that had characterized Mambu's teachings and became more purely nativist. Yali drew up a new law for the people and had it written down, incorporating the age-old totemic religion. His experiences in Australia proved crucial to this developing doctrine. In Brisbane—which, he explained, was the "Rome" often spoken of by missionaries—Yali had visited a museum. There he saw islander dance masks, hand drums, decorated skulls, and wooden statues of gods and ancestors. He recognized the latter as New Guinea deities seized by missionaries and sent away. Now the recollection of this visit furnished Yali with the key to the problem of the cargo.

Yali taught that Jesus was identical to Manup (an indigenous New Guinea deity) and since the crucifixion had been held prisoner in heaven, just above Sydney. Anxious to deliver cargo to his people in New Guinea, but unable to do so himself, Jesus-Manup had recently discovered the museum gods and had taught them the secret of making cargo. Thus would the goods come: from Australia. Yali preached that society was about to be transformed. The cargo would arrive in a few years at most.

The movement spread rapidly. "Haus-Yali" buildings, similar in design to the islanders' traditional spirit houses, replaced the mission churches as the social and religious focus of village life. Antiwhite feelings ran hot. Certain areas were practically in a state of rebellion. Cultists threatened missionaries, nonbelieving islanders were sentenced to jail, and illegal taxes were levied and paid to Yali. Violent outbreaks began to proliferate, exploding one after another like a string of firecrackers all through the region of Madang.

Frightened of the burgeoning nationalist movement, the government arrested Yali in 1950 and charged him with incitement to rape and extortion. The rape charge was an interpretation of certain sexual practices connected to the revived traditional religion. Extortion was the government's view of Yali's taxes. In an atmosphere charged with racial tension, the trial took place on July 3, 1950, before the district officer in Madang. Yali was convicted on both counts and was sentenced to six and one-half years in prison.

Initially, when Yali was removed from public view, believers were sanguine, even perversely enthusiastic. If the government executed him, people said, Yali would rise on the third day to deliver them. When he came it would be in glory and with a ship full of cargo, after an earthquake. People held firmly to this belief, so firmly that after a small earthquake in 1952, when a plantation worker saw a ship round the headland, he thought the day of Yali's return was at hand. He seized a machete and, whirling it above his head and shouting, dashed toward the plantation owner's home.

Hearing a noise, the planter exited the house to investigate. Before he realized what was happening, the man found himself in a fight for his life. Other laborers ran to help the planter and were able to pull his attacker from him before he could deliver the coup de grâce. Such was the intensity of belief in Yali, in the coming of the cargo, and in islander return to power.

Nevertheless, with Yali's imprisonment his movement lost momentum and his organization of lieutenants broke down and ceased to function. Within three years, Yali's cargo cult was dead on the Rai Coast, although as late as 1961 there were occasional outbreaks that rallied to his name. These were minor movements directed by local and independent leaders having no actual connection to Yali himself. They rose and fell in a matter of weeks. Soon the hopes of some islanders were to turn in another direction, to the American president Lyndon Johnson.

THE GHOST DANCE OF 1890

Another form of crisis cult erupted in the American West in the late nineteenth century, among Native Americans.[3]

As the last decade of the century commenced, the Sioux were the largest and strongest tribe of Native Americans within the United States. Their mastery of horses had made them masters in turn of a huge expanse of territory, extending from Minnesota to the Rocky Mountains and from the Yellowstone River to the Platte. Ranging hundreds of miles and feeding off the buffalo, the Sioux were the most militant of the western tribes in their response to the advance of white people.

Still, they preferred peace to endless war, so in 1868 the Sioux agreed to renounce all claim to most of their territory. In a treaty of that year the U.S. government granted them the whole present state of South Dakota "for their absolute and undisturbed use and occupation." The treaty further stipulated that the Sioux be permitted to hunt within their old range, outside the reservation, so long as the buffalo remained—forever, as they believed. But times were changing.

The building of the railroads ferried swarms of hunters and settlers onto the plains, and the extermination of the buffalo began. Within just a few years of signing the treaty, the Sioux realized that their eternal supply of food was about to vanish. Then gold was discovered within the reservation. Thousands of miners and outlaws rushed into the Black Hills in complete disregard of the government's promises and the protests of the tribe. The Sioux saw their one remaining hunting ground snatched away.

The result was war and the Battle of the Little Bighorn, George Armstrong Custer and his Seventh Cavalry massacred. A new treaty followed. By its terms the Sioux surrendered a further third of their reservation, including the sacred Black Hills. These forced concessions generated widespread dissatisfaction among the tribe's factions, both conservatives, who favored continued warfare, and progressives, who wanted peace but agreed with the conservatives that the U.S. government's promises were worthless. As the Commissioner of Indian Affairs wrote shortly thereafter, "Within eight years from the agreement of 1876 the buffalo had gone and the Sioux had left to them alkali land and government rations. It is hard to overestimate the magnitude of the calamity, as they viewed it."[4]

Yet somehow matters managed to deteriorate still further. Without the buffalo, the Sioux had to depend on cattle, crops, and government rations to survive, and in short order all three of these sources failed them. First, "black leg" struck the cattle in 1888 and many died; the next year the crops failed. This failure was followed without interruption by epidemics of measles, grippe, and whooping cough, all usually fatal to Native Americans. That same year, the Sioux made a new treaty with the U.S. government and turned over eleven million acres, half of their remaining land. In return, the government guaranteed the tribe rations of beef, which they expressly promised never to reduce. Drought struck in 1890 and the crops failed again. Sioux misery was compounded as Congress—the ink barely dry on the treaty—broke its promise and reduced the beef ration fully 50 percent. Starvation loomed.

It was at approximately this juncture that excited reports began filtering from the west, telling of the coming of a Native American messiah, Wovoka. He was a member of the Paiutes of Nevada. As the Sioux Turning Hawk later remarked, the reports "had the effect of fire upon the Indians."[5]

Wovoka was reportedly omniscient, spoke all languages, was invisible to white people, and came as a direct messenger from the Great Spirit.

The Sioux selected a group of delegates led by Short Bull, Fire Thunder, and Kicking Bear to go and talk with the messiah. These men hooked up with a multitribal delegation, including representatives from the Cheyenne and Arapaho, and crossed the mountains to Paiute country— Walker Reservation, just south of Virginia City. Here they encountered other tribal representatives streaming in from all directions.

Wovoka himself was just over thirty years old. As one delegate recalled, "When I first saw him [in the evening] I thought he was an Indian, but the next day when I could see better he looked different. He was not so dark as an Indian, nor so light as a white man. He had no beard or whiskers, but very heavy eyebrows. He was a good-looking man." Despite impressions, Wovoka was indeed a full-blooded Native American. His father, Tavibo, had been a visionary and was reputedly invulnerable, and he taught a doctrine much like what his son would go on to proclaim.[6] He died in 1870 when Wovoka was just fourteen, and the youngster attached himself to a rancher in the Mason Valley, David Wilson. The rancher bestowed on him the name Jack Wilson, under which he lived in obscurity until receiving the revelation that made him famous.

In 1889, a short time before he began to preach, Wovoka fell ill with a high fever, passing in and out of delirium. While he was sick, he later recalled, "the sun died" (an eclipse, immensely portentous among the Paiute), and he was taken up to see God. God gave him a message and sent Wovoka back to tell of it. As it was later rendered into halting English by a translator, the message was as follows:

> All Indians must dance, everywhere, keep on dancing. Pretty soon
> in next spring [Great Spirit] come. He bring back all game of every
> kind. The game be thick everywhere. All dead Indians come back
> and live again. They all be strong just like young men, be young
> again. Old blind Indian see again and get young and have fine time.
> When [God] comes this way, then all the Indians go to mountains,
> high up away from whites. Whites can't hurt Indians then. Then
> while Indians way up high, big flood comes like water and all white
> people die, get drowned. After that water go way and then nobody
> but Indians everywhere and game all kinds thick. Send word to all
> Indians to keep up dancing and the good time will come. Indians

who don't dance, who don't believe in this word, will grow little, just about a foot high, and stay that way. Some of them will be turned into wood and be burned in fire.[7]

Wovoka went on to declare that God had given him charge of the West, while "Governor Harrison" would oversee the East and God himself heaven. God also bestowed on him five songs for controlling the weather, one each for mist, snow, showers, storms, and clear skies. And, of course, God gave him the dance by which his movement became known—the Ghost Dance.

Reports of Wovoka and his revelation raced like a brushfire to the four winds. Tribes who heard of these things sent representatives to report back, and most of the assessments were favorable. In short order the Paiute, Mojave, Ute, Shoshoni, Crow, Assiniboin, Cheyenne, Comanche, Arapaho, and Caddo tribes began to dance—virtually all Native Americans of the West except for those living in parts of California, Arizona, and New Mexico. The Ghost Dance was everywhere. Though Wovoka urged peace, the U.S. government was nervous, and its representatives tried with varying degrees of success to stop the dancing.

As Short Bull and the Sioux delegation arrived at Walker Reservation, they were ushered in to meet with Wovoka. Such meetings had become common, and Porcupine of the Cheyenne described a typical one:

> Just before sundown I saw a great many people, mostly Indians, coming dressed in white men's clothes. The Christ [Wovoka] was with them. They all formed in this ring around [a place near the agency]. They put up sheets all around the circle, as they had no tents. Just after dark some of the Indians told me that the Christ was arrived. I looked around to find him, and finally saw him sitting on one side of the ring. They all started toward him to see him. They made a big fire to throw light on him. . . . He sat there a long time and nobody went up to speak to him. He sat with his head bowed all the time. After awhile he rose and said he was very glad to see his children. "I have sent for you and am glad to see you. I am going to talk to you after awhile about your relatives who are dead and gone. My children, I want you to listen to all I have to say to you. I will teach you, too, how to dance a dance, and I want you to dance it. Get ready for your dance and then, when the dance is over, I will

talk to you.". . . . We danced till late in the night, when he told us we
had danced enough. . . . [The evening of the next day] we all assembled again to see him depart. When we were assembled, he began to
sing, and he commenced to tremble all over, violently for awhile,
and then sat down. We danced all that night, the Christ lying down
beside us apparently dead.[8]

It was while he was in trances such as the one described that
Wovoka received continuing revelations.

SHORT BULL and the Sioux returned from their meeting with Wovoka
in March 1890 and immediately began to disseminate the new doctrine. In their version of the Ghost Dance, the tribe danced around a sacred
bow and arrows tied to an evergreen in the center of the circle. Before
dancing they took sweat baths (akin to saunas) for ritual purity. No white
people's clothes or metal were allowed; earrings and even belt buckles had
to be removed. While dancing, the men and women were placed alternately and held hands. Both sexes wore "ghost shirts," painted with the sun,
moon, and stars—rendering their wearers, it was believed, invulnerable to
white bullets.

In two crucial respects Short Bull, himself a visionary medicine
man, modified the messiah's teachings. Wovoka had set several dates for
the coming of the Great Spirit, but his firmest and most widely reported
one was spring 1891. In October of 1890, Short Bull declared at a large
gathering of the Sioux that he was advancing the time. It would happen
much sooner, he said, even within the next month. He urged the Sioux all
to gather in one place and to prepare for the messiah's coming. Even should
troops surround them, he declared, they must keep dancing. The guns of
the white men would be rendered harmless by the ghost shirts, and the
white race itself would shortly be annihilated.

The second doctrinal change was related to the first. Wovoka had
promised the elimination of white people, but in his teaching this destruction was entirely supernatural and in God's timing. This was the version of
the doctrine that all other Native American believers accepted. The Sioux,
however, at Short Bull's urging, decided that it might be possible to force

God's hand. If they cooperated with God and helped destroy the whites, they reasoned, heaven would arrive that much sooner.

Motivated in large part by the tribe's desperate circumstances, these changed teachings would lead to tragedy.

The most eminent Sioux supporter of the Ghost Dance and of Short Bull's modified doctrines was Sitting Bull. He was a medicine man famous even among the whites and had been present at the Battle of the Little Bighorn. He was also the foremost member of the conservative, warlike faction of the tribe. Sitting Bull was not entirely persuaded of the truth of Wovoka's claims, but he approved the direction things were going and so voiced no objections. In October, when Short Bull advanced the time of the End, Sitting Bull broke the "pipe of peace" that he had kept in his house since 1881. When asked why, he replied, "I want to die and I want to fight."[9] Henceforth he refused to cooperate with government agents. In the face of repeated orders to the contrary, Sitting Bull kept up the Ghost Dance in his section of the reservation.

Agents throughout the Sioux reservation began to grow increasingly alarmed at the Ghost Dance and their inability to control it. They repeatedly called for soldiers, and finally their requests were heard. In late November thousands of troops arrived on the scene without warning, and now it was the turn of the Sioux to be alarmed. Short Bull and Kicking Bear led a group of three thousand on a breakaway to the badlands. Sitting Bull prepared to join them, having received on December 14 a message from the group that "God is about to appear."

The troops, realizing the signal importance of Sitting Bull to any Sioux resistance, moved to arrest him before he could escape. At daybreak on December 15 a group of forty-three reservation police and volunteers surrounded Sitting Bull's home. Hundreds of his angry followers ringed the authorities and began to press them more and more tightly against the wall of the house.

Sitting Bull was calm at first and cooperated with the police, who entered his home and informed him that he was under arrest. But when he stepped outside and his eyes fell upon his followers, Sitting Bull became greatly agitated. He called out for rescue. One of the followers, Catch-the-Bear, opened fire. In the ensuing melee six of the arresting officers died; eight of Sitting Bull's followers likewise perished. The great man himself went down at the first volley, one bullet in his head and another in his side.

Some fifty of Sitting Bull's supporters then fled, making for the bad-lands. On their way they joined forces with another prominent chief, Big Foot, leader of one of the few remaining belligerent Sioux bands. Authori-ties met with Big Foot and urged him to surrender and to submit to arrest. He agreed. When the day came on which Big Foot was to turn himself in, however, troops discovered that he had broken camp and was on his way to the badlands. They moved to intercept.

On December 28, soldiers of Custer's old Seventh Cavalry suc-ceeded in intercepting Big Foot at the river known as Wounded Knee. Once again arrangements were made for him to surrender himself and his several hundred followers. Yet somehow, as the Sioux were in the process of being disarmed, things went terribly wrong. Yellow Bird, a medicine man and firm believer in the protection of the ghost shirts, was circulating among the warriors speaking in Sioux, urging them to fight. Some agreed. At his signal, the men threw off their blankets and leaped to attack the troops.

For a few minutes the Sioux were able to hold their own in hand-to-hand combat, bringing to bear their knives and war clubs. But the cavalry had earlier positioned Hotchkiss guns around the camp. Now they began to pour in two-pound explosive shells at the rate of fifty per minute, mowing down the Sioux, men, women, and children alike. Under this barrage most of the warriors were killed instantly.

A vengeful massacre followed. Fleeing women and children were hunted down and shot two miles from the encounter—pregnant women, those with babies in their arms, it made no difference. A few escaped, wounded, only to freeze to death in a blizzard that struck the next day. The sole survivors were a half dozen babies later found wrapped in shawls be-side their mother's bodies. One hundred twenty men and two hundred fifty women and children died at Wounded Knee. When the bodies of the adults were examined, virtually all were found to be wearing ghost shirts under their outer clothing—invulnerable shields perforated with bullet holes.

Spurred on by the doctrine of the Ghost Dance, the Sioux had taken actions that constituted the last violent Native American outbreak in the history of the West. By the turn of the century white people were every-where. Native American cultures were either disintegrating or gone. Wovoka, wracked with guilt over what others had done with his revelations, retreated into himself and died in relative obscurity. The pure Ghost Dance did not long survive, although transformed varieties persisted, eventually becoming the Earth Lodge and Bole Maru cults. The widespread belief in the imminence of the millennium died within a year of those at Wounded Knee.

KONRAD SCHMID AND THE SECRET FLAGELLANTS OF THURINGIA

Centuries before Wounded Knee and halfway around the globe, another crisis cult had its origins.

Amid famine, plague, war, and rumors of war in eleventh-century Italy, a strange and grim new practice arose: self-flagellation.[10] This novel form of penance soon spread throughout Europe. Its practitioners sought to wrest from God redemption for their sins on the eve of prophesied apocalypse. Over the next few hundred years it developed into a normal part of monastic life, and even lay people commonly took to beating themselves. For those of a certain mentality it could be a deeply spiritual experience, as a fourteenth-century friar's description of his own episode illustrates:

> [One winter's night he] shut himself up in his cell and stripped himself naked . . . and took his scourge with the sharp spikes, and beat himself on the body and on the arms and on the legs, till blood poured off him as from a man who has been cupped. One of the spikes on the scourge was bent crooked, like a hook, and whatever flesh it caught it tore off. He beat himself so hard that the scourge broke into three bits and the points flew against the wall. He stood there bleeding and gazed at himself. It was such a wretched sight that he was reminded in many ways of the appearance of the beloved Christ, when he was fearfully beaten. Out of pity for himself he began to weep bitterly. And he knelt down, naked and covered in blood, in the frosty air, and prayed to God to wipe out his sins from before his gentle eyes.[11]

Organized flagellant processions appeared in the Italian cities, the first in the year 1260. Priest-led columns of men and youths marched day and night, carrying banners and candles, moving from town to town. When they arrived somewhere new they would stand in array before the local church and flog themselves for hours. The effect upon the townspeople was profound: criminals confessed, robbers recompensed their victims, enemies reconciled and fell weeping into each other's arms. Whole villages joined the movements, and as the processions continued they grew longer and longer, twisting and meandering through the Italian countryside like columns of army ants.

In Italy the flagellant processions soon came to an end as people became disenchanted when their apocalyptic hopes failed to materialize. But the idea crossed the Alps and emerged in the towns of southern Germany, where it gained new life. And whereas in Italy the practice had been orthodox and enjoyed the support of religious and secular authorities alike, in Germany the situation was different. Here the communities were suspected of breeding heresy and revolutionary notions. German flagellants claimed that they were able to achieve salvation through the practice. Indeed, the mere act of marching in one of their processions, they said, absolved a person of all sin. What need had they of the Church?

The response of authorities was predictable. Archbishops and bishops began to excommunicate and expel the penitents right and left. Secular princes such as the Duke of Bavaria helped in the repression, so that by 1262 the movement seemed to have been eradicated. But reports of its demise were premature. What actually happened was that it went underground.

When in 1296 towns on the Rhine experienced the worst famines in nearly a century, uniformed self-flagellants appeared out of nowhere. And when the Black Death swept through Europe, killing in 1348–49 one out of every three people, vast numbers of flagellants emerged. They proved to possess rituals and songs and the central literature (the so-called Heavenly Letter) of the earlier movement. Thus some of the leaders must have come from a clandestine movement, from whose esoteric traditions they now drew.

The flagellant processions of 1349 were anarchic and often violent. They opposed the very ecclesiastical and secular authorities who had repressed the earlier marchers, ridiculing the sacraments of the Church and identifying the clergy with the Beast of the book of Revelation. For their part, authorities once more cooperated enthusiastically in extinguishing the movement. Flagellants were hanged and beheaded. Under this pressure virtually all the penitents abandoned their activities. Some literally tore off their uniforms and fled, "vanishing," as one chronicler put it, "as suddenly as they had come, like night phantoms or mocking ghosts."[12] Yet here and there the movement lingered on, and in the mid–1360s it erupted in a crisis cult centered in Thuringia, southern Germany. The leader was a man named Konrad Schmid.

IN AN AGE when literacy was exceptional, especially among laypeople, Konrad Schmid stood out. Through much effort he learned to read well enough to use monastery libraries, where he would pore over apocalyptic oracles and prophecies. After one protracted period of immersion in such literature, Schmid suddenly realized one day who he was. In the prophecies of the book of Isaiah—traditionally believed by Christians to foretell the coming of Christ—Schmid found himself. He announced that he, not Christ, was the divine bearer of the final faith. His was a higher dispensation than Christianity. Simultaneously, the flagellant leader assumed the title King of Thuringia.

This title resonated with echoes of the end of days, for it recalled the mythic emperor Frederick II. Frederick had come to the crown of Germany a century earlier amid prophecies that he would usher in the millennium. Brilliant and dashing, he went on a crusade to Jerusalem in 1229 and captured the holy city from the Turks. He was constantly embroiled in controversy with the papacy. Indeed, a famous *Commentary on Jeremiah* written in the 1240s predicted that Frederick would overthrow the Church twenty years hence. His sudden death in 1250, ten years before he was to assume this prophesied role, was a bitter blow to many Germans. Soon thereafter rumors spread that he was actually not dead; in southern Italy, where he had lived for most of his life, an opaque Sibylline phrase passed from lip to lip: *Vivit et non vivit* ("He is living and lives not"). A monk told of seeing Frederick enter Mount Etna, the abode of departed heroes such as King Arthur. Frederick became a Sleeping Emperor who would one day return as savior.

Thuringians recounted a similar story of a mysterious Frederick who was sleeping, not in Etna, but in the nearby Kyffhäuser mountain. One day he would return in glory to rule the world from their own region—the King of Thuringia. It was this myth into which Konrad Schmid tapped. He was at once incarnate God and the resurrected Frederick of the prophecies.

To become a member of Schmid's elect required confession of sins, an oath of absolute obedience, and flagellation at his hands. Salvation depended entirely on a right relationship to him. Followers were to be "soft and yielding as silk" in his hands and to pray only to him, addressing Schmid with the incipit of the Lord's Prayer: "Our Father." The least sign of disobedience would result in their being turned over to Satan for destruction.

Schmid taught his followers that the flagellant processions of 1349 had actually prepared the way for his own coming, just as John the Baptist had done for Jesus. As followers beat themselves, he further revealed, an angel named Venus watched over them. Where the Sioux were to wear ghost shirts while dancing, Schmid's followers donned "robes of innocence" for a bout of flagellation. And flagellation was to this movement what the Eucharist was to Christianity: the central continuing sacrament. It was a mystery into which angels longed to peer. King David, Schmid taught, had foreseen the Thuringian's rise at the end of days and despaired that he could not be a part of all that was to happen. Seeking a foretaste of the glory that was to be revealed in Schmid, David had taken up the whip and beat himself each night.

When the millennium arrived, Schmid assured his followers, they would be known as sons of princes. In an angelic choir they would take their places grouped about his person. Many members of the movement, impatient for that time, sold all their belongings and quit working. The resulting poverty increased the pressures on the group. After another outbreak of the plague in 1368, Schmid decided that the time for the last judgment had arrived. The millennium would begin the next year. But by now the Inquisition had taken an interest in the goings-on in Thuringia.

What happened next is not entirely clear. It is certain that an exceptionally active inquisitor arrived in the region and that many executions quickly followed. Apparently Schmid himself was one of them and was burned with six other heretics in 1368 at Nordhausen. But his movement was not so easily rooted out. People around Thuringia continued to believe in him, though with his unexpected death doctrinal adjustments were required. They now saw Schmid's life and death through the lens of the book of Revelation and its two "witnesses." According to the biblical book, these witnesses would arise at the end of time, preach against Antichrist, be killed by him, and then be resurrected.

Popular notions identified the witnesses as Elijah and Enoch, the two Old Testament figures who never died, being translated directly to heaven. The flagellants saw Schmid as Elijah and an associate who had perished with him as Enoch. So they were convinced that Schmid would rise from the dead to overthrow Antichrist (the Church) and preside over the last judgment. Since the two witnesses had already come, believers saw no obstacle to the notion that this Second Coming was imminent.

Over the next decades authorities continued to search out enclaves of secret flagellants in Thuringia. From time to time they would come upon one with a start, as though stumbling over a den of rattlesnakes. With a visceral horror they would strike out and destroy all they could see, only to find another den a few years later. Well into the fifteenth century flagellants preserved Schmid's doctrine and the Heavenly Letter unchanged, passing it from generation to generation in the privacy of individual homes. They formed a community both tightly organized and tight-lipped, baptizing into their membership all newborn babies by beating them until they bled. It was only in the 1480s that the last known cell was discovered and its members tried and burned at the stake.

WILLIAM MILLER AND THE GREAT DISAPPOINTMENT

In 1818 in upper New York State, a crisis cult of quite a different sort had its genesis. In that year William Miller, a farmer and Baptist layman of Low Hampton, concluded from personal Bible study that in about twenty-five years Christ would return and "all the affairs of our present state would be wound up."[13]

At first Miller kept his opinions largely to himself. As time went on, though, close friends urged upon him his obligation to announce his findings to the world. Things started slowly: a sermon here, a lecture there. By the early 1830s Miller was circuit-riding throughout small-town New England, presenting lectures illustrated with what was to become a famous diagram. Entitled "A Pictorial Chart of Daniel's Visions," in its day it represented the cutting edge of communications technology. No one had ever seen such an illustration of biblical concepts, and it always brought "oohs" and "aahs" when Miller unveiled it onstage. People would stare at its colorful portrayal of kingdoms and calculations and arching chronological trajectories.

As the 1830s gave way to the 1840s, many thousands of Americans were persuaded to watch expectantly for the Second Coming. Contemporary estimates of the movement's membership range as high as one million. Not all followers were committed believers, but the number was phenomenal nevertheless in a day when the population of the United States was only 17.3 million (today it is about 270 million). Millerism was a mass movement, the most dynamic millenarian group ever to spring up on American soil. It spread its tendrils throughout the Northeast and into the Midwest, from Maine to Michigan, to Iowa and Ohio. Only in the South did it encounter strong resistance, perhaps because many of the leading Millerites were also well-known abolitionists.

Millerism rose to prominence during the severe economic depression that gripped the United States in the late 1830s. While William Miller claimed no personal inspiration from God, he was commonly referred to by others as "the prophet."[14] Moreover, the movement boasted a "special revelation" in its new interpretive system, focused on the prophets of Israel. No one else had the system—called the "prophetic chronology"—and though no claims were made for its outright divine inspiration, it was seen as the only proper tool by which to draw out the meaning of texts that *were* divinely inspired, the Bible.

The engine of the movement's message was a rigorous logic relentlessly applied, snipping away finer and finer slices of uncertainty until the prophetic message stood bare, pared down to absolute certitude. The logic appealed to people, and though many skeptical church leaders of the day tried to refute Miller, all failed in the public forum. Once its presuppositions were accepted, the "prophetic chronology" proved very difficult to confute.

For a long time Miller refused to set a specific year for the return of Christ. He was content with the phrase "about the year 1843," for as he put it, "The day and the hour is not revealed, but the *times* are." Still, as the movement gained momentum the pressure to set a specific date mounted, and because he could see no error in his calculations, in December 1842 Miller relented. He set a year by the Jewish calendar: Christ would return between March 21, 1843, and March 21, 1844. Miller expected the fulfillment probably would be late in that Jewish year, since he "thought our faith would be tried."

As 1843 got under way Millerites were tense with excitement. Their principal newspaper, the *Midnight Cry,* adopted a three-month subscription policy. Excitement ratcheted higher in February when a comet, unexpected by astronomers, brilliantly lit the skies. Many saw it as a supernatural sign of the End. Press coverage of the Millerites increased manyfold as the predicted end drew nearer. On March 2, 1843, Horace Greeley's New York *Tribune* devoted an entire issue to a hostile report on the phenomenon.

In January 1844 Miller estimated that he had given over four thousand lectures to more than half a million people. The labor had broken his health, but he wrote that the cost was not too high and that with his "whole heart and soul" he looked forward to Christ's near return in the clouds of heaven. By March 14 Miller had returned home to Low Hampton to await March 21. While thousands of Millerites likewise huddled to wait, many of their neighbors derided them. Thus one "William Miller" wrote the following note to the only Millerite living in Sackets Harbor, New York: "The 'World' has commenced burning in Main [sic] in the North East corner. It does not burn verry [sic] fast, so I had time to write you a few lines before I got ready."

W HEN THE END failed to arrive on March 21, the Millerite leadership did not panic. They continued to wait in expectation. Miller observed that many of those who had looked forward to Christ's return "walk no more with us," but the movement did not at all collapse. George Knight has written:

> It went on. That continuity, in a large part, resulted from the fact that the Millerite leaders had been "soft" on the time. That is, they allowed for the possibility of small errors in their calculations and even in some of their historic dates. . . . Miller's "soft" approach to the exact time is evident in a letter he wrote on February 28, three weeks before the termination of his predicted end of the world. "If Christ comes, as we expect," he penned, "we will sing the song of victory soon; if not, we will watch, and pray, and preach until he comes, for soon our time, and all prophetic days, will have been filled."[15]

Shortly thereafter Samuel Snow, heretofore a minor actor in the Millerite drama, presented a new interpretation to explain the failure of the March 21 date. Snow's approach was based on typology; the Old Testament festivals, he said, found their "typical" fulfillment in the ministry of Jesus Christ. Snow drew upon portions of the New Testament to show that the festivals of Passover, Firstfruits, and Pentecost had been "fulfilled" by Christ during his earthly ministry, and at the exact same time in the year as their annual celebration.

Snow then pointed out that "those types which were to be observed in the 7th month, have never yet had their fulfillment." Consequently Snow predicted that Christ would come at the time of the biblical Day of Atonement, on the "tenth day of the seventh month" of "the present year,

1844." Millerite leaders then determined that the tenth day of the seventh month, according to the reckoning of the Karaite Jews (rabbinic Judaism being distrusted), would fall on October 22, 1844. That date now became the focus of Millerite enthusiasm. And this was not a soft prediction.

As autumn approached excitement intensified once again. Some Millerites sold all their possessions or even gave them away as soon useless. Joshua Himes, Miller's prosperous right-hand man, canceled all the debts owed him. Large numbers quit their jobs or let their fields lie untended as the hour drew near. But once again the End did not come. Again believers were crushed. One man, Washington Morse, later recalled:

> That day came and passed, and the darkness of another night closed in upon the world. But with that darkness came a pang of disappointment to the advent believers that can find a parallel only in the sorrow of the disciples after the crucifixion of their Lord. The passing of the time was a bitter disappointment. True believers had given up all for Christ, and had shared His presence as never before. The love of Jesus filled up every soul and with inexpressible desire they prayed, "Come Lord Jesus, and come quickly"; but He did not come. And now, to turn again to the cares, perplexities, and dangers of life, in full view of the jeering and reviling unbelievers who scoffed as never before, was a terrible trial.[16]

At Ithaca, at Dansville, at Scottsville and Rochester and elsewhere, mobs stormed the Millerite meeting places, but for Miller and his followers shock, grief, and confusion were the greater problems. As historian Whitney Cross has asked,

> Could any group in history have prepared for themselves a more vicious trap? A more sudden, more abysmal disenchantment? Not merely did the single doctrine of [Christ's soon return] come into question, but faith in the whole Bible, the literal reading of which had created their distinctive belief. If they admitted error, they must also place themselves in the dark concerning a large portion of the Scriptures.[17]

What happened to Miller's adherents? As Cross went on to observe, "The majority of those who had sought the very narrow path of perfect logic fell off the precipice." Like Jonah's gourd, Millerism had grown very rapidly, and it now withered almost overnight. Some individuals fell apart emotionally. Many became cynical about all religion and morality. A dwindling number continued, with ever decreasing enthusiasm, to set new dates for the Second Coming, each of which proved false in turn.[18]

Not all followers of Miller had been firm believers, of course; most had watched from a certain distance, never investing their entire selves in the movement. For them the cost of retreat was much lower. Thousands returned to their old churches. After a period of floundering, a substantial sprinkling of western New Yorkers, including Miller's own nephew—who first proclaimed the Millerite message in that area—joined a different, rising crisis cult, the Shakers.

Shaking off their stunned silence and confusion, the Millerite leadership finally issued a statement in the *Midnight Cry* of November 21, 1844. Admitting that they had twice been disappointed, they reasoned that God had overruled to make the disappointments serve an unknown divine purpose. Miller and his fellow leaders declared: "We now find ourselves occupying a time, beyond which we can extend none of the prophetic periods, according to our chronology and date of their commencement. . . . We admit that it is proved that we do not know the definite time."[19]

History was to demonstrate the utter inadequacy of this explanation. For the Millerites as a vital movement, it marked the end.[20]

THE STRANGE CASE OF SABBATAI SEVI

In the middle of the seventeenth century was born yet another crisis cult, the most extensive messianic movement in the history of the Jews. The focal point was Sabbatai Sevi, son of an undistinguished mercantile agent in an English firm. As Gershom Scholem, the great historian of these events, has observed, "Never before had there been a movement that swept the whole House of Israel."[21] Even while the Temple stood in Jerusalem, no messianic claimant ever achieved the broad acceptance that this one did. Faith in Sabbatai swept over every element of Jewry, from England to Persia, from Germany to Morocco, from Poland to the Yemen.

More remarkable yet, at the height of his acclaim this messiah apostatized from Judaism.

Born on the ninth of Ab (the anniversary of the destruction of the Jerusalem Temple) in the year 1626, Sabbatai Sevi received a traditional Jewish education. He was a good but not exceptional student whose real interest lay not in the Talmud but in the *kabbalah*. Among Sabbatai's Jewish contemporaries, the *kabbalah* was a mystical philosophy of great influence, especially the system developed by Isaac Luria Ashkenazi (1534–1572) and expressed in the writings called the *Zohar*.

Sabbatai threw himself into the study of these mysteries, and by the time he was twenty he had gained a reputation for cleverness. In Smyrna in 1648, Sabbatai revealed to a small circle of young scholars with whom he studied mystical lore that he was himself the long-awaited deliverer. On the question of how he arrived at his self-understanding the sources are silent, but in any event the rabbis of Smyrna banished Sabbatai from the city shortly thereafter.

According to a contemporary, Rabbi Joseph ha-Levi, Sabbatai "proclaimed himself a prophet and the whole congregation persecuted him. He and his friends were thoroughly beaten, and banished."[22] Sabbatai also "devoted himself to both the holy and the unclean names"; that is, he engaged in kabbalistic practices aimed at performing miracles and magic. He even invoked demons. Further, Sabbatai regularly transgressed the Jewish law, going so far as to speak aloud the holiest of God's names, YHWH, which only the high priest was to utter—and then only in the Temple on the Day of Atonement. The banished Sabbatai now began a long period of wandering from place to place.

The young messiah was tall, and according to one witness, "his face was very bright, inclining to swarthiness, his countenance beautiful and majestic, a black, round beard framed his face; he was very stout and corpulent." The rounded beard struck people as odd: "the hairs of his beard stood in one equal row from his upper jaw to his chin, not one hair protruded beyond the others."[23] And Sabbatai's beard was not all that was peculiar about him. In modern terms, he was a manic-depressive.

Adherents referred to Sabbatai's regular manic periods of ecstasy as his "illuminations." These were the times when he received his revelations and believed himself to levitate. His depressive phase they knew as "the hiding of the face," for in his agonies Sabbatai stayed in his chambers and refused to see anyone. Of course, his condition went unrecognized for what it was, and Sabbatai's agonies in the downswings of the condition's cycle became for believers the "sufferings of the messiah"—episodes when he wrestled with evil on others' behalf, as discussed eloquently, they explained, in scripture.

The illuminations convinced many that Sabbatai was indeed the messiah, for then his face burned red and he was like no one people had ever seen. One wrote that his face "was like the face of Moses, which was like the face of the sun." Leyb ben Ozer met with people who had eaten and drunk with Sabbatai, and afterward he reported:

> They told me that there is no comparison with his majesty; his face was like that of an angel of the Lord and all the time his cheeks were red. They also testified that whenever he was singing songs of praise to God, as he would do several times every day, it was impossible to look into his face, for it was like looking into a fire. . . . For this reason also many believed in him.[24]

In 1658, during one of his illuminations, Sabbatai received from God a new law and new commandments. This revelation sanctified Sabbatai's transgressions of traditional Jewish law. That the messiah might reveal a latter-day law was no unfamiliar notion; it could be found in the Bible. Traditional Jews looked to Isaiah 51:4, "for law shall proceed from me," and understood the words to speak of their deliverer. But they thought the reference was not to a new law as such but rather to a new understanding of the one, eternal Mosaic formulation. That sin should now be holy was shocking. Sabbatai's later followers expressed this confounding notion in a famous Hebrew dictum: *bittulah shel torah zehu kiyyumah,* "the violation of the Torah is itself its true fulfillment."

Sabbatai sojourned first in Salonica, then in Cairo, Jerusalem, and Gaza. While in Gaza he met Nathan Benjamin Levi, who was to become the prophet of Sabbatai as messiah. Nathan of Gaza cast himself as Elijah, forerunner of the anointed, and it was his own ecstatic visions that convinced him of Sabbatai's status. On September 5, 1665, Nathan heard a voice from heaven, as he said, "proclaiming that the messiah, the son of David, would become manifest to the world in a year and some months." There followed a vision, which Nathan set down in a long letter that soon began to circulate among all Jewish communities. The prophet wrote:

> Now I shall disclose the course of events. A year and a few months from today, [Sabbatai] will take the dominion from the Turkish king without war, for by the power of the hymns and praises which he shall utter, all nations shall submit to his rule. He will take the Turkish king alone to the countries which he will conquer, and all the kings shall be tributary unto him, but only the Turkish king will be his servant. . . . This will continue for four or five years. Thereafter

the aforementioned rabbi will proceed to the river Sambatyon, leaving his kingdom in the charge of the Turkish king . . . but after three months he [the Turkish king] will be seduced by his councilors and will rebel. . . . At that time the aforementioned rabbi will return from the river Sambatyon . . . mounted on a celestial lion; his bridle will be a seven-headed serpent and "fire out of his mouth devoured." At this sight all the nations and all the kings shall bow before him to the ground. On that day the ingathering of the dispersed shall take place, and he shall behold the sanctuary already built descending from above. There will be seven thousand Jews in Palestine at that time, and on that day there will be the resurrection of the dead that have died in Palestine. Those that are not worthy [to rise] will be cast out from the Holy Land. The [general] resurrection outside the Holy Land will take place forty years later.[25]

Here Nathan plainly prophesied that in 1667 the messiah would begin to reign. In 1672, the "messianic woes" would commence, and only Gaza would be safe. Next would follow all the miraculous events familiar from apocalyptic legends and the *Zohar*. Of course, within a few years all of Nathan's prophecies were to fail, and his letter would be discounted by believers as a forgery, but in 1665, as the missive spread through the Jewish communities, it touched off a frenzy. Redemption is at hand! The messiah is here!

The fervor gave birth to stories about Sabbatai's miraculous deeds, and the Jews of Europe halted in their labors to discuss the latest feats. Merchants in Italy and various North Sea ports wrote to their agents in the Levant, begging for new facts about the messiah. Sabbatai made his way back to Smyrna in a triumphal procession. The Jews of that city, who not so many years before had expelled him, now bestowed upon the prodigal absolute power as sole ruler of their community. Embassies began arriving from the four corners of the earth. In the synagogues he was publicly hailed as the messiah, and unbelievers were made to fear for their lives. In Persia, Jewish farm laborers sat down and refused to work, since their deliverer was about to lead them back to the Holy Land.

Excitement reached fever pitch when, at the beginning of 1666, Sabbatai journeyed to Constantinople. Supporters expected him to take the crown from the sultan's head and begin to fulfill the prophecies. Hebrew books of that time bore the date "the first year of the renewal of prophecy and the kingdom." But instead of following the script and submitting to

Sabbatai, the sultan had him arrested. He was held until September in prison near Gallipoli. During these months bribery allowed Sabbatai to continue receiving delegations from far and near, and no one considered his imprisonment an obstacle to imminent glory. Thus it was a totally unexpected catastrophe when the news went out: on September 16, 1666, brought before the sultan at Adrianople, Sabbatai Sevi, rather than be executed, had become a Muslim.

The disarray among believers was profound. They were literally speechless with shock. Soon thereafter most Jews repented of their attachment to this "false messiah" and returned to traditional Judaism. Sabbatai's own brother, Elijah, followed this course. But a substantial minority did not—could not—accept that all the miracles, excitement, and hope had been a delusion. In the midst of their quandary Nathan of Gaza came forward with a solution to the conundrum of an apostate messiah.

The prophet produced a synthesis of biblical verses and kabbalistic notions demonstrating that the apostasy of the messiah, far from proving him false, was in fact necessary—a requirement of his mission. Only in this way, Nathan explained, could Sabbatai attract the holy souls among the gentiles. To fulfill the redemption, the messiah, like Israel itself, must be cut off and must dwell for a time in exile. So Sabbatai was not really a Turk. He was, as ever, a Jew. But now he must inhabit two realities—one inward, the other outward—the two being reconciled only on that future date when he assumed the full splendor of messianic dominion. This idea quickly gained widespread support among remaining believers.

It fit well, too, with Sabbatai's mode of life in the next years. The Turkish government, expecting that they could use this important convert for their own purposes, tolerated for some time his double life as Muslim and Jew. Pilgrims continued to wend their way to Sabbatai at Adrianople. Among many groups and in many lands belief in Sabbatai flourished as an underground movement. Rabbinic officials opposed it and persecuted believers, but they were unable to exterminate the faith.

Eventually Sabbatai was banished to Albania, where he died in 1676. He had never achieved the glory prophesied for him, but that did not deter the faithful. They denied that he had failed or was dead; he had merely "gone into occultation." He was expected to return in forty years. When that time passed without his appearing, the doctrine was adjusted; his second coming was now placed at an indefinite time in the future. The belief in Sabbatai's return in messianic glory persisted among Sabbatians into the twentieth century.

The Sabbatian movement flourished for about 150 years after Sabbatai Sevi died. Only after 1815 did the cult peter out, and certain radical sects continued even longer. One of these, the Dönmeh, numbered between five and ten thousand in 1924.[26] The Dönmeh emerged after Sabbatai's death when believers faced the question: Should the apostasy of the messiah serve as a pattern for all? The great majority of Sabbatians answered this question with a resounding no.

The Dönmeh were among those who answered yes. They were a "crypto-Jewish" movement, outwardly Muslim, but among themselves Sabbatian Jews. During the first half-century of their existence, this group split and split again, always in response to the claims of new leaders. The first schism resulted when Sabbatai's brother-in-law, Jacob Querido, announced that the soul of the messiah had taken up residence in him. His claim had the support of Sabbatai's widow, and kabbalistic ideas allowed for reincarnation, but most Dönmeh rejected this particular instance.

The second schism erupted in 1716 among those who had rejected Querido's claim. Baruchya Russo was proclaimed the reincarnation of Sabbatai. Moreover, since a mystical theology very similar to Christianity had developed among the group, Baruchya as the messiah also asserted that he was an incarnation of God. Those circles of the Dönmeh who accepted neither Querido nor Baruchya remained faithful to the original authority of Sabbatai Sevi and his first prophets.

In Poland, meanwhile, there arose the so-called Frankist movement, centered in Offenbach and led by Jacob Frank. This group converted en masse to Catholicism while remaining Sabbatian at heart. Frank held court until 1791 and proclaimed the most radical and nihilistic of doctrines. For him, Sabbatai and Baruchya were the "first two," who had brought true revelation from God, but theirs was a limited mission. He would now complete what they had begun. Though Frank never said it in so many words, his disciples correctly understood his implicit assertion: incarnated on earth, he was the living God.

ANATOMY OF A CRISIS CULT

The movements that grew up around Mambu and Yali, Wovoka, Schmid, Miller, and Sabbatai Sevi illustrate many of the features typical of crisis cults. Hundreds of such movements are documented; thousands find at least some mention in the annals of history.[27] Comparative study discloses within them a structure of events that transcends culture.

A crisis cult takes its start when a body of people, whether small or large, comes to feel that their culture—or major aspects of it—no longer "work." They therefore seek to effect a new system, with new relationships and, often, new characteristics. The Melanesian cargo cultists, comparing their own Stone Age poverty to the shiny-metaled wealth of the advancing Europeans, grew radically discontent. Wovoka and his followers watched the Native American way of life fade away as more and more settlers pushed their way into the West. In response they sought a return to an idyllic past. Similarly, each of the other movements sought in its own way to create "the new person."

Crisis cults feed on human insecurity. Some aim to eliminate alien influences and values; others, to reinstitute customs thought to have existed in the past. Still others strive to effect a supernatural metamorphosis of the world. Often more than one of these motives appear in a single movement.

Crisis cults are thus a response to stress, but more than ordinary social tensions underlie most of them. In fact, shattering change is often required to bring them about—something that "radically destroys or reshapes an individual's most highly valued human and physical surroundings." Revolution, war, natural catastrophes, economic dislocation, contact with a seemingly invincible and imperialist foreign people: these are common catalysts. Disaster or perceived disaster leaves people confused, lost, often hopeless.[28] They need reasons for what has happened and a way to think about the world that points forward. They need hope. The old authorities are no longer fully respected. The situation is ripe for someone to arise with answers—answers that persuade, answers as certain as divine truth.

The stage is set for the prophet or messiah.

The modern study of such figures stands on a foundation laid by sociologist Max Weber. Weber defined the prophet as "a purely individual bearer of charisma, who by virtue of his mission proclaims a religious doctrine or divine commandment. The prophet's claim is based on personal revelation and charisma. This qualification must be regarded as the decisive hallmark of prophecy."[29] The prophet is an intermediary between human and God, bringing new revelation vital to the solution of the present difficulties. The Polynesians call such a person a "god-box." For the Black Caribs of British Honduras, the prophet is a "telephone exchange" between human and god.

Anthropologists often use the terms *prophet* and *messiah* interchangeably, but they are distinct.[30] A prophet is a person who claims to have had divine revelations and is conscious of a commission to tell people about them. A messiah, on the other hand, is a more exalted sort. He or she not only experiences revelations and receives a commission to proclaim the message, but also sees him- or herself as divinely ordained to establish a new order. The distinction hinges on the centrality of the messenger to the movement's aims.

Though every messiah is a prophet, not every prophet is a messiah. Mambu was a prophet, as was William Miller; Konrad Schmid and Sabbatai Sevi were messiahs.

The knowledge that prophets and messiahs claim is special in various ways. Most of all, it is absolutely unwavering. A statement from an October 1959 television interview with Carl Jung (who, though not conventionally religious, possessed this prophetic mind-set) illustrates the attitude:

Interviewer: "Do you now believe in God?"

Jung: "Now? Difficult to answer. I *know.* I don't need to believe. I know."[31]

This utter conviction is one aspect of the prophet's charisma. This person *knows.* Prophetic conviction lies outside most of our experience, but it is to everyday conviction as Michelangelo's painting of the Sistine Chapel is to graffiti. Anyone who has done public speaking has experienced the response that conviction in a speaker calls forth from the audience. Conviction breeds conviction. The prophet's certainty is thus immensely affecting. When people are in the needy emotional state that precipitates a crisis cult, its power is enhanced by an order of magnitude.

By *charisma* I mean something different from common usage, which has worn the concept's sharp edges smooth as a pebble. For most of us the word denotes little more than charm, but charisma in the technical sense is more a relationship than a quality. It denotes the mingling of a leader's emotional life with those of the followers. For example, the charismatic is able to compel, but this ability lies hidden even to the charismatic, until he or she encounters people willing to be compelled. When leader and followers come together, the result is akin to a chemical reaction: the leader compels, they are compelled—the emotional mingling begins.

Why are the followers willing to give the charismatic such control? In part, their willingness expresses the deep-seated human need to transcend ourselves and become one with others. In equal measure it results from the common yearning for a parental figure, a person who will shoulder our burdens, relieve us of life's decisions, and tell us that everything is going to be all right.

In our own time this charismatic chemistry has usually proved destructive. Adolf Hitler was a charismatic; so were Charles Manson and Jim Jones and David Koresh. These figures are deeply repugnant to us, yet their movements are documented in a way that has become possible only in the twentieth century. Consequently, one can learn a great deal about the phenomena of charisma by studying these men and their relationships with followers.

Charles Lindholm, analyzing the emotions flowing between Hitler and his listeners, wrote,

> Responding to Hitler's magnetic performance the audience members discovered themselves revitalized and powerful, merged in an active collective, and filled with devotion and awe for the man who had brought them together. He united them and gave them enemies to hate and comrades to love; above all, his intensity reformed their disintegrating world. As a convert put it, "We all gained something of this energy. We remained firm when everything wavered about us."[32]

Note the wording: the feeling that everything is wavering and insecure is the fertile soil of all crisis cults.

As the group members come to focus on the person of the prophet, so also—in extreme situations, at any rate—relationships and authority in the group radiate outward from that center. Any given member's situation depends on his or her standing with the leader. Whatever the prophet says, whatever the prophet asks is right, simply because it is he or she who has spoken. Consequently, organization tends to be fluid, based on the leader's decisions or whims, more personal than institutional.

The charismatic attracts others by drawing out and reflecting their own feelings. He or she becomes an "empathetic mirror" for their sufferings and desires. Through this dynamic the leader and followers become one. He or she is able to make them feel wonderful, important, as they may never have felt before. It is therefore no coincidence that most crisis cults draw their membership particularly from the poor.[33] Jim Jones often told his followers, "No one will ever love you the way I love you." They believed

him. Even those who later left the People's Temple testified to Jones's superhuman abilities to intuit their feelings. This is a common dynamic in
crisis cults. The binding glue is, if not love, a very convincing counterfeit.

Above and beyond the strong interpersonal connections lies the ar-
dent force of the leader. Weber observed that many charismatics possess
rare capacities to display highly colored emotions of all sorts. The episodes
of which they are capable precipitate fear, wonderment, and obedience in
their followers. Communion between a charismatic prophet and his or her
audience can be overwhelming even to those who choose not to follow. According to eyewitness testimony, the personal impact of Hitler was "a kind
of psychological force radiating from him like a magnetic field. It could be
so intense as to be almost physically tangible."[34] Manson's followers frequently spoke of his hypnotic eyes. Looking into Sabbatai Sevi's face was
"like looking into a fire."

YET CRISIS CULTS are more than mere emotional responses to stress
and disaster; they possess as well significant intellectual content. If
these movements look back to disaster or profound dissatisfaction, they
also look ahead, to a way out. The siren song that draws them along that forward path is the myth-dream. The anthropologist Kenelm Burridge coined
this term, explaining it as follows:

> As a concept "myth-dream" does not lend itself to precise defini-
> tion. Nevertheless, myth-dreams exist, and they may be reduced to
> a series of themes, propositions, and problems which are to be
> found in myths, in dreams, in the half-lights of conversation, and in
> the emotional responses to a variety of actions, and questions asked.
> Through this kind of intellectualization myth-dreams become "as-
> pirations." All peoples participate in particular myth-dreams . . .
> [although they] are not intellectually articulate, for they exist in an
> area of emotionalized mental activity which is not private to any
> particular individual but which is shared by many. A community
> day-dream as it were. But among literate peoples portions of the
> myth-dream may be intellectualized and set down in writing. . . .
> Eventually, such intellectualizations as are made may become the
> definitive principles upon which a group of persons may organize
> themselves into a viable party or movement. And by so organizing

themselves the group concerned puts itself into a position from which it may "capture" the myth-dream by symbolizing and putting into effect the propositions contained in the myth-dream.[35]

The myth-dream is any particular culture's ideal reality. In the case of Wovoka, the myth-dream included the resurrection of all dead Indians, the destruction of the whites through flood, and "game all kinds thick." A myth-dream is the assurance of things hoped for, the conviction of things not seen. And the crisis cult tries to make the myth-dream happen—to make Camelot real.

When the prophet emerges, he or she is able to dial into focus what has previously been blurred and inchoate in the collective mind. This role requires rare gifts of verbal expression, and prophets are commonly electrifying speakers. What this person says is not merely the sum of his or her own opinions or ideas but is, as noted, a revelation that has come in a dream, a vision, a pellucid flash of insight, or some other mystical experience.[36]

Moreover, the prophet's declarations always echo important features of the myth-dream, so the words resonate with listeners. These are things they are prepared to believe because they have long believed them, even without realizing it. They are hearing expressed openly what has lain largely unconscious in their minds, placed there through the process of socialization.[37] This revelation becomes the new law of the movement. In literate societies it is generally written down, as was the case with Sabbatai Sevi. In New Guinea in the days of Mambu and Yali's movements, the revelation inhered in certain treasured objects known as "the things of the ancestors." Consideration of the objects would evoke the revelation.

Burridge summarized the content of these crisis-cult revelations: "Promises of material prosperity, spiritual salvation, and political independence are made conditional on the observance of a series of commands, rites, and ceremonials; and, on the other side, there are threats of disaster if the content of the revelation is not accepted in its entirety."[38] The prophet also issues genuine prophecies, surety for the truth of the myth-dream in its fullness.

Yet however powerful, crisis cults cannot last forever. Like a piston, they have an upstroke and a downstroke.[39] The upstroke is the time of hope, of enthusiasm, and of transformative energy when the movement is on the rise. The downstroke is the period of decline. The typical life span is brief: a year, two years, almost always less than a decade. Greasing a movement's downstroke can be a variety of factors.

For one thing, it is impossible to stoke millenarian fires indefinitely. Either the movement transforms itself into some more stable entity, or it burns down to the last embers and flickers out. If a crisis cult can succeed in changing and stabilizing, it may enjoy long life—but as something else; it is no longer a crisis cult. That happened with earliest Christianity and Islam.

Also, governing authorities commonly decide to suppress a group. They recognize that at the core of many of these movements lies the potential for revolution. The latent violence may not easily find expression, especially in the modern world, because of lack of the resources—people and materials—needed to mount a military effort. Nevertheless, it is there. All that this potential needs to awaken and stir it into ferocious action is some glimmer of hope for success. As the early-nineteenth-century French statesman Tocqueville once observed, "Patiently endured so long as it seemed beyond redress, a grievance comes to appear intolerable once the possibility of removing it crosses men's minds."

Governments naturally tend to look with disfavor upon this simmering challenge. They prefer to rid themselves of a small problem rather than wait and face a big one. And the egos of powerful and arrogant people are often offended by these movements, because followers of the myth-dream refuse to acknowledge the supremacy of their this-worldly power.

Commonly the authorities kill or imprison the prophet. Contemplating how typical is this happening, one scholar has remarked, "Jesus standing before Pilate is just another messianic prophet standing before a District Officer." They try to scatter whatever followers survive the confrontation. Violence may now erupt, sometimes escalating into full-blown war. Government confrontation with crisis cults led to the Java War of 1825–1830; the Pai Maire Movement in New Zealand in 1864–1867; the Birsa Rising in India in 1899–1900; the Maji Maji Rebellion in German East Africa in 1905–1906, and the Saya San Rebellion in British Burma in 1930–1932. Events in Waco, Texas, involving David Koresh and the Branch Davidians are susceptible to a similar line of interpretation.[40]

Another element that can throw cold water on a heated crisis cult is failed prophecy. The leaders of these movements always prophesy in one way or another, whether they claim direct revelation from God or merely unparalleled insight into holy scriptures. Almost without exception real-world events fail to confirm the prophecies, and the failure becomes especially obvious when a given prediction is clear, specific, and open to empirical disproof. Firm dates can be as deadly to these movements as a snakebite. The 1844 Great Disappointment of the Millerites is a parade example here. Wovoka announced that his Native American paradise would arrive in the spring of 1891; when it did not, everyone could see that it did not. Nathan of Gaza, in his letter of 1665, issued a series of specific prophecies that failed.

Scholars call the phenomenon of disproved prophecy "disconfirmation." Minor disconfirmation involving peripheral group concerns is no real problem. Any number of explanations are available for such annoyances. The real problem is disconfirmation—and even more so, repeated disconfirmation—of a movement's central prophecies. Unless leaders can offer a truly convincing explanation for the apparent failure, members become depressed. They falter in their commitment. Many drop out. Thus the Shoshoni ceased believing in Wovoka's revelations after the End failed to come in 1891, and they quit performing the Ghost Dance. When Sabbatai Sevi converted, most of his believers fell away. Millerism melted away when its central prophetic claim was disconfirmed.

Rank-and-file members drift off, perhaps joining other groups that promise to meet the needs that gave birth to the original movement. By a process of evaporation membership dwindles down to a hard-core few who will never disbelieve, no matter what happens. Thus failed prophecy never results in the instant demise of a crisis cult, though, as with Millerism, it can lead to a swift end. More usually its effect is like an acute illness that leaves the patient weak and permanently bedridden. The patient lingers, declining and losing capacity, until finally death claims the atrophied husk. The death of the group frequently coincides with the rise of a generation that has not known the fervor of the upstroke.[41]

Often more than one of these factors weigh against a crisis cult. The group abandons its particular activities, for it is clear that they are not the solution. Nevertheless, the myth-dream remains intact, its basic notions still viable. In one sense the charismatic prophet has failed, for the movement has died out. Yet in another sense the prophet has succeeded, for the myth-dream that he or she passes on to subsequent generations is not the same as the one he or she received. The prophet has revised, refined, and qualified it. Eventually another prophet will arise and begin to articulate this new version. This prophet will introduce his or her own modifications in turn.

By this process the first prophet's movement becomes a precursor movement for that of the second. The second movement takes up elements of the first but considers itself distinct and modifies central themes. Mambu's movement collapsed a few months after he was deported, but he nevertheless had changed the myth-dream. He even entered it himself. He became a model for the new person, and when Yali arose he took up the shadowy notion of that figure as represented by Mambu and gave it new shape and substance. Wovoka began where his father had left off, only slightly adjusting the character of the early Ghost Dance and his father's ideas of the world to come. Yet there were twenty years between Wovoka's activity and his father's, and the two men spearheaded different though related movements. As predecessor to their actions, Schmid and his flagellants consciously harked back to the processions of 1349. Jacob Querido, Baruchya Russo, and Jacob Frank all regarded Sabbatai Sevi as a lesser precursor of themselves. While discarding some of Millerism's ideas, Ellen White elaborated other of its foundational concepts, leading to Seventh-Day Adventism.

This, then, is the true role of the charismatic: to feed the myth-dream.

IN 76 B.C.E. in the city of Jerusalem arose such a charismatic, in T. E. Lawrence's terms "a dreamer of the day." He would act Israel's myth-dream; if allowed, he would make it happen. The first messiah known to history, he was in a certain way the most important messianic claimant ever, because he was first.

This is his story.

CHAPTER 2

BEHOLD THE MAN

What did you go out into the wilderness to see? A prophet? Yes, I
tell you, and more than a prophet.

  Jesus, on John the Baptist

The originality of a prophet lies commonly in his ability to fuse into
a white heat combustible material which is there, to express and
appear to meet the half-formed prayers of some at least of his contemporaries.

  A. D. Nock, *Conversion*

A WELL-ORDERED silence reigned.[1] Using both hands, the priest-
king raised the libation of water high for everyone in the courtyard to
see. Towering behind him, the veil of the Jerusalem Temple flapped with
the breeze. The autumn sun glinted off the king's golden breastplate, and
the letters of the divine name YHWH inscribed in the same metal on his diadem flashed stabs of light. The air was filled with the smell of burned sacrifices. After a pause, the king began to pour the liquid out at his feet. The
crowd stirred. Murmuring, jostling, they pressed closer. Some began to
scream with fury. Others took up the taunts.

"Alexander, you are a bastard! You are not fit to rule!"

"Your mother was a prisoner of war! Whose son then are you *really*,
mighty king?"

"Shall a half-breed be priest in Israel?"

Goaded by their neighbors, a few among the crowd-becoming-mob twisted the hard lemons from the wands they carried and began to pelt the king. The notion gained momentum. Soon hundreds were raining fruit, seeking out their target on the altar above.

Backing away and shielding his face, Alexander turned to the altar's stairs. The golden bells on the hem of his vestments tinkled, their sweetness jarring, out of place. Hastening to descend, the king barked at the royal guard awaiting him at the foot of the stairs, "At them, you fools! At them! Attack!" At once the mercenaries—Pisidians and Cilicians, greaved and armored ancient Turks—leaped to obey. Swords drawn, swinging left and right, they waded into the ranks of the Jews, striking down anyone within reach.

Stumbling over fallen comrades, howling, the leaders of the mob now turned to flee. Their screams of rage had become cries of terror. In slow motion the wave of humanity reversed itself, surging outward from the altar in every direction. The guards swung and struck, swung and struck.

Within half an hour, silence reigned again. But this was not the silence of order. This was the silence of death. The corpses of six thousand festival goers lay all around, strewn in their rag-doll contortions with pieces of fruit. From a distance the scene resembled nothing so much as a macabre collage. Otherwise the courtyard was empty of humanity. The king had watched the slaughter from the Temple vestibule, making no move to halt the carnage. Now he walked to a basin and dipped his hands.

THIS WAS A DAY in the life of the Jewish nation as the second century B.C.E. came to a close. They were a people riven by faction and controversy, rent by a profound and protracted crisis—not unlike the Lebanon of recent times. In the year 94 B.C.E. their squabbling erupted into outright civil war. The events of the Festival of Tabernacles of that year, described above, were just the beginning.[2] Shortly thereafter and for six years Jew took up arms against Jew. Fifty thousand people died.

At the head of one faction stood the reigning king, Alexander Jannaeus (103–76 B.C.E.). Among his supporters were the Sadducees and many of the elite priestly families, with their extensive personal networks of allies and kin, lesser priests, minor princes, and sycophants. In modern terms the Sadducees and other priestly groups comprised a conservative party. They were heirs to ways of vast antiquity and—because it worked to their benefit—lovers of the status quo. Their adversaries included the

Pharisees, an innovative and largely lay movement on the rise whose strength was their popularity with the masses.

At the heart of the disputes was, as always, the question of power. But the issue came to focus in a way that was peculiarly Jewish: Whose version of religious law would control the Temple activities? Which understanding of the complicated—sometimes contradictory—and often incomplete biblical laws would govern the nation's sacrifices to God?

Temple laws may seem to be religious rather than political matters. No one in Judaea of the period, however, would have thought to make that distinction. The boundaries between these realms of their society were ill defined. Religion was political; politics, religious. Political power meant control of the religious institutions, principally the Temple. Religious ideas carried political implications. Thus, the political writing that survives from the period may be couched in the familiar rhetoric of *Realpolitik,* such as we find in Josephus (37–c.105 C.E.), who wrote in Greek two histories of these years. But it may equally well be inscribed in religious language, "psalms, hymns, and spiritual songs." The latter approach is the way of Hebrew authors. This is the method of the political writings among the Dead Sea Scrolls.

The fumes of popular disaffection with Alexander Jannaeus had been gathering for some time, but the spark that ignited them would strike most of us as hopelessly obscure and unimportant, a niggling matter of religious law. The question was where to pour a certain libation while celebrating the autumn harvest Festival of Tabernacles. When the time came to pour the libation, Alexander made a show of pouring the water on his feet, following the protocol—according to Sadducean understanding. The Pharisees held that the libation must be poured instead on the altar. Hence the people's anger when they saw what Jannaeus had done, for the general populace more and more favored Pharisee ideas.

With the slaughter of his opponents, Alexander guaranteed that priestly and Sadducean approaches to Temple law would continue to hold sway. But he also raised the stakes in the disputes by planting the seed of violence. Civil war became inevitable. From this moment the Pharisees and their supporters sought an opportunity for revenge. Not long thereafter they got one.

Alexander had launched a campaign against an Arab kingdom to the east, the Nabateans. Things went poorly, and when Alexander returned to Jerusalem at the nadir of his power, the Pharisees launched an open revolt. They were supported by a traditional enemy of the Jews, the Syrian Greeks to the north, whose forces were led by their king, Demetrius III. Alexander was eventually overwhelmed, his mercenary soldiers wiped out. The Jewish king was forced to flee for his life and to seek refuge in the mountains.

At this point the Pharisees had won, but now the cost of that victory began to impress itself on many of their Jewish allies. True, they had thrown off the yoke of a king they despised, but what had they really gained? The comprehension dawned that they had merely exchanged one master for another. Their new ruler would not even be Jewish but would be the Syrian, Demetrius. With a stunning illogic, six thousand of the Pharisees' allies changed sides and went over to Alexander. Demetrius calculated that with this shift in the balance of power his prospects for easy dominion over the Jews had dissolved. Besides, dynastic politics in Syria needed his immediate attention; he turned and marched back to Syria.

The Pharisees and their remaining allies fought on against Alexander and his revitalized army, but their window of opportunity had slammed shut. The civil war climaxed with Alexander's siege of the Pharisaic faction at a place whose name has come down to us, variously, as Bethome or Bemeselis.

Some eight hundred leaders of the revolt were captured and taken to Jerusalem. There Alexander killed their wives and children before their eyes, then crucified the revolutionaries while he himself (as Josephus tells it) caroused with his mistresses. Thus Alexander purged the wound of Pharisaic opposition, but rather than heal, the wound festered on for another decade. No other result was possible so long as Alexander continued to sponsor the dominance of priestly and Sadducean law in the Temple, and he did that as long as he lived. Consequently, the question became what would happen when Alexander died.

Would the crisis that had divided the Jewish house against itself for one generation live on into the next?

After the civil war and in the waning years of Alexander's reign, while continuing to oppose his policies, the Pharisees had gone on to garner still greater support with the masses. As that support became more and more evident even to the aristocratic elite, the Pharisees gained new allies within the ranks of the powerful. By the time of Alexander's death, their faction had become more potent than that of the Sadducees and priests. Political wisdom dictated that his successor recognize this new reality. So when Alexander died in 76 B.C.E., his queen, Alexandra, took the king's advice, did an about-face, and embraced the Pharisees. She appointed her elder son, Hyrcanus II, as high priest, and charged him with instituting the Pharisaic statutes in the Temple. The state now stood behind the Pharisaic vision of the law.

But as it turned out, the crisis was not thereby resolved. It had simply undergone a metamorphosis: the outs were in, and the ins, out. The issues remained, the enmity remained, the violence would continue.

THE JEWISH NATION was an animal caught in a trap, chewing off its own leg. The situation was ripe for what happened next. A millenarian prophet arose to lead a crisis cult. And he would become more than a prophet: he would be the first messiah of recorded history.

Before him the sources know no messiah. In the two centuries after him, like a mid-Atlantic hurricane, messianism fed upon the currents, growing, gaining force, sometimes swirling shoreward to batter those in its path with revolution. Twice the messianic idea helped propel its nation of origin into war with Rome and its legions. The first time, Jerusalem was burned to the ground and the Temple destroyed. The second time, half a million Jews lost their lives and the southern towns of Judaea were obliterated. In the decades following this archetypal messiah, other men repeatedly stepped forward to claim the role he debuted and to lead messianic movements among the Jews.

Jesus of Nazareth was one of them.

The name of the first messiah is nowhere stated outright, but a few clues in the Dead Sea Scrolls suggest that it may have been Judah. That is what I shall call him. His own followers called him the Teacher of Righteousness. This charismatic figure was able to express what many people were feeling but could not articulate. He began to caress, to shape anew, the inchoate notions of the myth-dream of Israel. The conceptual artifact that he created was beautiful and immensely powerful. Its repercussions reach to our own day.

ENTER THE PROPHET

Judah stepped forth from the highest ranks of the Jerusalem priesthood, a man well acquainted with the corridors of power and the politics of the royal court. About sixty years old, he was one of the greatest minds of his generation, and he had exercised that mind all of his life in the study of Holy Writ.

Now he confronted his weary nation with an urgent message from God. The nation's crisis had come about, Judah declared, because the people and their leaders had sinned, abandoning the ways of God that their forefathers had honored. They must now return to those ways. They must enter a *covenant of repentance,* a New Covenant.[3] Then would follow blessing, the wondrous era of peace and prosperity of which the biblical prophets had spoken.

But if the people refused, they would be destroyed and the nation would fall, for the Latter Days were at hand. Recognizing his as the last generation, the millennial generation, Judah called for decision. The time to repent was at hand.

Judah presented the people with Ten Commandments, the essence of his New Covenant, as Moses had done with the original covenant at Sinai. (Actually, there were more than ten, but if you examine the Bible carefully, you will find that the same is true of Moses' list.) In typical crisis-cult fashion, Judah's law encapsulated the divine message:

> *You shall separate yourselves from the Children of Hell.*
>
> *You shall renounce wealth acquired by wickedness, which defiles gifts and offerings dedicated to the Temple, and the Temple treasury as well.*
>
> *You shall not rob the poor of God's people, for that is to plunder widows and murder orphans.*
>
> *You shall distinguish between what is ritually unclean and what is pure, and so teach the difference between the holy and the profane.*
>
> *You shall observe the Sabbath as is proper, and the festivals and Day of Atonement according to the teachings of the New Covenant.*
>
> *You shall offer the sacrifices according to the exact rules for each.*
>
> *You shall love one another as yourselves.*
>
> *You shall fortify the poor, the needy and the stranger.*
>
> *You shall each of you seek the other's welfare.*

You shall not deal treacherously with your own flesh and blood.

You shall refrain from illicit marriage according to the law.

You shall reprove one another according to the commandment.

You shall not carry a grudge from one day to the next.

You shall separate yourselves from every type of ritual uncleanness in the proper way.

You shall none of you defile your holy spirit, avoiding that as God has taught.[4]

The first and foremost requirement of Judah's New Covenant was the one most provocative to authorities: *You shall not enter the Temple to kindle God's altar in vain.* By "vain kindling" Judah alluded to Malachi 3:10, which states that offering no sacrifices is preferable to offering them wrongly. With these words and without the slightest nuance, Judah condemned the Pharisaic laws taking hold in the Temple.

And he went further. He charged the people to refuse support to the Temple activities so long as the Pharisee laws held forth. Judah was convinced that the nation had gone awry in how it celebrated the festivals, especially that holiest day of the year, the Day of Atonement. Under Pharisee direction, these celebrations were taking place on the wrong days, which meant that they were null and void. Therefore, lacking atonement, the people were still in their sins, and they did not even realize it. This sin was provoking the crisis.

A long and bitter dispute lay behind Judah's charges about the festivals. For more than a century, priestly groups had been advocating that a solar calendar of 364 days be used in the Temple. This calendar, they argued, was once used by the patriarchs Abraham, Isaac, and Jacob; only later had Israel forgotten it. Theirs was a nationalist claim and also an implicit criticism of the calendar of the Pharisees, which was a variant of those used in the surrounding Gentile nations.[5] The Pharisee calendar, a 354-day lunar-based calendar, was more or less identical to the modern Jewish version. To the nationalist priests it was also a calendar of the Gentiles.

Despite the feuding about the calendar, earlier priestly groups had been willing to participate in the Temple activities; Judah himself had once been among them. But now, seeing with the clarity of new revelation, he thought differently. To obtain God's blessing, the nation must return to God's laws—all of them, including the proper calendar. Half measures were useless.

Judah's message was radical and divisive. No one could miss its implicit criticisms of the royal family's behavior. Controversy stirred within the most powerful circles in Jerusalem. The Pharisees—who were hardly, as Elizabethans would say, "secret in displeasure"—went on the attack.

UNAPPRECIATED by scholars for what they really are, Judah's words have come down to us in a work known as the *Thanksgiving Hymns*. A copy of this writing was among the original group of seven Dead Sea Scroll manuscripts discovered in 1947 by an Arab shepherd, Muhammad edh-Dhib, in a cave now known as Cave One. Later six additional copies of the *Thanksgiving Hymns* turned up in another cave (Cave Four), and a few postage-stamp-sized scraps of one more copy were salvaged from the original cave. By combining all eight of these fragmentary copies of the *Hymns,* it is possible to reconstruct the original form of the best preserved manuscript. It comprised twenty-eight columns (a column being the ancient equivalent of a page), on which were inscribed about forty separate hymns and discourses.

All but two or three of these hymns are couched in the first person. They share with the other Dead Sea Scrolls and 99 percent of all ancient Jewish literature something that strikes us as odd: they contain no signature; they name no author. Charles McGrath, editor of the *New York Times Book Review,* once opined, "In an ideal world every book would be anonymous—read for itself, not for who wrote or published it."[6] Perhaps. Still, that ideal world existed once, among the ancients of the Near East, only to give way before the Greek cult of personality. Anonymity has been unsatisfying to us ever since. We want to know.

Consequently, a notable problem of scholarship has been to figure out: Who was this "I" of the *Hymns?* The key that turned the lock has proven to be literary criticism, the techniques that eighteenth- and nineteenth-century scholars developed when they initiated the enterprise of modern biblical studies. Gert Jeremias was among the first to apply the method to the *Hymns.*[7] Writing in 1963, he showed that two distinct levels of authorship are mixed together in these writings.

On one level, the "I" of the *Hymns* is only representative. Here the pronoun stands for a group, not a single person. At other times, though, the "I" makes strong claims of authority and distances himself from others. Jeremias went on to note that the "authoritative" hymns also employ a vocabulary that is self-consistent and that differs from the rest of the hymns. For Jeremias, the individual "I" was the Teacher of Righteousness.

In a recent doctoral dissertation, Michael Douglas has advanced our understanding with a more comprehensive study of the levels within the *Hymns*. He has refined Jeremias's conclusions with a wealth of additional data and also has shown that the individual "I" hymns were transmitted as a unit. Subsequently, followers added materials fore and aft. These additions, the second level of authorship, are known today as Community Hymns. They are the writings where the "I" stands for a group. Thus we have Teacher Hymns and Community Hymns.[8]

So literary critics have been able to separate out two levels of authorship in the *Hymns*. And, granted, one level, one "I," is an individual of great authority. Still, how do we know that this "I" is the Teacher? How can we be sure that these are the words of Judah? Jeremias pondered this question long and hard. He studied other Dead Sea Scrolls that talk about the Teacher and compared their claims for the man to the claims being made by the authoritative "I." He then came up with a compelling argument, writing, "It is completely inconceivable that there could have been within the [same] company in a short span of time two men, each of whom came before the group with revolutionary claims to bring about redemption through his teaching, and that both men could have been accepted by the group."[9]

Had two such men arisen at the same time, Jeremias implied, there would have been conflict. No group could accept two such singular personalities as leaders simultaneously. And if the group had known two charismatic figures who lived at different times, evidence of that fact should be discernible in their writings. It isn't. Powerful logic indeed. But the best logic about what should have been in history is often overturned by later discoveries. The historian prefers evidence over logic. The historian wants a statement in the sources, something close to the time of the events. Fortunately, we have that in this case.

In their later writings, followers of Judah interpreted the "anonymous" words of his hymns and discourses as his.[10] They applied them to events in the life of a man they explicitly called the Teacher of Righteousness, so the conclusion is hard to resist: even though his name is not on them, Judah's followers believed that he had written the Teacher Hymns. They evidently possessed oral traditions about him and the early years of their own movement. When they wished to write about Judah, they turned to his very words.

Thanks to historical and literary criticism, we may be confident that in the *Thanksgiving Hymns* we do have the words of the prophet Judah. We have at least nine hymns from his hand. Together they constitute his spiritual testament—the Testament of the Teacher. They seem to have begun as personal meditations. These were Judah's reflections on events, poured out privately before his God in poetry and rhythmic prose. This origin explains much.

It explains why the hymns are sometimes concise to the point of obscurity, touching down on a notion only to fly on immediately to another, like a stone skipping over a pond. At other times the ideas are so overgrown with words that a machete is needed to hack through the verbiage and follow the trail. To this very personal origin the closest ancient parallel is the *Meditations* of the Roman Emperor Marcus Aurelius (ruled 161–180 C.E.). Like the twelve books of Marcus's *Meditations,* Judah's were personal writings composed at various times and places, only discovered and published after the author's death. Yet Judah's hymns were even more personal than the precepts set forth by Marcus Aurelius; they were akin to a modern diary.

Judah's hymns seem to have been arranged and transmitted in chronological order.[11] We can therefore map out the prophet's thought as it unfolded in response to changing circumstances. Though personal, these are also political writings, reflecting what Judah was saying and doing in the political situation in which he found himself. Once we understand that context, they leap to life. They allow us to follow matters closely from the time of the Pharisee takeover until events took a most unexpected turn.

THE TESTAMENT OF THE TEACHER

Once Alexandra became queen, Josephus reports, "She permitted the Pharisees to do as they liked . . . and commanded the people to obey them."[12]

But Judah did not obey them. Moreover, he urged others not to obey them either, declaring that God was behind his words. The Pharisee response becomes evident in Judah's first hymn, written in 76 B.C.E. (You are reading here the words of the first messiah; think of them as such while you read.)

> [I praise You, O Lo]rd . . . You have placed truth before my very eyes, and righteous men to reprove me . . . Those who, when I am sunk in mournful gloom, give me reasons to rejoice; they declare to me glad tidings of a peaceful result in the face of destructive rumors about me and [fears] so strong that my heart melts. They fortify me in the face of attack.

> You have given to my uncircumcised lips a tongue capable of reply, and You have supported me as I gird my loins and gather my strength. You have ordered my steps within the wicked realm. I am a snare to sinners, but healing to all who repent of sin; wisdom to the simple folk, and a steadfast mind to all the faint hearted. You have made me an object of scorn and derision for the unfaithful, but the very foundation of truth and understanding for the upright. Because of the iniquity of the wicked, I am defamed by the lips of violent men; scorners gnash their teeth. Sinners mock me in song, and the party of the wicked falls stormily upon me. They roar like mighty winds upon the seas; lifting up their waves, they spew mud and slime.

> Yet You have set me as a banner to the chosen righteous, a prophet given knowledge of wondrous mysteries. I test [the men] of truth, and try those who love instruction. I am an adversary to advisers of falsehood, but a man of [pea]ce to all seers of uprightness. I am become a spirit of zeal against all the Seekers of Accomm[odation, wherefore all] deceitful men bellow against me like the roaring of mighty waters. [All] their thoughts are so many schemes of Belial. Accordingly, they turn back to Hell the life of the man whom You had set aright by my mouth and taught. You placed insight in my heart whereby to open the fount of knowledge for all the initiated—yet they have exchanged this wisdom for an uncircumcised lip and a strange tongue, so becoming a people without understanding. Thus will they be ruined in their delusion.[13]

Judah was under attack; with this hymn he made the case for his leadership. His first defense was to focus attention on who he was. He wrote of himself, *I am a snare to sinners, but healing to all who repent of sin . . . a steadfast mind to all the faint hearted . . . a man of peace to all whose vision is righteous.* Note Judah's use of the term *all.* He was saying that what happened to him was crucial to the entire nation, to every Jew.

He stigmatized his opposition as all the unrighteous: *I am a spirit of zeal against all the Seekers of Accommodation . . . all deceitful men bellow against me.* Judah was not some fringe politician with a small group of extremist followers. He claimed to be a leader of national significance, and the ferocity of the verbal attack against him argues that he was. Again and again Judah defines himself: I am . . . I am. Clearly a focal point of the controversy was whether or not Judah actually was who he claimed to be.

So it was with Jesus, as the Gospels tell the story. "Who do men say that I am?" Jesus once asked his disciples, according to the author of Matthew's Gospel. The Gospel of John depicts Jesus, like Judah, using "I am" phrases to declare his sense of mission. Jesus says, "I am the light of the world" and "I am the way, the truth, and the life." John is often called the Gospel of the "I am" statements. Judah's various expressions of status and significance in the first hymn are analogous. These are the "I am" statements of the *Thanksgiving Hymns.*

Almost certainly Judah wrote in Jerusalem, for this controversy centered around religious law and the Temple. Jerusalem was the one religious and political center of significance in Judaea at this time. This is where *the party of the wicked,* that is, the Pharisees, had their headquarters. Judah subtly punned on the Hebrew name of Jerusalem when he spoke of being *within the wicked realm* (the second and third syllables of *Ye-ru-sha-layim* are assonant with the word for wicked, *ri-sha*). Furthermore, this phrase was a quotation from Malachi 1:4, whereby Judah invoked the broader context of the quotation. It was a portion familiar to everyone in the debate: "They will be called a *wicked realm,* a people always under the wrath of the Lord."

Judah vilified the Pharisees and their supporters with a variety of epithets, calling them *sinners, the unfaithful, violent men, scorners, advisers of falsehood, deceitful men.* The wording that most specifically refers to the Pharisees (*Pharisees* being a term the Dead Sea Scrolls never use) I have translated *Seekers of Accommodation.* The Hebrew is *dorshe halaqot;* the second word, *halaqot,* basically means "smooth." It plays on the technical term that the Pharisees and the later rabbis used for "religious laws," *halakhot.* By this wordplay Judah derided the Pharisaic laws as unreliable, slippery, insufficiently rigorous, and thus an accommodation—made, he implied, merely to gain popularity with the people, and at the expense of faithfulness to God's covenant with Israel.

Judah found himself the target of a war of words: *I am defamed by the lips of violent men; scorners gnash their teeth. Sinners mock me in song.* The first acts of Judah's public conflict with the Pharisees were verbal volleys. That accords with the natural order of human societies.

As the eminent sociologist Bruce Lincoln has written in *Discourse and the Construction of Society,* "Discourse and force are the chief means whereby social borders, hierarchies, institutional formations, and habituated patterns of behavior are both maintained and modified."[14] The Pharisees were dismantling social patterns that under Alexander Jannaeus had held sway for decades. In the process, they sought to intimidate Judah and others of his station in society (Judah's *righteous men to reprove me*) into shifting their allegiances, into following the lead of Alexandra and the ruling family. Moreover, this intimidation was working—Judah admitted to being terrified (*my heart melts with fear*). The Pharisees had succeeded in winning over some of Judah's allies and disciples: *they turn back to Hell the life of the man whom You had set aright by my mouth and taught.*

This seething war of words threatened to boil over. Social conflicts work themselves out through stages, as the research of the anthropologist Victor Turner has shown. Turner's stages are first "breach," then "escalation of crisis," "redressive action," and finally "reintegration or irreparable schism." Matters between Judah and the Pharisees were at the third stage. Actions were being taken that would either heal the breach, or widen it into irreparable schism. At this point, says Turner, "the group [to whom the action is addressed] is . . . at its most 'self-conscious' and may attain the clarity of someone fighting in a corner for his life."[15] Judah and his allies were being cornered.

Turner continues, "When redress fails there is usually regression to crisis. At this point direct force may be used."[16]

And the Pharisees did intend to force the issue.

THE CRISIS that now roiled around Judah drove him to write the first hymn. What he wrote gives us precious insight into the developing self-consciousness of a prophet. It also allows us to draw inferences about

Judah's situation before the Pharisee takeover. The critical phrase in both respects is the claim to be *a prophet given knowledge of wondrous mysteries*. This assertion invites closer inspection, for much lies beneath the surface of these words.

The term I have translated *prophet* is not the ordinary Hebrew word for such figures. In modern translations of biblical texts, the word that Judah used (Hebrew *melits*) is usually rendered into English as *interpreter* or *envoy*. For example, Genesis 42:23 uses the word in the context of the patriarch Joseph's meeting with his brothers. They first sold him into slavery and then, years later, came down to Egypt to buy grain. Thinking Joseph an Egyptian official ignorant of their native tongue, when in his presence the brothers conferred in Hebrew. The portion reads, "They did not know that Joseph understood them, since he spoke with them through an interpreter (*melits*)."

The term's use in Job 33:23 exploits a different nuance. The biblical writer employs it in parallel with a Hebrew word for *angel*. (The study of such poetic parallels is one of the best ways of determining the range of meaning for ancient Hebrew terms.) "Then, if there should be for one of them an angel, a mediator (*melits*) . . ." Here, a superhuman element intrudes.

In brief, analysis of biblical Hebrew usage shows that *melits* means, broadly, "one who speaks for another." Precisely how it ought to be understood in any one case depends on the parties involved: on who is spoken for, whom addressed.

The word's use outside of the Bible, in a Hebrew book composed just a hundred years before Judah set down his hymns, is especially instructive. About 180 B.C.E., Jesus ben Sira penned (quilled, actually; ancient writers used reed quills) a work known today by two names: *The Wisdom of Ben Sira,* and *Ecclesiasticus* (not to be confused with the biblical book Ecclesiastes). In chapter 10:1–2 of this book, Ben Sira ruminated on the connections between rulers and their subjects. He wrote, "A wise magistrate lends stability to his people, and the government of a prudent person is well ordered. As is the people's judge, so are his *ministers* (*melits*); as is the head of a city, so are its inhabitants."[17]

The Wisdom of Ben Sira shows that in the second century B.C.E., the word *melits* had taken on a connotation not clearly present in biblical usage. It had come to mean "minister" or "courtier." The term was a class marker, almost a title, describing someone of elite social standing. As a member of what sociologists call a "retainer class," this person evidently stood above the masses, but beneath the ruler, whom he served directly.[18]

The way Judah used the word drew on more than one of these meanings. (It is thus an excellent example of the double entendres frequent in Judah's hymns.) He had presumably served at the court of Alexander, advising the king on religious matters, so Judah was a courtier. On one level that is what he said about himself. Likewise, his Pharisaic opponents were also courtiers, though in Judah's view not the sort a king would want. Judah called them *advisers* (*melits*) *of falsehood*. Yet Judah was not merely a courtier—at least, not anymore.

The crisis of the Pharisees' rise to power had forced Judah to rethink everything that he believed. His thoughts about himself had also taken a new direction. Under the pressure of events he had come to see himself as *the* intermediary between the nation and God. That is why what happened to him mattered so much. Of course, the Pharisees, reputed (as Josephus says) to be the most accurate interpreters of the Bible, were also professing to be intermediaries. But they made the assertion in an attenuated sense. They claimed merely to possess the proper understanding of the authoritative writings that had come down through the ages.

Judah trumped that ace. His was no claim to explicate difficult biblical laws, though he could do that. Judah *knew*. He did not get his message only by studying the sacred texts. Judah got his message directly from God. The supernatural nuance we observed in Job's use of *melits* is a second element of Judah's intention in using the word. He had come as a messenger intermediary to deliver a message from God.

Few scholars have gotten Judah's point. According to Stephen Neill and Tom Wright, for example—they seek to represent the consensus of modern scholarship—Judah "had been the *Teacher* of Righteousness; he was of a different lineage, and no one had ever claimed for him that he was a prophet." No one, perhaps, but Judah himself.[19]

W HAT, PRECISELY, did Judah mean by the phrase *wondrous mysteries* (Hebrew *razze pele*)? This is not an easy question to answer, though an answer is essential if we are to understand Judah. Other than Judah's own use and a few derivative occurrences in the literature his crisis-cult followers composed after his death, the phrase appears in just one surviving work of Second Temple Judaism. This work was demonstrably influential on the movement Judah founded, though, so it is reasonable (though not provable) to conclude that he lifted this phrase from it.[20] The scroll in which it appears is a specimen of "wisdom literature."

Essentially, "wisdom literature" means how-to books on the topic of life. These writings search for understanding, trying to discover—and, once it is found, to communicate—the meaning of life. The idea that a basic order underlies the apparent randomness and injustice of day-to-day life was fundamental to the ancients. Several books within the Bible are wisdom writings (notably Proverbs, Ecclesiastes, and Job), and almost every culture of the ancient Near East developed similar books. The oldest collections of proverbs are not Israelite, but Egyptian; they antedate the Bible by more than a thousand years.[21]

In Israel the writing of wisdom literature did not cease when the biblical writers laid down their quills. Prominent among the nonbiblical representatives of the genre is one book we have already encountered, *The Wisdom of Ben Sira*. With the discovery of the Dead Sea Scrolls, a number of other nonbiblical wisdom books came to light. These works otherwise perished in antiquity, though they may have been widely known among the Jews of Jesus' time. It is one of these books that contains Judah's key phrase *wondrous mysteries*. We must therefore take a closer look at this writing.

The work is sometimes called, after one of its recurrent phrases, *The Secret of the Way Things Are,* and seven copies of it have emerged from the caves of the Dead Sea. Like the Sermon on the Mount in the New Testament, *The Secret of the Way Things Are* issues ethical instructions for the imminent end of the age.[22] In the shadow of this impending apocalypse, the work is much concerned with God's foreordained timetable. Its author urges the reader to *learn the secret of the way things are, the weight of eras.* He declares that *God has put into my heart true knowledge and understanding*—the result, he intimates, of *the vision I have seen.*

The author touches on a jumble of topics, including wisdom and folly, marriage and the proper respect for parents, borrowing and lending money (do neither), and the need to keep his teaching a secret from the wicked. Few modern women (and even fewer mothers-in-law) will be pleased to hear his admonition to husbands: he tells the man, *God has made you ruler over her . . . He has not made her mother ruler over her. He has separated her from her mother and given authority to you.* (These ideas are worth comparing with similar injunctions to husbands in the New Testament book of Ephesians, chapter 5).

An important element of *The Secret*'s teaching involved astrology, but this portion of the manuscripts has suffered great damage and it is no longer possible to extract the details of what was said about the royal science. Still, there can be no doubt of astrology's prominent role within *The Secret of the Way Things Are*. We may begin to suspect that astrological knowledge lay within the compass of Judah's *wondrous mysteries*. The portion of *The Secret of the Way Things Are* that uses that phrase now commands our attention.

Here the writer has been discussing good and evil and the enigmas of God's purposes. He goes on to say:

> *Seek these things with longing at all times; give careful thought to all their effects, and then you will experience [His eternal] glory, His wondrous mysteries and His divine wonders. By knowing the times, you are one who understands the best way to act.*
>
> *[For] the decree engraved in advance is coming. Every time of punishment has been inscribed. Indeed, what has been decreed is engraved for God in stone, concerning all the sins of the children of Seth. A book of remembrance stands written before Him, accessible to those who keep His words; and that book of remembrance contains the vision of meditation.*
>
> *God bequeathed the meditation to Enosh by spiritual perception, because his nature was patterned after the holy angels. Otherwise He has not given meditation to those of a fleshly nature, for they do not know the difference between good and evil in accordance with spiritual law.*[23]

This passage, with its sharply drawn distinction between "the spirit" and "the flesh," almost sounds like something the apostle Paul could have written. Occasionally what the author intended to say is obscure, but the general movement of his thought is clear. He describes a heavenly book, open before God. People with the proper spiritual cultivation can "read" it by *meditation*.

Through meditation the initiate seeks a particular *vision*. We have thus entered the realm of mystical experience, of esoteric revelation. The vision focuses on knowledge of the times—that is, the predestined course of history. The content of this book is one of God's *wondrous mysteries*.

Somehow the initiate can *experience* the mysteries. That experience also involves the glory of God, and—whether in a concrete or abstract sense—God's *divine wonders.* Miracles?

The writer goes on to say that this book is immensely old—older, by far, than the law of Moses. Given by divine revelation in the days of the patriarch Seth, knowledge of it was passed on to later generations, but not in writing. Rather it was *by spiritual perception,* beginning with Seth's son Enosh.

Now, Seth was the third child of Adam and Eve, born after Cain had murdered Abel. The Bible says that when Seth's son Enosh was born, "people began to call upon the name of YHWH" (Genesis 4:26). This portentous statement generated considerable speculation in later Judaism and among the exponents of early forms of Christianity. From it grew the notion of a pure line of Sethians carried on by Enosh. Gnostic circles included a group styling themselves "Sethians," and a Gnostic writing known as *The Three Tablets of Seth* was among a group of ancient Coptic texts discovered in 1948 in Nag Hammadi, Egypt.

Josephus also knew of a tradition connecting esoteric revelation with the line of Seth. He included in one of his books, *The Antiquities of the Jews,* something of what he called "the story of the children of Seth." These virtuous people, he says, "discovered the science of the heavenly bodies and their orderly array. Moreover, to prevent their discoveries from being lost to humankind, perishing before they became known . . . they erected two stelae, one of brick, the other of stone, and inscribed these discoveries on both."[24]

In outline Josephus's tradition of the Sethian line is similar to the statements of *The Secret of the Way Things Are.* The line that began with Enosh was virtuous, and because of that virtue they were granted the secrets of *the science of the heavenly bodies and their orderly array.* That means astrology and related knowledge. These secrets they preserved for posterity on two stelae (tablets set upright into the ground). Evidently Josephus and the author of *The Secret of the Way Things Are* were both acquainted with this tradition, though in variant forms.

With the explicit link between the Sethian secrets and astrology in Josephus we have even more reason to believe that Judah's *wondrous mysteries* did involve astrology. The heart of the secrets will have been the proper use of these sciences—as an adjunct, doubtless, to the study of scripture—to secure the *knowledge of the times:* foretell the future.

A SECOND PASSAGE in the Dead Sea Scrolls, this one in the introduction to the first edition of the *Thanksgiving Hymns* itself, appears to clinch the astrological connection.

This introduction to the *Thanksgiving Hymns* was inscribed by one of Judah's disciples soon after Judah's death. The disciple wrote in the first person. Judah, of course, had done the same in his own hymns. The result of this pronominal peculiarity was to make the disciple's introduction seem to be the words of the Teacher. This effect was intentional, but—fine as the line may seem—the ancients did not consider such writing fraud per se. Not that the ancients were blind to the possibility of literary forgery.

They knew it well, for it was not uncommon, and they condemned it. The church father Tertullian reports an instance of a presbyter in Asia Minor who was removed from office for composing a pious forgery. But the ancients made a distinction that we do not. This distinction hinged on integrity and intent. Provided that one wrote not to deceive, but in the spirit of the figure impersonated—carrying his ideas forward with integrity, making *his* point, as it were, in current controversies—no offense was involved. This was a common literary convention of the period. Reflecting our own sensibilities rather than ancient mores, scholars call the phenomenon *pseudepigraphy,* "false writing."[25]

Depending on how well the writing was done, modern literary analysts can often distinguish the true from the false. Michael Douglas has shown that not Judah, but a later follower, wrote the introduction. The situation parallels the common scholarly view of the apostle Paul's letters. Virtually all scholars agree that Paul wrote the New Testament books of Romans, 1 and 2 Corinthians, Galatians, and several others. But most also believe that the letters of Titus and 1 and 2 Timothy—though they seem to claim Paul's name—were written instead by disciples. If so, they were pseudepigraphs.[26] Parts of the *Thanksgiving Hymns* were likewise pseudepigraphy.

Working, as he believed, under the inspiration of the Teacher's spirit, this disciple poured forth praise to God in a long hymn on the creation.[27] *By your wisdom,* he wrote, *you established the generations of eternity. Before you created them, you knew everything they would do forever and ever.* These words laid the foundation for what follows, a long list enumerating the elements of God's creation, beginning with heavenly creatures, then turning to earthbound entities. The list includes various categories of divine beings—spirits, the heavenly host, principalities and powers, holy angels—each of which was said to rule its own domain. Of particular interest is the mention of God's creating *the sun and moon, together with their mysteries,* and *the stars, together with the paths they should take.*

What would have seemed mysterious about the sun and moon? It was their movements. Many believed that God had plotted out these movements aforetime and that they affected matters here on earth. Yet ancient observers of the heavens found them difficult to chart. Especially puzzling was the passage of the moon. (These motions are indeed highly variable. Only in modern times have they yielded to human efforts at a full and accurate understanding.) One reason to try to understand these movements was to design a calendar. Calendars, as markers of sacred time, were important and often controversial documents. We have seen how much weight Judah put on the proper calendar. The reference to the paths of the stars, on the other hand, was a straightforward ancient Hebrew way of describing astrology.

The writer went on to list other heavenly spirits: storms, thunder and lightning, and the storehouses of heaven (the latter, according to conventional notions, served as receptacles for rainwater). All of these entities he conceived as just that: living, moving beings who served at God's pleasure. And all of their deeds, everything they would ever do—every movement they would make, from everlasting to everlasting—was predestined. Thus, if one could break the code of their movements and deeds, one could know the end from the beginning. The key to the code, the disciple implied, lay in astrological and calendrical knowledge.

The writer next turned to human affairs. These, too, he asserted, God had purposed before creation, *according to the number of generations forever, for all the years of eternity.* God in his wisdom had established *their periods of existence before ever they came to be.* Then came the climax: *I know these things through understanding you have granted, for you have revealed to me your wondrous mysteries.*

What was the disciple-as-Teacher claiming to know? Not merely the fact of the creation of these celestial and earthly beings, for any reader of the initial chapters of Genesis could claim that much. Even children would scoff at a claim that such knowledge was special. That God had created the sun, moon, stars, and creatures of this world, culminating in humankind, would hardly qualify as a mystery at all, much less a wondrous one.

No, the real claim was to knowledge of the *patterns* of the creation. These patterns—whether celestial or chronological, whether involving the paths of the stars or those of a generation of humankind—were truly mysterious, and to know them was wonderful indeed.

Thus, writing not long after Judah's death, and doubtless with a firm tradition about what the Teacher had taught under the phrase in question, this disciple defined what the *wondrous mysteries* embraced. To know the mysteries meant to know God's creation and how it worked, where it was going. It meant an understanding of human destiny in the whole and in the parts. It therefore meant, among other things, being able to predict the future.

Ultimately this knowledge could come only through direct revelation from God, but full immersion in his wisdom, including an esoteric literary tradition, was the absolute prerequisite—the union card, as it were, without which one could not work. The means by which this revelation could come included astrology and (as *The Secret of the Way Things Are* suggests) visions induced by meditation.

By calling himself *a prophet given knowledge of wondrous mysteries,* then, Judah was asserting that he was of a stature comparable to that of any of Israel's ancient prophets. Isaiah, Jeremiah, Ezekiel, Daniel—these men had long ago spoken for God. All Jews held their written words to be divinely authoritative. But they had nothing on Judah. Had they declared the future from of old? So would he.

And he would do it in part using a method earlier prophets had condemned.[28] Judah well knew the words Isaiah 47:13–14 directed to Israel: "Let those who study the heavens stand up and save you, those who gaze at the stars and at each new moon predict what shall befall you. See, they are like stubble. The fire consumes them!" Yet Judah need not hew to what the ancients had laid down. As a prophet himself he was all that they were—and even more.

For when Judah wrote, *You have given to my uncircumcised lips a tongue capable of reply,* he was hinting that one greater than Isaiah was here. The only person in the Bible to whom the phrase *uncircumcised lips* is attached is Moses: lawgiver of Israel, greatest of the biblical prophets. Judah was intimating that he was a new Moses. Since he had a new law to give, and a New Covenant to inaugurate, the comparison was natural. It carried with it an implied threat. Any reader of the Bible would know the fate of those who had opposed Moses.

Fire came from heaven and incinerated some; the earth opened and swallowed others.

A SECOND TRAJECTORY emerges from Judah's hymn. The wording suggests that before the crisis of the Pharisee takeover, Judah had lived in Jerusalem as a wisdom teacher.

The hymn contains manifold references to wisdom, teaching, initiation into truth, and understanding. Judah wrote that he was the *foundation of . . . understanding*; his role was to *try those who love instruction*. We have seen that the phrase *wondrous mysteries* implies Judah's immersion in wisdom writings. Judah even went so far as to say that he was wisdom personified: *I am . . . wisdom to the simple folk*. (The idea of the personification of wisdom is central to modern research on the historical Jesus, for he also, according to many scholars, was first and foremost a sage.) These wisdom elements point us backward, telling us something of Judah's life in Jerusalem in the decades preceding the crisis of 76 B.C.E.

The life of a Jewish sage and wisdom instructor changed little in the years between 180 B.C.E. and the time when Judah held forth in Jerusalem. Therefore we can make inferences about Judah's life based upon our fuller knowledge of that earlier sage, Jesus ben Sira. Ben Sira labeled himself a "scribe," which in this period meant a wise man. Over his lifetime he devoted himself to study and meditation upon the books of Moses, the Prophets, and other holy writ, and in his later years he wrote his own book distilling those years of study.

Ben Sira was a man of leisure. He was free from manual labor, not a peasant as were the great mass of Jews, living as they did by subsistence farming. Indeed, only because he was wealthy enough not to have to toil physically could he hope to become a sage. Or at least, so Ben Sira thought, and doubtless it was the usual pattern. As Tevye of *Fiddler on the Roof* lamented, none but a rich man could discuss the holy books seven hours every day.

With the self-importance typical of many modern academics Ben Sira wrote, "By the scribe's profession wisdom increases; whoever is free of toil can become wise. How can he become wise who guides the plow, who thrills in wielding the goad like a lance, who guides the ox and urges on the bullock, and whose concern is for cattle?"[29]

Ben Sira belonged to the elite, to the educated and literate upper stratum of Jerusalem society. This group represented perhaps 5 percent of the populace. While the peasants labored in their fields, the sage spent his hours in the way Ben Sira described:

> He studies the wisdom of all the ancients and occupies himself with the prophecies. He treasures the discourse of the famous, and goes to the heart of involved sayings. He studies the hidden meaning of proverbs. . . . He is in attendance on the great, and has entrance to the ruler. He travels among the peoples of foreign lands to test what is good and evil among people. . . . He meditates upon God's mysteries. He will show the wisdom of what he has learned and glory in the Law of the Lord's covenant.[30]

As the leading scholars of their society, men such as Ben Sira and Judah were at home in lofty social circles. They tutored the youth of the aristocracy and royal family. Ben Sira ran an academy, and it is probable that Judah likewise met with students in a special venue, perhaps in the Temple courts or a private home.[31]

We must imagine that Judah had spent several decades in regular meetings with Jerusalem youth, instructing them and, naturally, building a following. He would have developed influence among the households whose heads imbibed his teachings, including the royal family. Disciples and supporters grew to respect and even love him. Like all eminent men, he also acquired enemies and stirred rivals who, given the chance, would seek his overthrow.

Ben Sira wrote that wise men were experts in the law. He meant that they were skilled in applying the scriptures to actual practice. In this connection they had to take stands on controversial points, so—as in many societies—among the Jews scholars were natural leaders for conflicting factions.[32] Despite this leading role, they did not comprise the very highest echelon of society. Ben Sira placed above them "the great": kings and queens, princes and members of the extended royal family, upon whose pleasure the wise men ultimately were dependent, and to whom they acted as advisers.

Attendance upon the great was like hang gliding: you took a big risk and had to be very sensitive to wind direction. The displeasure of the royals might be terminal. Ben Sira is replete with warnings about the care required when speaking with a king or queen.

Scribes studied more than biblical law. They cultivated the deeper mysteries of Moses and the Prophets. They delved into what lay beneath the surface of scripture. As the author of Ecclesiastes 8:1—himself a sage—put it, "Who is like the wise man? Who else understands the true import of a matter" (Hebrew *pesher davar*)? This search for the "true import" could easily lead to esoteric teachings, even give rise to mystical experiences. Some mystics traveled to heaven; Paul apparently did, and Judah himself would soon journey to that realm of "things unutterable."

T HE EVENTS OF 76 B.C.E. constituted a mortal danger to Judah's life and station in society and threatened to overturn years of his teaching in Jerusalem. A middle-aged or even elderly sage—in his hymns Judah refers to himself as "gray"—the first messiah came under attack because he dared to defy the new regime, publicly labeling it Satan's dominion. Asserting divine sanction, Judah sought to lead the nation from crisis to repentance, to create a new Israel, members of a New Covenant. He saw his contemporaries as the millennial generation.

So Judah looked backward to apostasy and forward to apocalypse. His own rise at the time of the End he believed forecast in scripture, to which he alluded in his first hymn: "In that day a *fount* shall be *opened* for the House of David and those who dwell in Jerusalem, in respect both to sin and to impurity" (Zechariah 13:1). Thus Judah wrote, *You placed insight in my heart whereby to open the fount of knowledge.* Zechariah had spoken of him.[33]

The Pharisees' initial response was to assail Judah's status, trying to undercut his prestige. The first hymn documents these attacks and the prophet's counterblasts. Remarkable as were the claims Judah made here, he would make others yet more remarkable.

The Pharisees weren't interested. They had heard enough.

CHAPTER 3

TO KILL
A PROPHET

Jerusalem, Jerusalem, the city that kills the prophets and stones
those who are sent to it!

Jesus (Matthew 23:37)

Aˢ ᴀ ʟᴇᴀᴅɪɴɢ Jerusalem priest and sage, Judah had once counseled
Alexander about religiopolitical problems like the Pharisees. He saw
that group as "sinning with a high hand"—that is, as intentionally trans-
gressing God's proper law: hardened criminals, as it were, impossible to re-
habilitate. But now the tables had been turned, and it was the Pharisees
who were in power. Now the Pharisees were the righteous, their enemies
the sinners worthy of death. Josephus reports that as Queen Alexandra
came to the throne:

> Throughout the entire country there was quiet, except for the
> Pharisees. . . . They tried to persuade her to kill those who had
> urged Alexander to put the eight hundred to death. Later they
> themselves slaughtered one of them, named Diogenes, and his
> death was followed by that of one after the other.[1]

Pharisaic groups were going from house to house, searching out opponents and putting them to the sword.

SNARES OF HELL
IN THE JERUSALEM COUNCIL

The prophet Judah was a primary target. He was on the run. In this atmosphere of mortal danger, Judah composed his next two hymns. Since their themes are similar, and because they were composed within a short time of each other, I consider them together.

The second hymn:

I praise you, O Lord, for You have preserved my life, and have protected me from all the snares of Hell. Indeed, violent men have sought my life because I uphold Your covenant. They comprise the fraudulent council of the party of Belial. They have failed to perceive that my office is ordained by You, and that You have saved my life because You are faithful to Your covenant. Surely You decree the direction of my life! Only because You decreed it have they attacked me, that You might be glorified by judging those wicked men, and that You might publicly manifest Your mighty power through me. Surely my station is by Your grace!

Though I have said, "Warriors have camped against me, surrounding me with all their weaponry. Arrows burst forth without cease, and the blade of the lance brings fire that eats away wood. Their clamor is like the roar of a flood, a thunderburst and downpour sweeping many to destruction. Wickedness and falsehood break forth to heaven as their waves billow high";—though I have said these things, and though my heart melts with terror and runs like water, still You fortify me to cling to Your covenant. The very net that they spread for me will trip them up; into the traps they set for me they shall themselves fall. Yet my feet will stand on level ground. From the very council they now control I shall bless Your name![2]

And the third:

I praise You, O Lord, because Your eye rem[ains] upon me, and You deliver me from the zeal of false advisors. From the party of the Seekers of Accommodation have You rescued the life of the poor one whom they plotted to destroy, whose blood they planned to spill over the issue of Your Temple service—except that they [had failed to per]ceive that You decree the direction of my life. I have been made an object of contempt and scorn in the mouths of all who teach deception. But You, O my God, have helped the poor and destitute one against those stronger than he, and redeemed me from the clutches of powerful men. In the midst of their reviling, You have not let me become terrified to the point that I would abandon the proper principles of Your Temple service, fearing ruin at the hands of wicked men, or that I would exchange for a delusion the steadfast mind [that You have established within me] . . . [3]

In these hymns Judah spoke for the first time of attempts on his life (*violent men have sought my life*). Evidently numbering more than one, these attacks frightened Judah so much that he almost joined the swelling ranks of the compromisers.

In the third hymn we also get Judah's first mention of the root of the crisis: how the Temple should be run (*the issue of Your Temple service*).[4] Judah held that by substituting their own laws for long-standing priestly traditions governing the Temple and its sacrifices, the Pharisees were breaching the nation's covenant with God. That covenant went back to the time of Moses. Refusing to surrender his principles, Judah remained faithful to that covenant, and therefore, he believed, God had so far protected him—for the covenant, as with any equitable arrangement between two parties, worked in both directions. Provided Judah was faithful, God was compelled to keep him safe (*You have saved my life because You are faithful to Your covenant*). It was at this point that Judah set down the first of his prophecies.

Only because You decreed it have they attacked me, that You might be glorified by judging those wicked men, and that You might publicly manifest Your mighty power through me. Judah linked God's judgment of the wicked— the Pharisees and their supporters—with a (supernatural?) act by which God would prove that Judah had been right all along. Judah predicted that it would happen in the light of day. Everyone would see it.

Judgment would fall, said Judah, because the nation's leaders had refused to recognize that he was God's prophet in this hour of crisis: *They have failed to perceive that my office is decreed by You.* In accordance with scripture, God had raised him up for this specific time in history—yet the Pharisees hard-heartedly denied it. So they would be judged and Judah would be exalted. And he did not have in mind some otherworldly vindication; Judah referred to the here and now. It would happen in this lifetime, it would happen in Jerusalem.

This was Judah's first prophecy.

Behind these words we can sense the prophet's anguished wrestling. Why had God permitted the recent turn of events? It was to explain this puzzle that Judah directed his first prophecy. The ultimate reason for the crisis, he concluded, was to prepare the way for his own exaltation before the nation—indeed, before the whole earth. For suffering must precede glory. By his suffering God would be honored and praised. God had decided to inflict this pain on his prophet, but not as a superficial response to recent events. The divine purpose for Judah had been foretold centuries ago by the prophet Isaiah.

As we shall see shortly, Judah found himself in such passages as Isaiah 53:10, "It was the will of the Lord to crush him with pain," and Isaiah 53:3, "He was despised and rejected by others, a man of suffering and acquainted with infirmity." Judah recognized the mysterious Suffering Servant of whom scripture spoke as himself. He thereby knew himself to be an immensely significant person—indeed, one of the principal actors in all human history. In him and by him climactic biblical prophecies would be fulfilled. As events continued to unfold, Judah would say more on this topic.

As with most effective prophecies, this first prophecy of the first messiah was vague. Judah chose to explain neither how the judgment would occur nor when or by what means God would manifest his power. But the import was undisguised: the ax was poised at the root of the trees.

Given that Alexandra, the high priest Hyrcanus, and much of the royal family had allied themselves with the Pharisees, Judah's prophecy was bold, forthright—foolhardy. As had the biblical prophet Jeremiah, Judah spoke despite the danger, undaunted. He was God's messenger. Yet he admitted again and again how frightened he was.

At the hands of the Pharisees, Diogenes and others among Judah's peers were already dead.

ANOTHER PROPHECY concludes Judah's second hymn: *From the very council they now control I shall bless Your name!* In gaining a controlling influence over the royal family, the Pharisees had also come to dominate the Jerusalem city council. This body (Hebrew *qahal*) advised the ruler on important matters. Judah's enemies had driven him from his former leading position there among its elders. He now predicted that he would prevail, return, and retake his rightful place. Like a seesaw, however, for Judah to rise, the Pharisees must fall.

We know little about the Jerusalem council during the reigns of Alexander and Alexandra.[5] The council's composition and function changed over the years. Josephus's descriptions of its processes in his own day, the late first century C.E., can only very cautiously be extrapolated backward to the period of Judah's prophecy.

Josephus once mentions a secretary of the council, so evidently it possessed a formal structure and, one supposes, various offices. How large it was we can only guess. A similar council in the Galilean city of Tiberias in the first century C.E. had six hundred members. Apart from the central fact that they served at the sovereign's pleasure, we know nothing about how the members of the council were chosen. We do know that they dealt with the affairs of Jerusalem, including taxation and the Temple. Inasmuch as many of Jerusalem's decisions affected the whole nation, the Jerusalem council was in effect a national institution.

Judah was therefore forecasting his own return to influence over the course of the nation. In the same breath he was threatening God's judgment upon the Pharisees, the queen, and the high priest.

If we understand Judah's prophecy in this sense, it is possible to see how some of the other Dead Sea Scrolls interrelate. In turn we can gain insight through those other writings into Judah's hymns. We can discover some specifics of the dispute that was imperiling his existence and that had now embroiled the Jewish nation in crisis and bloodshed for two generations.

SOME OF THE LAWS OF THE TORAH

Some thirty years after Judah's death, one or more members of the millenarian movement he would found sat down and wrote a commentary on the biblical book of Psalms. Unlike ourselves, this author did not regard the Psalms as timeless religious poetry. He read them rather as a series of prophecies, mysterious and so opaque that only God-given wisdom could elucidate their words. He believed that David, the ancient king of Israel, had composed the Psalms with gaze set firmly, not on the Israel of his contemporaries, but rather on a world that would exist centuries hence. The author of the commentary believed that when the hidden meaning of the Psalms was properly drawn out, it concerned Judah, his followers, his enemies, and the author himself.

For our present purposes the focus is one particular verse and its interpretation in the *Commentary on the Psalms*. The biblical portion is Psalm 37:32–33, and its interpretation follows immediately after the biblical quotation:

> *"The wicked man spies out the righteous man and seeks to have him killed. But the Lord will not leave him in his power and will not condemn him when he comes to trial."*

> *This portion refers to the Wicked [Pri]est who spied out the [Teach]er of Righteous[ness and sought] to have him killed [because of the legal pre]cepts and the law that the Teacher had sent to him.*[6]

Wicked Priest was the *Commentary's* code word for the high priest Hyrcanus II. *Teacher of Righteousness* was, as noted, one of the titles for Judah used by his later followers. The author of the *Commentary on the Psalms* held that when David wrote Psalm 37, he had bridged a millennium to prophesy one particular event: Hyrcanus, the wicked man, would try to have Judah, the righteous man, killed.

Through his circle's oral traditions the author was aware that such an attack had indeed taken place. He had also read the less explicit description of attacks in Judah's own hymns, of course, but the oral tradition supplied the missing detail of the high priest's personal involvement.

Had the sources not mentioned the fact, the historian would necessarily have to posit the high priest's involvement. The political realities of Jerusalem in these years required it. That Hyrcanus would respond to Judah's claims by seeking to erase this prominent agitator against his government—one who had a following—is a given; the high priest's mention is unsurprising. More striking is the *Commentary's* mention of *the legal precepts and the law that the Teacher had sent to him.* Apparently the attempts on Judah's life were prompted less by general factional animosity than by a legal treatise that he had sent to Hyrcanus.

And here fortune has cracked one of her rare smiles: that remarkable document seems to have survived.

The writing that is the likely candidate has come down to us in six fragmentary copies found among the Dead Sea Scrolls, all from Cave Four.

Taking their cue from a summarizing Hebrew phrase within the work, scholars have dubbed it *Miqsat Maase Ha-Torah,* "Some of the Laws of the Torah" (4QMMT or MMT for short). The ancient title is unknown.

MMT presented a cogent argument complete with illustrations and a closing exhortation. The basic thesis was simple and, given the historical circumstances, as predictable as addition: the wrong laws were governing the Temple. The Temple was therefore being desecrated through impurity, which was a by-product of all erroneous rituals. It threatened the efficacy of the entire Temple enterprise, for a sacrifice wrongly offered was an abomination to God—much worse than no sacrifice at all.

Two dozen examples of problems and solutions detailed this argument: Gentiles must no longer be allowed to sacrifice in the Temple; neither their grain nor their copper implements were to enter its confines; pregnant animals must not be sacrificed unless the fetus were offered separately, and that could not happen on the same day the mother was sacrificed; neither blind people nor deaf should be permitted to enter the Temple, since their limitations made it impossible for them to observe the purity laws; dogs must be banned from the Temple environs, lest they eat bits of meat still attached to the bones of the sacrificed animals.

These were the sorts of issues on which Judah considered compromise impossible. MMT declared: *We have separated ourselves from the majority of the peo[ple and from all their impurity], from being involved with these improper practices and from going al[ong with them] regarding these matters.*[7]

Judah and those for whom he spoke—like-minded priests among the Jerusalem elite, their disciples and supporters—had stopped participating in the Temple worship. They refused to resume until proper practice was restored. This boycott was in keeping with Judah's First Commandment, *You shall not enter the Temple to kindle God's altar in vain.*

Their nonparticipation was no mere religious protest. It was a political act and, moreover, a radical new turn in the nation's politics. So far as history records, the Pharisees had never refused to take part in Temple activities when they were out of power. Judaea was, after all, a Temple state, and being part of the state meant being involved with the Temple. In effect, MMT was a threat on the part of powerful Jews and their followers to secede from the union. In more modern terms, the situation facing Hyrcanus was analogous to what greeted Abraham Lincoln upon his election to the presidency in 1860. The news that Lincoln had been elected prompted first South Carolina, then Georgia, and finally every state in the lower South to move toward secession. Hyrcanus could not afford to respond with his nat-ural passivity.

Further, MMT was a bald-faced attempt at subverting the new Pharisaic Temple authorities. By the very act of its writing—surely no se-cret to his followers or others in Jerusalem—Judah and his colleagues sought to legitimate themselves to the broader populace. They would be the foremost arbiters of religious affairs. The work even included a policy recommendation to the high priest on what to do with the Pharisees once they were removed from power: [*Concerning anyone who intentionally vio-lates the precepts, it is writ]ten that "he despises and blasphemes."*[8]

The biblical reference behind this deceptively innocuous statement is Numbers 15:30. Implicit in the quotation is the biblical penalty, which MMT, with masterful indirection, left unstated—though it would have leaped to mind when Hyrcanus and his advisers read the work: "The person shall be cut off from among the people."

Kill him. MMT was laying the legal foundation for repeating the very course of action that Alexander had taken in the last generation: execu-tion of Pharisees.

For a right understanding of the practices MMT critiques, the prophet Judah was willing to risk death. For the maintenance of the new status quo, others were willing to kill. Such was the state of the union in Jerusalem in 76 B.C.E. These points of law—what may seem to us to be nothing but jots and tittles, the fine print—were the devilish details upon which hinged the fate of the nation.

Naturally, when they found out, Pharisee leaders did not take kindly to MMT. Nor could they ignore it. A solution to the "Judah problem" would have to be found.

T HE ROLL OF THE NAMES of Pharisee leaders in these years has been wiped nearly clean by the passing of centuries. The one place where such facts have sometimes been preserved, floating like ship-wrecked survivors, is the sea of rabbinic literature. The rabbis and rabbinic Judaism were heirs to the Pharisee sect. They arose near the end of the first century C.E., after the destruction of Jerusalem and the Temple by the Ro-mans. From time to time, their writings have preserved details about the ancestral movement. These writings—the Mishnah, the Tosephta, the Tal-muds, and wave after wave of other legal and biblical works—intermingle with their history liberal doses of legend. Yet they are what we have, and we must try our best to sort matters out and rescue any genuine facts that may be adrift.

These writings contain numerous reports of a leading Pharisee who lived during the reigns of Alexander and Alexandra. He was a contemporary of Judah, belonging like the prophet to the wealthy Jerusalem elite. Judging from rabbinic literature, he was the foremost Pharisee of his day. His name was Shimeon ben Shetah.

As you might suspect, while Alexander was king, Shimeon sometimes had his difficulties. Generally, though, Alexander left him alone. Politics dictated to both that they seek détente. Apart from the years of civil war with the Pharisees, things went more smoothly for Alexander if he got along with the Pharisee leadership. Occasionally he needed their help for purposes of state. Rabbinic sources include several versions of a story about one such occasion, when Alexander, despite his personal dislike of Shimeon, was forced to call upon him for help. Just prior to this time, Shimeon had narrowly escaped execution by the king, so for his part he was eager to oblige and shore up his own situation:

"Three hundred Nazirites came up to Jerusalem wanting to offer nine hundred offerings in the days of Shimeon ben Shetah," the story begins.[9]

Nazirites were people who had forsworn wine, grapes, and every product of the vine. They were forbidden to cut their hair or to approach any dead body, even that of the closest relative. At the end of a certain time after taking vows, they had to offer sacrifices in the Temple, after which they could return to normal life. The sacrifices consisted of three animals: a male lamb, a ewe lamb, and a ram, and the animals could be purchased near the Temple. Yet they were expensive and so beyond the means of many Jewish peasants.

The story continues, "For one hundred and fifty of them Shimeon found a loophole." Through his expertise in the Pharisaic interpretation of biblical laws, he was able to find an angle whereby to declare their vows invalid, so releasing them from the costly obligation to sacrifice. Unlike Judah's priestly law, whose interpretations favored the priests, the Pharisaic statutes favored their constituency, the peasants.

But for one hundred and fifty he was unable to find a loophole. He went up to Jannai [Alexander's Hebrew name] and said to him,

"Three hundred Nazirites have come up wanting to offer nine hundred offerings, but they cannot afford it. If you defray the expenses of one half from your resources, I will pay for the other half, and they can go sacrifice." Jannai paid for one half from his resources, and they went and sacrificed.

Tale bearers came to Jannai and informed against Shimeon ben Shetah, "Know that everything that was sacrificed, was sacrificed with your resources. Shimeon ben Shetah did not pay a penny." Jannai the king was enraged with Shimeon ben Shetah, who, upon hearing that the king was angry, grew fearful and fled.

Sometime later, men from the Persian court were sitting, feasting at banquet with Jannai the king. They said to him, "My lord king, we recall that there used to be a certain sage here, who would regale us with words of wisdom." Jannai said to his wife [Alexandra], "Send for him and bring him here."

She replied, "Give me the order, and send it with your seal, and he will come." He gave her the order and sent it with his seal, and Shimeon came. When he arrived, he sat between the king and queen.

Jannai said to him, "Why did you flee?"

"I heard that my lord, the king, was angry with me. I was afraid that you would kill me, so I fulfilled this verse: 'Hide yourself for a little while, until the anger is past' (Isaiah 26:20)."

"Why did you trick me?"

"God forbid! I did not trick you! No, you dispensed your money, and I my wisdom, as it is written, 'Either by the protection of wisdom, or the protection of money' (Ecclesiastes 7:12)." [Shimeon claimed to have kept his part of the bargain by finding loopholes for half the Nazirites.]

"Then why didn't you explain to me?"

"If I had explained to you, you wouldn't have defrayed expenses."

"Why do you seat yourself between the king and the queen?" [Shimeon's act was a brazen and dangerous breach of protocol.]

"In Ben Sira's book it is written, 'Cherish Wisdom and she will exalt you; she will seat you between princes' (Proverbs 4:8; *Sira* 11:1)."

Jannai ordered, "Fill his cup and let him recite the blessing." [The king pointedly offered Shimeon no food.]

Shimeon prayed, "Blessed be God for the food that Jannai and his friends have eaten."

"Are you still being difficult? I have never heard my name in the traditional blessing."

"What then? Am I to say, 'We bless you for what we have eaten,' when I have not eaten?"

Jannai ordered, "Bring him something to eat." And after he had eaten, he prayed, "Blessed be God for what we have eaten."

This story was crafted as it was passed down, tailored to please its eventual audience, the rabbis. People have always rooted for the home team, and the rabbis loved to hear about their Pharisaic ancestors outwitting enemies such as Alexander. But kernels of fact have survived the rabbinic tailoring.

For one, Shimeon ben Shetah is shown going into hiding at one point in his life. That is likely to be true, given the relations between Alexander and the Pharisees. For another, he comes back at the king's invitation with a guarantee of safety. That rings true because Alexander was negotiating with emissaries from Persia, then under the rule of the Parthians. Like Alexander, the Parthians were enemies of the Syrians. In fact, Alexander's nemesis, the Syrian king Demetrius III (the man who had invaded Judaea at the invitation of the Pharisees), was captured by the Parthians soon after his return home from that adventure. He died in captivity with them in 87 B.C.E.

If this story reflects events just a few years later—say, 85 B.C.E.—then Alexander's overture to Shimeon makes sense. In order to cement relations with the Parthians against a common foe, the king called upon the foremost Pharisee leader to support the negotiations. How better to convince the Parthians of Jewish sincerity than to obtain the pledge of this former ally of the Syrians? Shimeon's agreement would demonstrate to the Parthians that all factions of the Jews were on board.

Some of Shimeon's personal qualities also shine through in this story. They are the sort of qualities a man would need to rise to leadership in Jewish society in those years. He had a phenomenal command of biblical content and was renowned as a sage and master of Pharisaic biblical interpretation. He possessed a peasant shrewdness, the ability to get the better of every bargain, illustrated by his trickery concerning the Nazirites. And he was driven by overweening ambition, as shown by his taking a seat between the king and queen.

Another rabbinic story is told of Shimeon traveling to Ashkelon and hanging eighty women there for witchcraft. This happened under Alexandra's rule, though in those years Ashkelon lay outside Jewish territory. At the core of this legend lies the recognition of another facet of Shimeon's character: he would go to extraordinary lengths, even crossing into foreign regions, to enforce compliance with Jewish law. Nor would he hesitate to use deadly force.

Rabbinic literature recalled the reign of Alexandra as a golden age, for it was a time of Pharisaic dominion under Shimeon: "In the days of Shimeon ben Shetah and Shelamzion the queen [Alexandra's Hebrew name], it would rain on Sabbath evenings, such that grains of wheat became as an animal's kidney, grains of barley as olives, and lentils as golden dinars. The sages gathered some of them and preserved them for coming generations, to demonstrate the consequences of sin."[10]

The rabbis believed that in following Pharisaic ways less stringently after Alexandra's reign, the people had forfeited the fullness of God's blessing.

Naturally, Judah's later followers had a different view of the matter. According to the Dead Sea Scroll known as the *Damascus Document*, Alexandra's reign was the time of *turning from the Way*. This apostasy was connected with *the rise of the Man of the Lie, who baptized Israel in the waters of falsehood. He led them astray in a trackless wasteland.* In the *Damascus Document* the Man of the Lie is the foremost leader of Judah's enemies. Since these enemies were the Pharisees, it is reasonable to suspect (though in the nature of things unprovable) that the Man of the Lie was none other than Shimeon ben Shetah.[11]

He and his cohorts so far had no luck in murdering Judah, even though the queen and the high priest had blessed their intentions. Why had they failed? How could a courtier like Judah hope to defy, as he wrote, the efforts of *powerful men?*

The *Commentary on the Psalms* offered an answer, yet one so generic that it tells us only that its author did not know (or care to say?) how Judah managed to save himself: *This portion refers to the Wicked [Pri]est who spied out the [Teach]er of Righteous[ness and sought] to have him killed [because of the legal pre]cepts and the law that the Teacher had sent to him. . . . But God did not del[iver him into his power.]*[12]

The specific answer probably lies with Aristobulus, the queen's younger son, and his wing of the royal family. Unlike queen Alexandra and his older brother Hyrcanus, they had not embraced the Pharisees. They had not forsaken the priestly coalition that supported them during the wars of King Alexander. A leading figure in this wing of the family was Absalom, the dead king's brother. He had, according to Josephus, "preferred to live without taking part in public affairs." For that reason, Alexander held him in honor. (Another brother, who wished to "take part in public affairs," Alexander killed as a rival. Absalom's preference shows how well he knew his brother's character.)[13]

When Aristobulus came of age, he married a cousin, as was the frequent priestly custom. This woman was Absalom's daughter, making Absalom simultaneously uncle and father-in-law to Aristobulus. Absalom was a powerful figure in Jerusalem, and he had long been well disposed toward Judah.[14] It was thanks to Absalom's protection, and that of his network of lesser princes and hangers-on, that Judah had so far eluded the Pharisaic death squads.

Attempts on his life had failed because the prophet still had too many powerful friends. If Shimeon and his party were to rid themselves of Judah, they would need to adopt a new strategy. After the ancient equivalent of secret meetings in smoke-filled rooms, the plot was hatched.

D ESPITE THE TESTIMONY of the *Commentary on the Psalms*, the special impetus for the plot, MMT, was not the work of a single person. It had several authors. Here, for once, a conspiracy theory really is preferable to the notion of one man working alone. Judah could not have sent it by himself. That much is certain even though the names of the addressee and the authors have not survived among the fragments.

Group authorship emerges from the writing's Hebrew verb forms and from its use of the pronoun *we* at several junctures. What seems probable is that Judah collaborated on this treatise with allies—priests who, like himself, were unwilling to countenance Pharisaic domination of the Temple. Of course, Judah was the prime mover of the group, at least so far as his hymns suggest. Only of him could it be said,

> *You have set me as a banner to the chosen righteous, a prophet given knowledge of wondrous mysteries. I test the men of truth, and try those who love instruction. I am an adversary to prophets of falsehood, but a man of peace to all whose vision is righteous.*

The allies were some of the *chosen righteous* and *men of truth*.

The later author of the *Commentary on the Psalms* passed over Judah's allies in silence. They were less important than Judah; in the intervening years many had proven to be traitors. But at the time when Judah took up the quill to compose his initial hymns, these allies were his life support system. He referred to them gratefully in the first several lines of the first hymn: *Those who, when I am sunk in mournful gloom, give me reasons to rejoice; they declare to me glad tidings of a peaceful result in the face of destructive rumors about me and [fears] so strong that my heart melts. They fortify me in the face of attack.*

Three times in his second hymn Judah referred to the *covenant* between God and the nation. He considered himself faithful to it, the Pharisees the opposite. Yet these are very general notions, of limited use to the historian. Precisely how Judah conceived of this covenant is vital to our understanding of his situation, but in his hymns he never described the terms that were being broken.

MMT clarifies that problem by establishing a clear link between the covenant and the Temple laws. The covenant drew its substance from these laws, while the laws gained their more abstract significance from the covenant. The covenant gave them a religious context. But what precisely was that context in 76 B.C.E.? How were the biblical passages about the covenant then being understood? MMT provides an answer. In it Judah and his allies spoke plainly of the covenant's meaning. That understanding led them to warn Hyrcanus of the danger presently threatening the nation. They saw him, as the nation's high priest and representative before God, sitting squarely at a crossroads in the nation's history.

The biblical background to MMT's discussion of the covenant is found mainly in Deuteronomy 28–30. These chapters portray Moses delivering to the people of Israel "the words of the covenant that the Lord commanded him to make with the Israelites."

In structure Deuteronomy 28 is almost antiphonal. First comes a series of blessings that the people will enjoy if they obey God's commandments. This list is followed by a carnival-mirror image of those blessings, grotesquely and squatly transformed into the curses they will become if the people disobey. (Actually, the length of the list of curses is about twice that of the blessings. Such is the gloomy mood of the latter part of Deuteronomy.)

The point is stated bluntly: "If you do not diligently obey all the words of this law, those written in this book, and fear this glorious and awesome Name—the Lord, your God—then he will overwhelm both you and your offspring with severe and lasting afflictions" (Deuteronomy 28:58).

Judah and his developing crisis cult took these biblical threats at face value. The prophet and his peers truly believed that to compromise on the proper Temple laws would be tantamount to acquiescing in the nation's destruction. Thus Judah and his coauthors spoke of the covenant to Hyrcanus: *It is written that "If you [stray] from the Way, then calamity will befall you." And it is writ[ten,] "It shall come to pass, when all these things [be]fall you"—in the Latter Days, namely, the blessings and the curses—["then you will take not]ice and return to Him with all your heart and with all [your] soul."*[15]

These lines paraphrased first Deuteronomy 31:29, then Deuteronomy 30:1–2, but with a crucial difference. The new twist was the mention of *the Latter Days,* which is nowhere to be found in the passages in Deuteronomy.

As a prophet, Judah claimed to possess a *knowledge of the times.* Accordingly, he would know when *the Latter Days,* the end of the present reality, was at the door. He was saying that the time was now. This apocalyptic addition to the biblical text produced a declaration fully in harmony with the message the Gospels ascribe first to John the Baptist, then to Jesus: "The time is fulfilled, and the kingdom of God is at hand; repent!" MMT was saying what Judah had been proclaiming for some time.

A century before Jesus, the myth-dream of Israel was evolving in his direction through the charisma of an earlier prophet. The dawning of the kingdom might take place, said Judah, but was not guaranteed. Instead the curses of Deuteronomy might be activated. A disaster like that under Nebuchadnezzar (586 B.C.E.)—when the king of Babylon destroyed Jerusalem and the Temple and carried the nation's leaders into exile—was an equal and opposite possibility.

If the kingdom were to come, Hyrcanus must make the right decision.

At center stage in MMT's argument stood Deuteronomy, but the biblical book of Daniel was just offstage in the wings. This work portrays a series of four consecutive Gentile kingdoms that are to rule over the Jews. Afterward, at a time foreknown to God, "the holy ones of the most high shall receive the kingdom and possess the kingdom forever." This glorious but earthly Jewish kingdom of the Latter Days was what most people in Jesus' day thought of when they heard the phrase "kingdom of God." The prophet Daniel was told by God, as he tells us, to "keep the words secret and the book sealed until the time of the end. . . . Many shall be purified, cleansed and refined, but the wicked shall act still more wickedly. None of the wicked shall possess understanding, but the wise shall." These thoughts lay behind the next things said in MMT: *For we recognize that some of the blessings and curses written in the bo[ok of Mo]ses have already come to pass, signaling the arrival of the Latter Days. Many in Isra[el] shall return to the l[aw of Moses with all their heart] and never turn away again, but "the wicked shall act still more wi[ck]edly."* [16]

Judah and his allies thought they recognized in the foregoing years of crisis a fulfillment of Daniel's prophecies. The righteous were undergoing trials, while, all around, evil proliferated. Judah said as much himself in his own hymns. Daniel's time of the end was at hand, and it would be a time of sifting the righteous from the wicked.

This understanding of the character of that period is strikingly like that of Jesus, if it is true, as seems likely, that many of the parables contained in the Gospels go back to him personally. According to many parables Jesus saw the time of the kingdom's approach as one of sifting wheat from tares.

For MMT the tares of the Latter Days were primarily the Pharisees, the *wicked* of Judah's hymns. Not content merely to "blaspheme and despise" God's laws themselves, their recent installation of new Temple laws threatened to lead Hyrcanus and the entire nation down that same path to perdition. The authors of MMT urged Hyrcanus to be among Daniel's wise, possessed of understanding:

> *Understand all these things and beseech Him to keep your thinking straight, to keep far from you evil plans and the advice of Belial. Then you shall rejoice at the time of the end, when you find the essence of what we have said to be legally correct. And "it will be reckoned to you as righteousness"—your having done what is right and good before Him—to your own benefit and that of Israel.* [17]

The specific mention of the *advice of Belial* (a name for Satan) was a thinly disguised reference to the Pharisaic vision of the Temple laws. In his second hymn Judah had characterized the Pharisees as *the fraudulent council of the party of Belial.* In hymn after hymn he linked their party with

Satan. Given Judah's view of the Mosaic covenant, we can appreciate why he thought them the devil's spawn.

They would destroy not merely Judah, but the nation.

A CONFLICT OF VISIONS

MMT affords us precious insight into specific points of the dispute between Judah and the Pharisaic faction, something we do not find in his hymns. Yet his predicament was only one particular manifestation of a general phenomenon: the rent garment that was the Jewish society of his day. Judah was not alone in opposing the Pharisees. The Sadducees and other priestly factions who had things their own way under Alexander Jannaeus now stood to lose as much as he did. And, of course, in Alexander's reign the roles had been reversed and it was the Pharisees who were oppressed.

But why this division; how had the garment got torn to begin with? Surely the question of whether dogs should enter the Temple environs, however fiercely important in the particular context of MMT, was a mere incidental. What was the essence? Competing ideas about the Temple laws were but an outgrowth. What was the root, and in what soil had it anchored itself? What lay behind these seemingly obscure arguments, this reading between the lines of scripture that people clung to so tenaciously?

In large measure the answers to these questions lie in an understanding of the Pharisees. Thanks to the Dead Sea Scrolls, we are now able to chart more precisely the social revolution that was the Pharisaic movement. The Pharisees first arose about 150 B.C.E. among lay groups who, so far as history records, had not previously been a formal part of the political process. Their circles developed a characteristic new method for interpreting the Bible, using what Josephus calls the "ordinances of the Fathers" (probably to be understood as an early form of the rabbinic "oral law").

The Pharisees also held to novel philosophical ideas about the nature of the biblical revelation, ideas irreconcilable with older priestly theory.[18] And they developed laws that were consistently less harsh than those of the priests in their effect on the peasantry. This relative leniency fed their popularity with the masses.

Boiled down to its essence, Judah's crisis cult was an extreme form of conservative backlash against this rising movement. Grounded in the priesthood, Judah and those like him stood against the radical new ways of thinking and the rocketing rise to power that they propelled.

Josephus says of his people: "We regard as the most essential task in life the observance of our laws and of the pious practices, based thereupon, which we have inherited."[19]

Whoever decided how those laws must be observed, therefore, and developed the pious practices would derive immense prestige in Jewish society. And whoever controlled or helped control the Temple would reap manifold benefits.

Every society possesses diverse forms of capital: money, status, honor, hierarchy, place, precedence—things revolutions are fought to win. For centuries before the time of Judah, control over these social riches had resided mostly with the priests. We read odes to the priesthood in *The Wisdom of Ben Sira*. When Judah was a young man those words still rang true.

By the time of Josephus they sounded a quavering note. It was the Pharisees, he wrote in the late 70s C.E., "who were considered the most accurate interpreters of the laws." They, not the priests. Josephus made this statement even though he was himself a priest who neither liked the Pharisees nor believed their reputation.[20] Reality compelled his assent.

The Pharisees had seized prestige, and with it came power. The priests never went away, and they remained powerful. They were still in the game. They hadn't lost the whole pot. But by 70 C.E. the Pharisees, not the priests, enjoyed the gilded reputation of providing the most accurate understanding of the biblical laws. The pious practices were largely their domain.

So in the century and a half between Judah and Josephus, the priests lost substantial social capital. In Judah's mature years they were just beginning a retreat, and there was no reason to suppose that it was anything but strategic, that the priests could not rally and take the offensive again. But in fact they did not. The Pharisees never yielded the ground that they won in Judah's day. On the contrary, they went on to gain more.

The Pharisees were that rare historical phenomenon: a social revolution that won. Like winged ant queens out to found a new colony, most such movements die unsuccessful. Those that do succeed are naturally more famous, and they are the ones most of us recognize: the French Revolution, Spain in the 1930s, the German Reformation. In such terms the Pharisees equate with Martin Luther and his followers. Their priestly foils equate with Rome and the papacy. Judah arose to lead the Counter-Reformation.

Priest versus Pharisee, Pharisee versus priest: the two sides did not agree on what the Bible was, and they could not agree on the authority that should interpret it. The resulting rip in society's fabric was not the sort that could simply be drawn together and stitched up. As that premier negotiator Henry Kissinger once observed, there are some problems that cannot be negotiated. Thomas Sowell has written, "Policies based on a certain vision of the world have consequences that spread through society and reverberate across the years, or even across generations or centuries. Visions set the agenda for both thought and action . . . enduring historic trends have a certain consistency that reflects certain visions."[21]

The underlying problem among the Jews of Judah's day would never truly be resolved. It flowed from a sea change in society that could no more be turned back than can a tsunami. This was a conflict of visions.

The rise of the Pharisees continued. Within a decade of Judah's hymns, their social revolution would once again ignite armed conflict, pitting Jew against Jew, brother against brother. Alexandra's shuffling of the deck, bringing the outs in and throwing the ins out, did not work. Only the coming of the legions of Rome, overlaying this crisis with one even more acute, would bring it under control—and then, only for a while.

MMT DID NOT HAVE the desired effect. Shimeon and other Pharisee leaders prevailed upon Hyrcanus to hold the line. As the *Damascus Covenant* put it, *[The Man of the Lie] brought down the lofty heights of old, turned Israel aside from paths of righteousness, and shifted the boundary marks that the forefathers had set up to mark their inheritance. Therefore the curses of His covenant took hold on them.*[22]

Shimeon advised Hyrcanus to have Judah arrested. This was a brilliant stratagem. Judah's protectors might protest against the illegality of having him killed. They could not reasonably oppose a fair trial under the law. Whether it would actually be a fair trial was, of course, another matter, but appearances were important. They could not appear to oppose law and order.

No longer able to be protected by friends, Judah was taken into custody. The charge: false prophecy. The penalty if convicted: death by stoning.

CHAPTER 4

PROPHET ON TRIAL

Then they seized him and led him away, bringing him into the high priest's house. When day came, the assembly of the elders of the people, both chief priests and scribes, gathered together, and they brought him to their council. They said, "If you are the Messiah, tell us."

Luke 22:54, 66–67

As the first rays of the sun's light pierced the gloom of his musty cell, Judah was stirred from a sleepless night of prayer and reflection by the clanking of the guard and the grating of a key turning in the lock. The door creaked open, and two armored men entered the room. A glance at the first man was returned with a cruel smirk. The second was unable to meet his eyes, advancing with reluctant steps. A believer? "It's time, Teacher," he mumbled. "You must come with us." The first soldier took a firm grip on Judah's arm and pushed him roughly toward the door.

Their steps echoing as they climbed the rough hewn stairs from the dungeon, the soldiers directed Judah down the hall and out the door of the palace. Turning right as they emerged into the fog-filtered Jerusalem daylight, they marched him toward the Temple, the ancient city wall rising high on their left. David, Solomon, and their royal successors had taken pride in raising this rampart. With its strength and strategic position it was virtually impregnable.

Judah strode firmly, easily keeping up with the younger men. He breathed deeply of the sweet morning air. While earlier he had been sick with fear, now he was calm and felt little emotion; he knew what was true. God, by whatever means, would establish that truth. They arrived at the narrow bridge that connected the Upper City to the Temple environs and, crossing over it, took another sharp right, coming to a halt before the Bouleuterion.[1] How many times he had been here before, and in honor! As they paused outside this modest structure, the council's meeting chamber, Judah could hear the activity of the morning's first sacrifices beginning in the Temple beyond. The second soldier swung open the door to the chamber, and the first man thrust him stumbling inside, then pulled the door shut behind him.

Straightening and composing himself, Judah looked toward the seat where Hyrcanus, the high priest, perched, oil lamps throwing his shadow against the opposite wall. According to ancient custom, he would be the ultimate arbiter of Judah's fate. The hard set of his features encouraged no optimism. To the left sat the party of the Pharisees. Scattered here and there among them were members of the Jerusalem aristocracy whom they had won over to their views on God's laws. In the front row, in the position of the prosecutor, was Shimeon ben Shetah.

On the opposite side of the room were ranged members of the elite priestly families and Sadducees. Many of the seats on this side were empty. "My allies and kinsmen have abandoned me," Judah realized. He was numb; later the grief would make itself felt, as pain always follows a sharp blow to the face, but not right away. He glanced quickly to the spot where Absalom had reclined in council for as many years as Judah could remember. Absalom gazed blankly back at him, refusing to acknowledge his nod.

At a sign from Hyrcanus, Shimeon arose and gestured toward Judah.

"Fellow councilors and high priest, I do not myself know—nor do I suppose that you can name—anyone who, when summoned before us for trial, has ever presented such an appearance. For no matter who it was that came before this council for trial, he has shown himself humble and assumed the manner of one who seeks mercy, by letting his hair grow long and wearing a black garment. But look today at Judah, accused of false prophecy and seeking to lead the nation astray from God! He stands here clothed in his usual garb, his hair short and carefully arranged. Is he better, then, than those who have stood here before him?"

Shimeon paused, then took several steps forward into the center of the room, turning to acknowledge first one side of the chamber, then the other. He continued, "You are all familiar with the particulars of the case before us. This man, Judah, claims to be a prophet from God. That is a lie! I remind you of the words God gave by the hand of Moses, 'Any prophet who speaks in the name of other gods, or who presumes to speak in my name a word that I have not commanded the prophet to speak—that prophet shall die.'"

Whirling suddenly toward Absalom and the priestly group in the council, Shimeon fixed them with a glare: "You who are priests, let me quote for you your own statute, one that I do not acknowledge but that your own position requires you to consider: 'Any prophet who arises to urge you to apostasy, to turn you from following your God, must be put to death.' Surely Judah is guilty as charged, for he has claimed to speak as God's messenger while urging upon us all manner of falsehood. I will tell you of his lying words."

Now Shimeon swept his hand toward Hyrcanus, who leaned forward intently: "He has written to the high priest that one must give the tithe of cattle and goats to the priests. Now, it is true that this was for long the position of the priests, and Israel followed this law because it did not know better. In recent days, however, I and my colleagues"—here Shimeon indicated the Pharisees—"have produced evidence from the laws of Moses that this understanding was wrong. We have shown that the priests are not to receive this tithe because it nowhere appears in scripture in the lists of priestly gifts."

Walking up to Judah until their noses nearly touched and looking straight into his eyes, then turning back, Shimeon spat, "Everyone can agree that from time to time one may labor under a misunderstanding. God will not hold the misinformed to a strict accounting, for he is merciful. But to continue to uphold a falsehood once the truth has become known is a very different matter. Moreover, this man does not merely make a human argument for what is plainly false, but with perverted lips claims that this falsehood has come to him as truth from God himself! And this is just one of Judah's lies; there are many others. He claims to have a vision of knowledge; I say that it is not established! He claims to know the way of God's heart; I say that it is not the way!"

Shimeon continued in this vein for long hours, refuting point by point each of the legal positions that Judah and his peers had set forth in their position statement (MMT). Judah listened, alternately incredulous and furious, then finally weary. He resolved that the council should read in his posture neither his anger nor his weariness. The prosecutor drove on, weaving his arguments together in an intricate web of scriptural references and interpretation, sometimes speaking quietly, at other times red faced and shouting with passion.

Finally Shimeon ceased his peregrinations about the chamber and approached Hyrcanus: "Excellency, because you are the high priest of God, this man is yours to judge. I might continue for days demonstrating yet further that his law, which he claims to have received from God, is false. But you are a man who understands such matters, as is everyone in this room. I am confident, therefore, that I have made my case. Is Judah a prophet? Against my own wishes—for I have known him in better times—I am compelled to say yes. He is a prophet. But he is a false prophet! For such a crime the law of Moses knows but one penalty. I therefore urge you and this council to do your duty to God and our Temple. Sentence Judah to die!"

For a moment Hyrcanus sat motionless, making a show of pondering Shimeon's last statement. He reached up and scratched his ear. Then he stood: "I see that the oil has burned low in the council lamps. We are tired, and these are the gravest of charges that we must consider. I therefore require that we adjourn and meet again on the morrow to receive Judah's reply to Shimeon's arguments. At that time, also, I shall hear from any who wish to speak on Judah's behalf. Until the morning, then."

THE NEXT MORNING Judah stood gazing out over Hyrcanus and the council members. He had come prepared to speak the truth, though he knew that declaration would seal his indictment. The expressions of the council members, many of them longtime acquaintances and—some— even friends of earlier years, told him as much. He had taught these men, he thought, looking from face to face; had nurtured them in their youth; had led them to a true understanding of God's law. The words of Isaiah flashed into his mind: "I reared children and brought them up, but they have rebelled against me."

That had been the direction of things in the months prior to the trial. Hyrcanus's alliance with the Pharisee faction, his reaction to the position statement, the repeated efforts to kill him—these actions had made it certain that Judah would get no fair hearing if the Pharisees and his other opponents could help it. Before the trial began Judah, nevertheless, had trusted that his allies would support him, blunting the evident intentions of the Pharisees and their high priestly dupe. He had believed a fair trial possible. But yesterday had dissolved such hopes. His former allies were not even present. He determined to hold nothing back. What did it matter, the plots of human foes? Without question he would ultimately prevail. He had seen God, heard his voice, received the truth. Judah *knew.*

Hyrcanus rose and addressed him, "Judah, have you anything to say in reply to the charge of false prophecy that has been lodged against you?"

Moving to the center of the council chamber as the high priest re-seated himself, Judah nodded. "Indeed I have, Excellency; there is much that you and the councilors need to hear this day. I only wish that you were able to hear it, but it seems clear that Belial has your ear—not me, and certainly not the God who has raised me up for this time. You have rejected me, all of you; you have despised, not esteemed me—although God has manifested his mighty power through me.

"I see that my erstwhile allies, and even most of my family, have chosen to be absent from my trial. They evidently account me a broken vessel. So be it. They, like you, have fallen victim to the false prophets and seers of deception sitting here on my left, they who now lead God's people into error." Judah turned to face Shimeon and the Pharisees directly. Shimeon looked back with hooded eyes, regarding him coolly.

"You plot destruction against me so that you might better coerce Israel into exchanging God's law for your own accommodations, compromises with the truth. Yet God has spoken his law audibly to me, so I know you for what you are. You would stopper the drink of true knowledge from the thirsty of Israel and give them your own vinegar instead! You gaze upon their error and watch God's people practice idolatry at their festivals, for you deny the true calendar that guided Abraham, Isaac, and Jacob. You have them trapped, wrapped up neatly in your nets." Some of the aristocrats seated among the Pharisees squirmed and glanced about themselves uncomfortably. The Pharisees themselves began to twist in their seats with anger.

"Have you not seen? Do you not know? God despises every scheme of Belial. His counsel, not yours, will prevail. What God's mind has planned —*that* is what shall be established, and forever!" Now Judah pivoted and strode quickly toward Hyrcanus.

"These men are liars"—Judah emphasized the last word, trailing his voice out into a long, sibilant hiss—"who scheme the plots of Belial. Their plots will take root and blossom into poison and wormwood. Not being established in God's truth, they seek him only as hypocrites. They look about with a willful heart and go to idols to seek God. They seek his purposes from the mouths of false prophets corrupted by error. They have set before themselves the stumbling block of their own iniquity!" Hyrcanus listened, his expression betraying no sign that he was affected by Judah's words. Judah turned toward the small group of elite priests and Sadducees, stopping abruptly before Absalom. The old man recoiled as though struck a physical blow.

"With barbarous stammerings and a strange tongue, these men speak to Israel. By deception they render the nation's works so much madness. They have rejected the Way of God's Heart. They have spurned his word! They have repudiated the vision of knowledge that God has given me. Shimeon ben Shetah is most guilty of all. He would lead Israel into a wilderness of lawlessness. Surely you can see these facts; will you really say nothing and so countenance this evil? Do you not know that God will answer them in judgment, measure for measure as befits their idol worship and the multitude of their sins? They have abandoned God's covenant and will be entrapped by their own schemes. You are in danger of the same fate. You will all be cut off in judgment if you do not repent and, through me, enter God's new covenant." Fixing his eyes on Absalom's, Judah backed slowly toward the center of the room. He kept his eyes locked on Absalom's. A breath, two breaths—Absalom broke and looked down.

For a moment Judah paused and searched each face clustered about his former supporter. Then he raised his eyes, his hands likewise extending upward toward the heavens.

"O Lord, there is no madness in all your works, nor any deceit in your mind's plans. Those who cling to you shall abide in your presence forever; those who walk in the Way of your Heart will be established for everlasting. I thank you and praise you on high!"

Turning and dropping his arms, Judah once more addressed himself to the high priest, raising his voice and speaking in measured tones. "Because I have held fast to God, I shall be restored, no matter what you allow to happen here today. God has shown me that I will rise against those who hate me. One day my hand shall be against all who have despised me! Those who gather in support of God's covenant and seek him through me will never have their faces plastered with shame. They who walk in the Way of God's Heart will heed me and—because they do—array themselves before God in the heavenly council of the angels. The Lord will cause their rule to endure forever; their truth will spread abroad without obstacle. Do not think that he will countenance these scoundrels leading the true people of God astray, as they plan. No, he will put the fear of those who seek him through me upon all Israel! He will make the upright a war club against the nations, and so cut off in judgment all who transgress his commands, whether in Israel or among the Gentiles. Through me God will illumine the faces of many and multiply them without number, for he has given me what you, O high priest, lack: understanding of his wondrous mysteries. Do what you will. In the end it will not matter. God has fortified my standing in his wondrous council. That is why I am able to work wonders, demonstrating God's mighty deeds to every living person."

Judah approached and leaned in toward Hyrcanus. Sotto voce, his words audible only to the high priest, he added, "Whatever your judgment today, Hyrcanus, know that it is only temporary. God is my true judge, and yours. If you refuse his way still, it will not be because I have kept silent in the face of your intimidation. Your blood will be on your own head—and also the blood of every man here, and many in Israel. I do ask you, though— we have known each other these many years—I implore you, remember what once you knew so well! Do not let these prophets of deceit, these Pharisees, turn your heart from God." Straightening up and stepping back, Judah declared, "I have spoken the truth. Now you must decide."

A low murmur broke out among the Pharisees. Shimeon arose and hurried to Hyrcanus, whispering furiously in his ear. Absalom and those of his faction sat hunched and silent. Gesturing Shimeon back to his seat, Hyrcanus stood. "Is there any other here who would speak in favor of the priest Judah?"

JUDAH'S WORDS carried a depth of meaning to his audience that few of us are able to penetrate, for we lack the familiarity with the biblical text that the Jewish elite owned as a birthright. Virtually every sentence that Judah spoke resonated with biblical passages, often more than one, swelling his statements and giving them a much fuller semantic content than they seem on the surface to possess. Even after they have been translated, to us these statements remain an imperfectly understood foreign language. We recognize something of what is being said, but only that; the nuances—where communication truly lives—escape us. What did his contemporary peers understand him to say?

Most of what Judah had to say about his enemies, the Pharisees, related to three books of the Bible that speak of prophets false and true: Deuteronomy, Ezekiel, and Isaiah. Deuteronomy 18 constitutes the basic biblical definition of false prophecy, and it was to this portion that Shimeon ben Shetah alluded in his statement of indictment above.

But although Deuteronomy provided the framework for much of what Judah said, he chose to focus more specifically on Ezekiel, the relevant verses of which follow. It is important to have a look at them in order to begin to get a feel for the way the first messiah's mind worked. (The italicized portions of the verses are the Hebrew words that Judah quoted.)

> My hand [God is speaking] will be against the *prophets* who *see* false *visions* and utter *lying* divinations. They will not belong to the council of my people or be listed in the records of the house of Israel, nor will they enter the land of Israel. Then you will know that I am the Lord, YHWH.
>
> Because *they lead my people into error,* saying, "Peace," when there is no peace, and because, when a flimsy wall is built, they cover it with whitewash. (Ezekiel 13:9–10)
>
> Son of man, these men have set up *idols in their hearts and put wicked stumbling blocks before their faces. Should I let them seek* me at all?
>
> Therefore speak to them and tell them, "This is what the Lord, YHWH, says: *When any Israelite sets up idols in his heart and puts a wicked stumbling block before his face* and then goes to a prophet, I YHWH will answer him myself in keeping with his great idolatry.
>
> "*I will do this to entrap* the hearts of the people of Israel, *who have abandoned me* for their idols.
>
> "When any Israelite or any alien living in Israel *separates himself from me* and sets up *idols in his heart and puts a wicked stumbling block before his face and then goes* to a prophet *to seek me,* I YHWH will answer him myself.
>
> "*And if the prophet is corrupted* to utter a prophecy, I YHWH have corrupted that prophet, and I will stretch out my hand against him and destroy him from among my people Israel." (Ezekiel 14: 3–5, 7, 9)

When Judah quoted these phrases he did not mean to ignore the words that he left out. On the contrary: his purpose was to interpret the biblical text, both quoted and unquoted.[2] He and his audience could mentally fill in the context from which his words came, supplying the words that are not italicized.

Consequently, Hyrcanus and the council realized that, contained in the words surrounding his quotation, Judah was delivering a veiled threat: because they had abandoned God, Israel was facing judgment. Even more deadly—since they were willing to countenance false prophets, Judah intimated, God himself was entrapping them. The trap was the very false prophets in whom they trusted, the Pharisees.

In store for the Pharisees themselves lay the fate of the corrupt prophet of Ezekiel 14:9. God was about to "stretch out his hand against them and destroy them from among Israel." They would be eradicated from the land (Ezekiel 13:9). Note again: all of this content was in the words *not* quoted, implied by the words that *were* quoted.

The Pharisees were the "builders of a flimsy wall, covering it with whitewash" (Ezekiel 13:10). That was to say, their law was flimsy and insubstantial and could not be trusted as support, as much as it was enticing with its nice coating of white paint. For Judah's crisis cult this way of describing the Pharisees later became almost a cliché. They loved to refer to the Pharisees as "whitewashers" and "builders of a flimsy wall," and they derived this usage from the words that Judah implied.[3]

Judah referred to the Pharisees as corrupted prophets. His base text in Ezekiel baldly asserted that God was the source of the corruption. Judah's connection of prophecy and the Hebrew verb *corrupt, entice (pitah)* will have recalled to all council members the famous case of the biblical prophet Micaiah ben Imlah. The story appears in 1 Kings 22:1–38.

In this story the kings of Israel and Judah—Ahab and Jehoshaphat, respectively—are planning an attack on the Syrian kingdom of Aram. Before going out to battle, they seek the advice of prophets, for they want to know whether God will grant them victory. Ahab gathers four hundred of the prophets, and with a single voice they advise him to advance to the attack. Success is certain. But Jehoshaphat is troubled and asks, "Is there no other prophet of the Lord of whom we may inquire?" Ahab reluctantly calls in Micaiah, whom he hates because Micaiah always prophesies disaster for him.

True to form, Micaiah prophesies disaster once again, and Ahab refuses to believe him. Later in the battle Ahab is killed. This was precisely what God wanted to happen, but—so the story says—God had been unsure about how to force the king's death. Micaiah reveals how the divine plan developed:

> I saw the Lord sitting on his throne, with all the host of heaven standing beside him to his right and left. And the Lord said, "Who will entice (Hebrew *pitah*) Ahab, so that he may go up and fall at Ramoth-gilead?"
>
> Then one said one thing, and another said another, until a spirit came forward and stood before the Lord, saying, "I will entice (*pitah*) him."
>
> "How?" the Lord asked him.
>
> He replied, "I will go out and be a lying spirit in the mouth of all his prophets."

According to the story, therefore, to a man Ahab's four hundred were false prophets corrupted by an evil spirit. Only he whom none would believe, Micaiah ben Imlah, was true. To Judah the parallel with his own situation was patent.

This and similar biblical passages helped equip Judah and his contemporaries with their ideas about the mechanism of prophecy. Both kinds of prophets, they believed—true and false—were inhabited by a spirit. The razor-edged question in any given prophet's case was: Is this man or woman's spirit an evil messenger, or the Holy Spirit?[4] Outwardly the manifestations were identical.

Judah was navigating within this worldview when he charged that the Pharisees "scheme the plots of Belial." For him, they were literally possessed of the devil, inhabited by evil spirits. Naturally, Judah himself claimed to be an instrument of the Holy Spirit. (Implicitly this assertion appears several times in his hymns, and once, in hymn 7, explicitly.)

In charging the Pharisees, "You coerce Israel into exchanging God's law for your own accommodations," Judah referred to another biblical passage on false prophecy, Isaiah 30:10: "They say to the seers, 'See no more visions!' and to the prophets, 'Give us no more visions of what is right! Tell us accommodations, prophesy illusions.'" By applying this text to his enemies, Judah was saying that their wickedness was worse than self-delusion. They sought lies willfully. Isaiah 30:10 was an ingredient of Judah's thinking throughout his hymns. From it he derived his most telling epithet for the Pharisees, "Seekers of Accommodation." In the later literature of Judah's movement, the phrase became common coin to designate that enemy party.

In its thrust Judah's charge is strikingly reminiscent of the words of another prophet the Pharisees opposed, Jesus, who is reported by the Gospel of Mark to have said to them, "You have a fine way of setting aside the commands of God in order to observe your own traditions!"

O NE STRATEGY of Judah's defense, then, was to counter the charge of false prophecy by reversal. He sought to turn back the hand holding that potent weapon until those who would rob him of his position looked down its barrel themselves. Not he, but the Pharisees, were the false prophets. The problem was, how could the ordinary Jew decide whom to believe, Judah or the Pharisees?

The claim of either rival was likely to convince only someone who already recognized that claimant's authority. That reality put Judah in a hopeless position, because it was the Pharisees whose authority was in the ascendant. Since the antagonists expressed their messages in similar language, there was no obvious way for society to decide between them. Political factors would therefore become decisive. The prophet with the stronger political faction would become dominant and repress the one with weaker support.[5] Precisely that was already happening. Judah's approach was doomed to fail.

What he needed instead was to gain greater political support, but the opposite was happening. Absalom's departure signaled the loss of what little support Judah had among the council elite. His only prospect for victory in the trial was to bring Hyrcanus around to his side and then hope that the rest of the royal family would follow suit. That was not absolutely impossible; after all, Hyrcanus had already switched sides once. He was the sort whose dedication to principle never varied, though his principles were variable.

But would he convert to Judah's position? The possibility was vanishingly small. No, in reality Judah faced a kangaroo court, and he knew it. But that did not stop him from employing his second strategy of self-defense.

In addition to calling the Pharisees false prophets, Judah made grand claims for himself—again, partly by implication through his use of scripture.

In Deuteronomy 18—that fundamental passage on true and false prophecy—appear three verses perhaps more significant than any others. In the first Moses speaks, and he says, "The Lord your God shall raise up for you a prophet like me from among your own brothers; him you shall *heed*" (18:15; the italics mark the crucial term). In 18:18 and 18:19 God tells Moses, "I will raise up for them a prophet like you from among their brothers; I will put *my words* in his mouth, and he will tell them everything I command him. If anyone *does not listen to my words* that the prophet speaks in my name, I myself will call him to account."

These are the passages that lie behind two of Judah's statements in his defense. When he said, "They who walk in the Way of God's Heart will *heed* me," he was referring to verse 15. When he said of the Pharisees, "They have *spurned his word,"* it was the latter two verses that informed his statement.

As some Jews of that day read the Bible, scripture predicted the rise of a "prophet like Moses." Through these quotations Judah was casting himself in that role. Earlier we noted certain subtle indications of this same claim, and we will see many others in Judah's subsequent hymns. In the years after Judah the idea that a prophet like Moses would someday come to lead God's people became a major component of the myth-dream of Israel.

On at least four occasions under Roman rule in the first century C.E., Jews arose who claimed to be this prophet. They gathered followers and led abortive millenarian movements—crisis cults. One man was called Theudas, active in 45–46 C.E.; a second appeared while Festus was procurator, sometime during the years 52 to 60. This man was known simply as "the Egyptian." The other movements Josephus discusses with less detail. In each case, the Romans recognized the movement's potential for revolution and crushed it with their soldiers.[6] Some early Christians, too, expected a prophet like Moses to appear in the last days and thought that in Jesus he had.

Yet so far as we know, no one before Judah ever presumed to be that figure.

"YOU HAVE REJECTED ME; you have *despised, not esteemed* me." These words of Judah staked another claim equally fundamental and portentous.

They derived from a biblical portion, Isaiah 53:3, which reads, "He was *despised* and *rejected* of men, a man of sorrows, and familiar with suffering. Like one from whom men hide their faces he was *despised,* and we *esteemed him not."* Only here in the entire Bible do the Hebrew words Judah used—*bazah* (despise) and *lo hashav* (esteem not)—occur in collocation. Judah clearly had Isaiah 53 in mind.

By quoting Isaiah 53 and applying it to himself, Judah was asserting that he was the Servant.[7]

If one were to liken the myth-dream of Israel to a mountain range, the idea of the Servant would be among its highest peaks. Chosen by God as a teacher of truth, Isaiah indicates, he would appear as a deliverer to lead a new exodus. Predestined to his role from the womb, he was a weapon of God, to be brought out at a specific moment for God's use. He was also to be a "light to the Gentiles." The glory and honor that the nations possessed would be gathered into the Servant's Jerusalem.

Yet at first the Servant would be abhorred, despised by many of his contemporaries. According to some interpretations of the relevant passages, he would even undergo a trial and suffer violence at the hands of justice. After a period of suffering and persecution, God would vindicate him and destroy his enemies. Those who were not opposed to the Servant, the righteous remnant of Israel, Isaiah calls "the Many." They would profit eternally from the Servant's work.[8]

In his defense, Judah used the very same term to designate those he would benefit: "Through me God will illumine the faces of Many." "The Many" went on to become a premier self-designation for Judah's first followers.

Modern biblical scholars tend to limit Isaiah's Servant references to particular passages known as Servant Songs. (The passages usually so characterized are Isaiah 42:1–9, 49:1–13, 50:4–11, and 52:13–53:12.) But that is not the way some ancients saw the matter. For them, the Servant was present not only in the passages isolated by modern scholars, but also in many others. A final portion of Judah's defense exemplifies this observation.

Moreover, it brings to the fore a startling fact.

JUDAH SAID TO Hyrcanus, "God has *given* me an *understanding* of his wondrous mysteries."[9] The assertion is traceable to portions of Isaiah that Judah connected to the Servant passages. Yet the matter gets more complicated: Judah knew the relevant portions of Isaiah from a form of the book different from that translated in our Bibles.

The New International Version offers the following translation of Isaiah 40:13–14:

Who has understood the mind of the Lord, or instructed him as his counselor? Whom did the Lord consult to enlighten him, and who taught him the right way? Who was it that taught him knowledge or showed him the path of understanding?

These were the verses behind Judah's statements, but only in a sense.

Judah's radically different reading inheres in one letter of a single word in Isaiah. Whereas the traditional, or Masoretic, Hebrew text that the New International Version has translated has in 40:13 the word *yodiennu* (literally, "he [God] made him to know," or "instructed him"), a copy of the book of Isaiah found among the Dead Sea Scrolls has instead *yodiennah*, "he taught him it." The difference is so small, yet it changes the meaning of the entire passage.

The word *it* must by the rules of Hebrew grammar refer to some feminine entity in the preceding, and there is indeed a viable candidate. Processing the difference, Judah would have translated the verses into English something like this: "Whom has the spirit of the Lord prepared,[10] what man has he [God] taught his counsel?[11] With whom has he taken counsel and thereby taught him? Whom has he taught knowledge, whom has he *given* the Way of *understanding?*" (The italicized words are the ones Judah quoted in his defense statement.) In the traditional text, the question is rhetorical: "Has anyone taught God?" In the Dead Sea Isaiah, the question is real: *Whom has God taught?*

Judah would have attached these verses to other passages by analogy, which was the foremost method of biblical interpretation in his day. Analogy provided the links for any given interpretive chain. The steps in his reasoning would be as follows. First, Isaiah 40:13 mentions the "spirit of the Lord." Second, Isaiah 42:1 reports God saying, "Here is my Servant, whom I uphold, my chosen, in whom my soul delights; I have put *my spirit* upon him." Third, since Isaiah 42:1 is explicitly about the Servant, who receives the action of God's spirit, then by analogical inference 40:13 also concerns the Servant. By this method Judah would build up an entire chain of interlinked analogies, and a much fuller picture of the Servant would emerge than any one passage could contain.

So, by quoting Isaiah 40:13–14 in reference to himself, Judah was reinforcing his claim to be the Servant. His teaching came from God's spirit. He alone, of all people, knew the mind of God. God had been his teacher and supernaturally had bestowed upon him knowledge.

Yet Judah could get that meaning of Isaiah 40:13–14 only from the aforementioned copy of Isaiah found among the scrolls. It is contrary to the grammar of the traditional text.

The scrolls copy of Isaiah is technically designated 1QIsaiahᵃ. Another name for it is the *Great Isaiah Scroll.* This was among the first seven Dead Sea Scrolls discovered in Cave One by Muhammad edh-Dhib back in 1947. Today it is on occasional display in the Shrine of the Book in Jerusalem.

The broad correspondence between Judah's ideas and the text of this particular copy of Isaiah is startling. Consider a second example, the name that Judah used throughout his hymns for his prophetic message, "The Way of God's Heart." In his defense, Judah declared, "They who walk in the Way of God's Heart will heed me." In his prayer at the defense he voiced these words: "Those who walk in the Way of your Heart will be established for everlasting." Shimeon ben Shetah denounced Judah with specific reference to Judah's law, saying, "He claims to know the way of God's heart; I say that it is not the way!" When, years later, members of the movement Judah founded tried to define his role in God's plan, they wrote in the *Damascus Document, So he [God] raised up for them a Teacher of Righteousness to make them walk in the Way of his Heart.*[12]

One searches the traditional biblical text in vain for this phrase. It appears only in the *Great Isaiah Scroll,* at the point corresponding to Isaiah 57:17. According to the traditional Hebrew text of this verse, as translated by the New International Version, God says, "I was enraged by his sinful greed; I punished him, and hid my face in anger, yet he kept on in his willful ways." The last three words render the traditional Hebrew *derekh libbo.* At the same point in the *Great Isaiah Scroll,* the reading is instead *derekh libbi*—"the Way of My Heart." As before, this version of Isaiah requires a different understanding of the entire verse, such as: "I was angered by his sinful greed, and I smote him and hid my face and was angry. Then he repented and went in the Way of My Heart."[13]

This passage, in this scroll: it was here that Judah found the name for his message.

The examples of Isaiah 57:17 and Isaiah 40:13–14 are just two of at least ten instances where it can be shown that Judah quoted the *Great Isaiah Scroll,* not some other copy of Isaiah. The *Great Isaiah Scroll* in many places diverges from the Isaiah that we know from our Bible. Nearly a dozen of these disagreements surface in Judah's hymns.[14] We come thereby to a transfixing realization.

Reading the *Great Isaiah Scroll,* we are face-to-face with a book once consulted—or more likely, owned—by Judah, the Teacher of Righteousness. That he did own books is certain. After all, he was a scholarly member of the elite, a person who could afford to own books even though the average peasant could not. And in a still, small voice, another possibility clamors for recognition. Since Judah was a scribe and wisdom teacher, and since such people wrote and copied books, could it be that the *Great Isaiah Scroll* preserves Judah's own hand? Perhaps; he may indeed have written out part of this scroll himself (two scribes did the main work). And yet a third corollary emerges: the collection of books we call the Dead Sea Scrolls may have as its nucleus the personal library of this man, the first messiah.

From his mastery of this library emerged Judah's defense, attacking the Pharisees as false prophets and presenting himself as both the New Moses and the Servant.

H YRCANUS REPEATED his question. "Is there none who would speak in defense of Judah, charged as a false prophet? If convicted the sentence is death, so if you have anything to say, say it now."

Judah's eyes swept the chamber of the Bouleuterion. No one stirred. Not even Absalom, brother of King Alexander, his supporter—yes, friend. Absalom: the man who had saved him from the Pharisee death squads and had hidden him where Hyrcanus's agents could not reach. Absalom sat silent. Judah realized that in the period since his arrest, Hyrcanus and the Pharisees must have gotten to Absalom. His other friends, too; that was why they were not even here. They had abandoned him as politically impotent, and for the sake of their own political (and, probably, literal) survival sought new alliances. Some doubtless had fled the city.

After waiting a decent interval for further debate and finding none, Hyrcanus gestured to Judah to approach. "Judah, you have been charged as a false prophet. Having heard the charges and your defense, I have reached a verdict. I find you guilty as charged. I hereby sentence you to death by stoning." He paused and cleared his throat.

"Taking into consideration your station in life, however, I am prepared to commute the sentence. Instead you are to be permanently exiled from this land. You have two days to wrap up your affairs. Then you must leave and never return. You may take with you only what you can carry. The rest of your property is forfeit to the royal treasury. Your family and any others that you have deluded may accompany you or stay, as they will. Should you try to return to Jerusalem or any other part of this realm, you will be executed on sight."

BRUTA FACTA

At this juncture I must confess what the reader has undoubtedly suspected. We do not actually possess a transcript of what was said by the parties at Judah's trial. The foregoing has been a historical reconstruction.

Undoubtedly something like what I have just presented did happen. The reconstruction is based on what we know of ancient Jewish trials and where they were held in Judah's day.[15] We also have a record in the Bible of a trial for false prophecy that I have used as model. The prophet Jeremiah was tried for that crime and survived only because he could draw upon what Judah lacked—political support among the aristocracy (Jeremiah 26). For Judah's defense I have slightly adapted the wording from his fifth hymn. That hymn really was a defense, though it is not in the form of a legal brief. Judah must have expressed something like its contents in his oral responses to enemy attacks. And he did in that hymn make all the claims I have investigated above. (The full hymn is appended at the end of the chapter.)

What then are the brute facts? That Judah was put on trial we know from the testimony of a work of his later movement, the *Commentary on Habakkuk*. The author of that work discovered Judah's trial predicted in the words of the biblical prophet:

> *Why do you heed traitors and remain silent when the wicked swallows up one more righteous than he? (Habakkuk 1:13)*

> *The true import concerns the House of Absalom and the men of his party, who remained silent at the trial[16] of the Teacher of Righteousness and did not help him against the Man of the Lie, who rejected the law in the midst of the entire council.*

This passage also indicates that at the trial Absalom and his political friends and allies, *the House of Absalom*, did not support Judah as expected. If they had not been thought friendly, their silence in the presence of his accusers would not have been singled out for later censure. Thus we can deduce that Absalom had formerly sided with Judah. The trial was an occasion of treachery.

And the *Commentary* goes on to inform us that Judah's principal opponent at the trial was the *Man of the Lie*, whom we have encountered previously in the *Damascus Document*. The sobriquet was a cipher for the leading Pharisee, perhaps Shimeon ben Shetah. Moreover, the focus of the trial is explicit—it was a law associated with the Teacher and publicly assailed, in the Jerusalem council, by the Man of the Lie. By the implicit testimony of the *Commentary*, the charges for which Judah was condemned must have been connected with this law. That conclusion leads to the question of precisely what the charges were.

I think it very likely, based on several converging lines of evidence, that Judah was charged as a false prophet.[17]

First is the element of reversal so prominent in Judah's hymns. Recall, for example, the words of his second hymn: *The very net that they spread for me will trip them up; into the traps they set for me they shall themselves fall.* Judah is constantly slinging back at his enemies the very stones that they have hurled at him. In the first hymn Judah calls his enemies all sorts of names. They evidently have called him those same names or very similar ones: *Because of the iniquity of the wicked, I am defamed by the lips of violent men; scorners gnash their teeth. Sinners mock me in song.* So when Judah in his fifth hymn calls the Pharisees *prophets of deception, false prophets, seers of deception, deceivers,* and *seers of error,* it seems reasonable to suspect that once again reversal is at work.

He calls them false prophets because he believed it, but also because they had called him that. From the Pharisee perspective it would be the most natural label to pin on Judah. He presented himself as a prophet. If they did not accept him, he became a false prophet ipso facto.

Another reason to believe that false prophecy was the principal charge at Judah's trial emerges from a newly published Dead Sea Scroll. It is a legal work and a pseudepigraph (a "false writing" of the type discussed in chapter 2). The implicit claim is that Moses penned the work. Technically designated 4Q375, it reveals what the expression "false prophet" had come to mean:

> *Any prophet who arises to urge you [to apostasy, to turn] you from following your God, must be put to death. Yet if the tribe to [which] he belongs comes forward and argues, "He must not be executed, for he is a righteous man, he is a [trus]tworthy prophet," then you are to come with that tribe and your elders and judges [t]o the place that your God*

shall choose in one of the territories of your tribes. You are to come before [the pr]iest who has been anointed, upon whose head has been poured the anointing oil.[18]

Where Deuteronomy 18 leaves off, this work picks up. Deuteronomy provides only one way to know whether a prophet has truly spoken God's word. If his prediction comes to pass, then he is a genuine prophet (Deuteronomy 18:22). This is little help for people trying to decide about a prophet right now. If one has to wait years to determine the facts, what does one do in the meantime? And Deuteronomy gives no guidance for what would almost certainly be a common situation: people disagreeing about a prophet's veracity. After all, whether a prediction has come true or not might be a matter of interpretation.

4Q375 requires both the supporters and the detractors of a prophet to come to the high priest. In a badly damaged section, the work goes on to elaborate a ceremony performed by the high priest in order to determine the prophet's character. The ceremony involves procedures that could not actually have been performed in Judah's time, such as consulting certain divine oracles known from the Bible. Those oracles no longer existed. The work included these obsolete details to strengthen the literary fiction that Moses had written it.

Since the ceremony as described could not take place, presumably the statements of 4Q375 would have been subject, like Mosaic books of the Bible, to interpretation. One point that could not fail to emerge from such interpretation would be the high priest's role. Regardless of procedure, he would be the one to decide whether a prophet was true or false.

The other point that would clearly emerge would be this: a false prophet was one *who arises to urge you to apostasy, to turn you from following your God.* That definition would clear the way for filing a charge of false prophecy against anyone who had a view of Israel's law different from those in power. In this sense—if no other—the Pharisees could argue that Judah was a false prophet. Erroneous biblical interpretation had become, by definition, false prophecy. This meaning is not in the Bible, but 4Q375 shows that it was operative at least among priestly circles by 100 B.C.E. or so.[19]

Publicly rejecting Judah's biblical interpretation, his law, would be tantamount, therefore, to calling him a false prophet. The *Commentary on Habakkuk* recalls that Pharisaic rejection: *the Man of the Lie, who rejected the law in the midst of the entire council.* As is so often the case in historical investigation, certainty lies outside our grasp. Still, when Judah came to trial, it was probably as a false prophet.

IF JUDAH was indeed tried and sentenced as a false prophet, how likely is it that, rather than be executed (as the Bible requires), he was instead exiled?

The exile itself is a brute fact. Judah says in the fifth hymn, *I have been exiled from my country like a bird driven from its nest.* Also, the *Commentary on Habakkuk* knew of his banishment, mentioning at one point *the place of his exile* (Hebrew *beth galuto*).[20] Judah's exile is not at issue. The point is rather: Did it represent capital punishment commuted?

A passage from Josephus narrating events taking place in Jerusalem at this very time offers a clue. The Pharisees arraigned certain former advisers of King Alexander before Queen Alexandra, asking that they be executed. As members of the Jerusalem elite, the advisers appealed to the queen's son, Aristobulus, for help. (Recall, Aristobulus opposed the Pharisees.) Josephus says, "The most eminent people thus endangered fled to Aristobulus. For his part he persuaded his mother [Alexandra] to spare them because of their membership in the elite, and if she did not hold them guiltless, to exile them from the city."[21]

Here is a situation paralleling Judah's—former advisers to Alexander, on trial, turning for help to a royal member of Alexander's old coalition. The queen clearly believed that the men were guilty as charged. The prescribed sentence for their crimes was death. Invoking their lofty social status, Aristobulus urged his mother to substitute exile.

Alexandra acceded to Aristobulus, and, as Josephus reports, the men "dispersed around the country." Thus we discover that there did exist among the Jews of Judah's time a provision—whether formal or informal—whereby capital offenses could be punished instead by exile. The provision applied to the upper class, to judge from Josephus's narrative. What we know of the ancient world suggests that peasants guilty of the same crimes would have been executed forthwith.

The Bible contains no ordinance stipulating that criminals be banished, but traditions similar to what Josephus reports were in effect in the Hellenistic kingdoms of the Near East and all through the Greco-Roman world. Doubtless the Jewish legal practice was informed by these precedents. It was not for nothing, after all, that King Alexander had styled himself on his coins "Philhellene." Greek ways and legal practices had been leaking into Jewish life for decades. Thus on the model of the Hellenistic kingdoms, the Hasmonean priest-kings had instituted a secular tithe to support the state, despite the fact that such a tax is foreign to the entire ethos of the Bible.[22]

We have reason to believe that salient Roman legal ideas were also familiar to the Jews. To cite just one example: though the Bible is silent on the question of treason, the Dead Sea Scroll called the *Temple Scroll* prescribes crucifixion for that crime, just as did Roman law.[23] The parallel was no coincidence. The Jews of this time admired Rome. According to *First Maccabees* (composed during the reign of Alexander), they even signed a mutual defense pact with the Romans. Only later did the Jews come to consider the Romans enemies.

Thus Greek and Roman legal practice is potentially informative for understanding Jewish approaches in these years, particularly where extrabiblical Jewish law is at issue.[24]

Consider, then: among the Romans a person of high birth condemned to die might instead flee the country. The custom was in force already during the Republic, in the first century B.C.E. The Latin term for this option was *exsilium*; it denoted perpetual expulsion. The person could never return to Roman territory. After his escape (for which time was allowed under law), a decree issued by a committee or high magistrate sanctioned his killing by any person if he did return. This type of banishment entailed loss of citizenship and confiscation of all property by the state, except for what the condemned could carry away with him. To harbor an exile was a punishable offense; Romans could have nothing to do with him.

Another type of banishment in Roman law was *relegatio*. This broad term embraced various grades of exile. The mildest was temporary, without imprisonment or the death penalty in case of unauthorized return. Citizenship and property were usually retained. *Relegatio* entailed exclusion from a particular place—a city such as Rome, or all of Italy—or confinement to a particular place. Commonly, people were banished to Upper Egypt or to an island.

All forms of Roman expatriation applied to the upper classes alone; lower-class people convicted of identical crimes suffered forced labor or death. Among the Greeks, as well, exile was a penalty of privilege. It was a frequent punishment for elite convicted of intriguing against the government—which Judah's hymns, read aright, certainly show that he was doing.[25]

Josephus's *Jewish War* contains a second passage pertinent to the matter of Judah's exile. Again it concerns affairs at precisely the juncture of history we are considering. Describing Alexandra, the Jewish historian notes: "She was, indeed, the very strictest observer of the ancestral traditions, and would expel from the realm anyone guilty of offense against the sacred laws."[26]

Alexandra, Josephus explicitly informs us, used exile to punish people who offended her notions of the proper interpretation of biblical laws. And those notions came, of course, from her puppet masters, the leading Pharisees. Consequently, even without the formal charge of false prophecy, Judah—with his fixed, taproot convictions—might well have been banished. Judah's exile was probably in lieu of execution and therefore most likely permanent.[27] If contemporary Greco-Roman law is a valid indication, Judah would also have lost his property and been sentenced to die should he return unbidden.

In the case of Judah the prophet these, then, are the brute facts. After a lifetime of honor and esteem, he was ousted from power and publicly defamed, then nearly murdered, then accused of crimes involving Jewish law, tried—whereupon he was abandoned by allies and erstwhile aristocratic supporters—convicted, and exiled. Taken together, the psychic squeeze of these events must have been comparable to an extrusion press.

An Oxford psychiatrist has recently written, "It is frequently the case that [a prophet's] new insight follows a period of mental distress or physical illness."[28] When such a person emerges from the illness or personal crisis, he does not revert to what he was before. He is permanently changed, with a new set of beliefs about himself and the world.

So it was with Judah.

THE VISION OF KNOWLEDGE

Judah's fifth hymn:

> *I praise You, O Lord, for You lit my face with Your Glory as I received Your covenant . . . I seek You, and like an enduring dawn You have appeared to me in heavenly splen[dor.]*

But as for them, they [have led] Your people [into error] by pushing accommodation upon them, and prophets of deception have led them into error. Consequently, they shall be ruined, without understanding. Surely their works are so much madness!

I have been rejected by them, and they have not esteemed me when You manifested Your mighty power through me. Instead, I have been exiled from my country like a bird driven from its nest, and all my allies and kinsmen have distanced themselves from me. They account me a broken vessel. But as for them, false prophets and seers of deception, they plot destruction against me, wishing to coerce Your people into exchanging Your law (which You spoke so audibly within my mind!) for accommodation. They stopper the drink of true knowledge from the thirsty and instead force upon them vinegar, whereby to gaze upon their error as they madly practice idolatry at their festivals, and are trapped in their nets. Yet You, O God, despise every scheme of Belial. It is Your counsel that shall prevail, what Your mind has planned that shall be forever established!

As for them, they lie; they scheme the plots of Belial. Not being established in Your truth, they seek You as hypocrites. Their plots take root and blossom into poison and wormwood. They look about with a willful heart and go to idols to seek You. They set before themselves the stumbling block of their iniquity and go to seek Your purposes from the mouths of false prophets who are corrupted by error. With barbarous stammerings and a strange tongue they speak to Your people, by deception rendering all their works so much madness. For they have rejected the Way of Your [heart] and spurned Your word. They have repudiated the vision of knowledge, saying, "It is not established," and the Way of Your heart, saying "It is not the way."

But You, O God, shall answer them in judgment through Your miraculous power, measure for measure as befits their idol worship and the multitude of their sins, so that, having abandoned Your covenant, they are entrapped by their own schemes. You shall cut off in ju[dg]ment all the deceivers; seers of error shall be found no more. Indeed, there is no madness in all Your works, nor any deceit in Your mind's plans. Those who hew to You shall abide in Your presence forever; those who walk in the Way of Your heart shall be established for everlasting.

[I my]self, because I have held fast to You, shall be restored. I shall rise against those who hate me, my hand shall be against all who despise me. Surely they will not esteem [me un]til You manifest Your mighty power through me, appearing to me in Your might with heavenly splendor. You have not plastered with shame the faces of all who seek You through me, those who gather together in support of Your covenant. They who walk in the Way of Your heart shall heed me and thus array themselves before You in the council of the Holy Ones. You will cause their justice to endure forever, their truth to spread abroad without obstacle. You will not countenance scoundrels leading them astray as they had planned; rather, You will put the fear of these seekers upon Your people, and make them a war club against the peoples of all nations, so cutting off in judgment all who transgress Your commands. Through me You will illumine the faces of many and multiply them without number, for You have given me understanding of Your wondrous mysteries. You have fortified my station in Your wondrous council so that, for the sake of Your Glory, I work wonders while many look on, demonstrating Your mighty deeds to every living person.[29]

CHAPTER 5

THINGS UNUTTERABLE

I know a man in Christ who fourteen years ago was caught up to the third heaven. Whether it was in the body or out of the body I do not know—God knows. And I know that this man—whether in the body or apart from the body I do not know, but God knows—was caught up to Paradise. He heard things unutterable, things that man is not permitted to tell.

Paul the Apostle, speaking of himself
(2 Corinthians 12:2–4)

I N   H I S   F A M O U S book *The Varieties of Religious Experience,* William James wrote, "Our normal waking consciousness, rational consciousness as we call it, is but one special type of consciousness, whilst all about it, parted from it by the filmiest of screens, there lie potential forms of consciousness entirely different."[1] Jim Morrison of the Doors once spoke similarly of alternate consciousness, though in much earthier terms, when he urged a generation to "break on through to the other side." In Judah's fourth hymn, the ancient Judaean parted James's filmy screen. He broke through to the other side. It changed him forever.

AT THE BOUNDARY
OF SANITY AND MADNESS

Possibly the mystical experience this hymn tries to communicate happened while Judah sat brooding in the dark of his cell, awaiting trial.[2] Chronologically, then, what I am about to describe preceded the events of the last chapter and happened before the trial. Indeed, the very fact of Judah's arrest and imprisonment, together with his anticipation of the trial, may have served as the final emotional catalyst for his experience. In turn, the fact of the event may help explain Judah's claims at the trial.

This hymn is puzzling in many respects, and scholars have never understood it. In fact, the author of one major study of the *Thanksgiving Hymns* found it so difficult that she simply gave up and left the text untranslated. It does take real effort to come to terms with Judah's fourth hymn, and the narrative drive of Judah's story slows a bit here because everything he describes took place only in his mind.

Yet an understanding of this writing is worth some effort. For if I am right—and I am about to offer a novel interpretation of Judah's words—Judah tells us in his fourth hymn that he traveled to heaven. And if that were not enough, he also for the first time claimed to be the messiah.

The hymn reads as follows:

> O my God, [You] lit my face with Your glory as I received Your covenant . . . [I have w]alked in eternal glory among all [Your Holy Ones . . .

> Those who despise me] have considered me [an object of derision and mock]ing and I have been rendered as a ship upon the [r]aging sea, like a fortified city besieged by [her enemies.] I am in distress, like a woman in labor with her firstborn when her travail begins, when the mouth of her womb pulses with agony, when the firstborn of the woman writhes within her. Surely children come forth through the breakers of death, and she who gives a man birth suffers agonies!

> Yet through the breakers of death she delivers a male child, and through hellish agonies bursts forth from the bearer's womb: a Wonderful Counselor with His mighty power!

> But when the man comes safely through the breakers, they all rush upon his bearer: grievous agonies strike those giving birth, terrors come to their mothers. When he is born, the travails all turn back on the bearer's womb.

> She who bears wickedness also does so in pulsing agony, with hellish pains and the manifestations of terror. The foundations of the wall shake and break asunder, as a ship upon the face of the sea when a

mighty storm breaks out; those who dwell in the dust are like seafarers, terrified of the water's roar. Her wise men, all of them, are as sailors on a raging sea; surely all their wisdom shall be swallowed up as the seas rage, as the depths boil over and springs spout their waters.

The waves shall tower, the breakers of water soar while they clamor and cry out. As they are tossed by the swells, Sh[eo]l [and Abaddon] shall open wide, [and a]ll the arrows of Hell will dog their steps as they descend into the abyss. They will give a shout, and the gates of [Sheol] will swing open [to receive all] these handiworks of wickedness. The gates of Hell will close behind her who gave birth to perversity, and everlasting bars lock behind all those animated by wicked spirits.[3]

The first line of this hymn, *O my God, [You] lit my face*[4] *with Your glory as I received Your covenant,* alludes to Exodus 34, where the Bible re-counts Moses' descent from Sinai. Verses 29–34 of the biblical chapter are as follows:

> As he came down from the mountain with the two tablets of the covenant in his hand, Moses did not realize that the skin of his face shone because he had been talking with God. When Aaron and all the Israelites saw Moses with the skin of his face shining, they were afraid to come near him. But Moses called to them. . . . When Moses had finished speaking with them, he put a veil on his face. But whenever Moses went in before YHWH to speak with him, he would take the veil off until he came out. When he came out, and told the Israelites what he had been commanded, they would see the face of Moses, that the skin of his face was shining.

Like Moses, Judah had received a covenant, and so, like Moses, his face shone. But note especially the biblical explanation for why Moses' face shone: "He had been talking with God." What did that mean, and how did Judah take that meaning?

Moses did not get his message from God through dreams or visions, as did other prophets in Israel's history. Rather, as God says of Moses in Numbers 12:8, "With him I speak face to face—clearly, not in riddles; and he looks upon the image of YHWH." There was a physical aspect to the Mo-saic revelation that the Exodus text also embraces: "Moses went in *before*

YHWH to speak with him." Moses physically came into God's presence for discussion, as one might do with a human friend. At least, that was how many Jews of Judah's day read Exodus.

Thus Josephus narrates Moses' descent from Sinai with a telling difference of emphasis:

> On the third day, before the rising of the sun, a cloud settled
> over the whole camp of the Hebrews. They had not seen its like
> before. . . . While the rest of heaven remained serene, blustery
> winds and forceful rain came sweeping down. Lightning bolts were
> terrifying to the witnesses, and thunder indicated the presence of
> God as Moses required it. . . . The report circulating that God fre-
> quently visited this very mountain profoundly disquieted the He-
> brews. . . . Such was their mood when Moses appeared, shining
> brilliantly and in high spirits.[5]

Few people in Josephus's day would have argued with the idea that God lived in heaven. It was axiomatic—intellectual bedrock, as irrefutable as the observed fact that the sun and stars revolve around the earth. Josephus champions his notion that a portion of this divine residence had once descended, like a fog-shrouded express elevator, and had come to rest on Mount Sinai. This was the significance of the unearthly cloud and the historian's comment that "God frequently visited this very mountain." God only visited; he did not live there permanently, Josephus contends, as the ignorant might suppose from a superficial reading of the Exodus account.

Since God brought his divine surroundings down to the mountaintop with him in the manner Josephus describes, if Moses were to come before God and speak with him—to receive the Ten Commandments and the covenant for Israel—he had to enter those surroundings. He had to enter heaven. And this was something Moses did repeatedly. Any reader of the Sinai episode could affirm that Moses climbed the mountain fully seven times.[6]

So when Judah wrote, *You lit my face with Your glory,* he was making an extraordinary assertion. He meant to say that he, like Moses, had journeyed to heaven.

JUDAH EMPHASIZED his assertion through his wording in the fifth hymn. Recall his phrasing: *like an enduring dawn You have appeared to me in heavenly splendor.*[7] The Hebrew word I have rendered *heavenly splendor* (*urtom*) is very rare; in fact, before the discovery of the Dead Sea Scrolls, scholars had never seen it before. Finding new Hebrew words is not as uncommon as you might suppose. A substantial percentage of what once existed in the ancient Hebrew lexicon perished in antiquity, so almost every epigraphic or manuscript discovery restores some lost vocabulary. In such situations, we can deduce a word's meaning only by its use: Where is it used, and how?

One place the term *urtom* shows up is in a writing known as the *Songs of the Sabbath Sacrifice*. This bizarre work, produced by one or more members of Judah's movement, describes in thirteen songs the angelic worship and praise that were thought to take place in heaven. Earthly worship was but a shadow of that greater and ultimate adoration. By reciting these songs at the proper time and in the proper sequence, the worshiper might unite with the angels and so truly worship God.

Toward the end of the seventh song (unfortunately partially damaged) the architectural elements of the heavenly temple, which were conceived as living beings, are called to praise. I have underlined the song's use of *urtom* below:

> *Sing praises to the mighty God, make the choicest spiritual offering; make melody in the joy of God, and rejoice among the holy ones through wondrous melodies, in everlasting joy. With such songs shall all the foundations of the holy of holies offer praise, and the pillars bearing the most exalted abode, even all the corners of the temple's structure.*

> *Hymn the God awesome in power, all you wise spirits of light; together laud the utterly brilliant firmament that girds His holy temple. Praise Him, godlike spirits, lauding eternally the firmament of the uttermost heaven, all its beams and walls, all its structure and crafted design. The utterly holy spirits, living divinities, eternally holy spirits above all the holy ones . . . wondrous and wonderful, majesty and splendor and marvel. Glory abides in the <u>heavenly splendor</u> of knowledge . . .*[8]

Here our rare word is an element in a vision of heaven, describing the holy habitation wherein dwells the glory of God.

A second Dead Sea Scroll helps to clarify the term's meaning further. This writing, designated by scholarly nomenclature 4Q392, comprises an unknown wisdom teacher's ruminations on the creation narratives of Genesis 1–2. Only a few lines of one fragment of the work yield connected sense —but they include our word:

> He created darkness [and li]ght for Himself, and in His dwelling place is the light of <u>heavenly splendor</u>. All darkness rests before Him as well, but He has no need to distinguish between light and darkness. For the sake of humanity He did distinguish them—as the li[ght of] day, with the sun, and that of night, with the moon and stars. With Him is light that cannot be comprehended, whose [limit] cannot be known.
>
> All the works of God are paired. We who are flesh, should we not seek to understand them?[9]

This writer calls for contemplation of God's creation, even while admitting that our puny human intellect cannot conceive of things as they really are. Only God is able to do that. God does not even think about matters the way a human being must, by nature, seek to do. So the best we can hope for, the writer asserts, is to apprehend our world in the limited way made possible by divine concessions. The author's further notion that the entire creation is paired (literally: "doubled") reflects a wisdom tradition of the second century B.C.E., also known from *Ben Sira*.[10]

The author states that God dwells in *heavenly splendor (urtom)*. He helpfully offers a fuller definition: this is the *light that cannot be comprehended, whose limit cannot be known*. Hence in 4Q392, just as in the *Songs of the Sabbath Sacrifice*, our rare term characterizes the heavenly environs. This is the light that Judah invoked with his words. He meant that he had gone where that light was—at least, so it seems.

One might object that Judah's statement in the fifth hymn is ambiguous: *You have appeared to me in heavenly splendor.* Could he have meant to suggest, not his own ascension, but rather God's descent to make an appearance to him—a theophany? Scholars call such an experience of divine light a "photism." According to the book of Acts, the apostle Paul had such an episode on the Damascus Road. The literature on religious experience is full of them; sometimes, as with Paul, they accompany a dramatic religious conversion.[11] Was this what happened to Judah?

I do not think so, for two reasons. One is the very next line in hymn four: *[I have w]alked in eternal glory among all [Your Holy Ones]*. Even though the restoration of *Your Holy Ones* is uncertain, Judah still spoke of walking about in the realm of God's eternal glory. That could only mean heaven.

The second reason is related to the first, and it has to do with why the ancients described heavenly journeys at all. For a number of such descriptions have come down to us; stories of ascent were reasonably common in Hellenistic and Roman times, known in many different cultures.[12] By comparing them, scholars have been able to uncover commonalities of structure and purpose. A glance at one or two of these other passages to the celestial sphere can both explain my second reason and help us with a basic question.

Just what did Judah really believe had happened to him?

NO FIGURE in the Genesis narratives of the antediluvian age provoked more speculation among the ancients than Enoch. Twice he is said to have "walked with God." That phrase had the potential to sponsor all sorts of mystical trajectories. But still more fructifying for fertile imaginations was the cryptic comment, "then he was no more, because God took him" (Genesis 5:24). Many later readers interpreted this expression to mean that God had translated Enoch to heaven and that Enoch never died. What, they wondered, had Enoch seen in heaven? Did he ever tell anyone?

By the third century B.C.E. (if not earlier), literature ascribed to Enoch by literary fiction began to appear among the Jews. A fair number of different writings circulated. Several are referred to already by 200 B.C.E.[13] Five of the principal Enoch writings were later collected into a single book known today as *1 Enoch* or *Ethiopic Enoch,* the latter title because the complete book has survived only in an ancient dialect of Ethiopia. Ethiopian Christians considered *1 Enoch* scripture and included it as part of their Old Testament.

Certain circles of ancient Jews likewise considered the book authoritative. They took the Enoch writings at face value. For them, these were actual products of the biblical patriarch, kept sealed and secret, unknown until rediscovery in their own time. These circles included priestly groups of the late second century B.C.E., and among their ranks was Judah. In his final hymn Judah even alluded to an Enoch writing as holy writ.

Judah's later followers valued Enoch's revelations, as did many others. They were widely read in the first century C.E. Some twenty copies of Enochic literature found their way into the corpus of the Dead Sea Scrolls. In the front rank of the corps of believing first-century Jews stood Jude, the brother of Jesus, who in his New Testament book of the same name quoted *1 Enoch*.[14]

1 Enoch depicts the patriarch making several ascents to heaven before his final translation. The book presents itself as the written record of what transpired throughout these travels. In chapter 14 appears a pellucid description of an ascent:

> Winds caused me to fly and hastened me and lifted me up into heaven. . . . And I looked and I saw in it a high throne, and its appearance was like ice and its surrounds like the shining sun and the sound of Cherubim. And from underneath the high throne there flowed out rivers of burning fire so that it was impossible to look at it. And He who is great in glory sat on it, and his raiment was brighter than the sun and whiter than any snow. And no angel could enter, and at the appearance of the face of Him who is honoured and praised no creature of flesh could look. And the Lord called me with his own mouth and said to me, Come hither, Enoch, to my holy word.[15]

Enoch enjoyed an intimate audience with God, a privilege beyond even the highest angel. For the author of this writing, that was the meaning of the biblical statement, "Enoch walked with God." An experience akin to Enoch's may lie behind Judah's statement, *I have walked in eternal glory.*

And how was Enoch's tale intended to affect the reader? As one analyst has observed, "Enoch's ascent has the primary purpose of explaining some of the great evil on the earth while confirming that both the suffering of the righteous and the success of sinful forces will be righted hereafter." This is just the sort of message that members of a crisis cult needed to hear and that Judah would have sought out for help in explaining the catastrophes crashing about him.[16]

Almost as old as the Enoch writings was an Aramaic book purporting to be the last words of the patriarch Levi, third son of Jacob and the progenitor of the Jewish priesthood. This book dates to the period 200–150 B.C.E. *Aramaic Levi* recounts the prophecies and profundities of the model priest.

As such, it was a great favorite of the same priestly circles that treasured the
Enoch literature, and it was certainly known to Judah. As many as six copies
have been identified among the Dead Sea Scrolls (the exact number is not
entirely clear). Several medieval copies have also come to light.[17]

One passage of the book—by Murphy's law, damaged or missing in
every manuscript—chronicles Levi's ascent to heaven:

> *I laid down. And I remained . . . Then I was shown a vision . . . in*
> *the appearance of a vision, and I saw heav[en . . . and a mountain]*
> *under me so high it reached heave[n . . . and they opened] for me the*
> *gates of heaven and an angel . . . And he said to me, Levi, to you and*
> *to your descendants the priesthood is given, to serve the Most High in*
> *the midst of the land and to atone for the sins of the land.*[18]

Aramaic Levi was known and read by early Christian communities
in the first century C.E. and later. They passed it down, and eventually,
somewhat transformed, it found a final resting place in the work known as
the *Testaments of the Twelve Patriarchs*. This was a Greek book collecting
the last words of all twelve of Jacob's sons. Since the Christian version sup-
plemented and reconfigured *Aramaic Levi*, we cannot be sure how much of
the following rendition once stood in the older Jewish work. Still, it is sug-
gestive of the sort of material that has been lost from the damaged portions
cited above:

> I saw all men corrupting their way and that unrighteousness had
> built for itself walls and lawlessness sat upon the towers. Then a
> sleep fell upon me and I beheld a high mountain and behold, the
> heavens were opened and an angel of God said to me: Levi, enter!
> And I entered from the first heaven into the second one, and I saw
> there a water hanging between the one and the other. And I saw a
> third heaven, far brighter and more brilliant than these two; for in it
> there was boundless light. And I said to the angel, Why so? And the
> angel said to me, Do not marvel at these, for you will see four other
> heavens, more brilliant and incomparable, when you ascend there.
> For you will stand near the Lord and will be his minister and will de-
> clare his mysteries to men.[19]

As with Enoch's ascent, Levi's occurred at a time of crisis and corruption, "when lawlessness sat upon the towers." Heavenly visions and

ascents were (and still are) one response to such times. They are commonly associated with the charismatic leaders of crisis cults. Recall, for example, Wovoka, the Paiute messiah who journeyed to heaven and there received the Ghost Dance and other new teaching. To claim an ascent was the most formidable way for any charismatic leader to array authority behind his new laws. Provided one believes in the courier, a God-given message carried directly to its destination is as incontestable as a mud slide.

Another import of the journey was to present the faithful with a foretaste—a guarantee, a down payment—of future glory. The present journey was a rehearsal for the final and permanent one. As New Testament scholar James Tabor has written, "What the seer beholds or even experiences in some cases, mirrors what is expected at the end, whether of life [or of] history."[20]

Accordingly, Judah wrote in his fifth hymn, *Those who hew to You shall abide in Your presence forever;* these same would one day *array themselves before You in the council of the Holy Ones.* The *Holy Ones* were the angels, among whom Judah claimed already to have walked. So he said of himself in the same hymn, *You have fortified my standing in Your wondrous council.*

Judah taught his followers that after death they would unite with the angels. He himself had already done it, as the firstfruits, the firstborn among many. Judah almost might have written the words of Paul: "Whom God predestined he also called; and those whom he called he also made righteous; and those whom he made righteous he also glorified." So certain is the future glorification of believers that it has to be expressed in the past tense.

This, then, is the second reason that Judah's words should be understood to speak of a heavenly ascent, not a theophany. *O my God, You lit my face with Your glory as I received Your covenant. I have walked in eternal glory.* These words fulfilled a cardinal purpose of the heavenly journey. As Tabor concludes, "The ascent [looks forward]. What the figure sees and experiences is related to his expectations of a return ascent, and often that of the community as well."[21]

So it was with Judah.

SOMETIMES ANCIENT ascent was a literary fiction. It became a tried-and-true mechanism for the writer who wished to present ideas as more than his own. No hint of Levi's journeying to heaven is to be found in the

Bible. A second-century B.C.E. priest chose his identity and the topos of heavenly journey to create a megaphone for his own voice in the controversies of the day. Presumably that priest did not himself enjoy the sort of ecstatic vision that he granted his hero.

Yet we cannot be sure, for some people really did travel to heaven.

These are the people that William James had in mind when he spoke of a consciousness different from normal, waking consciousness. Such people have immediate and sometimes recurrent experiences of another dimension of reality. This human type is known from many different cultures and throughout recorded history. Their reports are too ubiquitous, too cross-cultural to be dismissed in every instance as nonsense or lies. In many cases, behind the stories lies something real. Marcus Borg, with equal parts evocation and description, has termed the individual who slips into this other consciousness a "spirit person."[22]

Borg elaborated, "What such persons know is the sacred. Spirit persons are people who experience the sacred frequently and vividly."[23] He went on to suggest that Jesus was one:

> The stories of his life in the gospels make this very clear. He had visions, including a vision at his baptism in which, like Ezekiel, he "saw the heavens opened" and the Spirit descending upon him like a dove. That vision was followed by a series of visions in the wilderness in what we typically call the temptation narrative, but which a cultural anthropologist would recognize immediately as a wilderness ordeal or vision quest, characteristic of spirit persons.[24]

How are we in this scientific age to come to terms with the visionary and heavenly voyager? We cannot avoid this question. Are we to label the spirit person delusional, a schizophrenic, or manic-depressive, mad? Few Christians would be comfortable saying such things about Jesus—or Paul, who by Borg's definition was another spirit person. They might have no qualms saying them about Jim Jones and David Koresh, who claimed heavenly journeys—but what about Ignatius of Loyola, yet another claimant?

From Borg's analytic perspective, all of these people can be grouped together. (Which is not to say, of course, that their characters, personalities, or ideas were otherwise alike at all.) Without question the spirit person is odd, different from most of us, but unlike ourselves the ancients were slow to castigate this difference. More often they celebrated it. Many of humankind's germinal ideas, they recognized, were generated by such people. So Socrates declared, "Our greatest blessings come to us by way of madness."

What Socrates meant by *madness* is not quite what modern psychology means. Spirit persons can only rarely be termed mentally ill, as the psychiatrist Anthony Storr has explained:

> Mental illness or "madness" is usually associated with "breakdown," with the inability to cope with life in our society, whereas many [visionaries] are effective social leaders, proselytizers and orators. Even if [such people] are deemed to be mentally abnormal, they do not usually become psychiatric patients or end their days in mental hospitals. The phenomenon of the [visionary] raises difficult questions about the nature of mental illness. Can people be regarded as psychotic merely because they hold eccentric ideas about the universe and their own significance as prophets or teachers? What are the boundaries between sanity and madness? What does labelling someone psychotic really mean? Are our current psychiatric classifications adequate? . . . Our dividing lines between sanity and mental illness have been drawn in the wrong place. The sane are madder than we think; the mad are saner.[25]

Storr concludes, "The diagnosis of mental illness *cannot be made on the evidence of beliefs alone,* however eccentric these appear. In the absence of other signs of mental illness, [a spirit person] cannot be deemed psychotic."[26] Perhaps someday psychiatry will develop a more nuanced way to talk about heavenly voyagers and visionaries. In the meantime, whatever else they may be, they are not crazy.

What then of the experiences they claim to have? Are they real? In any given instance this issue cannot be settled in a way that will satisfy all concerned. Perspective becomes all-important. From the insider's or believer's perspective, something objectively real takes place. The outsider by definition will be skeptical, for, lacking skepticism, he or she would no longer be an outsider. The outsider will argue that the experience is subjective.

No meeting of the minds is possible, since for either person truly to admit the other's position requires a "paradigm shift" whereby each simultaneously denies his or her own. The only way one pole can meet the other is to become that other. No compromise position exists; this is a zero-sum game. Our limitations as human beings come to the fore at this point: the boundary where madness meets sanity is also the boundary where faith meets knowledge.

Here the historian can do no more than describe what was believed. He or she cannot decide for anyone else what was true.

In the case of the spirit person Judah, we do not seem to be dealing with mere literary artifice. He seems to have believed that he had journeyed to heaven, received direct revelation, and returned to announce it to the millennial generation. And Judah himself told us about it—an important point. Except for one, all other stories of heavenly ascent that have survived antiquity are third-person accounts. Writers tell us about Enoch, about Levi, about Adam and others. Only the apostle Paul, in 2 Corinthians, tells us about himself.[27] Only Paul—until now.

With Judah we discover the second ancient autobiographical account of a journey to hear things unutterable.

WONDERFUL COUNSELOR

Reading beyond the first two lines of Judah's fourth hymn is like leaving a bright kitchen and going down the stairs into a pitch-black cellar. At first all one can see are ill-defined shapes. The language is disjointed. Images are fuzzy edged. Topics are brought up, dropped, then resumed without warning. Double meanings abound. But gradually the eyes adjust.

One can see clearly enough that Judah used various metaphors, first comparing himself to a ship (*I have been rendered as a ship upon the raging sea*), then to a city (*like a fortified city besieged*), and finally to a woman in labor (*like a woman in labor with her firstborn*). It further becomes clear that through these metaphors Judah meant to focus on his suffering. This focus was consonant with his self-identification as the Servant of the Lord, whose suffering, according to Isaiah, was central to all that he would accomplish. And Judah had suffered, and he was suffering right now as he languished in prison. So much is clear.

What remains blurred is the fourth metaphor: the baby born of the woman. Judah described this baby as a *Wonderful Counselor with His mighty power*. What could he have meant? If he was himself the woman, who was his child?

The fact that Judah was a spirit person can shed some light on this problem and, indeed, on the disjointed character of the entire hymn. Similarly odd language and imagery appear in oral accounts given by those tribal visionaries and spirit persons often called shamans. To draw on the comparative evidence that anthropologists have collected about modern-day shamans is legitimate, since various studies have demonstrated what I. M. Lewis called "the remarkable uniformity of mystical language and symbolism."[28]

Shamans function as mediums in societies that lack clearly defined political positions. The shaman becomes a powerful and often feared leader who regulates relations both among people and between people and the spirits. The medicine man of American western fame was a type of shaman. According to Mircea Eliade, a foremost expert on the topic, the diagnostic features of shamanism are specific: the shaman is an inspired priest who, in ecstatic trance, ascends to the heavens on trips.

As many cultures conceive of it, shamans are recruited by the spirits. That is, while they sometimes choose their vocation, more often they are themselves chosen. The initial experience of spirit possession is traumatic and commonly is a response to personal adversity such as severe illness, misfortune, or danger. As Lewis eloquently phrased it, "The road to the assumption of the shaman's vocation lies through affliction valiantly endured and, in the end, transformed into spiritual grace."[29] For example, one Chukchee was out harpooning seal on an ice floe and slipped into the water. He certainly would have drowned, he later reported, if not for the miraculous appearance of a friendly walrus. The animal comforted him and helped him hoist himself back onto the floe. After this close call the man made offerings to the walrus, and it became his tutoring spirit, transforming him into a shaman.

Eliade showed that the ecstatic experiences through which a man or woman becomes a shaman usually involve a tripartite schema: suffering, "death," and new life or "resurrection."[30] This is a kind of initiation, similar to those known from ancient secret societies. When the shaman is called by the spirits,

> Initiatory sicknesses closely follow the fundamental pattern of all
> initiations: first, torture at the hands of demons or spirits who
> play the role of masters of initiation; second, ritual death, experi-
> enced by the patient as a descent to Hell or ascent to Heaven;

third, resurrection to a new mode of being—the mode of "conse-
crated man," that is, a man who can personally communicate with
gods, demons and spirits. . . .

Whatever the nature of his sufferings may be, they have a role in
the making of the shaman only to the extent to which he gives them
a religious significance and, by the fact, accepts them as ordeals in-
dispensable to his mystical transfiguration.[31]

The parallels between shamans, with their sufferings and ascen-
sions, and Judah's situation are patent. And the parallels continue.

After their initial experience of "death" and heavenly ascent, shamans
describe in odd language what has happened to them. This is an attempt to
communicate what scholars call "disassociative thinking." They see themselves cut up by demons or spirits; their bones are scraped, the flesh
cleaned off, and so on. One Yakut informant related that the spirits cut off
his head and set it to one side so that he could, as required, watch his dis-
memberment with his own eyes. He was simultaneously victim and observer.[32]

Among the Tukano Indians of Colombo, shamans frequently report
ecstatic visions of a return to the womb. This again is disassociative thinking. Eliade noted similar descriptions in diverse cultures and commented,
"The novice's death signifies a return to the embryonic state. It is not only a
repetition of the first gestation and carnal birth from the mother; it is also
a return to the virtual, precosmic mode, followed by a rebirth."[33] So death
means birth.

Recall the considerable imagery of death in Judah's hymn. The first
half radiates menace. He was a ship in danger of being pounded to pieces by
an angry sea. He was a city about to fall to siege, after which in the ancient
world pillage and rape were standard operating procedure. He wrote, *Surely
children come forth through the breakers of death*. Again he wrote, *Through
the breakers of death she delivers a male child*. He spoke of travail, a pulsing
womb, hellish agony. Images of death are everywhere.

Yet Judah yoked all of this death imagery with birth. Just as in the
shamanic parallels, the two are linked, for both were aspects of the same
experience. Judah was at the moment of a "mystical transfiguration." His
language was odd—even, for some scholars, untranslatable—because he
was trying to give utterance to the unutterable. He was attempting to put
into words something mystical and strange, striving to bring under control a
psychic electric storm—his disassociative thinking.

Who then was the baby of the fourth metaphor? None other, I suggest, than Judah the mother.

As the Yakut shaman was in his vision both victim and observer, so Judah saw himself in two roles at once. And the power of this moment is graphically represented in the primary manuscript of the *Thanksgiving Hymns*.[34] The copyist left a space both before and after the phrase *Wonderful Counselor with His mighty power*.

This was a denouement.

AND YET: so accustomed are we to Aristotelian logic and linear thinking that it jars our sensibilities to suppose that Judah could represent himself as two entities simultaneously. Both the mother and the baby? Despite well-documented parallels in the present-day experience of other spirit persons, we rebel at this reading of his words. Nevertheless, a consideration of Judah's biblical sources brings us by a different path to that same conclusion.

Judah arrived at the metaphor of the baby by creating, as he so often did, an analogical chain of interpretation. Once we enter his loop, we can follow him from source to source and so reconstruct the way he was reading the texts. In this case Judah attached a portion of Isaiah 9 to a portion from Isaiah 11, playing on their similar content and related terminology. The attachment is telling, because he elsewhere applied the Isaiah 11 passage to his own person; therefore, we can infer that Judah also saw himself in Isaiah 9.

We shall consider his reasoning in detail below, but pay particular attention not just to the content of what Judah said, but to his method. Observe his brilliant mind in action, weaving passages together, jumping from place to place in the scriptures, creating new meaning, doing it all in his head. Even in a scripture-saturated society, very few people possess such capacities. Watch the prophet's mind at work.

Judah's words *Wonderful Counselor* derive from Isaiah 9:6, a verse familiar from Handel's *Messiah*. It has been a central messianic passage for Christians down through the centuries. With the terms Judah used in the fourth hymn italicized, Isaiah 9:6–7 reads:

> For *a child has been born* for us, a *son* given to us; the government
> shall rest upon his shoulders; and he shall be called *Wonderful*
> *Counselor* of the Mighty God, Everlasting Father, Prince of Peace.

> To the increase of his government and the peace there shall be
> no end as he establishes the throne of David and his kingdom,
> and upholds the throne with justice and righteousness, begin-
> ning now and until forever. The zeal of YHWH of hosts shall ac-
> complish it.[35]

This passage speaks of a mysterious person yet to come and bestows upon him several portentous titles, all of which in one way or another Judah appropriated for himself in his hymns. In addition to the words Judah actually quoted here, *Wonderful Counselor,* Isaiah's Everlasting Father and Prince of Peace also resonate with Judah's writings. We have seen that in his first hymn Judah said of himself, *I am an adversary to prophets of false-hood, but a man of peace to all whose vision is righteous.* In a hymn we have yet to consider, Judah wrote, *Indeed You, my God, have chosen me and made me a father to the pious.* Interpreting them in singular fashion, Judah applied all the titles of this portion of Isaiah to himself.[36]

Or almost all. One title from Handel's list is missing. As commonly rendered into English, the Hebrew *el gibbor* of 9:6 becomes another epithet for the child, "Mighty God." But Judah did not understand the phrase that way, as another title. Though his self-importance was nearly boundless, he stopped short of equating himself with God. Instead, he read *el gibbor* together with the preceding Hebrew phrase, so construing *pele yoets el gibbor* as "Wonderful Counselor of the Mighty God."

So he read the text; but this phrase was not the one he chose to put in his hymn. In place of *el gibbor* he inserted the Hebrew *gevorato* to arrive at what he actually said: *Wonderful Counselor with His mighty power.* Why this change?

The adjustment Judah made derived from Isaiah 11. Isaiah 9's word *gibbor* ("mighty") directed his thinking to Isaiah 11's *gevorah* ("mighty power"). The general contexts were similar, and the terms belong to the same word family, so this was a natural association. The first two verses of Isaiah 11 are the ones immediately relevant. Once again, I have italicized the key words and translated to spotlight Judah's understanding:

> A Sprout shall come out of the stump of Jesse, a Shoot flourish out
> of his Roots. The spirit of YHWH shall rest on him, a spirit of wis-
> dom and understanding, a spirit of *counsel* and *mighty power,* a
> spirit of knowledge and the fear of YHWH.

Like Isaiah 9, Isaiah 11 concerns a mysterious figure yet unknown. Besides that connection, Judah could weld chapter 9 to chapter 11 by two word links. In addition to the *power* family, the passages share the terms *counsel* and *counselor.* Judah lifted *mighty power* from Isaiah 11, added the Hebrew suffix meaning "his" (referring to God),[37] and joined it to Isaiah 9's *Wonderful Counselor.* He thereby intertwined the two passages and made it clear that both referred to the baby of his hymn.

Elsewhere Judah applied Isaiah 11 to himself very clearly. By here equating that chapter and chapter 9, he showed that in his view they *both* spoke of him. This is the Aristotelian logic we so love: if A equals B, and B equals C, then A must also equal C. Of course, the premise must be true. Where did Judah apply Isaiah 11 to his own person and circumstances? Where did he assert that A equals B?

To answer this question we must anticipate a bit and consider the wording of Judah's later hymns. They show that Judah understood the Shoot (Hebrew *netser*) of Isaiah 11 to be his followers. Consequently he wrote in hymn 8, *I have relied upon the abundance of Your compassion and waited upon the multitude of Your acts of lovingkindness, so to bring the plant to bloom, to raise the <u>Shoot</u> to maturity.* In the next hymn Judah complained of his circumstances: *He who nurtures the holy <u>Shoot</u> to become a planting of truth is himself hidden, without esteem, unknown, his secret sealed up.*[38]

The word *shoot* is uncommon in the Bible. It occurs but four times. Isaiah 11:1 is the solitary instance that could have given rise to Judah's statements. Reading the plural *roots* of the biblical passage as a singular in light of 11:10 ("On that day the *Root* of Jesse shall stand as a banner"), Judah focused on one Root, himself.[39] He was Isaiah's Root. Judah was the Root, his followers the Shoot.

Then he understood the ambiguous *him* of Isaiah's phrase ("the spirit of YHWH shall rest on *him*") as referring to the Root, not the Shoot. Consistent with this view, Judah put quill to leather and inscribed (again in hymn 8), *You have upheld me by Your might and have poured out <u>Your holy spirit</u> within me.*[40]

And there is more: in his first hymn Judah laid claim to special wisdom, knowledge *(daat)* and understanding *(binah)*, all qualities ascribed to the figure of Isaiah 11. Recall his words: *I am <u>wisdom</u> to the simple folk;* and, *You have set me as a banner to the chosen righteous, a prophet given <u>knowledge</u> (daat) of wondrous mysteries;* and, *You have made me the very foundation of truth and <u>understanding</u> (binah) for the upright;* and yet again, *You placed*

insight (_binah_) _in my heart whereby to open the fount of_ _knowledge_ (_daat_).
The evidence is strong enough to get a conviction even in Los Angeles.
Judah saw himself in Isaiah 11.

And thus we arrive back at the conclusion we reached earlier on the
basis of comparative anthropology. Strange as it seems, Judah was both the
mother and the baby of his hymn.[41]

THE ROOT OF JESSE
SHALL STAND AS A BANNER

As Judah languished in prison, cockroaches scurrying over his hands, and
then later stood trial as a false prophet, something happened to his thinking. His fourth and fifth hymns testify to the development.[42] After intense
psychological and physical suffering, and one or more journeys to heaven,
Judah now stood in possession of a complete vision of himself.

It was a vision at once religious and political, a vision as newborn in
human experience as the baby of whom Judah wrote. The Jerusalem sage
recognized in himself the reification of an idea that a mere two or three generations before had been unknown. It was an idea that would go on to inspire art, literature, and music the equal of any ever produced, but also
genocide and wars of inhuman cruelty. It was the idea of the messiah.[43]

Gershom Scholem once pondered "the price which the Jewish people
has had to pay out of its own substance for this idea which it handed over to
the world."[44] By his fifth hymn, Judah saw himself as something momentous and new to recorded history. He was the first messiah.

This is a strong statement, made stronger by the fact that I have said
it several times already. But only now have we seen enough of Judah's story
that a defense of it can begin to make sense.

THE ESSENTIALS of a concept always bear repeating. Thus, though I
have touched on the matter above, reconsider: What is a messiah? One
cultural anthropologist specializing in crisis cults, M. I. Pereira de Queiroz,
wrote:

> Those religious doctrines which [are] used to foretell the dawning
> on earth of an age of perfect happiness are called "millennial"; they

oppose the existing society, which is considered as unjust and oppressive, and proclaim its impending downfall. These doctrines are called "messianic" whenever the inauguration of this perfect world is dependent upon the arrival of a "son of God," a divine messenger, or a mythical hero; in fact, of a "messiah." The messiah is he who announces and inaugurates on earth a "Kingdom of Heaven."[45]

The ideal reality of which de Queiroz spoke, I have called the myth-dream. Many cultures have them, perhaps all. But not all myth-dreams have agents. Not every millennium needs a messiah.

Some do, and here her definition fogs up; de Queiroz has juxtaposed *messiah* with *divine messenger* (prophet) as though they are one and the same. Her locution is standard practice among cultural anthropologists, but for our purposes it is not sufficiently precise. I repeat the distinction I suggested before: every messiah is a prophet, but not every prophet is a messiah. The messiah does more than announce God's plans. The messiah makes them happen. Without the messiah there is no kingdom. Apart from that fine-tuning, de Queiroz's definition is admirable.

Writing as a theologian rather than an anthropologist, James Charlesworth has characterized a messiah as "a divinely appointed, and anointed, supernatural man. . . . This eschatological figure will inaugurate the end of all normal time and history."[46] Again, a bit of fine-tuning: the adjective *supernatural* can be jettisoned; it is not applicable to the majority of ancient Jewish sources touching on messianic ideas. Charlesworth's Christianity is showing. Otherwise the substance of his definition, whereby he consciously seeks to represent a wide scholarly consensus, differs little from that of de Queiroz. Either definition will do nicely. The question is, how well does Judah fit them?

The Jews had long been a literate culture, and over the centuries much of their myth-dream was committed to writing. By the second century B.C.E. the works of Israel's prophets largely constituted its repository. These books were considered collections of prophecies—not reactions to their own time and circumstances so much as encrypted oracles of what would happen in the Latter Days.[47]

Some of the prophecies had been fulfilled, but many yet remained.[48] These spoke of the permanent deliverance of the Jews from foreign rule, from exile and dark happenstance; they predicted the advent of a special leader, sometimes identified as a son of David but often called by other names; they promised that Israel would be raised to the head of the nations and that conversion of the Gentiles to the worship of Israel's God would follow; they spoke of a new Jerusalem wherein would stand a new and supremely glorious Temple; they promised a permanent era of peace, the resurrection of the dead, and the recompense of the wicked.

This, in brief, was the myth-dream of Israel. By the time Judah finished his fifth hymn, he had filed claim on much of it.

Judah knew himself to be the prophesied future ruler. He implied this role in asserting that Isaiah 9 and 11 referred to him. Isaiah 9:6 says of the *Wonderful Counselor*, "the government shall rest upon his shoulders." Isaiah 11 says of its figure that he must rule (11:3–4).[49] Yet on the critical point of his future rule Judah was not content merely to imply by context. By the time he wrote his later hymns, Judah was explicit: Jerusalem and those in power there would be overthrown. He would ascend to rule in their place. Accordingly, he wrote in hymn 5, *I shall be restored. I shall rise against those who hate me, my hand shall be against all who despise me.*

By the eighth hymn he would become yet more explicit: *You shall exalt my horn above all who despise me; the remnant of those who waged war against me and who prosecuted me shall be scattered like chaff before the wind, and I shall rule over my house.*[50] To speak of God exalting the horn was good biblical idiom; it meant raise to power—in political contexts, raise to political power.[51] Thus 1 Samuel 2:10, "The Lord judges the ends of the earth; He gives power to his king, and *exalts the horn* of his anointed [the king]."

Judah expected to rule in Jerusalem in place of his enemies, and his subjects would be his "house"—what Isaiah 11 and other biblical passages call "the remnant." These were the loyal followers whom Judah described as *those who gather in support of Your covenant* and of whom he prophesied, *You will cause their justice*—the word can also be translated "rule"—*to endure forever, their truth to spread abroad without obstacle.* And when his followers spread the truth abroad, Judah imagined that he would be their commander.

Judah foresaw leading an army of the remnant against the wicked in Israel who denied him, then campaigning against the Gentiles until all bent the knee to the God of Israel. Thus in his fifth hymn he said, *You will put the fear of these seekers upon Your people* (the wicked Jews) *and make them a war club against the peoples of all nations, so cutting off in judgment all who transgress Your commands.* He continued, *Through me You will illumine the faces of Many and multiply them without number.* The last phrase alluded to a central idea of Israel's myth-dream, God's already ancient covenant promise to Abraham: "I will make you exceedingly numerous" (Genesis 17:2). Through Judah it would at last be fulfilled. By virtue of sheer numbers, Judah's Israel would be an irresistible juggernaut on the battlefield.

What about the expected New Jerusalem? In his seventh hymn Judah would broach that topic, picturing Jerusalem as a fortress city:

> *You will establish a foundation on stone and place rafters with an accurate plumb line and a true level, laying down tested stones to raise an impregnable wall that cannot be moved. None who enter it will stumble; surely no foreigner will pass its gates—doors preventing entry, cross-bars mighty and shatter-proof. No raiding party shall enter with weapons of warfare, and the arrows of the wicked shall cease to fly in battle.*[52]

Judah connected this city's establishment with the extirpation of evil Jews by forces loyal to him:

> *The eternal rampart will open into an endless expanse, and the everlasting gates will swing wide to usher forth the weapons of warfare. They will spread their forces from one end of the land to the other, shooting their arrows and allowing the guilty no retreat. They will be utterly trampled down, none taken alive, without hope among the stacked corpses. Not one of the mighty warriors shall escape.*[53]

The *mighty warriors* was a stock term in Judah's writings, representing the soldiers supporting Hyrcanus and the Jerusalem establishment.

And finally, Judah went on to describe the resurrection of the righteous, who would rise to fight shoulder-to-shoulder with the living in this great war of the Latter Days: *Those who lie in the dirt will raise a standard, and worm-eaten men will lift high a banner for the army.*[54]

How well does Judah fit the accepted definitions of a messiah? In his hymns Judah accounted for every major element of Israel's myth-dream, promoting millennial doctrines, and always with himself at the center of it all, ready to make it happen as God worked through him. Before him had been divine messengers, numerous prophets, in Israel and throughout the world—but that is all they were. None made claims comparable to Judah's. He would inaugurate the Kingdom.

Functionally, Judah claimed to be a messiah.

THE GOSPEL OF MARK tells the story of Jesus' triumphal entry into Jerusalem as the time of his clash with the city's authorities drew near. In its typical spare style, the Gospel relates:

> Then they brought the colt to Jesus and threw their cloaks on it; and he sat on it. Many people spread their cloaks on the road, and others spread leafy branches that they had cut in the fields. Then those who went ahead and those who followed were shouting, "Hosanna! Blessed is the one who comes in the name of the Lord! Blessed is the coming kingdom of our ancestor David!"

Reading this text and other portions of the Gospels, the casual student of this period in Jewish history might well conclude that the Jews held in common a well-defined messianic theory and that this theory required its principal actor to be a son of David. And not just the casual student; for centuries this view was a commonplace among scholars as well.

Only within the last two decades have scholars begun to take account of how diverse Judaism was in the period 200 B.C.E. to 100 C.E. Indeed, so different were the ideas from group to group that some scholars today prefer to speak of "Judaisms." The "normative Judaism" of nineteenth- and earlier twentieth-century historiography has disappeared, to be replaced by a kaleidoscope of groups with shifting intellectual and political allegiances. The Judaism of this time was wrestling with itself, twisted and shoved by intellectual moves and countermoves. This world was not the masterful and orderly progression of a Bach concerto; this was the cacophony of two cats and a trash can.[55]

The diversity extended to concepts of the messiah. Though the messiah's connection with David was central to some beliefs, and "son of David" was for adherents of such beliefs a basic messianic title, "there was considerable fluidity among the various titles that could be or become messianic titles."[56] Perhaps surprisingly, "messiah" was not prominent among them; its use was limited and late. One might easily claim the role of "messiah" without ever using the term itself. And in the period of the second century B.C.E. in particular, there is almost no evidence for the hope that the Davidic line would one day be restored. Instead, as John Collins has observed, "We find a range of figures who are viewed as agents of salvation by different groups."[57] (Collins was referring to literary descriptions, not actual human claimants.)

This was the state of the myth-dream when Judah came onstage. Consequently, it was no difficulty that he was a priest rather than a member of the tribe of Judah and descendant of the house of David. He could claim to be the messiah without having to finesse the fact that he was no "son of David." Indeed, in the years preceding Judah, what messianic interest there was (and it was neither strong nor widespread) focused on a priestly figure as the leader of the Latter Days. When Judah appealed to the myth-dream and echoed it, as all charismatic leaders do, he could direct himself to these priestly expectations and so relate to what his hearers already believed.

A work that we have already encountered, *Aramaic Levi,* testifies to these priestly notions. Discussing the birth of his several sons, Levi is made to say at one point: *Once again she conceived by me at the proper time fitting for women, and I called his name Kohath. [I saw] that all [the people woul]d gather to him, and that the high-priesthood [over all Isra]el would be his.*[58]

This may seem an innocent passage, but it makes a subtle and subversive argument. Levi explains that he named his son Kohath because he *saw that all the people would gather to him.* The priestly author has thus connected the name "Kohath" to the verb *qahat,* "gather."

This is the same punning interpretation given to the verb by the biblical writer in Genesis 49:10, a passage that later Jews understood as prophetic. On his deathbed, Jacob bestows a final and definitive blessing on his sons. Speaking of his son Judah he says, "the peoples will gather (*qahat*) to him." What has happened is this: *Aramaic Levi* has lifted Jacob's blessing for his son Judah and reapplied it to Kohath, a founder of the high-priestly line.[59]

Since this Judah's line gave rise to David and later kings, *Aramaic Levi's* reapplication had the effect of making the royal priestly. Following this precedent any biblical portion that spoke of "David" might be recast, applied instead to a priestly leader. The first messiah almost certainly would have construed biblical prophecies—such as that found in Isaiah 9, "he establishes the throne of David and his kingdom"—along such lines. This sort of passage could be made to speak of him, priest though he was.

That the myth-dream should focus on a priestly agent when the messianic idea first stirred in Israel is understandable. For several centuries prior to the second century B.C.E. priests had headed the government. First Persia, then Egypt, then Syria had ruled the Jews; but the immediate leader, living in Jerusalem and representing the people to their foreign over-lords, was the high priest. It became natural to think of his office as the highest in the nation. *King* was a title no Jew had borne for hundreds of years. In all but name, the high priest was the king.

Accordingly, in his book Ben Sira praised Simeon ben Johanan (high priest from 219 to 196 B.C.E.) by drawing attention to his building and military activities. Ordinarily in the ancient Near East, these things were royal concerns:

> [Simeon], in whose time the house of God was renewed, in whose days the temple was made strong. In his time also the wall was built facing the Dwelling, in the Temple of the mighty King [i.e., God]. In his day the reservoir was dug, the pool vast as the sea. He took care for his people against bandits, and strengthened his city against the foe. (50:1–4)[60]

The priest Shimeon acted like a king and was applauded for it. Other examples from the second century B.C.E. also show the process whereby priests were assigned or took on royal prerogatives.[61] These texts, composed a generation or two prior to Judah's years in Jerusalem, show that his claim to be the first messiah would not have seemed inherently implausible to contemporaries. No clear notion of a Davidic messiah yet existed. For his followers, Judah was—like charismatics generally—telling them what the myth-dream had primed them to hear.

The messiah was to be a priest.

"A DISTINCTION must be made between messianism as a complex of ideas, doctrines, hopes and expectations on the one hand, and messianic movements on the other."[62] So wrote one scholar recently, and he was right.

Obviously the possibility of a messiah must precede the identification of one. In this regard a perusal of the literature and history of the Jews from the second century B.C.E. to the end of the first century C.E. reveals how important Judah really was.

Before Judah, there existed few literary descriptions of messiahs—contemporary "ideas, doctrines, hopes and expectations" were limited.[63] Portions of the Enoch writings from the second century B.C.E. and earlier mention no messiah.[64] Nor do other Jewish literary works of the second century: the *Assumption of Moses,* the *Sibylline Oracles, The Wisdom of Ben Sira, First Maccabees, Second Maccabees.* In this period only the few priestly writings noted above concerned themselves with divine agents of the Latter Days.

Yet after Judah, literary references rapidly began to proliferate.

The *Psalms of Solomon* from the mid–first century B.C.E. constitute a prominent example. This writer hopes for a messiah who will cleanse Jerusalem of the Gentiles and return the city and Temple to their former cultic purity. Another work of that time or a little later is the final addition to *1 Enoch,* known as *The Similitudes.* This late Enoch writing features an exalted figure variously designated "the Chosen One," "the Righteous One," "the Anointed One" (Hebrew "messiah") and the "Son of Man." Two works of the late first century C.E., *Fourth Ezra* and *Second Baruch,* also contain substantial messianic descriptions. Finally, Judah's own movement would produce in the years after him a number of messianic texts.

The literary picture that emerges is clear and startling: before Judah, almost nothing; after Judah, a proliferation of texts concerned with the messiah. To judge from literary remains, no group with "a strong and developed interest in messianism" arose until the mid–first century B.C.E.[65] The writings of Judah's own later movement and the *Psalms of Solomon* date to that time. And recall: with the *Psalms of Solomon* and subsequent writings, we are talking only about the *idea* of a messiah, not an *actual* messiah. The authors of those works identified no one as the messiah. They wrote only of their hopes.

Judah represented the next step—not just "ideas, doctrines, hopes and expectations," but a flesh-and-blood messiah, leading a messianic movement. None had existed in Israel before him. After him, in contrast, more than half a dozen appeared in staccato fashion (though they are not always certainly identified as messianic rather than prophetic).[66]

The movements led by Theudas (45–46 C.E.) and the man called "the Egyptian" (sometime between 52 and 60 C.E.) were probably messianic. Theudas and his counterpart both claimed to be the New Moses. Theudas persuaded people to follow him to the Jordan River, which he intended to part. By the definition of de Queiroz, that sounds like the act of a messiah: he was about to inaugurate a new and ideal era. Likewise, the Egyptian swept the masses along with him to the Mount of Olives, intending to overthrow the walls of Jerusalem by a word. Afterward his forces would invest the city and destroy the Romans. He was to be the agent of the change, not merely its herald; so a messiah, not just a prophet.

Other first century C.E. movements were led by self-styled kings who seem to have appealed to the Davidic ideology. Athronges, once a shepherd like David, led a powerful resistance movement when Herod died in 4 B.C.E. He held councils, organized his forces into military units and subdivisions, and may have claimed to be anointed by God's spirit. At the same time across the Jordan in Perea, a man named Simon, a former royal servant, stirred up a peasant-based movement and, according to Josephus, "assumed the diadem." The movement was significant enough to draw the attention of the Roman historian Tacitus, who wrote in garbled fashion of Simon's messianic pretensions: "After the death of Herod . . . a certain Simon usurped the name of king."[67]

Later, at the time of the First Revolt against Rome (66–73/74 C.E.), at least two messianic claimants led parties of the resistance. The first, Menahem ben Hezekiah, went to the Temple one day attended by a bodyguard and put on the royal purple. Disaffected members of his own coalition put a swift end to his pretensions, but there can be little doubt that he was claiming by his actions to be the long-awaited leader of the Latter Days. A more substantial messianic movement centered on Simon bar Giora, whom the Romans executed when the war was over as the principal commander of the Jews. According to Josephus, after the Romans had destroyed the Temple and burned the city and were seeking Simon, "[He] dressed himself in white tunics, and buckling over them a purple mantle arose out of the ground at the very spot whereon the Temple formerly stood."[68]

The leader of the Second Revolt against Rome (132–135 C.E.) also probably made a bid for the messianic mantle. His name was Simon bar Kosiba. Jewish sources of the next generation styled him Simon bar Koziba, while Christian sources dubbed him Simon bar Kochba. Both the name changes were derogatory puns: the Jewish version meant "son of the Liar" (it turned out he was not who he said he was), and the Christian one "son of the Star." The latter was an allusion to a biblical passage in the book of Numbers: "a star shall come out of Jacob." This verse was interpreted as a messianic prophecy already by the first century B.C.E. Since they presuppose the messianic assertion, these puns could hardly have arisen if Simon never claimed to be the messiah.

All of these messianic figures followed Judah. None came before; then at least seven followed after him—and I leave to one side the movements of John the Baptist (perhaps only prophetic) and Jesus.

Why this watershed? Why are there few literary references to messiahs before Judah and relatively many after him? And why no messianic claimants before him, then a substantial number in the decades immediately afterward? Why is it the case that "Jewish [messianism] exploded into the history of ideas in the early first century [B.C.E.] and not before?"[69]

Two probable explanations for this development were the disastrous reigns of the last of the Maccabees—the family of Alexander, Alexandra, Hyrcanus, and Aristobulus—and the Roman conquest of the Jews in 63 B.C.E. Scholars have long recognized the importance of these events as occasioning the rise of Jewish messianism. Judah's own movement was a crisis-cult reaction against Hyrcanus, his family, and his policies. He prophesied that he would replace Hyrcanus; since Hyrcanus was both king and high priest, that was what Judah saw for himself. Judah's example itself argues the truth of the view that Maccabean failures (and, later, Roman oppression) were major catalysts for the rise of messianic hopes and movements.

But another factor must be recognized: Judah himself. The rise of literary activity and actual movements in the years after him was no coincidence. The fact of Judah, the reality of the first messiah, had entered the myth-dream. We should not forget the point made by Pascal: once any given thing has happened, it then becomes much easier for it to happen again. History repeats itself constantly.

The events that swirled around one Jewish leader in 76 B.C.E. did not happen in a corner. Judah's movement became—apart from early Christianity—the most dynamic and enduring crisis cult of these centuries of Jewish civilization. If similar events happened later among others who resonated with the Judah-inspired, revised myth-dream of Israel, it was only to be expected. This is the way the myth-dream works.

One justly renowned scholar who specializes in the study of messianism recently lamented, "It is unfortunate that we have no writings from the hands of messianic pretenders, or even from their followers, which would illuminate their ideology."[70] He wrote unaware that in Judah's writings we do possess precisely that.

Beguiled by the conventional explanation of the Dead Sea Scrolls, scholars have recognized almost nothing of Judah's significance. Charlesworth, who has devoted much of his career to the scrolls and to messianism and who has produced considerable valuable research, lately set down the following: "The [Thanksgiving Hymns] probably contains psalms composed by the Righteous Teacher, but none of them is messianic."[71] After reading just this much of Judah's story, you can judge the merits of that statement for yourself.

Judah was to write in his final hymn that he was hidden, unrecognized for what he was by most of his contemporaries. No less has the first messiah been hidden from modern scholarship.

CHAPTER 6

STRANGER IN
A STRANGE LAND

Let no one attack and kill any Gentile for the sake of property or
profit, nor take anything from their property, lest they blaspheme—
except on the decision of the Council of Israel.

Damascus Document 12:6–8

But now I will send for many fishermen, declares the Lord, and
they will catch them. After that I will send for many hunters, and
they will hunt them down on every mountain and hill and from the
crevices of the rocks.

Jeremiah 16:16

IMMEDIATELY after his sentence on the charge of false prophecy,
Judah left Jerusalem and headed into permanent exile. To judge from
later events, he was accompanied by fifty to one hundred men and their
families, followers so certain of Judah's claims that they were willing to forsake hearth and home and take their chances with the first messiah. Most
likely some members of Judah's own family—his wife, sons, daughters, and
their spouses and children—left with him.[1]

Of his property, Judah took only the few movable goods that he
could carry. The items he managed to bring along included book scrolls.
Among these were the *Great Isaiah Scroll* and, evidently, a copy of the

Minor Prophets.[2] (The Minor Prophets, also known as the Twelve, are the short books extending from Hosea to Malachi in English Bibles. In Judah's day they could all fit on a single scroll.)

A GRIM-FACED NATION

In the ancient world exile was a dangerous and uncertain situation. State-less, the citizen of no country or city, reduced to poverty by confiscation of lands and property, one had to decide where to go and, once there, what to do to survive. Judah had to solve those problems for what amounted to a small colony. Judging from his words, he made his decision on those points shortly before composing his sixth hymn:

> I thank you, O Lord, that You have not abandoned me while I sojourn among a grim-[faced] people . . . [nor] have You judged me as my guilt might have required. You have not deserted me when, as is my nature, I acted wickedly. Instead, You have protected my life from destruction and made [Your servant a fugiti]ve among lions who are appointed for the children of guilt—lions who are about to break the bones of powerful men, about to drink the blo[od] of warriors. You have made me a sojourner among many fishermen who cast their nets upon the water; among hunters of the children of perversity. As a judgment You have established me there. Yet You have actually fortified the secret truth within my mind—the water of the covenant for those who seek it.
>
> You have closed the mouths of lions whose teeth are keen as the sword, whose fangs are like sharp spears. Their plans to capture me are deadly as the venom of serpents, so they wait in ambush, but cannot open their mouths wide to pounce. For You, O my God, have hidden me right before their eyes, while concealing Your Law within [my heart] until the time ordained, when You will reveal to me Your salvation. Surely You have not abandoned me in my distress! You have heard me cry out in my bitterness, in my sighing recognized my anguished cry. You have saved the poor one in the lions' den; they whet their tongue like a sword. You Yourself, O my God, have closed their jaws, lest they tear the poor and destitute one to pieces. Their tongue

has withdrawn like a sword into its sheath, without st[rik]ing Your servant.

So that You may publicly manifest Your mighty power through me, You have done miracles on behalf of the poor one. You have brought him into the crucib[le, like g]old to be wrought by the flame, as silver is refined in the furnace of the smith, becoming sevenfold more pure. Just so the wicked of the Gentiles rush against me with their afflictions, seeking every day to crush me. Yet You, O my God, have settled the storm to a whisper! You have rescued the poor one like a bir[d from a trap], like prey from the mouth of lions.[3]

Where did Judah go?[4] This is a problem that can be solved in either of two ways. The first is to examine the explicit testimony on the matter contained in the *Damascus Document,* a principal writing of Judah's later followers. Scholars often have been unwilling to take its testimony at face value (although, in my view, without good reason). The second approach corroborates the first and is the method whose potential has already been demonstrated: a consideration of Judah's biblical sources. For in this hymn, read in the light of biblical sources, Judah plainly said where he had gone.

Beyond the problem of Judah's location, this second approach uncovers other aspects of the meaning of Judah's sixth hymn, aspects that for Judah's followers were to prove of incalculable significance.

SEVEN TIMES the *Damascus Document* speaks of Judah and his followers taking up residence in "the Land of Damascus." The phrase is so central to the writing that it has given the work its name.[5] In that land, it is said, they *swore to a sure covenant, that is, the New Covenant.* The group is called *the repentant of Israel, who went out from the land of Judah to sojourn in the Land of Damascus.* Judah's hymn used similar language, minus the specific proper noun: *You have not abandoned me while I sojourn. . . . You have made me a sojourner.*

A commentary inserted as a gloss on the narrative of the *Damascus Document* spoke more fully of this movement into exile:

As Scripture says, "I will exile the tents of your king and the foundation of your images from My tent to Damascus" (Amos 5:27).[6]

The books of the Law are the "tents of your king," as Scripture says, "I will re-erect the fallen tent of David" (Amos 9:11). "The king" means the congregation. And the "foundation of your images" means the books of the prophets whose words Israel despised.[7]

This commentary demonstrates that Judah's later followers discovered in the prophet Amos a specific prediction of what had happened to them. This was a tremendously reassuring discovery, for it showed that despite appearances—their political defeat in Jerusalem, their present exile—things were proceeding according to God's purposes. It may be that Judah himself taught them from these passages.

They read in the scriptures of themselves, exiled, carrying their scrolls of the Law and Prophets to the Land of Damascus. The unquoted context of the Amos citation, present as usual in the minds of the readers here, included these words: "Did you bring me sacrifices and offerings forty years in the wilderness, O house of Israel?" The answer to this question was, of course, no.

So Judah's followers found in Amos a precedent for faithful Jews who offered no sacrifices. This was their own situation, one that would continue until they assumed power in Jerusalem. That, they believed, would happen at the end of "forty years," but this is a doctrine that developed only later and so will not occupy us at present. What did apply from the moment of exile, however, was Amos's fortification of Judah's First Commandment: *You shall not enter the Temple to kindle God's altar in vain.*

The designation "Land of Damascus" presents a fundamental problem of identity. The phrase never occurs in the Bible, although the name of the Syrian city Damascus is common, appearing forty-four times. In the Bible, one never goes to the "Land of Damascus"; one simply goes to "Damascus" (for example, 1 Kings 11:24). Why did the writers of the *Damascus Document* not say "Damascus," if that is what they meant?

Evidently that is not what they meant. Their choice of words was precise. They intended to distinguish the "Land of Damascus" from Damascus plain and simple. Biblical Hebrew usage can help us understand their point.

In biblical idiom a principal meaning of the phrase "the land of X" (where X stands for any city name) is "the area ruled by X." For example, 2 Kings 23:33 mentions "the land of Hamath." Hamath was, like Damascus, a Syrian city and in biblical times the capital of an Aramean kingdom. It ruled the land around it. Or again: Zechariah 9:1 refers to "the land of Hadrach," which meant the area ruled by that north-Syrian city. Accordingly, the expression "Land of Damascus" designated the region of which Damascus was the capital city. This was a political expression.[8]

Now, it so happens that for three decades partially overlapping Judah's mature years, from 95 to 64 B.C.E., Damascus was the capital of a small kingdom known as Coele-Syria. Both before and after, this kingdom was swallowed up by larger Syrian political entities, but for this brief window of time it stood on its own. We know from the coins minted in the kingdom that a rapid succession of rulers held sway there. Two of them in particular—Aretas III, king of the Arab realm of Nabatea to the south and east, and the great Armenian empire builder Tigranes I, King of Kings—may have figured in Judah's sixth hymn, as we shall shortly consider.[9]

The geography of Coele-Syria no doubt figured prominently in Judah's decisions about where to live and what to do. Since the *Damascus Document* stipulates that Judah's exile was merely in the "Land of Damascus"—Coele-Syria—he need not have been in close proximity to the city of Damascus.

He might have wished to be. Travelers down through the ages have spoken in rapturous terms of the city's beauty on first view. It lies at the eastern base of the Anti-Lebanon mountains, in the midst of a lush plain carpeted with gardens and orchards. Oranges, lemons, citrons, pomegranates, and many other fruits flourished in its environs. So beautiful was its initial appearance that Muhammad is supposed to have refused to enter it; a man is granted only one Paradise, he said, and if he chose this one, he would have none above. Once past the first view and inside, though, the city was less Edenic: squalid, a stinking germ-broth like all ancient cities, it was crisscrossed by narrow streets that were shadowed by buildings and crowded with people and animals. Damascus was famous as an entrepôt. Caravans came and went along international highways, bringing goods from the four corners of the Near East and beyond.

To the west of the city, Coele-Syria extended some fifty kilometers. Much of this mountainous western region was thick with cultivation, with particular emphasis on the raising of livestock and fruits.

Forty-five kilometers south of the city, approximately at the northern extent of the modern Golan Heights, Coele-Syria shared a border with the Jewish kingdom that Judah had just quit. Imagine a map pinned to a wall: if you were to suspend a weighted string tacked to the Damascus city-dot and follow the string south to that border, right or east of the string you would find steppe lands. A mere fifteen kilometers farther east this steppe graded into the great Syrian Desert.

The steppe was an area of nomadic sheepherding, lightly settled in antiquity, just as it is today. The modern population is less than ten people per square mile. The steppe-desert to the southeast of Damascus was precisely the region known in ancient times as the Wilderness of Damascus (1 Kings 19:15). This was an area where the biblical prophet and miracle worker Elijah had been active, and it may be that this is where Judah settled. He could be very close to Jewish territory—right across the border—yet still in the "Land of Damascus." The writings of his later followers persistently connected their foundational period to exile in "the wilderness."[10] The Wilderness of Damascus would be an excellent place to hide oneself, particularly the southeastern region known as Trachonitis.

And, as a reading of Judah's sixth hymn indicates, he needed to hide.

WHEN JUDAH WROTE *You have not abandoned me while I sojourn among a grim-faced people,*[11] he was alluding to two passages in the Bible, Deuteronomy 28:49–50 and Daniel 8:23–24 (itself an application of the words in Deuteronomy). The two passages read as follows (italics as usual):

YHWH will bring a nation from far away, from the end of the earth, to swoop down on you like an eagle, a nation whose language you do not understand, a *grim-faced* nation showing no respect to the old or favor to the young. (Deuteronomy)

At the end of their rule, when the transgressions have reached their full measure, shall arise a *grim-faced* king, skilled in intrigue. He shall grow strong and powerful and cause fearful destruction, and do as he wishes; the *powerful* he shall destroy, even the people of the holy ones. (Daniel)

The portion from Deuteronomy was set in the context of those same chapters (28–30) that had informed the theology of MMT. In MMT, recall, Judah and his former allies had proclaimed the dawn of the Latter Days. They recognized its arrival because of the outbreak of wickedness and the

Pharisee-led departure from God's covenant that Deuteronomy, as they believed, predicted. And recall, Daniel and his vision of four succeeding kingdoms that would rule over the Jews played a strong supporting role in MMT's declarations. With his sixth hymn's allusions, Judah revisited those ideas.

Deuteronomy warned that if Israel violated its covenant with God, conquest by a merciless foreign nation would figure among the consequent divine curses. Judah was saying that he now lived in exile among those who would carry out the conquest, the *grim-faced nation*. He further implied with the connection to Daniel 8 that the last of Daniel's four kingdoms was on the scene. After the last of four kings of that realm—so Daniel had foreseen and inscribed—a final monarch would arrive on the scene, mightiest of all. This king would attack and destroy the *powerful* of Israel. Leading the army of the grim-faced nation would be the grim-faced king.

Judah thought the stage was set, and so he spoke of *lions who are appointed for the children of guilt—lions who are about to break the bones of powerful men, about to drink the blood of warriors*. The *children of guilt* was an expression Judah used several times in his hymns for his enemies; so too, the *powerful* and the *warriors* were part of that inimical triumvirate.[12] The *children of guilt* were probably the Pharisees, the *powerful* their accomplices among the Jerusalem elite, and the *warriors* the soldiers of Alexandra and Hyrcanus's regime.

In choosing *lion* to designate enemy kings, Judah might have referred to any number of biblical passages, for the king of beasts was a frequent biblical symbol for human sovereigns. His wording suggests that Jeremiah 50:17 was prominent in his thinking: "Israel is a scattered flock that lions have chased away. The first to devour him was the king of Assyria; the last to *break his bones* was Nebuchadnezzar king of Babylon." Judah knew that Nebuchadnezzar had been a king who invaded Israel as a divine judgment. The mention of breaking bones in the Jeremiah passage would have led Judah's mind to Isaiah 38:13 and the judgment of God: "like a lion he *broke all my bones*."

When Judah inscribed the words *lions whose teeth are keen as the sword, whose fangs are like sharp spears,* he employed a rare Hebrew word for fangs, *metaleot,* so signaling his integration of Joel 1:6: "A nation has invaded my land, powerful and without number; it has the *teeth* of a *lion*, the *fangs (metaleot) of a lioness."* Once again the biblical text cast the lion as a metaphor for an enemy invader. Composing this hymn, Judah mentally drew together all the passages where that equivalence existed and wove them together into a mélange.

These lions were *appointed* for invasion, he wrote; Judah meant that they were predestined, like Nebuchadnezzar, to serve as an instrument of God's wrath. They would *drink the blood of warriors,* an allusion to the prophet Ezekiel. Mixing his metaphors, he said they were also fishermen and hunters (*You have made me a sojourner among many fishermen who cast their nets upon the water; among hunters of the children of perversity*), allusions to portions of Jeremiah that Judah chained to the words of Ezekiel by his usual method of verbal association (italics mark Judah's words; underlines show verbal links):

> This is what YHWH the Lord says: Call out to every sort of bird and all the wild beasts: "Assemble and come together from all around to the sacrifice I am preparing for you, the great sacrifice on the <u>mountains</u> of Israel. There you will eat flesh and *drink blood.* You will eat the flesh of *warriors* and *drink the blood* of princes of the earth as if they were rams and lambs, goats and bulls. . . . At the sacrifice I am preparing for you, you will eat fat until you are sated and *drink blood* until you are drunk." (Ezekiel 39:17–19)
>
> But now I will send for *many fishermen,* declares YHWH, and they will catch them. After that I will send for *many hunters,* and they will hunt them down on every <u>mountain</u> and hill and from the crevices of the rocks. (Jeremiah 16:16)

The passage from Ezekiel invokes the context of that book's chapters 38–39, prophecies directed to "Gog, of the land of Magog, the prince; head of Meshech and Tubal." According to Ezekiel's prophecies, this mysterious king would one day mass his armies against God's people: "After many days you shall be mustered; in the Latter Years you shall go against a land restored from war, a land where people were gathered from many nations on the mountains of Israel" (38:8). Ezekiel went on say: "You will rouse yourself and come from your place out of the remotest parts of the north, you and many Gentiles with you, all of them riding on horses, a great horde, a mighty army; you will come up against my people Israel like a cloud covering the land. In the Latter Days I will bring you against my land" (38:14–16). Judah saw the attack as a punishment against his enemies, all foreordained more than four hundred years before he was even born.[13] It was finally about to happen, in these Latter Days whose arrival Judah had already publicly proclaimed.

Identification of the Jeremiah passage's influence on the hymn is certain, since the noun *hunter* (Hebrew *tsayyad*) occurs nowhere else in the Bible. And in this one occurrence it is paired with the other term Judah used, *fisherman* (Hebrew *dayyag*). Jeremiah 16 describes a horrible judgment that is decreed upon Israel because of its wickedness and violations of God's covenant. It constitutes a reiteration of Jeremiah's prophecy that God has ordained disaster against Israel from the north (for example, Jeremiah 1:13–15, 4:5–10).[14]

So: Judah was identifying the hunters and fishermen as the invader from the north, just as the Ezekiel context invoked the far-northern armies of Gog. The lion Nebuchadnezzar had led his Babylonian forces west from Mesopotamia and then had turned and marched upon Jerusalem from the north. North, north, north—that was where the constellation of Judah's biblical usage intimated that he had settled. This was exactly what the *Damascus Document* said. The two approaches have arched together, completing the circle.

It was in the Land of Damascus that Judah was living, but he was not at rest.

THE FIFTH MODE

The ancient world greatly mistrusted the wanderer, the person who belonged to no city. Aristotle condemned them: "Someone who is cityless . . . is either a rogue or more than human, like the 'kinless, lawless, heartless' person Homer complained about. That sort of man is by nature also a warmonger, since he is like a stranded piece in checkers." It was a commonplace that people who lived away from home were disreputable characters. Wandering privation was the usual fate of exiles, who therefore did favor a war as Aristotle charged, since that might overthrow the government that had exiled them and they could return home. As one scholar has commented, "The exile who left his native land was expected to encounter poverty, shame, dishonor and hostility."[15]

What the exile needed most desperately was an income, some means of survival. The options were few. We must remember that in the ancient world, work for a wage was uncommon, the more so if one had no home city and so had to wander. Only a few highly trained specialists made their living by combining travel and wages: builders and sculptors who worked in expensive materials and unusual techniques, so that they quickly exhausted the work in any one locale; medical practitioners; traveling philosophers; high-class prostitutes; cooks, traders, and actors.

None of these occupations would have been feasible for Judah, who had devoted his life to the study of wisdom and the sacred books. The market for itinerant Jewish wisdom teachers was hardly that for famed Greek philosophers; we have no evidence it existed at all. Moreover, Judah was not alone. He had with him a large group, whose own laws required them to live together, separate from Gentiles.[16]

But sometimes exiles could find sponsors in their new land, wealthy people who would ease the wanderer's poverty. Could Judah?

A sizable number of Jews lived in Damascus. The New Testament (Acts 9:2, 2 Corinthians 11:32) reports the existence of this community in the period about 50 C.E. Josephus records that at the outbreak of the First Revolt with Rome in 66 C.E. more than ten thousand of them were slain.[17] The Damascus community almost certainly included individuals wealthy enough to help Judah and his people. Yet the latter had separated themselves from the mass of Jews in Judaea. Could they get along any better with the Damascene Jews? We have come to know Judah well enough to be certain: only if the Damascene Jews accepted Judah's teaching en masse would it be possible for the exiles to settle among them. And Judah's later hymns make it clear that such never happened.

All these constraints limited Judah's possibilities even more than those of the ordinary exile. What remained to him?

Returning to Aristotle, the foremost classifier in antiquity: according to his *Politics*, ancient people produced their subsistence in five basic ways.[18] The first was pastoral nomadism. That lifestyle held little attraction for Judah and his followers, since they were city dwellers from Jerusalem. Few had ever owned livestock, though wealthy Jerusalemites sometimes raised sheep and goats on their scattered estates outside the city. Judah numbered at least a few such aristocrats among his supporters when his showdown with the Pharisees began. But these rich people, having the most to lose, probably would have been the least likely to follow Judah into exile. As the crisis escalated, most would have dropped away and deserted him. Any who did stay the course—and as we shall see, a few probably did—would have lost their animals when their estates were confiscated.

A second way to live, said Aristotle, was by hunting. Unfortunately, the Land of Damascus offered limited prospects for this pursuit. The western half was under intensive cultivation, the eastern too barren to support much wildlife. It might be possible there to hunt wild deer, snakes, lizards, birds, and rabbits as an adjunct to other means of subsistence, but Judah and his group faced a strong practical disadvantage. They were ignorant of the country. To learn where and how to hunt indigenous game would take time. And how kindly would the native Syrians take to poaching newcomers? Moreover, many of the animals Judah's people might find were "unclean" according to Jewish food laws (Leviticus 11). They could not be eaten. To live by hunting alone was impractical for fifty or one hundred men and their families.

Aristotle's third and fourth modes of livelihood were fishing and agriculture. Given the geography, fishing was no real possibility. The Land of Damascus was an inland kingdom and embraced no large lakes.

By far the majority of people in Judah's time lived by agriculture. But farming presented an insuperable obstacle to Judah and his followers: they owned no land. They owned no property at all that they could not carry. Even if they had managed to secrete money in their movable goods, they still would have needed to find a farmstead large enough to support their numbers, owners willing to sell to outsiders from a nation often hostile to their own, and authorities willing to let them settle down. Then time would have been needed—a year or more—for crops to be planted and harvested. And we must bear in mind: the strong tradition of the later movement was that Judah and the first members settled in the wilderness. Agriculture is not likely in deserts.

Wherever they chose to settle, a group as large as Judah's would have made the locals very nervous. They would appear threatening and difficult to control. Records of the period show that colonies of exiles such as Judah's encountered hostility and engendered anxiety because people knew they might resort to Aristotle's fifth mode of livelihood—brigandage.[19]

And indeed, it does seem (although the evidence is inferential and hence far from certain) that Judah and his followers began to live by this fifth mode. It would fit well with a wilderness existence. And in considering how the exiles decided to support themselves, we must factor in another element: Judah's arrival in Syria was no secret. The dominant motif of Judah's sixth hymn is flight and escape. Judah not only dwelled among lions; he was their prospective prey.

He wrote, *You have closed the mouths of lions.* He wrote, *Their plans to capture me are as deadly as the venom of serpents.* He wrote, *They wait in ambush, but cannot open their mouths wide to pounce.* He wrote, *You have hidden me right before their eyes.*[20] He wrote, *You have saved the poor one in the lions' den; they whet their tongue like a sword.* He wrote, *You have closed their jaws, lest they tear the poor and destitute one to pieces.* He wrote, *The wicked of the Gentiles rush against me with their afflictions, seeking every day to crush me.*[21] And finally he wrote, *You have rescued the poor one like a bird from a trap, like prey from the mouth of lions.*

Judah was fleeing the authorities of the Land of Damascus, who sought, as he believed, to destroy him. Why? If it is correct to connect this trouble with his new way of life, it was because he was practicing Aristotle's fifth mode. The prophet had gone the way of Pancho Villa.

Judah was a bandit.

ARISTOTLE CONSIDERED brigandage to be respectable, little more than a form of hunting, and in such views he was far from alone. The historian Thucydides testified that for many Greek communities of his time and earlier it was a perfectly acceptable way of life.[22] Writing at the tail end of the fifth century B.C.E., he observed of former days, "At this time such a profession, so far from being regarded as disgraceful, was considered quite honorable." He went on to specify that in certain regions of Greece in his own time, "the custom of carrying arms still survives from the old days of robbery; for at one time, since houses were unprotected and communications unsafe, this was a general custom throughout the whole of Hellas [Greece] and it was the normal thing to carry arms on all occasions, as it is now among foreigners." Much of the rural world was then as lawless as the old American West. It paid to be fast on the draw, for one never knew when outlaw raiders might swoop down.

Even religious groups like Judah's sometimes took to this way of life. Four centuries after the first messiah, the Church Father Jerome (348–420 C.E.) warned against long-haired, chained ascetics in Syria called *catenati*. They lived by brigandage. The rhetorician Libanius (314–c.393 C.E.), a native of Syrian Antioch, likewise warned of fanatic monks who, he alleged, went about in bands, robbing and pillaging. Regardless of religious attachment, many in antiquity who suffered a drastic downturn in their fortunes perforce became brigands. This fact is presupposed by an order that the prefect of Egypt circulated during the reign of the emperor Antoninus Pius (138–161 C.E.).[23]

The order stipulated that all who had suffered proscription should now return home. (Proscription was a declaration that a person was an outlaw, whereupon all property was confiscated and the person had to flee to avoid arrest and, often, execution. The legal situation thus closely paralleled Judah's.) Soldiers should cease arresting these people, the order required. But after the period of grace expired, remaining wanderers were to be seized as brigands self-confessed. Clearly the operative assumption was that wanderers became bandits.

This assumption was rooted in the realities of ancient life. An almost axiomatic connection existed between any type of movement, or wandering, and banditry. Most people were peasant farmers, after all, fixed and immobile. The literature of the period particularly connected shepherds with banditry: for all of antiquity "shepherd equals bandit" was almost always true.

Even people who belonged to higher stations than Judah's resorted to brigandage when fate tore them from home and kicked out from beneath them their political and social props. For a period after the assassination of Julius Caesar and following a defeat at the hands of the Nabateans, the Roman client king Herod the Great was forced to this way of life. Josephus relates:

> Then King Herod, in despair of the outcome of the battle, rode off to get aid. But in spite of his haste he was not quick enough in bringing help, and the Jews' camp was taken. . . . From then on, Herod resorted to brigandage and overran many parts of the Arabs' territory, which he damaged in his raids. Camping in the mountains and always avoiding open battle, he still did considerable damage by his incessant and energetic movements, and he was also very careful of his own men, using every means to make good his losses.[24]

With Caesar's death, Herod lost Roman support. Consequently, he lacked a political base among the Jews. He lived for some time as a raider, strategically directing his attacks against the Nabateans, never the Jews, for he hoped to return to power among the latter.

If a man of Herod's wealth and political prominence could wind up a bandit, so could Judah. If he was now being pursued by the Syrians, it was only to be expected: "The 'correct' response of a king, or of his representatives, to bandits was to repress them."[25] The authorities of the Land of Damascus sought to kill Judah and his men either because they actually were brigands or because it was feared that they would become such. This is a reasonable inference from the evidence at hand.

For authorities all during antiquity, banditry was an untamable migraine headache. The emperor Justinian (c. 482–565 C.E.), in the section of his *Digest* entitled "On the Duties of a Provincial Governor," set the burden squarely on their shoulders: "It is the duty of a good and serious governor to see that the province he governs remains peaceful and quiet. . . . He must hunt down desecrators and pillagers of sacred property, bandits, kidnappers, and common thieves, and punish each one in accordance with his misdeeds."

By modern standards, ancient political control—even in the most repressive regimes—was amazingly relaxed. The problem lay with the technology; authorities of the day suffered from more technical difficulties than a third-rate television network. To control rural terrain with the primitive instruments of communication at their disposal simply was not possible. Brigandage therefore enjoyed a healthy existence in the interstices between local army commanders, town rulers, private landowners, state officials, and the general populace of town and countryside. Controlling bandits was just hard to do.

Often those charged with maintaining order hired others to deal with the problem. About 150 C.E. the senator Fronto, ready to depart to take up the government of the Roman province of Asia, wrote a letter to the emperor Antoninus Pius. He discussed his plans to employ a man named Senex. Senex was an ancient hired gun, the bounty hunter who rides into town in the typical western. He was a specialist in hunting down bandits. Such men existed because our modern infrastructure of local police and investigative agencies did not. Towns sent guards on the round of their territory, which might include publicly owned estates. The sources mention mountain, country, and night wardens as well.

Another way to cope with bandits was by using soldiers. Areas with substantial numbers of soldiers used them as police. They served everywhere as investigators, enforcers, torturers, executioners, and jailers. The routine way of using soldiers against brigands was to station them in guard posts along the highways.

Raider targets included public granaries and storehouses, temples, tombs, and ordinary houses, not to mention trade caravans. The caravans coming and going from Damascus were a tempting target, and the sources describe brigand attacks on them as a recurring plague. Bandit attacks could be very violent. The familiar Gospel story of the Good Samaritan presupposes this grim reality. Epigraphic evidence for death at the hands of brigands is widespread. Tomb inscriptions show that victims included personal slaves and household managers, municipal officers, soldiers, and whole families. One family—father, mother, and six-year-old child—was killed, according to their tomb, *causa ornamentorum* ("on account of their finery").

A POSSIBLE OBJECTION to the notion that Judah and his men became bandits is the self-righteous mind-set evident in Judah's writings, surely emblematic of those he attracted. Despite the analogy of the *catenati* and bandit monks, still one must wonder: Could such uncompromising followers of biblical law consider turning to this way of life, even *in extremis?* After all, the law of Moses addresses theft, personal injury, and murder in no uncertain terms. Could a group such as Judah's rationalize brigandage?

The evidence we have on this point is indirect, but it shows that a life of banditry was not beyond the pale even for very pious Jews—provided that the targets were not Jewish. One element of this evidence comes from the *Damascus Document* produced by Judah's own followers.

The *Damascus Document* has a complicated literary history. Some of the laws it contains were promulgated by Judah himself. Some were the later products of his followers. And some originated in the priestly circles where Judah came to maturity; these were, therefore, older than his movement. One of these very early laws was retained by Judah and his followers as a part of the *Damascus Document* through all the stages of the book's evolution. The fact of its retention suggests that the law had some continuing purpose, for otherwise it simply would have been dropped, no longer copied.

How people interpreted this law as their circumstances changed we cannot be sure, but it reads as follows: *Let no one attack and kill any Gentile for the sake of property or profit, nor take anything from their property, lest they blaspheme—except on the decision of the Council of Israel.*[26]

This law was a clear statement of brigandage. To attack and kill for property, to take from property—this was what bandits did. The fact that the law was formulated at all shows that brigandage against Gentiles was an issue in the late second century B.C.E. The statute regulated this practice without outlawing it altogether. In general, it said, one should not engage in raids on Gentiles because they might blaspheme God as a result. Yet the law allowed for the possibility of raids, provided that the *Council of Israel* approved.

What was this *Council of Israel?* The exact expression—Hebrew *hever Yisrael*—appears in no other source of the period. Yet it is strongly reminiscent of a phrase that is common on the coins of the Hasmonean rulers, both before and after Judah: *hever ha-Yehudim,* "the Council of the Jews."[27] This council, together with the individual Maccabean high priest or king, constituted the mint authority that issued the coins. Only the second terms in these phrases are different, and the different terms are equivalent. Corporate "Israel" was the "Jews."

"Council of the Jews" was an official designation of the Jerusalem council to which Judah had once belonged and to which he prophesied he would return. The Jerusalem council, then, was empowered by this old priestly law to regulate raiding on Gentile neighbors. Whether it ever approved such banditry the sources do not say, but during the reign of Alexander ample opportunity existed. The warrior king waged several bitter campaigns against the Gentile nations surrounding Judaea. In the ancient world brigandage and war were related activities, so we may suspect that officially sanctioned brigandage did occur at these times, if at no other.

What would this law mean to Judah and his followers after they left Jerusalem? Certainly they would no longer recognize the authority of the Jerusalem council, controlled by the Pharisee liars and false prophets that Judah so roundly condemned. As a charismatic prophet and messiah, Judah himself now represented the ultimate political and religious authority to his group. Presumably, therefore, Judah either formed his own council at this juncture and styled it the true *Council of Israel* or arrogated to himself all decisions that were formerly the province of the Council of the Jews. Either way, Judah and his followers could decide to raid Gentile properties in full conformity to older legal precedent.

Years later, when Judah had passed the scene, members of his movement were guided by officials they called *maskilim,* "instructors." The role of these men was modeled after that of the ideal *maskil,* Judah. It is significant, then, to read in a text composed to guide these leaders, *[the instructor] shall work God's will when he attacks the wicked [Gentiles], and exercises authority as He has commanded.*[28] Even in the years following Judah, when raiding was no longer essential to survival, provision existed in his movement's legislation for violent action against non-Jews. Indeed, it was expected to happen—the law reads *when he attacks.* Of course, we have already seen that Judah believed he would someday lead the army of Israel in a *jihad* against the Gentiles. A few such attacks in the desperation of his present circumstances would seem to pose no theoretical difficulty.

So Judah's group probably could rationalize a period of banditry. Other Jews in these years certainly did, raiding Gentiles without censure from fellow religionists. A notable example was Hezekiah, a brigand chief who hid out in Galilee and operated against Syria, Tyre in particular. Josephus reports that in 47 B.C.E., Herod hunted this man down on the Galilee-Syria border and put him and many of his men to death.[29] For this action he was praised effusively by the Syrians, but not by the Jews of either Galilee or Jerusalem. On the contrary: members of the Jerusalem elite took up the cause of Hezekiah when his mother and mothers of his fellow brigands appeared wailing in the Temple precincts. They charged Herod with acting illegally. He had executed the men without trial. As a result Herod himself was tried but through Roman intercession escaped conviction. It was a close call.

The whole incident throws a spotlight on mainstream Jewish attitudes toward raiding Gentiles. While respectable people might not do it themselves, they did not condemn those who did. Aristocrats could support an arch brigand and look good doing it. The mothers of Hezekiah and his horde could successfully portray themselves and their sons as pious Jews grievously wronged by Herod. And Herod's actions were considered so scandalous that Hyrcanus—still the high priest—could not ignore them even though he wanted to.[30] Their way of life entailed theft and, sometimes, murder, but brigands who attacked Gentiles were not considered outright criminals. All knew that they themselves might someday be reduced to poverty, by politics, war, or taxation, and set on the same path.

Josephus records several other examples of Jewish bandit hordes who preyed on Gentiles with the covert support of fellow Jews. He tells us of Tholomaeus, an arch brigand "who inflicted very severe mischief upon

Idumea and upon the Arabs." In the mid–40s C.E. he was captured, brought before the Roman procurator Fadus, and sentenced to death. In another incident "on the road leading up to Bethhoron, some brigands attacked one Stephen, a slave of Caesar, and robbed him of his baggage."[31] This attack happened some time between 48 and 52 C.E.

Yet another prominent episode involved Herod once again. This time the brigands were from Trachonitis, and they were specifically despoiling the region of Damascus. This case deserves a closer look.

IN BIBLICAL TIMES there were two major international highways in the Near East. One was the Via Maris, or Way of the Sea. This road snaked north from Egypt along the Mediterranean coast, passed through the Jezreel Valley to Hazor, and then came to Damascus, branching out from there. The other was known as the King's Highway. This route also connected Egypt and Damascus but via a more southern path. It skirted the Dead Sea and passed through the region of Transjordan, skimming by some forty kilometers east of the Sea of Galilee. The King's Highway was important especially because traders in Arabian spices and aromatics traveled this way from Yemen to Damascus. As the road approached Damascus, it passed a mere ten kilometers west of Trachonitis.

Trachonitis was one of two major bandit strongholds in the greater Syrian region. The other was the mountains of Lebanon. Unlike Lebanon, Trachonitis lay within Coele-Syria, the Land of Damascus. Trachonitis was situated just northwest of what is today called Jebel Druze, an epicenter of massive volcanic outflows, whereby the entire region was composed of hard basalt. In modern times the region has come to be called *el-Leja*—"the refuge" par excellence—because of the difficulty of negotiating it.[32] The *Great Britain Admiralty Handbook of Syria (including Palestine), 1920* described the area well:

> The passes, fissures and caverns in this black and desolate region
> are so inaccessible that the Bedouin robbers by which El-Leja has
> been infested for centuries, continue to find secure refuge from the
> law. . . . At only a few points are the rocky borders penetrable and,
> there, the tracks are hewn out of the rock. The secrets of internal
> communication are carefully guarded by the inhabitants. Tracks
> over and around deep fissures or through narrow passes and con-

fused masses of fallen or upheaved rocks, can only be followed in daylight with the help of local guides whose knowledge is confined to particular localities.[33]

If Judah and his followers settled in the Land of Damascus and practiced brigandage, this was where they would have wanted to hide out. The bandits of Trachonitis were parasites of the King's Highway trade, preying especially—as the historian and geographer Strabo (63 B.C.E.–21 C.E.) informs us—upon the Nabatean spice traders.[34]

In 23 B.C.E. the Roman emperor Augustus bestowed Trachonitis upon Herod as an addition to the client-king's realm. As ruler, Herod took up the task of rooting out the region's bandits, some of whom were Jewish. Despite considerable efforts—including settling three thousand of his fellow Idumeans in the region to help out—Herod failed. He eventually decided to plant another colony of settlers as a buffer between Trachonitis and the King's Highway, but even this solution was only partial. As always, controlling bandits proved as hard as caging the wind.

Josephus provides a contemporary description of Trachonitis as a bandit hideaway that is strikingly similar to what the *Admiralty Handbook* had to say twenty centuries later:

> The inhabitants of that region led desperate lives and pillaged the property of the Damascenes. . . . It was really not easy to restrain people who had made brigandage a habit and had no other means of making a living, for they had neither city nor field of their own but only underground shelters and caves, where they lived together with their cattle. They had also managed to collect supplies of water and of food beforehand, and so they were able to hold out for a very long time in their hidden retreat. Moreover, the entrances to their caves were narrow, and only one person at a time could enter, while the interiors were incredibly large and constructed to provide plenty of room. . . . The whole place consisted of rocks that were rugged and difficult of access unless one used a path with a guide leading the way, for not even these paths were straight, but had many turns and windings.[35]

Did Judah and his fellow exiles settle for a time amid the basalt and brigands of Trachonitis, living the life of bandits? We cannot be sure.

We can say that, like all exiles, Judah would have faced the pressures of poverty and hostility and would have needed to find a way to survive. We can say that he evidently did settle, if not in Trachonitis, at least in the vicinity. We can point to the fact that he was living among "lions," according to tradition living in the wilderness and in the Land of Damascus. Evidently he was somewhere in the Wilderness of Damascus. He was being pursued. Of these facts we can be certain. To say that the exiled Jews became bandits is an inference that fits well with all the facts we have and fits what we know about the harsh realities that ancient exiles faced. But we must be clear that the facts are few.

In any event, the importance of Judah's sixth hymn does not lie primarily in its suggestion of brigandage. No, the outstanding element is something else: the prophecy of enemy invasion that Judah first set down here when he wrote, *You have protected my life from destruction and made Your servant a fugitive among lions who are appointed for the children of guilt—lions who are about to break the bones of powerful men, about to drink the blood of warriors.* What Judah said would happen, what his later followers said he said would happen, and what actually did happen—these were to be fundamental to the future of Judah's crisis cult.

When Judah made his prediction, his followers numbered at most one hundred men and their families. The total number of people could not have exceeded four or five hundred. Two years later only a tiny minority— fifteen men—would still be at his side. Analogy with other crisis cults argues that the group should have been administered last rites then and there. The death rattle was in the throat. But what should have happened next did not. Twenty-five years later, far from dead, Judah's movement numbered in the thousands. It had become a major force in first century B.C.E. Judaism. Judah's prophecy was the main reason.

What, precisely, did Judah envision?

APOCALYPSE WHEN?

"God has revealed things to come, by visions, in figures and parables, and in this way the same things are oftentimes revealed again and again, by different visions, or in different figures, and parables. If you wish to understand them, you must combine them all in one."[36] So said William Miller, prophetic leader of the most dynamic millenarian movement of nineteenth-century America. His insight is counterintuitive.

The ordinary reader of the Bible would more naturally suppose that Israel's writing prophets, spaced out over half a millennium and living under the most diverse historical circumstances, addressed distinct issues, persons, and events. That they constantly rerevealed the same message, and always in cryptic terms, seems a strange notion.

Yet this view emerges easily once the interpreter is convinced that the prophets had little or nothing to say to their own times. If their words are viewed as coded predictions, all directed toward the future, Miller's position suggests itself. It must be so, because Miller's view was shared by Judah and any number of other biblical interpreters down through the ages, all working without knowledge of the others and yet all arriving at the same basic conclusion. The principle is alive and well today; for example, it lies at the heart of Hal Lindsey's *The Late Great Planet Earth,* reportedly the best-selling book in America for the decade of the 1970s.[37]

The principle of rerevelation guided Judah's later followers in their various commentaries on biblical prophecies. The *Commentary on Psalms,* the *Commentary on Habakkuk,* the *Commentary on Nahum,* various more fragmentary works on Isaiah, Zephaniah, Micah, and others all evidence this perspective. It shines through Judah's hymns. One cannot but conclude that this interpretive method was one of the first messiah's primary teachings. Certainly it provided the underpinnings for his prophecy of invasion from the north.

Judah's collective allusions implied that Deuteronomy, Jeremiah, Ezekiel, Joel, and Daniel all foresaw the same event. Indeed, one additional prophet, Nahum, must be added to the list. Judah quoted Nahum 2:11 ("Where now is the *lions' den,* the place where they fed their young?") when he said, *You have saved the poor one in the lions' den.* So Nahum, too, had known aforetime Judah's exile among those who later would invade.

In recognizing Judah's method and through constant immersion in his words and their biblical sources, the historian analyzing Judah's hymns begins to arrive at a synthetic understanding. It becomes possible to speak—though only in general terms, for the evidence is incomplete—of Judah's doctrines. When it comes to his doctrine of invasion, the basic questions are: Who did Judah think would invade? And, When did he think it would happen?

To both questions Judah's writings, seen in the proper historical perspective, suggest answers. In both cases his later followers, while claiming to represent the master's teaching, gave different answers.

As JUDAH SURVEYED the Near East in the year 74 B.C.E., he could not have failed to be aware of events in northern Syria. Tigranes I, king of Armenia, had marched in. Beginning in 83 B.C.E., working his way farther and farther south, he conquered Syria piecemeal. By 72 B.C.E., just two years after Judah wrote his sixth hymn, Tigranes made himself master of Coele-Syria, the Land of Damascus.

In Jerusalem, as Josephus reports, Tigranes and his conquests were matters of grave concern. The Jerusalemites believed he had an army of three hundred thousand men. It was also clear to Alexandra and her advisers that Judaea was a potential target for the kingdom builder. To buy valuable time, the Jewish queen sent Tigranes gifts and parlayed through envoys. As one historian of Rome notes, "Doubtless Judaea lay in the long-term plans of Tigranes, but the delay in advancing on it [he stopped to conquer regions in Phoenicia] proved permanent. His departure in 69 B.C.E. occasioned fervent sighs in Judaea."[38] Tigranes had to retreat because of reverses suffered in battle with Roman forces.

If Alexandra and the Jerusalem aristocracy feared Tigranes and recognized the danger he represented, Judah, too, may well have anticipated the Armenian's advance into Judaea. Was Tigranes his invader from the north? This possibility would square nicely with "Gog, of the land of Magog" and Ezekiel 38:14–15, the context to which Judah had alluded: "You will rouse yourself and come from your place out of the *remotest parts of the north,* you and many Gentiles with you, all of them riding on horses, a great horde, a mighty army." For a Judaean, Armenia lay much more remotely to the north than did Syria. The possibility that Judah had Tigranes in mind cannot be excluded.

It is also possible that the first messiah thought of Aretas III, the king of Nabatea. He was ruling the Land of Damascus when Judah arrived there and had been for a decade. Aretas was the monarch of Coele-Syria from 84 to 72 B.C.E. Furthermore, the Arab kingdom of the Nabateans and the Jews had a history of warfare between them and were often enemies in the years of Judah's maturity. Alexander, the king whom Judah advised, fought them fiercely. Aretas was certainly the lion nearest to hand, and it was his underlings—minor Damascene figures, though, not Arabs—who would have been the ones chasing Judah. One cannot rule out Aretas as Judah's invader. Yet strictly speaking, most of the Arab's realm lay to the west and south of Judaea, and he was less likely than Tigranes to be styled a northern enemy.

In evaluating Judah's prophecy, we must try to think about matters as he would have. Both Tigranes and Aretas are possibilities, but the best option, the lions Judah most likely intended, are the Seleucid Greeks. In the second century B.C.E., a dozen members of this Syrian dynasty crossed paths with the nation of the Jews, mostly as unwelcome rulers. Repeatedly these Greeks warred with Judah's people.

One of them, Antiochus IV Epiphanes, sacked Jerusalem in 169 B.C.E., spilled the blood of its citizens in the streets, and looted the Temple —facts that Judah surely knew, for his followers later wrote of that dark time. The Maccabean uprising followed Antiochus IV's attack. In 135/134 B.C.E. another of these Syrian monarchs, Antiochus VII Sidetes, invaded Judaea, devastated the entire country, and finally besieged the Hasmonean high priest and ruler, Hyrcanus I, in the capital city.

Antiochus forced Hyrcanus I to capitulate. The Jews had to surrender their arms, pay tribute, give hostages, and raze the city walls of Jerusalem. This encounter may well have fallen in Judah's earliest years; gray in 76 B.C.E., he was probably born about 135. In Judah's mature years, during the reign of Alexander, the Seleucids mostly exhausted themselves in internal squabbles. But the Judaean invasion of Demetrius III in 88 B.C.E. must have been seared into Judah's memory. As noted earlier, he likely had some involvement in the aftermath of the civil war it christened.

For a Jew of Judah's age and experience, the Seleucids represented a bête noire, and what could be darker than a lion? Lately they had been kings of the Land of Damascus. Judah would have no reason to doubt that they would rule again. The Syrians had invaded Judaea from the north time and again. To predict that it would happen once more and finally, as a judgment on his enemies, the Jerusalem power structure—this seems a natural extrapolation for a person in Judah's situation. The Seleucid Greeks are therefore the most likely candidates for identification as Judah's northern invader.

If so, he was almost right.

Throughout his hymns, Judah spoke repeatedly of vindication, of personally witnessing the demise of his enemies, of his own coming power in Jerusalem. But when? Unlike some crisis-cult leaders, Judah presumably had a short time line for the events of the apocalypse, for everything the scriptures predicted must happen in his own lifetime—and he was no longer a young man. He clearly did not expect to have to wait another generation. What, then, did he expect?

The answer to this question lies in Judah's understanding of a passage in the book of Daniel, an understanding that Judah's hymns allow us to ferret out.

Daniel was perhaps the most important of the biblical prophets for the Jews of this era, for a reason that Josephus relates: "Not only did he prophesy about what was going to happen—other prophets did that, after all—but he also fixed the time when these things would come to pass."[39]

Daniel *fixed the time when*—that is, Daniel was believed to supply a chronology for the Latter Days. The passage of his book that Josephus has in mind is 9:24–27, a notoriously difficult and ambiguous section that has catalyzed crisis-cult dreams for two thousand years. For Judah's ideas, too, the passage provided a megawatt spark, though all we can unravel with the evidence he left behind is his view of the last verse, 9:27.

Judah's signature phrase *(that You might publicly manifest Your mighty power through me)* derived from his interpretation of this verse of Daniel.[40] In Hebrew, the initial three words of 9:27 are *higbir berit larabbim*, "he [an unspecified actor] will make a strong covenant with the Many." Compare the first of these words with the Hebrew of Judah's phrase, *hagbirekha. Higbir/hagbirekha*: even with no knowledge of the language, one can see that Judah's verb form is a variation on Daniel's first word.

Moreover, Judah asserted throughout his hymns that God had given him a covenant (Daniel's *berit*). He also designated his followers the Many (Daniel's *rabbim*). Thus Daniel 9:27 collocates three concepts that lie at the very heart of Judah's understanding of who he was and what he was to do. Judah must have interpreted the first three words of Daniel 9:27 as, "He [identifying the actor as God] will make a strong covenant with the Many"—into which he inserted his signature *through me* (Hebrew *bi*). By this reading the prophet Daniel had predicted that God would use Judah to make a covenant with certain people, the faithful Many. Once again the first messiah found himself in a biblical passage.

The next words in Daniel 9:27 are, "for one week." Daniel employs the word *week* to mean "seven years," drawing on a system of mystical chronology common to a number of Jewish writings of the Second Temple period. The entire time span that Daniel 9:24–27 delineates is seventy of these week-years, or 490 ordinary years.

By casting his mission in terms of Daniel 9:27 and the last of these seventy week-years, Judah exposed the tip of an exegetical iceberg. We can only speculate about the mass below water level: how he construed the sundry chronological elements and other things Daniel says. But what does seem clear is that Judah located himself at the end of Daniel's 490 years. Accordingly, he believed that from start to finish his mission of calling the Many to the New Covenant was to occupy a seven-year span of time.

How would the invasion from the north figure in that span? It is hard to ignore the previous verse, Daniel 9:26: "The troops of the prince who is to come shall destroy the city and the sanctuary. Its end shall come with a flood,[41] and at the end there shall be war. Desolation is decreed." Recognizing Judah's principle of rerevelation, the general import these verses would have for him is obvious. He would have tied them in with the passages from Deuteronomy, Jeremiah, Ezekiel, and the other prophets. The "prince" was Judah's invader, and he would come at the "end" for war. Whether Judah would say this end was the conclusion of the seven-year final week or merely sometime within that span, none can say.

What we can determine is this: within seven years of Judah's promulgation of the New Covenant, the northern army was to descend on Jerusalem. Would Judah begin counting in 76 B.C.E., with the outbreak of the Temple crisis? Or would he begin only in exile in 74 B.C.E., when in the Land of Damascus he and his followers, according to the *Damascus Document,* sealed their allegiance to the New Covenant? Or would he conjure some subtle reason to commence the countdown at another point in time? However he proceeded, the time when he believed the prophecy would be fulfilled must lie somewhere between approximately 73 and 65 B.C.E.

With this short-range forecast, Judah was taking that most hazardous of prophetic steps, making a Millerite move. By identifying a date, he was staking his authority on a concrete, empirically verifiable prediction. Everyone would know whether this prediction came true. Judah was like a mastodon grazing on the edge of the La Brea tar pits. One false step and he—and his crisis cult—would be a fossil.

As a matter of fact, Judah's prophesy did not come true. But he came *so close* to being right—as history was to show, close enough.

Few of Judah's Near Eastern contemporaries could have recognized that a new player shoving his way into the rugby-scrum of the region's politics had come to stay. He would do more than stay. He would dominate the game. Rome: within a few short years, most of the Hellenistic kingdoms of the Near East would fall to its legions. When Judah issued his prophecy about the northern invader, Rome's advance was—at least from a Judaean standpoint—just over the horizon.

It was Rome's army that would simultaneously disconfirm Judah's prophecy and provide a foil for the reinterpretation supplied by later followers, proving that the prophecy had actually come true.

The Seleucids of Syria never marched on Jerusalem. If they had ever intended to, their hand was stayed by the Roman imperium. The Romans swept aside Tigranes I and the various Seleucids; they bullied and eventually conquered the Nabateans. All of Judah's lions were reduced to simpering kittens. A greater lion than these had come. So it was Rome itself that, in 63 B.C.E., marched on Jerusalem.

Strictly speaking, Judah's prophecy of invasion was disconfirmed. First, no invasion occurred during the years when he was expecting it. Second, when it did happen, the invader was not the one Judah identified. But Judah's prediction had not been off by much, and crisis cults do not speak strictly. The invaders came only three or four years too late, and they did come from the north.

By then Judah was gone, and his followers consequently had been forced to develop a new chronology for the events of the Latter Days, expanding his seven years to a forty-year "final generation." The details of their method do not concern us at present. Within that new, reinterpreted framework, Judah's slightly mistimed invasion worked just fine. Far from being disconfirmed, Judah's prediction, as his followers claimed, was all too accurate.

Reinterpretation is to crisis cults what a blood transfusion is to a heart surgery patient. As we have seen with the Millerites, success or failure in reinterpreting disconfirmed prophecies—for they almost always are disconfirmed—determines whether groups remain healthy or sicken and die. Judah's followers were adept at adjusting his slightly incorrect prophecy and turning it into their greatest triumph, making it the anchor of their far-reaching claims.

That Judah was so close to being right chronologically helped immensely. Perhaps what he predicted did not happen, but it was easy to say that what happened was what he really meant. On the question of who would invade, note Josephus's description of the advance toward Jerusalem of the Roman armies in 63 B.C.E., led by Pompey: "Pompey took the army that he had prepared against the Nabateans, and the *auxiliaries from Damascus and the rest of Syria,* and marched."[42]

The Roman army, said Josephus, included native elements, non-Roman auxiliaries, from Damascus and Syria.

So in a sense the Seleucid lions came after all. Judah had never scripted the Romans as his invader, but his followers could point to this organic connection between the eventual invaders and Judah's lions and could claim that this had been his meaning all along. That was precisely what they did.

One place where we can observe their reinterpretation in action is the *Damascus Document.* In a passage that has never been truly understood, the authors of this work described the Jerusalem leadership, under the thrall of Pharisaic error:

> *Truly they were too sick to be healed; every kind of galling wound adhered to them because they did not turn away from traitorous practices; they relished the customs of fornication and filthy lucre. Each of them vengefully bore a grudge against his brother, each hating his fellow; each of them kept away from nearest kin but grew close to indecency; they vaunted themselves in riches and in ill-gotten gains; each of them did just what he pleased; each chose to follow his own willful heart.*
>
> *They did not separate from the people, but arrogantly threw off all restraint, living by wicked customs, of which God had said, "Their wine is <u>venom of serpents</u>, the cruel poison of vipers" (Deuteronomy 32:33). "The serpents" are the kings of the <u>Gentiles</u>, and "their wine" is their customs, and "the poison of vipers" is the head of the kings of Greece, who came to wreak vengeance on them. But the "Shoddy-Wall-Builders" and "Whitewashers" [i.e., the Pharisees] understood none of these things.*[43]

Scholars have been unable to explain why the *Document's* explanatory gloss on Deuteronomy 32:33 took the direction it did. Why should the elements of this verse be interpreted as relating to kings and Gentile customs and an invasion by "the head of the kings of Greece"? The attentive reader will recognize an aspect of the solution: the *Damascus Document* intended the passage from Deuteronomy as more than a simple quotation. It was a double allusion. The second reference was to Judah's sixth hymn (the underlined words).

Judah had written, *Their plans to capture me are as deadly as the* <u>venom of serpents</u>, *so they wait in ambush.* He had also written, *The wicked of the* <u>Gentiles</u> *rush against me with their afflictions, seeking every day to crush me.* The authors behind this passage of the *Damascus Document* knew Judah's hymns very well, as well as they knew the Bible. They tracked Judah's first statement to its biblical inspiration and quoted the full verse. They then unpacked his reasoning.

Those seeking to capture him were, he said, *serpents.* Since the authors knew that Judah had been in exile in the vicinity of Damascus, they concluded that these *serpents* must be the rulers of the *Gentiles* of that region. And that was, indeed, what Judah had meant: the *serpents* were another metaphor for his hymn's lions. Hence the authors derived their kings.

The writers went on to connect the kings/serpents with the vipers mentioned in Deuteronomy. By this move the vipers, like Judah's serpents, were understood as the kings of Gentile realms, and so—combined with some wordplay, a method of biblical interpretation their culture considered legitimate—they cleverly brought the Romans in the back door.

The Hebrew word for *poison* in Deuteronomy's *poison of vipers* is *rosh.* But *rosh* has another meaning in Hebrew, "head." Thus the authors read Deuteronomy here as referring to the "head of vipers," and since vipers were equated with rulers or kings, they derived their *head of the kings.* But how did they show that scripture specifically predicted the coming of *Greek* kings?

Pursuing the double meaning of *rosh* (poison/head), the authors linked Deuteronomy by analogy to yet another scripture, one whose context they knew Judah had implicated in his sixth hymn, Ezekiel 38:2. That verse spoke of our old friend, "Gog, of the land of Magog, the prince; *head (rosh)* of Meshach and Tubal." So Gog, the *head* of Ezekiel, was the *poison* of Deuteronomy. Then to connect Gog, Meshach, and Tubal to the Greeks required forging one final word link, this time with Genesis 10:2.

Genesis 10 is a chapter devoted to genealogies. Its second verse reads, "The descendants of Japheth [Noah's third son] were: Gomer, Magog, Madai, Javan, Tubal, Meshach, and Tiras." *Javan* was the Hebrew word for Greece. Reading this verse together with Ezekiel 38:2 told the authors of the *Damascus Document* that "the land of Magog" was a Greek land or bordered one, since Javan was listed with Magog. Even more closely connected to Javan, since they followed immediately in the list, were Ezekiel's Tubal and Meshach. The conclusion followed: since Gog was ruler of Magog and the *head* of Meshach and Tubal, he must be a Greek or, at least, a ruler of Greek lands.

Pompey, the Roman general marching at the head of Greek auxiliaries, the man who had made Syria a Roman province, met all the criteria. He became Gog. So they called him *the head of the kings of Greece.*

Since Judah, by implication, had equated Gog with the northern invaders, his followers could argue through this elaborate chain—Judah's words linked to Deuteronomy to Ezekiel to Genesis—that he had predicted the Roman invasion. True, *we* know Judah had not really meant what they were claiming. But his followers did not see things that way. Acolytes of a charismatic leader rarely do. They know he cannot be wrong. He had spoken of Greeks, they would find Greeks.

Moreover, by 63 B.C.E. what Judah really meant was not what mattered. What followers said he said, what people could be persuaded to believe he meant—that was what mattered.

His followers were doubtless sincere, but even in ancient times, spin could be more important than substance.

A NOTHER INSTANCE of Judah's movement reconfiguring the invaders of his sixth hymn appears in the *Commentary on Nahum.* On the basis of internal evidence, we can assign this work to a period just months after the Romans had taken Jerusalem, to late 63 or early 62 B.C.E. A portion of this commentary related to Nahum 2:11, the verse that Judah alluded to when he wrote, *You have saved the poor one in the <u>lions' den</u>* (Hebrew *meon arayot,* the only occurrence of the phrase in the Bible). The *Commentary's* method was to quote a biblical portion then attach its explanation:

["*Where now is the lions' den, the place where they fed their young?"*]
(2:11a)

[Its true import concerns Jerusalem, which has become] a dwelling for the wicked Gentiles.

"Wherever the lion goes to enter, there also goes the cub [without fear."] (2:11b)

[Its true import concerns Deme]trius, king of Greece, who sought to enter Jerusalem through the counsel of the Seekers of Accommodation; [but Jerusalem never fell into the] power of the kings of Greece from Antiochus until the appearance of the rulers of the Kittim.[44]

In the *Commentary's* interpretation, Judah's Damascene *lions' den* had advanced to Jerusalem, just as he predicted. In the Judaean capital now resided the *wicked Gentiles* from whom Judah once fled (*The <u>wicked of the Gentiles</u> rush against me with their afflictions*). Note the deciphering: Nahum's *lions* equals the *Commentary's wicked Gentiles*.

There is no textual basis for that equation, no particular reason for it at all apart from Judah's sixth hymn. Pursuing an implicit connection with Damascus—a pursuit that likewise cannot be explained apart from the writer's knowledge of Judah's hymn—the writer identified the specific *lion* of Nahum 2:11b with *Demetrius, king of Greece*. This king was none other than Demetrius III, ruler of the Land of Damascus and Pharisee ally who tried to enter Jerusalem in 88 B.C.E.

The writer knew that Demetrius III had failed to take the city twenty-five years earlier. He believed that Jerusalem had never fallen to any of the *kings of Greece* in the years between Antiochus IV Epiphanes (169 B.C.E.) and his own present, 63/62 B.C.E. Now, unfortunately, it lay under the control of the *Kittim*, a common cipher in the Dead Sea Scrolls for the Romans.

In full possession of these historical facts, the writer declared: *Jerusalem never fell into the power of the kings of Greece from Antiochus until the appearance of the rulers of the Kittim.* The correlating expression he used was crucial and intentional; by means of it, he inserted the *Kittim* (Romans) among *the kings of the Greeks.* Thus: as Antiochus was a Greek (*from Antiochus*), so were the Romans (*until the Kittim*). The purpose was to assert that Judah's apparently disconfirmed prophecy—Syrian Greeks would take Jerusalem—had not been disconfirmed after all. Accordingly, the writer's interpretation of the second half of Nahum 2:11b was that the lion's *cub* referred to the Romans. Where the *lion* had sought to enter but failed—Jerusalem—there the lion's *cub* now dwelled undisturbed. And mother and cub are always one flesh.

JUDAH HAD WRITTEN, *You have made Your servant a fugitive among lions who are appointed for the children of guilt—lions who are about to break the bones of powerful men, about to drink the blood of warriors.* His followers could show that this prophecy came true. The lions had come, had taken Jerusalem, had killed many Jewish aristocrats, had drunk the blood of warriors. To any Jew of the time, the evidence of Judah's truthfulness was everywhere to be seen. Romans marched the streets. They had established an occupying force in the city (though it lasted only a few months). Tribute had been levied; though it was heavy now, the ordinary person would soon became aware just how onerous and unceasing its exactions were to be.

The definition of a true prophet was agreed: what he predicted had to come true. The false prophet must be dispatched, as Judah had been. But now the evidence was all around that Judah actually had not been a false prophet. What more demonstration did anyone need? This prophecy-proved-true became the touchstone of his movement's message for the rest of its existence.[45]

And a potent message it was. If Judah had been proved right on this central tenet of his teaching, an invasion to destroy Jerusalem as a judgment of God, then had not one better pay attention to the rest of what he said? At the time of his trial, perhaps it was hard to choose between the Pharisees and Judah. Jerusalem had since fallen to wicked Gentiles, and the Temple of God had been desecrated. Was the choice any easier now? Hundreds, even thousands found that it was.

Yet all of that lay fifteen years in the future. The first messiah had more immediate concerns. Whether Judah and his followers were living by banditry is uncertain; in any case, two social principles that apply to brigands were about to make themselves felt. One principle is that in large raider bands the center can almost never hold. Conflict splits the group like a cue ball striking the rack. The second principle is equally natural. Given their strike-and-flee existence, the usual end of bandits is by betrayal.

Judah was about to feel the sting of the traitor's kiss.

CHAPTER 7

THE DOG
TURNS BACK

Suddenly a crowd came, and the one called Judas, one of the twelve,
was leading them. He approached Jesus to kiss him; but Jesus said
to him, "Judas, is it with a kiss that you are betraying the Son of
Man?"

Luke 22:47–48

WITHIN THE FIRST YEAR of exile in the Land of Damascus, a
substantial number of Judah's beloved followers—people he considered his spiritual children—deserted him and returned to Jerusalem. Their
apostasy was a specimen of the most profound challenge that a crisis-cult
leader can face: insider denial of his charisma. For these people had tasted
Judah's truth, had known his secret revelations, and still chose to leave.
This choice was a much more potent attack on the first messiah than the
easily deflected verbal slings of outsiders. How could such desertion be explained?

For those who remained behind, the apostasy was akin to a death in
the family. It could not fail to raise feelings of insecurity and, more omi-
nously, doubts about Judah. Many would begin to rethink their own commitment. Morale was bad. The wound had to be stanched or it would bleed
out and death would be swift.

Yet threatening as this apostasy was, the return to Jerusalem gave impetus to a second problem, more immediate and—if possible—even more dangerous.

Judah's seventh hymn (really more of a discourse) tells us of these problems:

I thank You, O Lord,[1] *for You have not abandoned the orphan, nor despised the poor one. Surely Your miraculous power [cannot be fath]omed, and Your glory has no bounds! Wondrous warriors serve You, and assist the poor when [their] feet are swept out beneath them. [They shall as]sist those eager for righteousness, to bear them up from the din of battle, together with all the faithful poor.*

As for myself, because of the ini[quity of all] who judged me, I have become a source of contention and dissension among my allies, of jealousy and fury among those who entered my covenant. They who had assembled to me all murmur and grumble; ev[en those who sh]are my bread have turned insidiously against me. All those who joined my council have played me false and spoken perversely. The men of my [coven]ant have rebelled and go about grumbling. They have traitorously gone to the children of destruction and defamed the mystery that You had hidden in me! For in order that You might man[ifest Your mighty power] through me, and because of their guilt, You have hidden from the children of destruction the fount of understanding and secret truth.

These children of destruction are the very ones who plot destruction and open their mouths only to teach the laws of Belial, whose lying tongue is like the venom of serpents, giving flower to thorns. Like those that glide in the dust on their bellies they strike, seizin[g with the cruelty] of cobras that cannot be charmed. This venom has become an incurable pain and sharp agony in Your servant's inmost being, crushing [my spirit] and draining my strength so that I cannot carry out my office.

They overtook me at the pass, where there was no place to escape, and it was impossible to separate [from our fa]milies. They played the lyre against which I had contended, and mingled music with their mockery, ruin and destruction. Chest pains se[ized me], and agonies

*like the birth pangs of a woman in labor; my heart was pounding
wildly within my chest. I was dressed for mourning, and my tongue
clove to the roof of my mouth. For they had surrounded me with plans
[of destruction], and their intention appeared bitterly clear to me. The
light of my countenance grew dark, and my face turned deathly pale.*

*You, O my God, had given me respite from distress, but they
supplanted it with oppression, and closed me up in deadly darkness.
I ate the bread of groaning; my drink mingled with unending tears.
Surely my eyes were wasted from grief, my very self from that day's
bitterness! Grief and misery did surround me, and shame was upon
my face. My own bread turned into an adversary, my drink contended
against me. They entered my bones only to destroy my spirit and to
sap my strength.*

*As the mysteries of transgression somehow permit, they are guilty of
altering the very laws of God!*

*I was indeed bound with ropes that could not be burst, with fetters
impossible to break. A mighty wall [surrounded me], secured with
iron bars and [bronze] door[s] that could not [be opened]. My prison
was like the very depths, from which none can [be lifted up . . . The
agonies] of [Be]l[i]al surrounded me . . .*

*I know that there is hope for those who repent of sin, and forsake
wrongdoing through the mul[titude of Your mercy] . . . and to walk in
the Way of Your Heart without sinning. So I am comforted concerning
the throng of Gentiles and the din of kingdoms mustering for war.
[For] I know that You will raise up a small group of survivors among
Your people, a remnant within Your inheritance; You will refine them
and purify them from guilt—for everything You do is by the canons of
Your truth; by Your covenant mercies You will judge them, in Your
bounteous mercy and abounding forgiveness; You will teach them by
Your mouth according to Your veritable uprightness, establishing them
in Your counsel. For Your own glory and purpose have You acte[d], so
as to magnify the Law, and . . .*

*[You have established] the men of Your counsel in the midst of
humankind to recount Your wonders to the generations of eternity,
and to [me]ditate on Your mighty deeds without ceasing. Thus shall all*

nations come to know Your truth, all peoples Your glory. Indeed, You have brought the men who follow Your counsel [into] Your divine council. They share a common lot with the Angels of the Presence, and no intermediary stands between them and [Your] Ho[ly Ones] . . . They will give reply by Your glorious mouth, and be Your princes in [an eternal] heritage.

The sprout [shall bud] like an everlasting flow[er of the field], the Shoot will grow into the boughs of an eternal Tree. It will cast its shadow upon the whole earth; its [summit] will brush the clouds, its roots stretch down to the depths. All the rivers of Eden will [water] its branches. It will become a measureless sea, it will pour out an unceasing downpour upon the earth. To Sheol . . . It will become a source of light, an eternal, never-failing fount. By its bright flames shall all the perverse be consumed. [It will] become a fire lapping at all guilty people until they cease to be.

Those who once gathered to my testimony have been deceived by advisers [of falsehood and turned their ba]cks on the laws of right service. Though You, O God, commanded them to benefit from going in the ho[ly] way in which they went, on which neither the uncircumcised, the unclean nor the violent might travel, yet they have slipped from the Way of Your Heart, and they [stum]ble because of the destructive urge of their [own] he[arts.] Belial is the advisor of their minds—oh, it is an evil purpose! They wallow in their guilt.

And I am like a sailor in a ship on a storm-tossed sea; their waves and all their breakers thunder against me—a staggering wind, [without] a calm wherein I might revive. There is no path to guide my way on the face of the sea. The abyss resonates to my groan, and I [am at] the very gates of death. Yet I am like one who has entered a fortified city, protected by a wall that none can scale.

I rel[y] on Your truth, O my God. Certainly You will establish a foundation on stone and place rafters with an accurate plumb line and a true level, laying down tested stones to raise an impregnable wall that cannot be moved. None who enter it will stumble; surely no foreigner will pass its gates—doors preventing entry, cross-bars mighty and shatter-proof. No raiding party shall enter with weapons of warfare, and the arrows of the wicked shall cease to fly in battle.

Then the sword of God will hasten to the appointed time of judgment.
All those who have held to His truth shall be stirred up to extermina[te]
the wicked, and the children of guilt shall be no more. The warrior
will draw his bow, and the eternal rampart will open into an endless
expanse; the everlasting gates will swing wide to usher forth the
weapons of warfare. They will spread their forces from one end of the
land to the other, shooting their arrows and allowing the guilty no
retreat. They will be utterly trampled down, none taken alive, without
hope among the stacked corpses. Not one of the mighty warriors shall
escape.

For the po[wer] belongs to the Most High God . . . Those who lie in
the dirt will raise a standard, and worm-eaten men will lift high a
banner for the army . . .

I have been struck dumb . . . [I am like an a]rm broken off at the
joint; my feet have been mired in muck. My eyes have grown weary
of seeing evil, my ears from listening to the shedding of blood. I am
stupefied by the evil plotting. Surely Belial is manifest when their
destructive intention shows itself! All the foundations of my frame
have crumbled, my bones separated from one another. My inmost
being is like a ship in a raging storm. My heart is heavy almost to the
point of death, and faintness has swallowed me up because of their
sin-driven destruction.[2]

APOSTASY FROM CRISIS cults like Judah's is not unusual. On the contrary, a certain amount of defection is the norm. It even follows semipredictable patterns. The group's later literature shows that Judah's movement had to fight defection throughout its history.[3]

Judah's was what sociologists term a "high-tension" movement. The tension register measures the degree of social separation between a movement or religious group and the larger society. The higher the degree of social separation, the higher tension a movement is. As the sociologist of religion William Sims Bainbridge has remarked, "By definition, a really high-tension religious movement would reject major societal institutions, like the family and the market, replacing them with some kind of radical alternative."[4]

Judah's movement had done precisely that. They first rejected the Jerusalem Temple and its cultus, then denied the legitimacy of the current representatives of the ruling family, Alexandra and Hyrcanus II. As for replacement, Judah had himself in mind. Short of outright revolt, a movement within ancient Jewish society could scarcely position itself in higher tension with the nation than had Judah's.

People join high-tension movements because they believe that the return on investment will ultimately exceed the present cost. If the cost is very high—that is, the degree of commitment required is extreme—people often find the movement attractive nevertheless. The high cost seems reasonable given the value of the promised eternal rewards. To put it another way: if the cost people are asked to pay is too low, they tend to doubt the value of what they are being asked to buy. For this reason, movements that require their members to make many sacrifices are often more attractive than those making few demands. A total immersion movement like the Branch Davidians, Heaven's Gate, or the Aquarians will seem more appealing to some than the low tension of their local Episcopalian church or Reformed synagogue.

But high-tension movements have more difficulty retaining their members than do low-tension groups. After all, the cost is not paid using credit cards or deferred payments; this transaction is C.O.D. The greater part of the reward, on the other hand, *is* deferred. For this reason, "substantial numbers of long-term members of [high-tension] new religious movements leave of their own volition."[5]

The cost for Judah's followers had been high indeed. They paid for membership with the loss of their homes, their property, their friends and family. After suffering the deprivations of life in exile, the continuing, day-by-day cost of their decision undoubtedly came into sharper focus. Some no longer felt themselves sufficiently compensated by the first messiah to make the cost worthwhile. These people decided to cash out their investment and return to the city. (That they could do so shows that they were under a less severe legal interdiction than Judah, for whom return was not an option.)

So attrition is normal for groups like Judah's. But the sickness that infected Judah's ranks was more serious than routine defection. His wording shows that he faced the cancer of large-scale, open rebellion: *They who had assembled to me all murmur and grumble; even those who share my bread have turned insidiously against me. All those who joined my council have played me false and spoken perversely. The men of my covenant have rebelled and go about grumbling.* At least one heated and public confrontation must have taken place, during which Judah failed to overpower the opposition. The first messiah continued to lose every decisive conflict: first in Jerusalem, now in the Land of Damascus. The leaders of the rebellion departed, taking with them to Jerusalem an unknown—but judging from the sequel, substantial—percentage of the total adherents to Judah's New Covenant.

The departure was anything but amicable, and his opponents did more than just go their own way. They went straight to Jerusalem and there threw in their lot with Judah's enemies. They now began to work positively for their former leader's destruction: *They have traitorously gone to the children of destruction and defamed the mystery that You had hidden in me!*

What caused this rebellion? Why was it so effective? And why did such a malevolence seize Judah's former devotees? The answers to these questions lie in a close consideration of how Judah dealt with the fact of the apostasy.

A COMMON STRATEGY for crisis-cult leaders in such situations is to attack the genuineness of the defectors' commitment. If it can be shown that they never really belonged to the group, then it follows that they never experienced the charisma of the leader. The attack by insiders on the leader's person and revelations is thereby blunted. Since they were not true members, their acid testimony is diluted, watered down. Its potency becomes no greater than the criticism of outsiders.

This was the strategy of the group behind the New Testament book of 1 John when they suffered defection: "They went out from us, but they did not belong to us; for if they had belonged to us, they would have remained with us. But by going out they made it plain that none of them belongs to us" (2:19). This same strategy was probably effected by Judah, though we have only hints to that end from the later *Damascus Document*. The key wording appears at one of the junctures where the work considered the issue of general disobedience to the group's laws: *When his actions become evident, he shall be sent away from the company as if his lot had never fallen among the disciples of God.*[6]

If a person were regarded as outside the elect because he disobeyed this or that individual law, then a fortiori he would be so defined if he expressed the most profound disobedience possible and left altogether. Since this person was never among the elect, defection was simply an expression of his true nature. Judah would have agreed with the writer of 2 Peter: "It has happened to them according to the true proverb, 'The dog turns back to its own vomit.'"

A second rhetorical strategy commonly brought to bear against crisis-cult apostates is to brand them as deceived. This was a heavy component of Judah's response. He blamed the defection on the insidious effect of his enemies' lies, which, like a slow-acting toxin, had finally dissolved his erstwhile followers' resolve: *Because of the iniquity of all who judged me, I have become a source of contention and dissension among my disciples.* He went on: *They who once gathered to my testimony have been deceived by lying counselors.*

Lying counselors, as we have seen, was one of Judah's terms for the Pharisees. He laid some of the blame on the fallible humanity of the disciples but even more on Satan's blandishments: *They stumble because of the destructive urge of their own hearts. Like a counselor, Belial is with their hearts.* Judah's words counterposed Belial, the infernal *counselor* (Hebrew *yoets*), to himself, the Wonderful Counselor.

Of course, Judah's attack was not a reproach shouted at the backs of those who left. He had lost their ear. He offered his antidote to those who stayed but were wavering. Any thoughts that the Pharisees' laws seemed attractive, he assured them, were Satanic. Early Christianity likewise used this argument against the path of least resistance represented by another way of life: "Be self-controlled and alert. Your enemy the devil prowls around like a roaring lion looking for someone to devour" (1 Peter 5:8).

Judah's third and final strategy for combating apostasy was, again, common to the arsenal of almost all crisis cults. His rattling of this biggest of guns was somewhat muted, but the weapon was there, between the lines, camouflaged. Later, his followers wheeled it into command position when they denounced defection in the *Damascus Document.* The weapon was simply this: deny salvation to any apostate. This was not a stand-alone weapon; it was more like the second barrel of the "deceived" gambit, for in the thinking of Judah and his followers, to be deceived *was* to be doomed to Hell. Therein lay the urgency of Judah's new revelation.

Again, this third approach did not really concern those who left. They no longer cared what Judah said, and by leaving they had denied Judah's authority over their eternal destinies. Like Judah's other responses, this salvation stratagem targeted the remaining members.

The *Damascus Document* said as follows:

> So it is with all the men who entered the New Covenant in the Land
> of Damascus, but then went back and played the traitor, and so turned
> away from the fountain of living water. They shall not be reckoned
> among the council of the people, and their name shall not be written
> in their book . . . Such is the fate for all who reject the commandments,
> whether old or new, who have turned their thoughts to false gods and
> who have lived by their willful hearts; they have no part in the House
> of Law. They will be condemned along with all their companions who
> went back to the Men of Mockery, because they have uttered lies
> against the correct laws and rejected the sure covenant that they made
> in the Land of Damascus, that is, the New Covenant. Neither they
> nor their families shall have any part in the House of Law.[7]

The *Men of Mockery* were those who followed the Man of Mockery,
another name Judah's movement developed for the Man of the Lie, Shimeon
ben Shetah (if, indeed, he was the Man of the Lie).

Judah's own volley against the salvation of apostates was, as so often,
implicit in his use of biblical sources. Thus Judah wrote, *They who had assembled to me all murmur and grumble.* The word he used for *grumble* (Hebrew *telunah*) is special, appearing in the biblical books only where the
people of Israel grumble against Moses. By choosing this word, Judah continued to cast his role for the Latter Days in terms of the myth-dream,
drawing one more parallel between himself and the archetypal lawgiver of
Israel.

All through Israel's wilderness journeys, according to the books of
Exodus and Numbers, the people grumbled against Moses. For example,
Exodus 16 tells the story of their protest against him for lack of food, after
which they received the famous manna. Israel's murmuring against Moses
was portrayed by the biblical writers as directed in reality against the one
who had chosen Moses, God. So Moses charges in Exodus 16:8, "You are
not grumbling against us, but against the Lord." And in Numbers 14:27 we
read of God saying, "How long will this wicked community grumble against
me? I have heard the complaints of these grumbling Israelites." The penalty
for continued complaint emerges in Numbers 17:10: "Put back Aaron's
staff in front of the covenant, to be kept as a warning to rebels, so that you
may make an end of their grumbling against me, or else they will die."

Through his well-considered choice of words, Judah captured the resonance of these biblical passages and directed it against his own defectors. He implied that they rebelled not against him, the New Moses, but against God. He did not have to say that the biblical penalty—death under God's curse—would descend upon such rebels. For Judah's remaining followers, who, like all ancient Jews, took biblical precedents seriously, these reminders were a chilling challenge to apostasy and an intimidating rebuke even to dissent.

Judah's word was law. There was no court of appeal.

NEVERTHELESS, for all the weapons Judah brought to bear against the apostates, he was—as his hymn reveals—somewhat desperate and profoundly depressed because of what had happened. To assuage his desperation and soothe his depression he turned to the Bible, where he knew that he would find, encoded, the course of all the events of the Latter Days, even his defeats. He sought the strongest weapon of all: proof that this apostasy had to happen, that it was always supposed to happen this way. And Judah found what he sought. He found himself, his allies, and their apostasy in what would later become a central biblical text for his followers, Zechariah 11.

This passage informed his charge, *I have become a source of contention and dissension among my allies, of jealousy and fury among those who entered my covenant.* The passage reads (italics as usual):

Thus said YHWH my God: "Shepherd My sheep who are in danger of slaughter. Those who buy them, kill them without compunction, and those who sell them say, 'Blessed is YHWH, for I am rich,' and their own shepherds have no pity on them. Accordingly, I will have no more pity on those who dwell in the land," says YHWH. "I will cause each one to fall into the power of his neighbor and his king; they will devastate the land, and I shall rescue none from their hand."

So I shepherded the sheep in danger of slaughter, that is, the oppressed of the flock. And I took two staves: the first I called "Pleasantness," and the second I called "Corrupters," and I shepherded the sheep.

In one month I eliminated three *allies,* for I became angry with them, and they tired of me. So I said, "I will not be your shepherd;

let the sheep who is to die, die; who is to be destroyed, be destroyed; and let the rest devour each other's flesh." Then I took my staff named "Pleasantness" and broke it, so nullifying *my covenant* that I had made with the peoples.

So it was annulled that day, and the oppressed of the sheep, who obeyed me, knew that it was the word of YHWH (Zechariah 11:4–11).[8]

Perhaps the single most important term in Judah's seventh hymn is *my covenant* (Hebrew *beriti*). For a Jew of the first century B.C.E., such language was the pure distillate of hubris. It was to equate oneself with the patriarchs: Abraham, Isaac, and Jacob, or Moses—the select few through whom God had made covenants with Israel, and so the most important people in the nation's history. Judah's usage, then, was yet another brick in the edifice of his claim to be the New Moses. It constitutes further evidence that he considered himself a messiah.

The only biblical lode from which Judah could have mined *my covenant* (where the possessive *my* attached to *covenant* refers to someone other than God) is Zechariah 11. Even a cursory glance at its content impresses: this passage could fit the contours of Judah's present circumstances as tightly as a bodysuit. So he now drew to himself more of the myth-dream of Israel; here was the notion of the Good Shepherd. (Jesus would later make the same application, according to the Gospels. Note especially John 10:1–18.)

Judah would appeal to the image again in his eighth hymn, when he wrote of his followers, *They are like children who play in the embrace of their foster father.* Here he referred to Isaiah 40:11 (in the *Great Isaiah Scroll* version) and its use of the Good Shepherd motif: "He will feed his flock like a shepherd: he will gather the young in his arms and carry them in his *embrace,* and gently lead the *children.*"[9]

Judah's later followers recognized his self-recognition. They knew that in some mysterious way their founder was the Voice that spoke in Zechariah's words. An early form of the *Damascus Document* applied Zechariah's "oppressed of the sheep" to Judah's movement. They were the followers of the Shepherd. In two different, fragmentary *Commentaries on Isaiah* they likewise connected their Teacher to the Shepherd.[10] We shall see how important this connection was when it became necessary for them to explain the messiah's death.

Judah's choice of the term *allies* (*I have become a source of contention and dissension among my allies*) and his reading of an ambiguous spelling in Zechariah 11:8 as *allies,* is significant.[11] It leads us to the heart of the apostasy from his movement and helps explain both why it happened and why its leaders were able, when confronting Judah, to gain support. It explains something of the structure of his movement to this point.

You may recall that Judah used the word *allies* earlier, when he wrote in the fifth hymn, *All my allies and kinsmen have distanced themselves from me.* In the politics of the period—and Judah's hymns are political writings—the Hebrew word *rea,* which normally means "friend," had taken on the specialized meaning "ally." It was a technical term. In fact, so was the Hebrew behind *kinsmen.*

Josephus employs the Greek equivalents of both of these Hebrew words in his chronicle of Herod's rise to power in the 40s B.C.E. After a study of Josephus's use of those equivalents, the historian Brent Shaw concluded of Herod:

> His power was pyramided "internally," based on various coalitions
> of lesser men of local power. The circle of men around him upon
> whom he depended was comprised of two parts: (a) "friends" [allies]
> and (b) relatives or kin. Relatives, that is kin relations of the royal
> [house], were expected to give their support to the king—they were
> his first line of defense against those who threatened his power, and
> were ideally supposed to be those whom the king could trust to
> handle his affairs for him. . . . It was with this group of "friends and
> relatives" that Herod consulted on important courses of action, and
> upon whom he depended as surrogate leaders and commanders in
> dubious situations. These "friends," however, were not mere civil
> servants, but men of real power and capabilities and who, since they
> were powerful in themselves, simultaneously acted as a constraint
> on his powers.[12]

Herod and other men of power in Judah's day were thus the central attachment of a reticulate structure of *allies and kinsmen,* the latter being members of their own families. The *allies* were themselves powerful, and their relationship with the focus figure had to be negotiated so that both parties benefited. Shaw's term *friend* (Greek *philos* = Hebrew *rea*) is therefore better rendered "ally," since mutual feelings of goodwill were not the binding glue here. This was a political relationship based upon expediency. When politics changed, so would the variables in the expedient equation. "Friends" would reassess their relationship and act accordingly.

Such reassessment had twice bedeviled Judah. True, he was never at the very highest level in the pyramid of power—belonging to the next tier down—but those of his station organized themselves to imitate the system that governed the highest circles. These were the proven political methods in the Near East of the day. When at Judah's trial the crisis in Jerusalem reached its climax, some of his *allies* reassessed and decided to abandon their leader. It was expedient. That decision Judah recorded in his fifth hymn.

Now a second wave of these elite social peers had elected to desert. Shaw's last sentence probably explains why. All along, these men had acted as a certain "constraint on his powers," but as Judah's self-assertion grew, these constraints had to either stretch or break. They broke. Judah overstepped the agreed boundaries of "friendship."

The elite status of those who led the revolt against Judah goes far in explaining why the rebellion against the first messiah was so successful. After all, the common element among Judah's followers had thus far been their willingness to forsake everything because of belief in him. Only a powerful counterforce might prevail against his charismatic magnetism.

The leaders of the opposition were indeed such a force. These were not just any followers, they were Judah's social peers. Like him, they had been at home in lofty Jerusalem circles. These were the remnants of the priestly elite who, with Judah, had drafted MMT as an early response to the Pharisee takeover in the Temple. These men had been subsidiary leaders in Judah's movement, a movement that began in Jerusalem with multiple leadership but was now, with Judah's growing self-realization, more and more becoming an autocracy. Not everyone was happy with the change.

We must recall that the things Judah wrote in his hymns were private. While they certainly reflect what he taught his followers, we cannot always know just when the prophet revealed his private new understandings to the acolytes. We may suppose that the ideas expressed in the hymns often remained private for some time, shared by Judah only with his God.

At any rate, it was only now that Judah's messianic consciousness became apparent to his followers, and some of them—perhaps most—were unwilling to accept it.

Armed with this understanding, we can appreciate how Judah must have read Zechariah 11 as a thinly veiled prediction of the present circumstances. Judah saw himself as raised up by God to come to the Jews in a time of crisis, when the "sheep were in danger." For Judah the "danger" was what he had been warning against all along: abandoning God's truth, abandoning priestly interpretation of the Bible, especially the Temple laws. The nation's leaders—the buyers and sellers of the sheep, "their own shepherds"—had been unfaithful. Judah said of them in this discourse: *As the mysteries of transgression somehow permit, they are guilty of altering the very laws of God!* So God had decided to bring punishment against the land.

Each Jew would "fall into the power of his neighbor and his king." Here Judah discovered reinforcement for his prophecy of an enemy marching from the north. Only the "oppressed of the sheep" were to prove faithful, though originally Judah's covenant also embraced the people of the staff called "Pleasantness." (The second staff, "Corrupters," Judah would take as the Pharisaic faction; Zechariah never classifies this group as within the covenant.)

Judah equated the defection of the moment with the apostasy prophesied of the people of the staff called "Pleasantness." "Pleasantness" represented those who followed only while it was "pleasant," until the testing grew truly severe. They failed to stay the course. And so in the mirror of Zechariah we see reflected how Judah believed he should seal that abrogation. Those who departed he would curse.

Let them die; let them be destroyed; let them eat one another's flesh. These words of Zechariah Judah reserved for his erstwhile *allies.* Their salvation was forfeit, the New Covenant annulled for them. The last words of Zechariah became Judah's benediction to his remaining followers: "And the sheep, who obeyed me, knew that it was the word of God."

What a beautifully phrased threat.

MIRED IN MUCK

Judah wrote in this discourse, *I am like a sailor on a storm-tossed sea,* and the structure of the discourse itself is something like a wavy sea. Judah moved alternately from the throes of despair to a mountaintop giddiness. As he contemplated recent events his emotions fell and rose, fell and rose. The discourse followed those movements.

Judah had good reason to be depressed. Not only had his following been decimated by apostasy that threatened to snuff out his movement in its infancy, but a number who remained faithful had suffered a violent, literal death. Judah himself barely escaped alive. Just before he wrote, the group had been attacked.

But before we consider what may be known of that occasion, it is worth focusing briefly on a few of the other waves of Judah's present writing. These ups and downs tell us important things about Judah's changing movement and the first messiah's self-understanding. We see how continuously he was able to discover the purpose behind anything that happened by contemplating the Bible. So profound was his knowledge of Israel's scriptures that with every twist and turn in the road, passages leaped to mind, their true significance now clear at last, but only because he was able to connect passage to passage and passage to event with unparalleled mental agility.

A deep emotional trough is reflected by Judah's words: *I was indeed bound with ropes that could not be burst, with fetters impossible to break. A mighty wall surrounded me, secured with iron bars and bronze doors that could not be opened. My prison was like the very depths, from which none can be lifted up.* Some scholars have been led by these and similar phrases in the discourse to suggest that Judah's enemies had seized him and thrown him into prison. But his enemies' actual intent was more deadly; if they had succeeded in laying hands on the aged priest, the sequel would have been a sepulcher, not a cell.

A more likely understanding emerges from Judah's biblical usage. He probably had in mind here Jeremiah 6:28, "They are all hardened rebels, *traitorously going to defame.* They are all *bronze* and *iron*, acting destructively." Judah also echoed this passage when he said, *They have <u>traitorously gone</u> to the children of destruction and <u>defamed</u> the mystery.* The references to *bronze* and *iron*, together with Judah's other expressions for binding and imprisonment, were metaphors. They were intended to represent the way that his followers' treachery made him feel: helpless and weak, closed in from every side.

Judah drew from the Bible many other expressions for desertion. They appear everywhere in this discourse, as for example Judah's *My feet were mired in muck.* This was not a way of describing the hideous conditions of an ancient dirt-floored prison pit. It was rather a reference to Jeremiah 38:22, "All the women left in the palace of the king of Judah will be brought out to the officials of the king of Babylon. Those women will say to you: 'They misled you and overcame you—those trusted friends of yours. *Your feet are mired in muck;* your friends have backslid.'" Judah appropriated for his discourse the emotional ambiance of this verse and others like it, pouring out before God his own bleak feelings of despair, for his friends, too, had backslid.

But Judah surged up and crested above those feelings as his thoughts moved to the few remaining faithful sheep and the great plans God had for them through him. Even the prospect of foreign invasion of his beloved Jerusalem could elicit praise, for it was a part of the purpose of God: *I know that there is hope for those who repent of sin, and forsake wrongdoing through the multitude of Your mercy . . . and to walk in the Way of Your Heart without sinning. So I am comforted concerning the throng of Gentiles and the din of kingdoms mustering for war.* Judah now launched into his most protracted description of his followers and their destiny yet. In the two years or so since his earliest hymns, Judah's ideas about these followers had clearly ripened.

As important as Judah was, God's approaching kingdom, he indicated, was not only about him. His followers were another focus of the prophecies. They were the remnant (Hebrew *sheerit*) heralded by the prophets of old. He wrote, *You will raise up a small group of survivors among Your people, a remnant within Your inheritance.* This statement drew on scriptures such as Isaiah 37:32, "For out of Jerusalem will come a *remnant,* and out of Mount Zion a band of survivors. The zeal of God Almighty will accomplish this." Judah described how God was even now purifying his remnant through their trials: *You will refine them and purify them from guilt.* All that had happened to them was by God's design, to make known his truth: *For Your own glory and purpose have You acted, so as to magnify the Law.*

This purified remnant, Judah contended, existed to glorify God and to make him known to all nations: *You have established the men of Your counsel in the midst of humankind to recount Your wonders to the generations of eternity, and to meditate on Your mighty deeds without ceasing. Thus shall all nations come to know Your truth.* Judah meant that his own new revelation, the content of the New Covenant, would by the agency of his followers spread throughout the whole earth.

And Judah returned in this discourse to his favorite themes of union with the angels and the destruction of the wicked. These notions caused his heart to sing: *You have brought the men who follow Your counsel into Your divine council. They share a common lot with the Angels of the Presence.* The Angels of the Presence were the highest angels, the only ones among the multitude of heavenly beings privileged to enter God's presence. Judah's followers were to be like them, exalted on high.

On the destruction of the wicked, the prophet characterized his followers as the light of the world: *They will become a source of light, an eternal, never-failing fount. In its bright flames all the perverse shall be consumed. It will become a fire lapping at all guilty people until they cease to be.*

Judah also portrayed his group as an enormous tree, an image he would develop further in his last written words. This tree he conceived as the maturation of the Shoot of Isaiah 11; the Shoot, as we have seen, was Judah's group: *A sprout shall bud like an everlasting flower of the field, the Shoot will grow into the boughs of an eternal tree.* I shall discuss this arboreal motif at length below, so it will occupy us no further now.

All of this forecasting about his disciples made Judah's thoughts spiral back once more to the defectors, and with this gyre he crashed again into depression: *They have slipped from the Way of Your Heart . . . The abyss resonates to my groan, and I am at the very gates of death.* Almost without pause, however—so swiftly and without segue that one must question Judah's emotional stability—the first messiah surged from his anguish to a new crest.

This swell drew its force from his contemplation of the New Jerusalem.

"IN THE TWENTY-FIFTH year of our exile," wrote Ezekiel the prophet, "the hand of the Lord was upon me, and he brought me by means of angelic visions to the land of Israel, and set me down upon an exceedingly high mountain."[13]

The mountain was Zion, and from it Ezekiel looked out upon what none other could see, for sometimes a city set on a hill *can* be hidden. This was what he described. His visions of a new Temple set within a new temple city comprise Ezekiel 40–48. Isaiah, too, looked for a New Jerusalem, encrusted with all manner of precious stone (54:11–12); and the apocryphal book of Tobit longed for the day when "Jerusalem and the Temple of God will be rebuilt in splendor, just as the prophets have said" (14:6–7).

In part these ideas were a reaction to the comparatively modest Temple the Jews were able to build upon their return from exile in Babylon. It was no match, said contemporaries, for the splendid structure of old, erected by Solomon and destroyed by Nebuchadnezzar. For centuries notions of a future, wondrous Temple were nurtured and grew, particularly in priestly circles. The hope for this Temple became a cornerstone of the myth-dream.

The New Jerusalem with its magnificent Temple were aspects of the Kingdom of God, in its essence an earthly, Jewish kingdom. It was thoughts of this city and the kingdom that comforted Judah as he brooded over his recent reverses and that laid his heart to rest over the prospect of the nations mustering for war. For Judah that war, the first volley in the final war of wars, was but a part of the divine plan for the Latter Days. Ultimate victory for Israel was likewise predestined, a victory that Judah now believed he would lead. This was why he could write, *I am comforted concerning the throng of Gentiles and the din of kingdoms mustering for war.*

The New Jerusalem that Judah contemplated was Augustine's City of God, and Judah believed that God was in the details. He associated the city's foundation with the dawn of the millennium. His heart exulted in its near approach:

> *You will establish a foundation on stone and place rafters with an accurate plumb line and a true level, laying down tested stones to raise an impregnable wall that cannot be moved. None who enter it will stumble; surely no foreigner will pass its gates—doors preventing entry, cross-bars mighty and shatter-proof. No raiding party shall enter with weapons of warfare, and the arrows of the wicked shall cease to fly in battle. Then the sword of God will hasten to the appointed time of judgment.*

Judah's ideas on the coming eternal city may have been shaped partially by one of the Dead Sea writings known as *The Vision of the New Jerusalem*. Preserved in six copies, this work consists of an elaborate verbal blueprint for the future city and its Temple.[14] *The Vision of the New Jerusalem* dates to the early second century B.C.E., and there is good reason to believe that Judah knew the work. It was a source for another Dead Sea writing called the *Temple Scroll,* which Judah's own followers produced (possibly with his input).[15] If they knew the *Vision* then Judah probably did, too, since it antedated them all.

The writer picked up where Ezekiel left off and, in a work some fifty columns long (much less is extant), provided details of temple-city architecture and protocol sufficient to satisfy the most fastidious priestly reader.

The initial surviving portions of the work described the wall surrounding the holy city and the twelve gates that pierced it. As in Ezekiel's visions, an angel guided the anonymous seer (Ezekiel himself?). While the angel measured the structures with a cane some ten feet long, the seer wrote down each and every particular. Listing these details in what strikes the modern reader as stultifying fashion was intended to convey certainty:

God would surely bring to pass all of his promises—including those of the New Jerusalem—as proved by how precisely even the minutiae had been foreordained:

> He measured from the northeastern corner to the south, to the first gate, thirty-five stades [1 stade = 2/15 of a mile]; and the name of this gate is called the gate of Levi. From this gate he measured to the south, thirty-five stades, and the name of this gate is called the gate of Judah. From this gate he measured to the southeastern corner, and he measured from this corner westwards thirty-five stades; and the name of this gate is called the gate of Joseph.

The work continued in this vein for all twelve gates. Then the angel ushered the seer into the city, laid out like a Brobdingnagian checker-board.[16] This New Jerusalem was a rectangle whose long sides measured about nineteen miles, short sides thirteen miles. It was larger than any ancient city, dwarfing the actual Jerusalem of the author's time:

> Then he brought me into the city, and measured all the city blocks. Length and breadth, they measured fifty-one canes by fifty-one canes, making a square three hundred and fifty-seven cubits to each side. Each block had a sidewalk around it bordering the street: three canes, that is, twenty-one cubits.

> So he showed me the measurement of all the blocks: between each block was a street six canes wide, that is, forty-two cubits. The main streets that passed from east to west were ten canes wide, that is, seventy cubits—for two of them. A third street, which was on the north of the Temple, he measured at eighteen canes in width, that is, one hundred twenty-six cubits.

The author of The Vision of the New Jerusalem went on to describe more of the outer wall with its gates, towers, and stairs. Then he filled in his outline of the structure of the city blocks, detailed the fifteen houses within each block, offered still more on the city towers—they were seventy-five feet high and constructed of electrum, sapphires, chalcedony, and gold—and spent some time discussing the proper priestly procedures in the Temple.

The work ended with a prophecy of the kingdoms to come, climaxing in a final apocalyptic war between Israel and the Gentiles, much as Judah himself prophesied would happen (only he specified *when:* in the next few years). Invoking the New Jerusalem in his discourse, Judah focused almost exclusively on this Armageddon and the city's martial function as a stronghold against Gentiles.

These clearly were his predominant interests in the seventh hymn. The final damaged fragments of the *Vision* read:

> . . . *shall rise up in place of it, and the kingdom of Persia . . . and then shall rise up the Kittim [originally probably meaning Greece, and so Judah would read it; but his followers would later decode the name as Rome] in place of it. All these kingdoms shall appear one after another . . . others numerous and lordly with them . . . with them Edom and Moab and the Ammonites . . . of the whole land of Babylon, not . . . and they shall do evil to your descendants until the time of . . . shall come . . . and then shall appear among all the peoples the Kingdom.*

That Judah in his darkest hours should dwell on apocalyptic prophecies such as the New Jerusalem text is highly significant from the standpoint of understanding the first messiah's mind. His focus reinforces the inference that he had long known and cogitated upon apocalyptic writings, for such behavior is a common pattern with charismatic prophets and messiahs as they are known from history. The historian Norman Cohn summarized his magisterial study of medieval millenarian movements and their leaders thus:

> Sometimes [the leaders] were petty nobles; sometimes they were simply impostors; but more usually they were intellectuals or half-intellectuals—the former priest turned freelance preacher was the commonest type of all. And what all these men shared was a familiarity with the world of apocalyptic and millenarian prophecy. Moreover, *whenever the career of one of them can be traced, it turns out that he was obsessed with eschatological phantasies [sic] long before it occurred to him, in the midst of some great social upheaval, to [lead a movement.]* (emphasis mine)[17]

Cohn's model of the millenarian prophet holds true for many figures besides those of his study. One example: David Koresh. Well before he became the messiah of the Branch Davidians, Koresh was known in Seventh-Day Adventist circles as a young man who was well versed in the Bible. He had a particular interest in, and command of, biblical prophecy. Koresh spent hours trying to solve the riddles of the New Testament's apocalyptic book of Revelation.

In a 1984 letter to an acquaintance, he expressed something of an obsession with the seventh messenger mentioned in Revelation 10:7. According to the biblical text, this figure would come from God with a "final message." Koresh specifically said in the letter that the messenger was yet to come.

While visiting Israel in January 1985, Koresh underwent a profound "experience," the pivotal and defining moment of his life. An elderly survivor of the Waco tragedy, Catherine Matteson, knew Koresh both before and after this experience. Even after the tragedy she remained a believer. According to James Tabor's and Eugene Gallagher's study of Koresh, she recalled:

> Prior to 1985 Vernon [Koresh's given name] often told the group that the "full message" was coming, but it hadn't arrived yet. When he returned from Israel in February 1985, Catherine remembered, everything about him had totally changed. He told her and others that he had now received the full message and that the mystery of all the Prophets, as indicated in Revelation 10:7, was beginning to unfold.[18]

Like Cohn's medieval prophetic figures, Koresh possessed the "facts" of prophetic and apocalyptic texts for a long time before he knew their meaning. During that revelatory moment common to charismatics, all these facts swam into focus. It was a sudden and absolute shift, almost like changing state, as when water becomes ice: different and yet the same. Koresh himself now became the hero of his holy drama, the seventh messenger he once pondered and struggled so hard to identify. He even journeyed to heaven to receive truth.

Something similar almost certainly happened in Judah's case. After decades as a wisdom teacher and scholar of biblical prophecies and apocalyptic writings, during a dark night of the soul, the soft focus of the facts sharpened into crystal clarity. Judah underwent an "experience" catalyzed by the psychological pressure of the Pharisee takeover.

After this shift, Judah knew himself to be the Voice of Zechariah 11 and other scriptures: the expected Suffering Servant, the New Moses, the Wonderful Counselor, the Good Shepherd, and other figures of the myth-dream of Israel; in short, the messiah. Earlier, Judah had been one of numerous priestly expositors of the holy writings—a leading light, true, but still only first among equals—looking for these figures yet to come. They were other than he. But like Koresh, like the flagellant messiah Karl Schmid, and like other prophets down through history, with a burst of insight Judah ceased to stand outside the text. Now he inhabited the scriptures. He became himself.

Judah's mention of the New Jerusalem in this discourse thus opens a window into the first messiah's apocalyptic self-understanding. Yet we might have known nothing of it or of the *Thanksgiving Hymns,* Judah, or his movement had his enemies succeeded in their aims. For Judah's seventh hymn was written in the wake of an attack intended to kill him.

And it was his own apostate followers who spearheaded the effort.

THE MYSTERY OF UNGODLINESS

In the autumn of 74 B.C.E. (or possibly 73 B.C.E.), shortly after the wholesale defection led by his priestly allies, Judah and his remaining faithful gathered together: men, women, and children. Brigands do not normally travel with their families, for obvious reasons, so this occasion was special in more ways than one.[19] The group was preparing to celebrate the Day of Atonement, which they designated by a term otherwise unknown from surviving sources, *yom ha-taanit,* "The Day of Self-Affliction."

The Bible requires this holiest day of the Jewish calendar to be celebrated every year on the tenth day of the seventh month. The purpose is to atone for the people's sins of the foregoing year. While any list of Judah's reasons for opposing the Pharisees would have to be long, the fact that they advocated a new way of observing the Day of Atonement must stand near the top. His hatred of their novel approach even helped inspire one of his Ten Commandments, wherein he declared, *You shall observe the Sabbath as is proper, and the festivals and Day of Atonement* [literally, "Day of Self-Affliction"] *according to the teachings of the New Covenant.*

In the several decades leading up to Judah, as the Pharisees' social revolution gathered steam, an older, priestly understanding of the character of the Day of Atonement was brought forward to try to put the brakes to their momentum. This older view appeared in the book of *Jubilees,* a work that, as we have observed, was beloved of Judah and his movement. This book's understanding apparently became that of Judah's New Covenant as well. And what was that understanding? *Jubilees* conceived of the Day of Atonement as a day of mourning.

The day was instituted, the book asserted, to commemorate the occasion of Jacob's grief when he was told that Joseph had been torn to pieces by a wild beast. Genesis 37:34 says of his reaction: "And Jacob rent his garments, and put sackcloth upon his loins, and mourned for his son for many days." The Bible gives no date for this occasion and never links it to the Day of Atonement, but *Jubilees* did both:

> *This is why it is decreed that the people of Israel should afflict themselves on the tenth of the seventh month (on the day that the news which made him weep for Joseph came to his father Jacob), and that on it they should make expiation for themselves with a young goat—on the tenth of the seventh month, once a year, for their sin (for they had resented their father's affection for his son Joseph). And this day has been set apart so that on it they should grieve for their sins and for all their transgressions and for all their misdeeds, and so cleanse themselves, once a year, on that day.*[20]

Conceiving of the Day of Atonement as requiring mourning, Judah and his followers abstained from all food and drink, wept, and donned sackcloth. Probably they also afflicted their bodies with sleeplessness, preferring to read the scriptures, pray, and recite hymns day and night. They also may have stood on their feet continuously, thus exhausting themselves; diverse Jewish groups are known to have followed such customs.[21]

Pharisaic observance concurred with the priestly doctrine that one should fast on the Day of Atonement, but there agreement ceased. For the Pharisees, far from being a day of mourning, the Day of Atonement became a day of festivity, of music and merriment. This perspective lived on after the Pharisees in rabbinic circles. One famous rabbi, Rabban Shimeon ben Gamaliel, is said to have commented, "There were no more joyous days in Israel than the fifteenth of Ab and the Day of Atonement, on which the daughters of Jerusalem, garbed in white borrowed garments (so as not to shame the poor), would dance in the vineyards."[22]

Naphtali Wieder, writing about this changing conception of the Day of Atonement, noted:

> It is easy to picture in one's mind the striking contrast between worshippers cloaked in sackcloth and covered with ashes, worn out through lack of sleep and continuous standing, and fainting from loud and excessive weeping, on the one hand—and on the other, people dressed in white festive garments with the women wearing their precious ornaments and maidens and young men dancing and singing—a telling picture indeed of the wide gulf separating the two conflicting conceptions regarding the nature of the holiest day in the Jewish calendar.[23]

In reality the gulf was wider still. Judah, recall, urged a solar calendar that had developed among the priests, attacking the luni-solar calendar that the Pharisees championed. Now in exile, Judah was free to follow his calendar. It differed from the Pharisaic version used in Jerusalem, being longer by ten days a year. Over three years, the difference between the two calendars grew, from a single day in year one, month one, to thirty days by year three, month twelve. Then the two were reconciled but immediately began to diverge again. Accordingly, in 74 B.C.E. the celebration of the Day of Atonement in Jerusalem preceded that of Judah's group in the Land of Damascus by at least four days, and possibly by as many as twenty-four.[24]

It was these differences in the manner and timing of the day's observance that dictated Judah's enemies' strategy. The variation between the two calendars gave them enough time to celebrate in Jerusalem and still march to Judah's hideout in the Land of Damascus. All they needed was a guide to his whereabouts, and with the return of the apostates, they had even that.

JUDAH AND HIS FOLLOWERS had camped in a narrow ravine, possibly in one of the twisting basalt corridors that defined the rocky redoubt of Trachonitis. While they were praying, wailing, and confessing their sins, there suddenly appeared a military force led by Hyrcanus. The soldiers burst upon them, shouting and swinging their swords. Arrows rained down in deadly arcs.

So swift and unexpected was the attack that the women and children among Judah's group were caught up in the combat, helpless. The men were nearly as helpless, for they were unarmed. The Day of Atonement was, in biblical terms, a "Sabbath of Sabbaths." That meant that no work was allowed, and the use of weapons—even picking up and hurling stones—was defined by priestly convention as work.[25] Of course, Hyrcanus and his men knew they would catch Judah in this most vulnerable condition. That was the whole idea.

Judah's men, unarmed, exhausted from their self-afflictions, and paralyzed by shock and uncertainty, were no match for their merciless foes. Many of them fell where they had stood in prayer. The last sounds they ever heard were the dulcimer tones of lyres played by members of Hyrcanus's force. This was a cruel defilement of the sacred day's mourning, intended by its merrymaking to drive home Pharisaic legal dominance.

Somehow—and the sources are silent as to the method—Judah managed to escape. If the attack occurred in Trachonitis, the topography helps explain how that would be possible. Slipping between two boulders, diving into a hidden pocket—the region was a maze even for its regular inhabitants. Outsiders might as well be blind when it came to uncovering the places to hide. Others of Judah's faithful also got away in the confusion, but many women and children perished with their men in the slaughter.

Prominent in Hyrcanus's ranks were one or more of the first messiah's erstwhile allies. These were Judah's Judas, traitorous guides to his location without whom the attack would have been impossible. Guides offered the only hope of finding a person or place in Trachonitis. These men had probably purchased reentry into Jerusalem—and with it, perhaps, repossession of their forfeit property—with the information about Judah that they brought back with them.

Following the butchery, Hyrcanus and his force combed the vicinity looking for the first messiah. Judah had been their principal target. If his neck were allowed to slip from the noose, the battle could not be called a victory. Finally, frustrated and furious at their failure to kill the man who would be king, the high priest and his men turned and headed back to Jerusalem. They might hunt forever in the fast of Trachonitis and never track down the old priest. They consoled themselves that at least most of his group now constituted a problem solved.

Why did Hyrcanus attack? The probable answer is that he found out about Judah's most recent claims, particularly that Judah believed he would rule in Jerusalem. As we have noted earlier, this prophecy was yet undeclared at the time of Judah's trial. For the traitors, Judah had overstepped what they were willing to believe of him. So they returned to Jerusalem and offered to trade the rulers information for amnesty. Part of their information was Judah's prophecy of his own rule.

This was what Judah meant when he wrote, *They have traitorously gone to the children of destruction and defamed the mystery that You had hidden in me!* The *Damascus Document* described the same actions when it spoke of the apostates: *all the men who entered the New Covenant in the Land of Damascus, but then went back* [to Jerusalem], *and played the traitor, and so turned away from the fountain of living water* [Judah's laws]; these were the *warriors who went back to the Man of the Lie.*[26] The apostates went back, and several of the leaders offered their services to Shimeon ben Shetah and the Pharisee sage's royal backers, Hyrcanus and Alexandra.

The high priest and queen were happy to make the trade, for the information the priestly deserters offered was of great value. Judah had been permitted to go into exile rather than be stoned when he was a mere false prophet. But now he was something else: he openly preached sedition and spoke of becoming high priest and king. He had not learned his lesson. Judah was clearly unwilling to let well enough alone. This agitation, if allowed to spread, might spell disaster.

Certain circles in Jerusalem, the rulers knew, would turn a ready ear to Judah's ideas, if for no other reason than their unhappiness with the new regime. Matters were still sensitive. Provided with inspiring leadership, priestly circles might yet rally against the forcibly installed Pharisaic order. War could result. (These were not paranoid fears; in 67 B.C.E. precisely these things happened. But by then it was too late for Judah.)

Political unrest could be given no opportunity to breed. The capital punishment Judah had earlier been spared, Hyrcanus and the queen decided, would have to be carried out after all. They began to plan the attack.[27]

"HE WHO WALKS righteously and speaks what is right stops his ears from listening to the shedding of blood and shuts his eyes from seeing evil." So Judah knew from Isaiah 33:15, and so he cast himself as that righteous man and speaker of truth: *My eyes have grown weary of seeing evil, my ears from listening to the shedding of blood.* He ended his discourse as he had begun, deep in the trough of depression.

The attack had left him stunned, but even that reaction, he believed, had been ordained of old. He wrote, *I was struck dumb,* adopting the language of the Servant from Isaiah 53:7 (which he now knew referred to the attack): "He was oppressed and afflicted, yet he did not open his mouth; he was led like a lamb to the slaughter, and as a sheep before her shearers is *struck dumb,* so he did not open his mouth."

He found a further prediction of his situation and explanation of what it meant in Ezekiel 3:26: "I will make your *tongue cleave to the roof of your mouth* so that you will be *struck dumb* and unable to rebuke them, though they are a rebellious house."[28]

In this hymn Judah also quoted the first part of Ezekiel's verse: *I was dressed for mourning, and my tongue clove to the roof of my mouth.* His suffering was required by his God-given role, but it nevertheless drove him to a new strategy: silence. And even that strategy, he considered, was foreordained.

He would now be silent and cease to address himself in any way to the *rebellious house,* the leadership and people of Jerusalem. Yet members of his own group had likewise denied the truth. They, too, were part of that *rebellious house.* How could he be sure of any individual among the few scattered sheep that survived and with whom, regathered, he now huddled? He could not. With them, too, he now began a policy of selective silence, one they would resent.[29] From now on, the most explosive of his ideas Judah would keep to himself.

The attack drove Judah to retreat into himself, but it also drove him to discover more precisely what his role was to be and how his followers' destiny would unfold. A silent messiah? A messiah denied? Were these things really God's plan for him? Could it be that the messiah was to be secret all along?

Judah knew that God would tell him.

CHAPTER 8

THE SECRET
MESSIAH

Jesus asked them, "But who do you say that I am?" Peter answered
him, "You are the Messiah." And he sternly ordered them not to tell
anyone about him.

Mark 8:29–30

As JUDAH sat to write his eighth hymn, the utter depression that had
characterized much of the previous hymn lifted. He wrote with renewed confidence of his eventual, earthly vindication and of a future, glorious transformation into an eternal being of light. He made some truly
remarkable statements.

Now some two years into his exile, Judah lifted his eyes to a longer
horizon. He began to express a longer-range view. Thus his thoughts here,
and in the ninth hymn that he wrote somewhat later, devolved ever more
decisively upon his followers. He also reflected on his roots, thereby placing himself in a very particular historical context. In the ninth hymn Judah
spoke of both forerunners and followers.

OF ROOTS, SHOOTS, AND TREES:
THE PRECURSOR MOVEMENT

Millenarian movements typically issue from a social stream or continuity in
which appears over time a succession of prophetic figures. Thus Yali followed

Mambu in one particular region of Melanesia. Wovoka walked in the foot-steps of his father; Karl Schmid and his flagellants harked back to the move-ments of 1349; Jacob Querido, Baruchya Russo, Jacob Frank, and other Sabbatian prophets all saw themselves as finishing what Sabbatai Sevi had begun. Whole series of Islamic prophets frequently have emerged from Mus-lim brotherhoods and schools run by *hadjis* or mystics.[1]

The same was true in earlier Semitic culture. Judah had his origins in a school of wisdom teachers and mystics located in Jerusalem. Journey-ing to its porticoes, we will find his precursor movement. And at the head of their ranks we will find his precursor prophet—Judah's John the Baptist.

Judah's eighth hymn:

I thank You, O Lord, for You have upheld me by Your might and have poured out Your Holy Spirit within me so that I cannot falter. You have braced me for battles against wickedness, and in the midst of all their destruction You have not allowed me to become so terrified as to abandon Your covenant. You have made me like a mighty tower in a wall set on high. You have secured my frame on bedrock, laid eternal foundations for my support. All my walls are tested and cannot be shaken. You have given me as holy counsel to the weary. You have re[inforced m]e in Your covenant and emboldened my tongue according to Your teachings.

But the spirit of destruction has no mouth, the sons of shame possess no tongue capable of reply. Lying lips shall be struck dumb! Surely You shall ring in the guilty verdict against all my adversaries, and so by me separate the righteous from the wicked!

For it is You who know the intention of every created thing. You recognize the tongue capable of reply, and have firmly established me [in] Your teaching and truth. You have directed my steps aright to the paths of righteousness, so that I may walk in Your presence in the realm of [lif]e, on paths of glory and peace measure[less] and [un]ceasing forever. For You know Your servant's nature! I have certainly never relied up[on wealth or gain] and so become arroga[nt], secure in my own strength. I have no fleshly refuge, [for apa]rt from Your forgiveness, [human beings] lack the righteousness that delivers from s[in].

I have relied upon the abund[ance of Your compassion] and waited upon [the multitude of] Your acts of lovingkindness, so to bring the

*Tree to blossom, to raise the Shoot to maturity—secure in Your might
—and to [make the Branch fruitful. For it is by] Your righteousness
that You raised me up to establish Your covenant—and I have laid
hold of Your truth. Indeed You, [my God, have chosen me] and made
me a father to the pious—a guardian, as it were, to the men who are a
sign of things to come. They open their mouths like a suckl[ing at its
mother's breast.] They are like children who play in the embrace of
their foster father.*

*You shall exalt my horn above all who despise me; the remnant of
those who waged war against me and who prosecuted me shall be
scattered like chaff before the wind, and I shall rule over my house,
fo[r You], my [G]od, have helped me. Thereafter You shall exalt me on
high, and I shall blaze with a light of sevenfold brilliance by the very
lig[ht that] You have [es]tablished as Your glory. Surely it is You who
are my [et]ernal light; You have set my feet firmly on level ground
[for everlasting]!*[2]

And Judah's ninth hymn:

*I th[ank You, O Lord, for] You [s]et me at the source of streams in a dry
land, of gurgling springs in a parched land, irrigating the garden—
of po[ols] of wa[t]er [in] a field. You set me among a stand of cypress,
elm, and pine assembled for Your glory, trees of life alongside a secret
spring, hidden amidst all the well-watered trees. Their destiny was
to nourish a Shoot, which would become an eternal Tree, but if they
were to nourish it, they had first to take root, so they stretched forth
roots to the strea[m].*

*The Shoot's trunk also opened to the water of life, and it became an
eternal source of life. Every beast of the forest shall graze on the Shoot's
leafy branches; its trunk will be a gathering place for all passersby, its
foliage shelter every winged creature. All the well-watered trees may
tower above it, growing uncontrolled in their stand, but they have not
stretched forth their root to the stream.*

*Yet he who nurtures the holy Shoot to become a Tree of truth is himself
hidden, without esteem, unknown, his secret sealed up.*

*But You, O God, have protected his fruit with mysterious mighty
warriors, holy angelic spirits and a whirling flame of fire, so that no*

outsider may enter the fountain of life, or drink holy waters with the everlasting trees, lest his fruit blossom along with the [T]ree that reaches to the clouds. For he has seen, yet not recognized—considered, yet not believed in—the source of life. The eternal [sp]rout gives forth its produce, while I have become as torrents against those who despise me, flooding over when they spew their filth upon me.

For You, O God, have put Your words in my mouth like spring showers to satisfy all who un[derstand]—a fount of living water, and the heavens will never fail to pour forth. The showers will never depart, but will swell to a river overflowing its [ba]nks, becoming fathomless seas. Hidden in secret, they shall suddenly burst forth . . . becoming a fl[ood of] water [for every tree], both green and dry, and a lake for every beast and bir[d]. Then the [well-watered] trees [will sink] like lead in the mighty waters, [and be cast] into flaming fire and wither. The Tree will [produce] fruit, [and become an] eternal [source of life], a glorious and maj[estic] Eden [for everlasting.]

By my hand You have opened up its wellspring with all its channels. [You have planted i]t facing the true measuring line; the planting of its trees aligns with the plumb line of the sun . . . becoming glorious branches. When I extend my hand and dig out its channels, its roots stretch forth even into flinty rock and [it anchors] its trunk in the earth. Even in a season of heat it remains strong.

But were I to withdraw my hand, it would become like a bus[h in the wastelands], its trunk as nettles in a salt flat. Its channels would nourish only thorns and thistles, briars and weeds. [The trees] on the banks would become trees yielding bad fruit. In the heat its leaves would wither, unrenewed by [gushing] rain.

[As for me,] I sojourn with sickness and [my] heart is st[rick]en with afflictions. I am like a man forsaken in his anguish [and moan]ing. I have no strength left. Surely my afflictions have ripened into bitterness and incurable pain so that [strength] is gone! [My heart po]unds like those who descend to Sheol, and my spirit is adrift with the dead. My life draws near to Hell, and I waste away day and night without repose. My affliction spreads like a fire, a fire shut up in [my] bone[s]; the flame eats away until daybreak, exhausting my strength for celebrating ordained times, and spending my flesh before festivals.

Breakers have assailed me and I am cast down for annihilation. My strength has been cut off from my body; my heart flows like water and my flesh melts like wax. The strength of my loins has become trembling, my arm is broken from its joints; I cannot lift my hand. My feet are fettered, my knees are weak as water; I cannot take a step. When my leg summons my foot it does not move. My arms are shackled by chains of stumbling. Though You ceaselessly empower my tongue, I am unable to lift my voice, unable to proclaim the teachings that revive the stumbling spirit, unable to sustain the weary with a word. The flow of my lips has been struck dumb . . .

[For] breakers of death have [surrounded me], Sheol is upon my couch. My bed lifts its voice in lament, [my couch] its cry in mourning. My eye is like a moth in a kiln, my tears are as rivers of water; my eyes waste away for repose. My [strength] stands afar off, my life is distant.

Though I go from ruin to destruction, from pain to affliction, from agony to breakers—still shall I meditate on Your wonders. In Your lovingkindness You have not rejected me, so I shall delight in the abundance of Your mercy from one ordained time to the next. I shall reply to those who seek my destruction, and rebuke those who were ashamed of me. I shall condemn my judges, establish against them Your righteous judgment—for I know Your truth.

I have chosen my punishment. My afflictions actually please me, for I wait upon Your lovingkindness and You grant prayer to Your servant's mouth. You have not rejected me, neither deferred my well-being nor abandoned my hope. Before affliction You fortify my spirit—indeed, You established my spirit and know my every plan. In my distress You comfort me, and I take delight in Your forgiveness, consoled about former sin.

Indeed, I know there is hope only in Your lovingkindness, assurance only in Your abundant might! For none is justified when You sit to judge, none acquitted when You bring a case. One man may be more righteous, one person wiser [than] his fellow; one body may be more glorious than another of fl[esh], this spirit mightier than that—but none compares in might to Your power. Your glory is [fathomless], Your wisdom beyond measure; Your truth has [no equ]al, and apart from it is n[o deliverance]. I have hew[n out my step] by You, and my standing is [by Your lovingkindness. My enemies] do not pre[vail against me, nor] do my prosecutors . . .

You—because of [Your] many [acts of lovingkindness], my adversary will not prevail over me, to destroy me . . . [a]ll who waged war [against me, my prosecutors], will meet shame, and those who complained against me, disgrace. For You, My God . . . will prosecute my case against them.

Surely it was in Your mysterious wisdom that You rebuked me, as You have hidden the truth until the time ordained [for its revealing, and righteousness until] its appointed time. Your rebuke will become my joy and rejoicing, and my afflictions will become ever[lasting] healing and eternal [peace]. The scorn of my adversaries will become my glorious crown, and my calamity, eternal might. Indeed, [You have made Your] wisdom [known to me], and by Your glory has my light shone. For You have made the light to shine out of darkness, light[ing my] fa[ce and healing] my wound. In place of my stumbling is wondrous power, and the broad expanse displaces my confinement. Surely [You are my deliverer], my escape and refuge, my mighty rock and fortress. In You I trust at every agony, [for You] are my deliverance for everlasting!

Surely You knew me before my father begot me; [You set me apart] from the womb. I was yet [inside] my mother and You lavished kindness upon me; Your mercy came to me at my mother's breast, in the arms of my nursemaid [I received] Your [lovingkindness]. From my youth I perceived You in the wisdom of Your law. Your sure truth upheld me. You delight me by Your Holy Spirit, and still today You lead me. When I have [been per]verse, Your righteous reproof is there, and You deliver me by Your peace. Abundant forgiveness has accompanied my steps, and when You judge me it is with [me]rcy overflowing. Even in hoary age You provide for me. My father did not know me and my mother abandoned me to You, yet You are a father to all the children of Your truth. You rejoice over them like a mother over her infant, like a foster father over the baby in his arms. You provide for all Your creatures.

To find Judah's John the Baptist, we must analyze the first portion of Judah's ninth hymn, which has never been rightly understood. With that data in hand, we can turn for additional information to three passages in the *Damascus Document*. The combination of all these elements will unveil the precursors to Judah, as well as their leader.

The first messiah set down his thoughts in the ninth hymn in his usual allusive style:

> I thank You, O Lord, for You set me at the source of streams in a dry land, of gurgling springs in a parched land, irrigating the garden—of pools of water in a field. You set me among a stand of cypress, elm, and pine assembled together for Your glory, trees of life alongside a secret spring, hidden amidst all the well-watered trees. Their destiny was to nourish a Shoot, which would become an eternal Tree, but if they were to nourish it, they had first to take root, so they stretched forth roots to the stream.
>
> The Shoot's trunk also opened to the water of life, and it became an eternal source of life. Every beast of the forest shall graze on the Shoot's leafy branches; its trunk will be a gathering place for all passersby, its foliage shelter every winged creature. All the well-watered trees may tower above it, growing uncontrolled in their stand, but they have not stretched forth their root to the stream.[3]

The actors in Judah's complex minidrama are sometimes hard to separate and keep straight, but they were four in number: the prophet himself, the *trees of life*, the *well-watered trees*, and the *Shoot* that becomes an *eternal Tree*. Each of the actors had a particular role to play.

The *trees of life* were those among whom Judah grew to manhood and maturity; they were the *pools of water* in a *dry land*. He drew his imagery from Isaiah 41:18–19, which, of course, he understood as prophetic, Isaiah foreseeing Judah and his times (italics highlight words that Judah quoted):

> I will open up rivers on barren heights, and springs within the valleys. I will turn the desert into *pools of water,* and the *dry land* into springs. I will put in the desert the cedar and the acacia, the myrtle and the olive. I will set *cypress* in the wasteland, *the elm, and the pine together.*

These trees represented the remnant, those Jews who had remained true to God when the rest of the nation apostatized. They were water, the nation a dry land, a desert. That the *trees of life* were in essential continuity with the *Shoot* (Judah's present followers) is clear from the seamless segue of his hymn. He placed both under a single umbrella motif, "tree of life." Judah derived this image from Genesis 3:24, "[God] placed on the east side of the Garden of Eden cherubim and a *whirling, flaming* sword to guard the way to the *tree of life.*"

The priestly prophet alluded to other elements of Genesis 3:24 as well, constantly intertwining water imagery with that of trees: *But You, O God, have protected his [the Tree's] fruit with mysterious mighty warriors, holy angelic spirits, and a whirling flame of fire, so that no outsider may enter the fountain of life, or drink holy waters with the everlasting trees, lest his fruit blossom along with the Tree that reaches to the clouds.* With this imagery Judah shifted to what was his primary focus throughout the hymn, the second actor—the *Shoot*, and what it would become: *The Tree will produce fruit, and become an eternal source of life, a glorious and majestic Eden for everlasting.* This *Shoot* become *Tree* was nothing less than the Kingdom of God. (According to the Gospels, Jesus also likened the Kingdom to a tree.)

The function of the first actor, the *trees of life,* was to give the second actor, the *Tree,* its vital sustenance: *Their destiny was to nourish a Shoot.* The *Shoot/Tree* would arise from them but then outgrow them, reaching the heavens and leaving them behind.

Judah saw himself, the third actor, as one of the *trees of life* but also as distinct from them. Taking over where the other trees left off, he was the one directly responsible for bringing the *Tree* to maturity: *He who nurtures the holy Shoot to become a Tree of truth.*

As to the fourth actor: on one level Judah's *well-watered trees* represented the Jewish nation, and on another their false leaders, the Pharisees. He drew the image from Ezekiel 31:14, with a single interpretive stroke heralding the fate of these leaders and the unbelieving nation:

> Therefore no *well-watered trees* will ever tower proudly on high, and they shall not lift their tops among the *clouds.*[4] No *well-watered trees* are ever to reach such a height; they are all destined for death, for the earth below, among mortals, with those who go down to the Pit.

Though they now towered above the *Tree,* the *well-watered trees* were fated for destruction, implied Judah, because *they have not stretched forth their root to the stream.* What the *well-watered trees* would not do, the *trees of life* did: *they had first to take root, so they stretched forth roots to the stream.* Likewise, *the Shoot's trunk also opened to the water of life.*

As often in his hymns, Judah employed water imagery to symbolize truth, God's true laws—known already in germinal form in the time of the *trees of life* but now come in their glorious fullness to fertilize the *Shoot.* This fullness of the law was Judah's New Covenant; as he said in his sixth hymn, *You have actually fortified the secret truth within my mind—the water of the covenant for those who seek it.* Any refusing the New Covenant would perish; those who embraced it, live.

To summarize Judah's intricate scenario: the first messiah said that he had begun life among God's remnant, the *trees of life.* From that group emerged a related but not precisely identical entity, the *Shoot.* Judah's role was that of gardener, bringing the *Shoot* to mature form in the *Tree.* That would happen by means of his law, elements of which had evidently already been known to the *trees of life.*

Thus Judah was the person who would inaugurate the Kingdom of God, and as such he was the messiah, but he stood in continuity with both earlier and later recipients of God's blessing.

A similar scheme appears in the *Damascus Document,* but with an important difference. As Jesus spoke to the crowds only in parables, yet forswore allusion to speak to his disciples plainly, so the *Damascus Document* speaks plainly where Judah spoke in riddles. Thus it gives us more straightforward historical information than Judah did in his hymns, filling in the picture of the *trees of life,* the precursors.

From its descriptions we can isolate an earlier Jerusalem prophet.

T HE INITIAL PORTIONS of the *Damascus Document* have endured the ravages of time, but just barely. At the point where unbroken text survives and one can securely follow the thought, the work reads as follows:

> *Now listen, all you who recognize righteousness. Consider the deeds of God. For He has a case against all flesh, and shall execute judgment against all who spurn Him.*
>
> *When Israel abandoned Him by being faithless, He turned away from them and gave them up to the sword. But when He called to mind the covenant He had made with their forefathers, He left a remnant for*

Israel and did not allow them to be exterminated. In an era of wrath—
three hundred and ninety years after He had handed them over to the
power of Nebuchadnezzar, king of Babylon—He visited them and
caused to grow from Israel and Aaron the root of a Tree, destined to
inherit His land and grow fat on the good produce of His soil.

They understood their iniquity and knew they were guilty men. For
twenty years they became as blind men, like those groping for the way.
Then God considered their deeds, that they sought Him with a whole
heart, so He raised up for them a Teacher of Righteousness to make
them walk in the Way of His Heart.[5]

This portion of the *Damascus Document* launches one of three sermons that together comprise the section of the work called the Admonition. Here a wisdom teacher speaks, someone like Judah. Much of what is
said could even be the prophet's words. Yet the *Damascus Document* was
only composed after—and in light of—Judah's death.

At the Admonition's core probably lies Judah's public instruction.
These were the things he taught his disciples, whereas the Teacher Hymns
were his private meditations. Because of that connection, many of the terms
and ideas familiar from Judah's hymns naturally appear also in the *Damascus Document*. To this core of his public teaching, later followers added
substantial material in successive stages. Often it is difficult, sometimes
impossible, to peel the onion and separate the layers.

Whoever produced the *Damascus Document*'s final form, the message of the first sermon is clear. In the time just before Nebuchadnezzar
(586 B.C.E.), God turned against his people because they had abandoned
him. He determined to destroy the nation using foreign armies. Still, he
preserved a remnant. Three hundred and ninety years after the Babylonian
king Nebuchadnezzar killed or carried into exile many of the unfaithful, God
visited the remnant, composed of both laypeople (*from Israel*) and priests
(*and Aaron*).

This remnant the *Damascus Document* called *the root of a Tree*. The
Tree, the author parenthetically remarked, was *destined to inherit His land*
and grow fat on the good produce of His soil. The *root of the Tree* was more
righteous than the mass of the people, because those who belonged to the
root were penitent: they *knew they were guilty men*. For twenty years after
coming to exist as a group, they sought God but lacked a sufficient guide,

and so they *became as blind men, like those groping for the way.* Yet they were trying.

Recognizing their sincerity, God took pity on *the root of a Tree* and raised up for them a *Teacher of Righteousness.* This man revealed to them what they had been groping to find, the *Way of God's Heart.* The latter phrase was, of course, Judah's own name for the teachings of his New Covenant.

The *Damascus Document*'s representation of the *dramatis personae* is fully consonant with Judah's veiled description in the ninth hymn. The precursor group, called in his hymn the *trees of life,* are here designated *the root of a Tree.* That is, they were not the *Tree* itself, but from them the *Tree* emerged. The *Tree* figures in both narratives and represents Judah's follow- ers, both as they are in the present and as they will be in the future when in their maturity they take power and the Kingdom has come. The boundary between the present and future forms is virtually nonexistent and is not drawn distinctly even in Judah's hymns—though he tended to call the pres- ent followers the *Shoot (netser)* and the future, vastly expanded nation of those who believed in him the *Tree.*

Judah's *well-watered trees* stand in the background in the *Damascus Document* presentation, where they are never called by any name other than *Israel.* In the *Damascus Document, Israel* designates both those destroyed in the time of Nebuchadnezzar and the disbelievers of the time of the *root.* Judah himself is here the *Teacher of Righteousness.* It was he who guided the blind gropers into all the truth.

What does this first sermon of the *Damascus Document* tell us? It tells us that the precursor group comprised both laypeople and priests, thereby implying—given what we know of social prestige in the Judaea of those years—that it was a priest-led movement. It tells us that the move- ment existed for twenty years as a social force before Judah came on the scene. This number is not schematic. It can probably be taken as rounded off but more or less precise.[6]

The entire *Damascus Document* is a retrospective and selective por- trait by Judah's later followers. They regarded their forebears as we might a partly cloudy day: there was much to appreciate, but still, there were the clouds. To Judah's followers, the precursor movement had known some of the truth but was clouded by error.

The precursors themselves would doubtless have taken a different view of matters.[7]

A PASSAGE FROM a second sermon in the *Damascus Document* reca-
pitulates certain ideas about the precursors that appear in the first sermon and in Judah's hymn, and it furnishes further important details:

> *In the time of destruction of the land [586 B.C.E.] the Boundary-*
> *Shifters appeared and led Israel astray and the land was devastated, for*
> *they had spoken rebellion against the commandments of God given*
> *through Moses and also through those anointed by the Holy Spirit*
> *[i.e., the Prophets]; and they prophesied falsehood to turn Israel from*
> *following God. But God called to mind the covenant of the*
> *forefathers; and He raised up from Aaron men of understanding and*
> *from Israel wise men, and He taught them and they dug the Well of*
> *which Moses spoke, "the well the princes dug, the nobility of the*
> *people dug it with a staff" (Numbers 21:18).*
>
> *The Well is the Law, and its "diggers" are the repentant of Israel who*
> *went out of the Land of Judah and sojourned in the Land of Damascus,*
> *all of whom God called Princes because they sought Him, and not a*
> *single mouth denied their honor. And the Staff is the Interpreter of the*
> *Law of whom Isaiah said, "God fashions a staff fit for His work" (Isaiah*
> *54:16). The "nobility of the people" are those who came to sink the*
> *Well, using the laws that the Staff inscribed for them to follow during*
> *the entire wicked age (and apart from those laws, none would succeed)*
> *until there should arise in the Latter Days the Teacher of*
> *Righteousness.*[8]

Like the first sermon, this one describes the land's destruction by
Nebuchadnezzar because of general rebellion, and it notes God's designation of a remnant. But in contrast to the first sermon, here the author skips
over the centuries after Nebuchadnezzar and jumps right to the remnant,
the precursors of Judah's movement: *He raised up from Aaron men of under-*
standing and from Israel wise men.

The boundary between the precursors and Judah's own followers is
hard to distinguish in this sermon. That fact is significant in itself. Despite
the effort that the *Damascus Document* makes to distance its own group
from the precursors, it was hard to do because they were very much alike.
Like Judah himself, the precursors received special instruction from God,

so fulfilling—according to the sermon—a prophecy from the book of Numbers. They received true Law, symbolized by a watery image, the *Well*.

The author then begins to backtrack, starting with the more recent past, then receding to the more distant.

More recently, emerging from the precursors to go into exile, *the repentant of Israel* had done some digging in the Land of Damascus. These people were Judah's original followers, the ones who left Jerusalem with him. They flourished at least one or perhaps two generations before the author of this layer of the *Damascus Document*. He focuses on the honor due them as the founders: *not a single voice denied their honor.*[9] The designation of this group (*shave Yisrael*) derived from Judah's own phrase for his followers, used in the first hymn and elsewhere: *those who repent of sin (shave pesha)*.

Then the author steps further back in time and introduces a figure he calls the *Staff*.

The *Staff* was a person of great importance, for his role, even as Judah's own, had been forecast by Isaiah: *God fashions a staff fit for His work*. The strange name is not an actual birth name, of course, but a pun. The Hebrew for *Staff* can also be translated "Lawgiver," and the double entendre was intentional. The Staff was a foundational figure. He was a prophet who had received revelation from God.

The Staff was Judah's John the Baptist.

His followers, *the nobility of the people,* were the precursors from whom Judah's immediate disciples eventually emerged. They followed the *laws* given by the *Staff,* laws so important that without them even a partial knowledge of God was impossible: *and apart from those laws, none should succeed*. The first sermon had described these same people less positively: *They understood their iniquity and knew they were guilty men. For twenty years they became as blind men, like those groping for the way*.

The *Staff*'s laws had been superseded only by Judah's own: *until there should arise in the Latter Days the Teacher of Righteousness*. What follows immediately after this passage of the *Damascus Document* is in fact Judah's laws in précis, his Ten Commandments, which we met in chapter 2.[10]

The Staff passage in the *Damascus Document* is difficult and has given rise to diverse explanations by scholars. But the present analysis finds support in yet a third parallel portion of the *Damascus Document*. Comparing the pattern in these three passages eases the difficulties in each, for the repetition clarifies uncertain details.

Following the scheme we have come to expect, after detailing a history of Israel's unfaithfulness to God, this third sermon goes on to isolate the remnant:

> But with those of them who remained, who held firm to the commandments of God, He instituted His covenant with Israel forever, revealing to them things hidden, in which all Israel had gone wrong: His holy Sabbaths, His glorious festivals, His righteous laws and truthful ways, His pleasing sacrifices—"which, if a man do, he shall live" (Leviticus 18:5). He opened up before them and they dug a Well, yielding much water. Those who reject this water shall not live.

> But as for them, they wallowed in human sin and ways of impurity, all the while saying, "Surely the covenant is ours." Nevertheless, God in His mysterious ways atoned for their iniquity and forgave their sin. And He built for them a faithful House in Israel, whose like never appeared before or since, to this very day. Those who hold firm to it shall receive everlasting life. All the glory of Adam is rightly theirs.[11]

This version of the story, by explaining what the rest of Israel did wrong, tells us plainly what the remnant precursors did right.

They were right about a whole list of fundamentals: statutes for the Sabbath, sundry laws regulating the biblical festivals such as the Day of Atonement, Temple sacrifices, and in general God's *truthful ways*. By stating that they rightly celebrated the festivals, the author implies that the forerunners at least acknowledged the proper calendar.

The list of fundamentals is an allusion to a passage in *Jubilees*, the work that we met earlier and that Judah and his followers treasured. *Jubilees* is a polemical pseudepigraph featuring an Angel of the Presence, whom it portrays as addressing Moses on Sinai, "predicting the future" (including details about the actual second-century B.C.E. author's present). The work claims to reveal secret laws that Moses kept from Israel at the time of their original revelation. Only now, says the book, can these secrets be known.

The underlined words of the Jubilees passage below are those that appear in the *Damascus Document* summary:

*They will be captured and fall into the hand of the enemy because
they will have abandoned My <u>laws</u> and My <u>commandments</u>, the
<u>festivals</u> of My <u>covenant</u>, My <u>Sabbaths</u> and My <u>holy things</u> [i.e.,
sacrifices] that they will have sanctified to Me among them, My
tabernacle and My Temple that I shall have sanctified to Myself in
the land by placing My name upon it.*[12]

By alluding to this list, the *Damascus Document* linked the precursors to the book of *Jubilees*, essentially saying that they were privy to its secret revelations, knew its many laws, and fulfilled some of its "predictions." This statement ties in with the earlier portion from the second sermon, which was less specific about the content of the precursors' laws but more specific about their source: the Staff. Putting the passages together shows that the writers of the *Damascus Document* saw a connection between the laws of *Jubilees* and the Staff.

More specifics on the relation between Judah's own laws and those of the *Staff* emerge from something else the third sermon says: *But as for them, they wallowed in human sin and ways of impurity.* The precursors, gropers for the way, knew some laws but were blindly ignorant of others. Their lawbreaking occurred because of that blindness.

Their ignorance, says the text, involved two distinct elements: *human sin (pesha)* and *ways of impurity (niddah)*. These were therefore the leaks in the legal dike; these were the places where Judah made his repairs. The wording recalls Zechariah 13:1, "In that day a <u>fount</u> shall be <u>opened</u> for the House of David and those who dwell in Jerusalem, in respect both to *sin (hattat,* a synonym of *pesha)* and to *impurity (niddah)."* Recall that Judah saw himself in this very verse of Zechariah and wove it into the composition of his first hymn: *You placed insight in my heart whereby to <u>open</u> the <u>fount</u> of knowledge.*

The synonyms for sin, *hattat* and *pesha,* are too general to permit us to dig out any legal specifics, but *niddah* is more yielding. In the legal parlance of the Hebrew Bible, the type of impurity called *niddah* refers to things such as illicit sexual intercourse, laws of menstruation, and defilement caused by contact with a corpse.[13] All had repercussions for Temple purity.

According to the *Damascus Document,* then, these specific types of impurity were the areas Judah's laws addressed that the *Staff's* laws had neglected. Not by coincidence, the sermons of the *Damascus Document* highlight several examples of just such laws. These laws almost certainly go back to Judah's own teaching.[14]

Where the first sermon says: *Then God considered their deeds, that they sought him with a whole heart, so He raised up for them a Teacher of Righteousness to make them walk in the Way of His Heart,* the present portion parallels, *God in His mysterious ways atoned for their iniquity and forgave their sin. And He built for them a faithful House in Israel, whose like never appeared before or since, to this very day.*[15] The author would not have described any movement flawed by *human sin and ways of impurity* as a *faithful House* enduring to his own day. Hence, the *faithful House* cannot refer to the precursor movement as such; it refers only to the offshoot, the believers cultured by the perfecting work of the Teacher, Judah.

As Jesus is pictured in the Gospels as building on a foundation laid by John the Baptist, so years earlier the first messiah, Judah, brought to perfection the work begun by a still earlier precursor figure, the Staff.

What then can we say about Judah's precursor, his John the Baptist, the Staff?

T HE STAFF PREPARED the way for Judah. Judah's second-generation followers could not deny this truth. It spawned for them, as a similar fact later did for the disciples of Jesus, an awkward problem: Was the earlier man the greater? The ancient world gave all honor to the founders of movements and philosophic schools. "Shall the student be greater than the master?" Jesus himself is quoted as asking. Before the followers of Jesus confronted this dilemma, Judah's met it head-on. They acknowledged the Staff's importance yet argued the inadequacy of his laws. This strategy was not intended merely to reassure themselves. The message of the *Damascus Document* was purposely crafted to address an audience that included followers of the Staff.

When Judah's crisis cult was born, the precursor movement did not thereby cease to exist, any more than did John the Baptist's followers disperse with the birth of the Jesus movement. Though Judah had lived among the precursors for many years, though he was their self-described leading light, in the crisis of 76 B.C.E. the first messiah drew after him only some of the earlier group. The majority remained behind.

The precursor movement was thus alive and well when the *Damascus Document* was composed. Its leaders, rather than follow Judah, had

adopted an alternate strategy for overthrowing the Pharisees and reinstitut-
ing priestly Temple laws, one that for a time was much more successful.[16]
When that success proved short-lived, they in turn proved ready to consider the "Gospel of Judah" presented in the *Damascus Document.*

The following facts about the Staff seem secure. He was the original
founder of the movement from which Judah emerged, the foremost among
Judah's *trees of life.* He catalyzed a movement around himself by promul-
gating laws that addressed Sabbath observance, proper methods of Temple
sacrifice, and the observance of Israel's holy festivals. Judah and his later
followers conceded that the Staff's laws on these fundamental points were
correct. They themselves followed them and used them to evolve new legislation.

The Staff had embraced the proper calendar, though he was not its
originator. Its origins were much older. Within the precursor movement he
probably bore the title "Interpreter of the Law." Since after Judah's death
his own movement designated leaders by that same title, it was probably
the ready-made name of an older, traditional office, borne by the foremost
intellectual in the Staff's Jerusalem wisdom school, whoever he might be at
any given time.[17] Judah himself, following in the footsteps of the Staff, had
doubtless once occupied this position.

The Staff had flourished some twenty years before Judah's own rise to
leadership. So when did the precursor movement begin? Though certainty is
impossible, approximation is not (granting a few reasonable assumptions).

In years to come, Judah's movement would require that a man assume no position of command or leadership until he was at least thirty years
old. If we stipulate that Judah, brilliant as he was, came to lead his movement shortly after that minimum age; and if we recall that in the mid–70s
B.C.E. the prophet described himself as aged; and if we factor in the "forty
years" that the *Damascus Document,* in its schematized view of history, assigned to Judah's ministry (the number really meant "a generation"), we arrive at a date of about 110–105 B.C.E. for Judah's rise to preeminence.[18]

Subtracting twenty years from Judah's rise brings us to 130–125
B.C.E. This was when the Staff strode onto the stage of history. He stirred
up a following that included both priests and laypeople. These were the
early years of Hyrcanus I (ruled 135/134 to 104 B.C.E.), and this was as far
back as Judah's movement later traced its origins.[19]

By the time that Judah assumed leadership, the Staff's movement
had already become a political force. That inference follows from Judah's

situation at the Pharisee takeover in 76 B.C.E. He was a threat to the Pharisees, important enough for them to want to destroy him. Head of his school, Judah had been a confidant of Alexander. He and his peers were comfortable in the corridors of power, at home in elite circles. How else could they have dared to pressure the new high priest, Hyrcanus II, on Temple policy (MMT)? For such political involvement a foundation must be laid. That takes time.

The Sadducee-dominated coalition to which Judah and his priestly peers belonged had coalesced in the last years of Hyrcanus I, just before Judah rose to prominence.[20] Though Josephus portrays it as dominated by the Sadducees, the coalition embraced other priestly groups. It counted as its own many of the elite priestly families. The coalition included the Staff and the precursor movement.

It was the Staff who laid the first course of bricks for Judah's superstructure. In terms of influence, therefore, he was a major factor in Jewish history of the second century B.C.E. And the Staff certainly satisfies the definition of a prophet: about 130 B.C.E. he brought a new revelation, one related somehow to the book of *Jubilees,* a message from God that told the people where they were going wrong. A crisis cult formed with him as the nucleus. Then, twenty years later, a new prophet arose, Yali to the Staff's Mambu: Judah. He redefined the myth-dream as he received it from the Staff and eventually took the crucial step and crossed the boundary into messianism.

Prophet though he was, the Staff was fated for the shadow realm of Lethe, in whose darkness is shrouded almost all of humanity's past. One branch of Judaism did remember for a time that he had lived and taught, though no one ever bothered, so far as we know, to record his real name. Then the very fact of his existence slipped from human memory.

Nevertheless, a distant, very faint echo, his influence presses itself upon us still.

For in history it is often true that behind the profound lies the obscure. Consider: if the Staff had never been, Judah could not have been the first messiah. And if Judah had not been what he was, had not lived the first messianic life, then the myth-dream of Israel would have been something different—perhaps much different—when a young carpenter from Nazareth began to give it new voice. Had that been the case, then the message of that carpenter could not have invoked the precise combination of elements that it did.

And absent that precise combination of elements, what might the Jesus movement have become—and what might have become of it?

"THE DESTINY OF MEN"

In the Wilderness of Damascus, Judah faced a problem. Perhaps it was his disciples who first broached the question, with tremulous voices and downcast eyes. Perhaps Judah came to realize the need for an answer himself, as a result of his own inner wrestling with repeated setbacks.

The question was this: If Judah were indeed who he said he was— the man to raise the curtain on the millennium, the magnetic North of the Prophets of Israel, foreseen and predestined to his role a thousand years before his birth, the climactic personality of all history—then why did so few recognize him?

Judah's answer came straight from the Servant Songs of Isaiah. *He who nurtures the holy Shoot to become a Tree of truth is himself hidden, without esteem, unknown, his secret sealed up,* he wrote in his final hymn. This was an expression of the theme of nonrecognition, basic to the biblical portrait of God's Servant: "He was despised, and we did not esteem him," Isaiah had said. "He had no form or majesty that we should look at him, nothing in his appearance that we should desire him."[21]

In short, Judah came to believe that the nation had refused him because that was the way God had always planned it. He was the messiah, but he was also a secret. Soon would come the denouement. The Jews would recognize their error and Judah for who he was. Until then he would remain, as Sabbatai Sevi centuries later, in "occultation." Judah had already adumbrated this doctrine in his fifth hymn: *Surely they will not esteem me until You manifest Your mighty power through me.*[22]

The idea that when he came the messiah would go unrecognized until God explicitly made him manifest became thereafter a stanchion of the myth-dream of Israel. One of the latest of the Enoch writings, the *Similitudes of Enoch*—composed perhaps a generation after Judah, shortly after 40 B.C.E.—said of its messianic figure, "He was chosen and hidden before Him before the world was created, and forever. But the wisdom of the Lord of Spirits has revealed him to the holy and the righteous." Elsewhere the same work added, "And the kings and the mighty and all who possess the earth, will praise and bless and exalt him who rules everything which is hidden. For from the beginning the Son of Man was hidden, and the Most High kept him in the presence of His power, and revealed him only to the Elect."[23] Judah, too, was only known to his followers, the Elect.

Another apocalyptic writing originating in very different circles, *Fourth Ezra*—composed, says scholarly consensus, in the late first century C.E.—also played on the theme of the hidden messiah. In this work, God explains to a visionary who writes in the name of Ezra: "Just as no one can explore or know what is in the depths of the sea, so no one on earth can see My son or those who are with him, except when his time and his day have come." Some fifty years later, the early Christian apologist Justin Martyr reported hearing the same general idea from the mouth of Trypho, a Jew with whom he conducted an extensive dialogue. Trypho argued against Jesus as the messiah on the grounds that "The messiah, if he had been born and was anywhere, would be unknown. Even he would not know for certain that he was himself the messiah until Elijah should come, anoint him and make him manifest to everyone."[24]

Some scholars believe that the idea of the hiddenness of the messiah also explains a variety of vexed problems in the Gospel accounts of Jesus.[25] For example, the repeated commands of Jesus reported in the Gospel of Mark, to the effect that his disciples should keep to themselves what they have seen him do and heard him say (in spite of clouds of witnesses)—the so-called "Markan Secret"—seems to be related to this idea.

Judah was the first messiah. He was likewise the first hidden messiah. Before him, so far as we have evidence, the tenet did not exist. After him, diverse types of Judaism embraced it. Here as in so much else, the first messiah fed the myth-dream and defined for the Jews what *messiah* was to mean.

O NE OF THE TRULY remarkable statements that Judah made in his writings appears in the eighth hymn. Here he wrote, *You shall ring in the guilty verdict against all my adversaries, and so by me separate the righteous from the wicked!* According to their reaction to him, Judah maintained that first the Jewish nation, then all humankind, would be judged. Through him *(by me,* Hebrew *bi),* God would separate the wheat from the chaff. To refuse Judah's teaching was to throw in one's lot with the wicked and so go to Hell.

This was certainly what Judah's followers understood him to mean. The *Commentary on Habakkuk* said as much when explaining Habakkuk 2:4:

["But the righteous live by their faith."]

Its true import concerns all the Doers of the Law in the House of Judah, whom God will deliver from damnation because of their true works and faith in the Teacher of Righteousness.[26]

This same verse in Habakkuk was later to prove central in the thought of the apostle Paul, who gave it his own interpretation in the book of Romans: "For I am not ashamed of the gospel; it is the power of God for salvation to everyone who has faith, to the Jew first and also to the Greek. For in it the righteousness of God is revealed through faith for faith; as it is written, 'The righteous live by their faith.' " For Paul, Habakkuk 2:4 meant that faith, not works of the Law, was the basis for salvation. For Judah's followers, works of the Law were inseparable from faith, and that Law was defined by Judah's revelations.

Therefore, only those who entered Judah's New Covenant and practiced its teachings, so producing *true works,* would be saved. Further, they believed, one must have *faith in the Teacher of Righteousness.* This phrase meant that one must receive his revelations as true, which entailed unwavering conviction of his role as peerless mediator between God and humanity.

Fearing that the uniqueness of Jesus might somehow be compromised, many scholars have labored to distinguish the *Commentary's* concept *have faith in* (Hebrew *heemin be*) from what later Christians came to hold of Jesus. Representative are the words of William Brownlee: "Faith in him [the Teacher of Righteousness] is not due to his personal righteousness, but to the rightness of his teaching, which if followed will bring salvation. . . . This contrasts sharply with faith in Christ as a redemptive figure."[27] The Christians' basis of salvation, these scholars argue, was the person of Jesus, not his teaching; salvation would come because of his act of redemption at the cross, as a substitute sacrifice on behalf of believers.

The contrast that Brownlee and others urge is valid in itself but rather fine-tuned; it can easily sponsor an exaggerated sense of the difference between Judah's role and that of Jesus. For one thing, a survey of the biblical use of Hebrew *heemin be,* "have faith in," shows that when it is used positively the reference is always to God or, much less often, his spokes-men Moses and the prophets.[28] Thus one trusts God either directly or through his representatives, and that trust is redemptive. A good example is 2 Chronicles 20:20: "Listen to me, people of Jerusalem! Have faith in YHWH your God and you will be upheld; have faith in his prophets and you will be successful." This verse parallels faith in the prophets with faith in God. The practical equivalence is clear. Ultimately God is always the re-deemer. The Christian faith in Jesus is but a variation on this greater theme, for as orthodoxy developed Christians came to believe that Jesus was God.

Yet among the early Christians this orthodox notion was only one way of viewing Jesus. There were others; it is important to remember that Christianity in the first century C.E. was a Jewish movement and no more monolithic than was Judaism more generally. In this historical context the argument scholars such as Brownlee make is anachronistic. Their distinc-tion is that of academic theology, divorced from the social realities of at least some early Christian communities. Are we really to imagine that early Christians denied Jesus' teachings an intrinsic role in the salvation he was thought to bring? How could that be, when teachings such as the Sermon on the Mount defined life in the Kingdom, and life in the Kingdom was it-self an aspect of salvation?

Many Jewish Christians, in particular, saw the issue of good works differently than did the Pauline Christianity that Brownlee is representing. As with Judah's followers, for these Christians good works were an inextri-cable part of salvation, the proof of conversion. The Jewish-Christian book of James, for example, seems to argue against the Pauline notion, conclud-ing, "You see that a person is justified by works and not by faith alone" (James 2:4).

Judah claimed to be, and was received by his followers as, a redeemer figure no less than Jesus. Within the religious system each established they were functional equivalents, though the modalities differed. Neither sys-tem was possible without the central, charismatic revealer of the way to sal-vation. And both were exclusive: Judah claimed that God would divide all humanity into two camps using him. The Gospel of John proclaimed the same of Jesus: "I am the Way, the Truth and the Life; no one comes to the Father but through me" (John 14:6).

In the words of two prominent New Testament experts, "Jesus him-self lived in the categories of the Old Testament, which is the record of the great acts of God in history; he was aware that he himself was the greatest act of God in history; in him and by him the destiny of men would stand and fall."[29] If Jesus actually thought such things—and to my mind he did, though many modern scholars question or deny it—he was not unique in those thoughts.

Judah had thought them first.

DEATH OF A MESSIAH

Judah privately expressed a powerful conviction in his coming vindication in his eighth hymn with statements such as, *You shall exalt my horn above all who despise me; the remnant of those who waged war against me and who prosecuted me shall be scattered like chaff before the wind, and I shall rule over my house.* He must have expressed similar sentiments to his small group of remaining followers when he taught them publicly. We can therefore scarcely imagine the force of the blow to all their hopes when the first messiah died—or, more probably, was killed.

Two passages in the *Damascus Document* mention Judah's death explicitly but say nothing about how it happened. These portions look back on Judah's demise from a distance, as a fact; they are not commenting on the death itself. They nevertheless yield crucial information. To bring this information to the fore, a third passage of the *Damascus Document* must be considered alongside them (underlines show connections):

> *When this foreordained period is complete, <u>according to the number of these years</u>, there will be no further need to be connected to the House of Judah, but instead each will stand on his own tower: "the wall is built, the boundary removed" (Micah 7:11) . . . And <u>during all these years</u> Belial will be loosed in Israel.*

> *So also is the judgment against all the men who entered the New Covenant in the Land of Damascus but then returned (to Jerusalem) and traitorously turned away from the Well of Living Water. They shall not be reckoned among the Council of the People, and their names shall not be written in their Book, <u>from the day</u> that the <u>Teacher of the Yahad was gathered</u> to his fathers <u>until</u> there appears the Messiah of Aaron and Israel.*

> Now *from the day* that the <u>Teacher of the Yahad was gathered</u> to his
> fathers <u>until</u> the perishing of all the warriors who went back to the
> Man of the Lie will be <u>about forty years</u>. And <u>during that foreordained
> period</u> God's anger will burn against Israel.[30]

The idiom these passages use for Judah's death is the biblical expression, "gathered to his fathers." It tells us nothing about the manner of death, for biblical usage applies the idiom to violent and peaceful passings alike.[31] But taken together, the *Damascus Document* passages reveal more than a first reading may suggest.

They focus on a foreordained period when Satan will be given free rein, when he will be—as the New Testament says—the Prince of This World. The *Damascus Document* implies that the concept of this period was well known, because it could be referred to without particulars or explanation, simply as *these years*.

Yet twice the *Damascus Document* does define the period more fully, and it is precisely here that it speaks of Judah's death. His death was a signal, a landmark on the march of history toward its predetermined ends. On both occasions the work uses Judah's death as part of a bracketing for the phrase *these years*. The death serves as an element in two "from . . . until" statements.

At the near or "from" end stood the recognized event, Judah's demise. At the far end—the "until" end—it was prophesied that the Messiah of Aaron and Israel would come. This was a figure in whom Judah's movement later came to believe. Indeed, while in his time they believed only in him, they later came to embrace a theory of multiple messiahs, still including him.[32]

The *Damascus Document* says that the bracketed period's total length will be *about forty years*. This was the era during which God's wrath would spend itself on the nation. During this time no apostate could return to the group. The period was also the author's present. But why the imprecise number? Why "about" forty years?

Historians usually despise imprecise numbers, but this one is different. This one is welcome, for it conceals a precious datum about Judah's death.

To understand the point, we must step back for a moment and canvass the ideology of the *Damascus Document,* some of which is already familiar. Because Israel has disobeyed God's commandments, it argues, God has a legal case against it. Only a remnant has remained faithful to him.

This remnant will one day inherit the land, but for now the land's inhabitants are mainly those whom God has rejected. The remnant does not yet have the land and so is in exile.[33]

The remnant was Judah's movement. They believed themselves to be "in exile," a notion whose genesis was the literal exile of Judah and his first followers. After Judah's death, under the pressure to reinterpret prophecy and so avoid disconfirmation, the literal seed had grown into a pattern, a typology. The genesis had become an exodus.

The typology equated the movement's present situation with that of Israel wandering in the wilderness, waiting to enter Canaan, the Promised Land—waiting, like Judah's followers, to inherit the land. Based on this equation, salient details of the original exile to Egypt and, especially, the subsequent Exodus to the land were reapplied to the new situation. And one of those details was length.

The length of the wilderness wandering was forty years. Forty years, therefore, became the time "in the wilderness" for Judah's followers; it was the length of *these years* in the *Damascus Document,* the time they had to wait before receiving their inheritance—power. The *Commentary on Psalms* that we have met earlier explicates this doctrine while annotating a biblical portion: "Its true import concerns all wickedness at the end of *the forty years,* for it shall be blotted out and no wicked man will be found in the land." That the author wrote *the forty years* (not merely *forty years*) proves that this chronology was a well-rehearsed teaching.[34]

Consider in that light the following comparison, which puts one of the *Damascus Document* portions alongside its informing biblical passage (italics mark key phrases):

> *For forty years* the children of Israel traveled in the wilderness, *until the perishing of all* the people, *the warriors who* came out of Egypt who did not listen to the voice of YHWH. (Joshua 5:6)
>
> Now from the day that the Teacher of the Yahad was gathered to his fathers *until the perishing of all the warriors who* went back to the Man of the Lie will be *about forty years.* (*Damascus Document*)[35]

The original Israelite warriors perished in the wilderness because they refused to believe that God would give them the Promised Land. They trembled with fear after they had spied out its giant inhabitants. Consequently, God refused them entry and waited until the next generation, as the biblical narratives tell the story, before permitting Israel into Canaan.

In the *Damascus Document* typology, the apostates from Judah are equated with these unbelieving warriors, since both failed to "listen to the voice of YHWH." What is striking in the comparison of these passages that share so much language is the difference of time: *forty years* in Joshua becomes *about forty years* in the *Damascus Document*.

The reason for the difference is not hard to find. Joshua's narrative was counting all the time spent in the wilderness, whereas the *Damascus Document* count began only with Judah's death (*from the day that the Teacher of the Yahad was gathered to his fathers*). The latter number was naturally lower, since Judah did go into exile with his followers. Judah was there at the beginning of the forty years. Therefore, to count from his death as the *Damascus Document* did, one had to subtract the time Judah was with the exiles.

Yet even after subtracting this time, the book still described the exile's span as nearly forty years.

One can only conclude that Judah died relatively soon—within, say, two or three years—after the exile began. Otherwise the *Damascus Document* would have specified "about thirty-five years" or "about thirty years" or some other appropriate number. Even after Judah's death, the figure was still nearest forty.

Since the Pharisees came to power with Alexandra in 76 B.C.E., and within a short time—two years, maybe less—matters in Jerusalem came to a head with Judah's trial, he must have been exiled by 75 or 74 B.C.E. Two or three years later he was dead.

Elsewhere the *Damascus Document* tells us something else about the circumstances of Judah's death, something crucial, but almost in a whisper. It addresses the subject only obliquely, quietly, even furtively. And it mentions no names.

WE SAW IN THE last chapter that Judah portrayed himself as the biblical Good Shepherd. He did that partially on the basis of the prophet Zechariah, where he found predictions both of his covenant and of his follower's apostasy (Zechariah 11:4–11).

In a section later consciously removed—censured by excision—the earliest level of the *Damascus Document* presupposed the identification of Judah as the Shepherd and interwove two other Zechariah passages about that figure into a prophecy of judgment:

And all who reject the commandments and the laws will suffer the recompense of the wicked when God visits the earth, when the word spoken through Zechariah the prophet is fully complete: "O sword, awake and smite My Shepherd and the man loyal to Me," says God. "Strike down the Shepherd and the sheep will scatter; but I will draw back My hand from the Oppressed" (Zechariah 13:7). "Those who obeyed him" (Zechariah 11:11b)—they are "the oppressed of the sheep" (Zechariah 11:11a). They will escape in the time of visitation, but all the rest will be handed over to the sword.[36]

The purpose of the author of the *Damascus Document* at this juncture is to reassure believers while threatening outsiders. Only believers will be saved when, at the end of the forty years, God visits the earth for judgment. All unbelievers, Jew and Gentile, will be *handed over to the sword*. The image of the sword looms large in this vision. Indeed, the two-edged thrust of the passage concerns whom the sword will strike and whom it will spare.

The *word spoken through Zechariah* has already begun to be fulfilled but is not yet complete. It will be complete only when God visits the earth. The word involves smiting. Thus, of the three characters in this scenario, one—the Shepherd—has already been smitten, because the sheep—the second character—have been scattered as a result. This is their present condition. They (the author and his companions) are scattered, weak, fearful. Yet God has drawn back his hand before striking them, too. They are the *Oppressed*. The third character, *the wicked*, will yet be smitten. Thus the sword runs throughout the passage, and its action is what makes the plot cohere.

The *him* of the phrase *those who obeyed him* is the Shepherd of Zechariah 11:11. The biblical verse is in the first person: "So it was annulled that day, and the oppressed of the sheep, *who obeyed me*, knew that it was the word of YHWH." By the *Shepherd* the *Damascus Document* means Judah, giver of the *commandments and laws* whose rejection was fatal to eternal life.

Accordingly, the evident meaning of the passage is that Judah had been "smitten by the sword." The same action had dramatic consequences for his followers, now "scattered." Since the wicked are threatened with literal destruction by the sword at God's visitation, a consistent reading requires that the same is the meaning of the smiting throughout. This is no metaphor for suffering. As the Suffering Servant, one might suppose, Judah had been smitten in that he suffered; but the passage rules out that weaker interpretation by applying the same penalty to the wicked. To be smitten here means to die.

The quotation from Zechariah 13 (a chapter Judah earlier quoted in his hymns and applied to himself) suggests both that the *Damascus Document* author recalled Judah's death as violent, and that he believed it was somehow part of God's plan. The event had been predicted of old (though we have no warrant for thinking that Judah himself had ever interpreted the verse that way). The later author was reinterpreting central scriptural passages that Judah had used to teach about himself in the light of a shocking, actual episode. This incident absolutely required some explanation.

Therefore he quoted the whole of Zechariah 13:7, which was unnecessary to his ostensible purpose—the discussion was about the sheep and the wicked, not the Shepherd. For that discussion the author might well have quoted merely the last half of the verse. Yet he felt it important to mention the Shepherd, for by affirming that the death had been predicted, he affirmed that it was part of God's plan all along.[37] He then declined further explanation, passing immediately to the sheep.

This is the one place in all the writings of what became a widespread movement that the founder's death is in any way "described." And this, the single description, is reticent, almost embarrassed, restrained as though straitjacketed. Why?

Historical analogy suggests an answer to this question. When Sabbatai Sevi died in the fall of 1676, more than six months were required for the news to reach Italy. When it did, one Sabbatian leader, Meir Rofe, wrote to another, Abraham Rovigo:

> And now I will announce to you great news but keep it secret and for God's sake do not divulge it to anyone. A letter arriving from Sofia from R[abbi] Samuel Gandoor says that it is true that the Beloved has been asked to the Celestial Academy on the very Day of Atonement. . . . [Meanwhile] you should ask a question how his words may come true after this, and why and for what reason this has happened, and whether this is a real death.[38]

Other circles of Sabbatian faithful also imposed silence on themselves, one member commenting, "Even our master, the Holy Rabbi, the Holy Lamp [Nathan of Gaza, Sabbatai's prophet] whose light shines from one end of the world to the other, and from whom this great mystery is possibly not hidden, is silent and does not want to speak for the time being." Within another year or so, by 1678–1679, various explanations of the apostate messiah's death began to develop. The silence was broken; but for nearly two years the principal reaction to Sabbatai's demise was to say nothing. The shock was too great, the apparent disconfirmation of all the prophecies too hard to explain. Besides, who knew what might happen next? Perhaps the messiah would shortly be manifested in his glory.[39]

The reaction to Judah's death was similar: shock, utter dismay, silence in the face of the inexplicable. The embarrassment that shines through the early version of the *Damascus Document* was real. Not much was said because not much could be said. Later, for reasons we shall see, Judah's death was no longer an issue, whereupon the *Damascus Document* was reworked. The Zechariah passage and all reference to the first messiah's end were removed altogether.

Two possible agents for Judah's smiting suggest themselves. Perhaps the Damascene lions of his sixth hymn finally caught up with him and his brigand band, and Judah and some of his men received the usual penalty for banditry. Or it may be that Hyrcanus and the Jerusalem authorities, having tried once unsuccessfully to rid themselves of the threat posed by the first messiah, tried again. This time they achieved their aims.

Either way, the remaining followers faced a defining crisis.

72 B.C.E.; the aged priest Judah, dead, none of his central prophecies come to pass. After a lifetime of teaching and engagement at the highest levels of Jerusalem politics, after refusing to countenance the new Pharisaic regime in the Temple, after trial and exile, anguish and apostasy, the first messiah had died, far from his home, almost alone. Only fifteen followers and their families remained, these now "scattered." By all the canons of reason, this should have been the end of things.

But it was not. For whatever Judah had been in his lifetime, he was about to become far more in his death.

CHAPTER 9

RECKONED
WITH THE GODS

Let us run with perseverance the race that is set before us, looking
to Jesus the author and perfecter of our faith, who for the joy that
was set before him endured the cross, scorning its shame, and has
taken his seat at the right hand of the throne of God.

Hebrews 12:1–2

THE FIRST MESSIAH died intestate, never having expressed his will
on how matters should continue after him, because for Judah the concept of succession could have no meaning before his prophecies' sure fulfillment. He held in prospect his enthronement by God as king and high
priest in Jerusalem. Judah expected to rule, expected to bring his enemies
to account, expected to march on the Gentile nations to force every knee to
bow, every tongue to confess the God of Israel. Judah expected to found the
Kingdom of God. His acolytes were likewise convinced.

A CUNNINGLY DEVISED FABLE?

When he died leaving these things all unrealized, Judah ignited within his
disciples a ferocious energy that somehow had to find release. Generating
this energy was the friction between his predictions and the group's beliefs,
on the one hand, and, on the other, actual events. Judah had said that he

would rule; how could that be true now? Judah had said that they would rule with him; how could that happen now? Judah had spoken of the destruction of the wicked, of the return of the Jewish nation to its rightful place at the head of the nations. What of these prophecies now? To judge by appearances, all that Judah had said was false.

And yet that could not be. His followers truly believed that when Judah spoke, God spoke. In the crisis of their day they found meaning and hope through that word. So Judah could not be false, not so much because of what he was, but because of what his followers were. They could not believe that Judah was false without casting profound doubt on their ideas about God and the meaning of their own lives. So deep was their investment in Judah that to declare him false would be to commit spiritual suicide.

Thus his death left the first followers in limbo, in acute psychological pain. The diagnosis: disconfirmation distress.

A crisis-cult member closer to our own day once wrote eloquently of the sort of anguish that now gripped Judah's followers. Hiram Edson, a Millerite, captured his group's own disconfirmation distress when the Second Coming failed to materialize in October 1844 as the Millerites had been predicting:

> Our fondest hopes and expectations were blasted, and such a spirit of weeping came over us as I never experienced before. It seemed that the loss of all earthly friends could have been no comparison. We wept, and wept, till the day dawn. I mused in my own heart, saying, My [Millerite] experience has been the richest and brightest of all my Christian experience. If this had proved a failure, what was the rest of my Christian experience worth? Has the Bible proved a failure? Is there no God, no heaven, no golden home city, no paradise? Is all this but a cunningly devised fable? Is there no reality to our fondest hope and expectation of these things? And thus we had something to grieve and weep over, if all our fond hopes were lost. And as I said, we wept till the day dawn.[1]

Judah's followers now had to ask whether everything Judah had said was but a cunningly devised fable. Were all their fond hopes lost? If not, they had to show in a manner convincing to themselves (and persuasive to future members of the group, if there were to be any) that, despite appearances, Judah's prophecies were true. We saw in the last chapter that Judah's early followers turned to Zechariah and found there reassurance that Judah's death was a part of God's plan. Yet that discovery was an incomplete solution to the problems his demise presented, leaving unresolved the tension of the apparent disconfirmation.

How did Judah's followers handle this tension? It would not dissipate on its own. From their subsequent writings, we know that Judah's movement thought and talked about him a lot.[2] Such constant contemplation, like sunlight through a magnifying glass, could only intensify the problem. The focused heat was almost certainly too great for the group to reduce by the method of demotion. Konrad Schmid's followers opted for that solution, recall, demoting him from "Christ" to "Elijah the forerunner" and expecting thereafter a new ultimate figure.

Another possible solution in the circumstances the followers faced would have been to invoke the mechanism of "the second coming." At that time, it could have been argued, any prophecies still unfulfilled would be resolved. Did the followers assign Judah a future role? Many crisis cults do anticipate the return of the founder. Yali was expected to return. So was Konrad Schmid. So was Sabbatai Sevi. After David Koresh died in April 1993, his resurrection was anticipated in December 1996. What about Judah?

Was Judah coming again?

T HE CLEAREST EVIDENCE of what Judah's followers believed about his postmortem status is found in the *Thanksgiving Hymns* themselves, in the final form of that work.

Judah's Teacher Hymns had been swallowed up and now sat whole and undigested in the stomach of the *Thanksgiving Hymns*. In the eight columns that preceded Judah's writings, a variety of the later leaders of his movement inscribed their own hymns. As had Judah, they wrote in the first person. In the ten columns that trailed Judah's book, followers placed a series of hymns of somewhat different character from those of the first eight columns.[3] Like the writings that preceded Judah's book, though, this second group also spoke in the first person.

Once the initial columns of "I" hymns had been paired with the second grouping of "I" hymns like bookends around Judah's own writings, the result was an entire scroll in the first person. Technically, this was what scholars call a "redaction;" it was a reworking of earlier material to create a new thing. Redaction went on constantly in the ancient world. It was one way of keeping older materials vital, speaking afresh to new generations and their newly risen concerns. Redaction was a way of retelling a story.

As a result of the redaction involved in the *Thanksgiving Hymns,* the whole now comprised nearly thirty columns of first-person speech. Judah's hymns were the anchor, the central and historically primary element, so evidently the intended effect of the redaction was to expand the revelation that Judah had given, thereby claiming his authority for new ideas that had arisen in the group.

The whole of the *Thanksgiving Hymns* was now presented as Judah's voice; it was a greatly expanded Book of Judah.

Near the end of the surviving portions appears a hymn unlike any other, tantalizing for what can be read yet very badly damaged. We may call it the Hymn of the Exalted One. Only recently has it become possible to reconstruct it with the help of two of the other copies of the *Thanksgiving Hymns,* which preserve more of the hymn. In addition, a shorter version has come down to us in another work discovered among the Dead Sea Scrolls.[4] By combining all four witnesses, nine of the original nineteen lines of the Hymn of the Exalted One can be reconstructed. It emerges as a reflex of Psalm 89:6: "For who in the heavenlies can array himself with YHWH? Who is like YHWH among the angels?"

But this newly discovered hymn offers an unexpected twist to the biblical sentiments, claims now placed in the mouth of the first messiah:

> I am reckoned with the angels, my dwelling place is in the holy
> council. Who has been regarded with scorn like me? And who has
> born oppression like me? And who is like me, lacking evil, so that he
> can compare to me? I have never been instructed, yet no teaching
> compares to my teaching. I sit on [high, exalted in heave]n . . . Who is
> like me among the angels? . . . The utterance of my lips, who can
> endure? Who can challenge me in speech and so compare with my
> judgment? [I] am beloved of the King, a companion to the Holy Ones,
> and none can oppose me. [To my majesty and my glory] can none
> compare, for my station is with the angels. Neither glory [nor majes]ty
> have I laid up as treas[ure] at the price of gold, neither of fine gold.
> None can compare with me, and no [iniquity] has been reckoned
> against me.[5]

In all creation, Judah was made to say, he was second to God alone. Indeed, even that distinction was a bit fuzzy. Psalm 89 had asked, "Who is like YHWH among the angels?"; Judah as speaker responded with a counterquestion: "Who is like me?"

The immensity of his implied claim falls little short of the Philippian Hymn that the apostle Paul included in his letter to the Philippians. The Philippian Hymn affirmed "Jesus Christ is Lord," using the word for *Lord* that commonly rendered YHWH (the holiest Hebrew name for God) into Greek. By this equation the Philippian Hymn essentially asserted the divinity of Jesus. Similarly, the reconstructed *Thanksgiving Hymn* applied scriptural God-language to Judah.

The first lines of the Hymn of the Exalted One echoed the Servant Songs, which were so central to Judah's own writings. By redaction, Judah was made to apply the Servant motifs, notably those of Isaiah 53, to himself. He went on to assert that his teaching was incomparable, incontestable. His judgment in legal matters (the picture is the forensic setting of God's heavenly court) was incontrovertible.

As depicted by the words of the Hymn of the Exalted One, Judah had once lived on earth, where his relations with contemporaries had been troubled: *Who has been regarded with scorn like me? And who has born oppression like me?* But now he had been raised up, yet not to become a member of the rank-and-file host of heaven, grand as that might be. He had been raised still higher, higher even than the archangels. So close was Judah's rank to God that only divine language sufficed for accurate description. What had happened to Judah after his death? According to the redaction of the *Thanksgiving Hymns,* just what Christian tradition was to claim for Jesus.

He had taken his seat at the right hand of God.

FOR JUDAH'S FOLLOWERS, he was now semidivine, the highest angel, just as for certain early Christian groups—among them the Jewish-Christian Ebionites—Jesus assumed that role after the resurrection. As justification for their claims of apotheosis, the followers could cite pointed words from Judah's own eighth hymn, where he had written: *Thereafter You shall exalt me on high, and I shall blaze with a light of sevenfold brilliance by the very light that You have established as Your glory.*[6]

Judah, they could claim, had prophesied his own exaltation. By using the term *blazing* Judah meant to say that upon death he would literally become a star. In Jewish thought of this period it was a way of describing transformation into an angel. The enlightened of Judah's Jerusalem would have derided any modern suggestion that stars are enormous, inanimate balls of flaming hydrogen becoming helium. Everyone knew that they were heavenly beings. They were alive.

Thus Judah and his followers—and many other Jews—saw no metaphor in the words of Daniel 12:3: "And the wise shall shine like the brilliance of the firmament, and those who make the Many wise, as stars, forever and ever." They found in Daniel's words support for the notion of astral immortality. For the righteous, to die was to become a star.

Having been so taught by their Teacher, Judah's followers held that after death they would become angels (another notion shared by certain early Christian groups). Such was the thrust of various passages that we have seen in Judah's hymns, for example the fifth hymn: *They who walk in the Way of Your heart shall heed me and thus array themselves before You in the council of the Holy Ones.*[7]

So also the seventh hymn: *You have brought the men who follow Your counsel into Your divine council. They share a common lot with the Angels of the Presence, and no intermediary stands between them and Your Holy Ones . . . They will give reply by Your glorious mouth, and be Your princes in an eternal heritage.*[8] The greatest hope of these most hopeful of people was to be one with the angels.

What, then, could be more natural for Judah's followers than to imagine that upon death he had become the greatest of angels? For surely Judah's reward would be more glorious than that of any ordinary believer. The language of the remarkable hymn they placed in his mouth was merely an expression of the sentiments the group might be expected to have: Judah was at the right hand of God.

So the earliest followers could take comfort from Zechariah that Judah's death was providential, planned from the very beginning. And they could glory in their conviction that Judah was now exalted above all other created beings. Yet even these soothing affirmations did not entirely resolve the problem of the unfulfilled prophecies, most especially that of Judah's central prediction: his own coming rule. Moreover, while the hymn placed in his mouth perhaps implied an answer, it did not directly address the question.

Was Judah coming again?

To find out, we must turn to another of the writings his movement later produced. This was an extremely important book—not least because this one, alone of all the surviving writings his followers set down, alluded to Judah using that specific term, *messiah*.[9]

SEVENTY WEEKS ARE DECREED

When it was first discovered, the manuscript of the work known as the *Melchizedek Book* was in a very bad state. It was written about 50 B.C.E., and over the years scholars have succeeded in reconstructing substantial portions. The greater part of the remains can now be read as follows:

> And concerning what scripture says, "In [this] year of jubilee [you shall return, every one of you, to your property" (Leviticus 25:13) and what is also written, "And this] is the [ma]nner of [the remission:] every creditor shall remit the claim that is held [against a neighbor, not exacting it of a neighbor who is a member of the community, because God's] remission [has been proclaimed:] (Deuteronomy 15:2)

> [The true import] is that it applies [to the L]atter Days and concerns the captives, just as [Isaiah said: "To proclaim the jubilee to the captives." (Isaiah 61:1)] . . . and from the inheritance of Melchizedek, f[or . . . Melchize]dek, who will return them to what is rightfully theirs. He will proclaim to them the jubilee, thereby releasing th[em from the debt of a]ll their sins.

> [He shall pro]claim this decree in the fir[s]t [wee]k of the jubilee period af[ter nine j]ubilee periods. Then the D[ay of Atone]ment shall follow af[ter] the [te]nth [ju]bilee period, when he shall atone for all the Sons of [Light] and the peopl[e who are pre]destined to Mel[chi]zedek. . . . For this is the time decreed for "the year of Melchiz[edek]'s favor," (Isaiah 61:2, modified) [and] by his might he w[i]ll judge God's Holy Ones and so establish a righteous ki[n]gdom, as it is written about him in the Psalms of David, "A godlike being has taken his place in the divine council; in the midst of the divine beings he holds judgment." (Psalm 82:1) Scripture also s[ays] about him, "Return to [it] on high; A divine being will judge the peoples." (Psalm 7:7–8)

Concerning what scripture s[ays, "How long will y]ou judge unjustly, and sh[ow] partiality to the wick[e]d? [S]el[ah]" (Psalm 82:2), the true import applies to Belial and the spirits predestined to him, becau[se all of them have rebe]lled, turn[ing] from God's precepts [and so becoming utterly wicked.] Therefore Melchizedek will thoroughly prosecute the veng[ea]nce required by Go[d's] statu[te]s. [Also, he will deliver all the captives from the power of B]elial, and from the power of all [the spirits predestined to him.] Allied with him will be all the ["righteous] divine beings." (Isaiah 61:3) [The . . .] is that wh[ich . . . al]l the divine beings.

This vi[sitation] is the Day of [Salvation] that He has decreed [through Isai]ah the prophet [concerning all the captives,] inasmuch as scripture sa[ys, "How] beautiful upon the mountains are the fee[t of] the heral[d] who [an]nounces peace, who brings [good] news, [who announces salvat]ion, who [sa]ys to Zion, 'Your [di]vine being [reigns].'" (Isaiah 52:7) This scripture's true import: "the mounta[ins" are the] prophet[s,] they w[ho were sent to proclaim God's truth and to] proph[esy] to all I[srael.] "The Herald" is the [An]ointed of the Spir[it,] of whom Dan[iel] spoke, ["After the sixty-two weeks, an Anointed One shall be cut off." (Daniel 9:26) The "Herald who brings] good news, who announ[ces salvation"] is the one of whom it is wri[tt]en, ["to proclaim the year of YHWH's favor, the day of vengeance of our God;] [to comfo[rt] all who mourn." (Isaiah 61:2) This scripture's true import:] he is to inst[r]uct them about all the periods of history for eter[nity . . . and in the statutes of] [the] truth . . . [dominion] that passes from Belial and ret[urns to the Sons of Light] . . . by the judgment of God, just as it is written concerning him, ["who says to Zi]on 'Your divine being reigns.'" ["Zi]on" is [the congregation of all the Sons of Righteousness, who] uphold the covenant and turn from walking [in the way] of the people. "Your di[vi]ne being" is [Melchizedek, who will del]iv[er them from the po]wer of Belial.[10]

The *Melchizedek Book* was a topical biblical commentary. Rather than interpreting consecutive portions of one book of the Bible, it correlated diverse biblical materials believed to concern the Latter Days. To express its chronology, the work reckoned by jubilee periods of forty-nine years, each jubilee subdivided into "weeks" of years. A week was seven years, so seven weeks comprised a jubilee. This chronological system is akin to the one we have seen earlier in Daniel; indeed, the *Melchizedek Book* built its temporal superstructure upon the 490 years (= ten jubilees) of Daniel 9:24–27.[11]

The book featured two protagonists, the Herald and Melchizedek. The author looked back to the Herald as a figure of the past, while his expectations of Melchizedek were primarily directed to the future.

The Herald bore a special relationship to the biblical prophets, for he "stood upon" (went beyond, perhaps, or completed?) their writings. To make this point the author drew upon Isaiah 52:7, "how beautiful upon the mountains are the feet of the Herald," glossing the first phrase, *The mountains are the prophets,* and adding afterward, *The Herald is the Anointed of the Spirit, of whom Daniel spoke.* Another way to render *Anointed of the Spirit* into English is *Messiah of the Spirit.*

This Herald was a messiah.

The author also quoted Isaiah 61:2 as a prophecy about the Herald. He had come to "comfort all who mourn," which he did by *instructing them about all the periods of history for eternity . . . and in the statutes of the truth.* Almost certainly this pivotal figure of the past was Judah, the Teacher of Righteousness. Michael Douglas has written:

> The purpose of the Herald's coming is to announce the imminent fulfillment of the Day of Salvation, which was prophesied by the prophets from a distant vantage point. The Herald's message was that the exile was coming to a close and the dawn of a new age was breaking. In order to make such an announcement, the Herald had to believe that he had been granted a revelation of the knowledge of God's timetable. . . . With this knowledge he surpassed the prophets who did not know *when* their prophecies would be fulfilled.[12]

Douglas pointed out that this claim to know *when* was precisely the assertion made on behalf of the Teacher of Righteousness by the *Commentary on Habakkuk:*

> God told Habakkuk to write down what would happen to the generation to come; but <u>when</u> that period would be complete he did not make known to him. When it says, "so that with ease someone

can read it," this refers to the Teacher of Righteousness, to whom God
made known all the mysterious revelations of his servants the
prophets.[13]

The Herald's apocalyptic teaching function also resonates with the
Damascus Document's characterization of the Teacher: *[God] raised up for*
them a Teacher of Righteousness to guide them in the Way of his Heart. He
taught to later generations what God was about to do to a generation deserving
wrath. And Judah had tied the Herald verses (Isaiah 61:1–4) to himself
through his oft-repeated claim to be the Servant of the Lord.[14]

The author of the *Melchizedek Book,* as a learned member of Judah's
group, knew Judah's hymns. He recognized these connections. By his characterization of the Herald, he intended to evoke Judah.

And by using the term *messiah* of the Herald, he intended to apply it
to Judah as well.

T HE BOOK'S OTHER protagonist, Melchizedek, dominated the first
half of the book, and truly momentous claims were made on his behalf.
He was first said to *proclaim to them* [Judah's followers] *the jubilee.*[15]

In the Bible the jubilee was a feature of the laws of ancient Israel,
which required the people to proclaim a jubilee once every fifty years. This
requirement was a mechanism to slacken the cords of debt slavery and
avoid permanent alienation of the citizens' patrimony. At the jubilee, land
that had passed from its owners for whatever reason reverted to the original
holder. Hebrew slaves were set free. Signaled by the blowing of trumpets,
the jubilee year began on the Day of Atonement.

But the *Melchizedek Book* completely changed what the Bible meant
by the jubilee year. Our author linked two biblical passages relevant to the
jubilee (Leviticus 25:13 and Deuteronomy 15:2), then wrenched from them
a far-from-literal interpretation. In the past, he said, Melchizedek had inau-
gurated the jubilee year by proclaiming liberty. Unlike the biblical version,
though, this liberty was not freedom from slavery. For our author it meant
forgiveness of sins: *releasing them from the debt of all their sins.* That any Jewish text in these years could suggest that someone other than God might forgive sins is astonishing (though the reader of the New Testament will
perhaps recall that the Gospels grant that power to Jesus, in Mark 2, for example).

In our author's interpretation, the biblical Day of Atonement also underwent radical surgery. First he severed it from its biblical connection with proclaiming the jubilee year. Then he grafted it onto a future, apocalyptic event, when Melchizedek was to *atone for all the Sons of Light and the people who are predestined to Melchizedek.* Melchizedek would not merely forgive sins but also atone for them once and for all.

This is another astonishing notion in a Jewish text—though once again, early Christians believed the same of Jesus and said so in the New Testament (for example, Hebrews 9:26–28).

On the Day of Atonement, the text continued, Melchizedek was to judge the wicked angels *(he will judge God's Holy Ones)* and so, in effect, establish the Kingdom of God, stretching from the heavenly realm to the terrestrial. Melchizedek would employ as his assistants a variety of angels, *all the righteous divine beings.* In that day he would cast down the Prince of this world, Belial, and all his wicked spirit attendants *(Therefore Melchizedek will thoroughly prosecute the vengeance required by God's statutes).* By overthrowing these principalities and powers, Melchizedek would deliver believers from Satan's power.

Beyond these explicit statements about Melchizedek, the *Melchizedek Book's* treatment of biblical quotations is remarkable for what it affirms implicitly. In its biblical quotations the *Melchizedek Book* recast what the Bible presents as an act of God by inserting a new agent—Melchizedek.[16] This sleight of hand occurred even where the Bible used God's holiest and most particular name, YHWH—the Tetragrammaton, the ineffable Name. In the Bible, Isaiah 61:2 says, "He has sent me to proclaim the year of YHWH's favor;" the *Melchizedek Book* rewrote the verse: "For this is the time decreed for the year of Melchizedek's favor."

By this replacement the author implicitly dubbed Melchizedek "YHWH" and so created what the rabbis later called a "second power in heaven." The comments of Alan Segal unpack the significance of the move: "Sharing in the divine name is a recurring motif of early Jewish apocalypticism, where the *principal angelic mediator* of God is or carries the name Yahweh."[17]

So Melchizedek was the highest angel, and he was coming in the future to atone for the sins of Judah's followers and to establish the Kingdom of God. But what did those actions have to do with Judah?

To answer that question, we must take a glance at the chronology of the *Melchizedek Book,* represented on the next page in figure 1.

Figure 1. The Week-Years of the Melchizedek Book *Aligned with Daniel's Seventy Weeks (Daniel 9:24–27; One Week = Seven Years)*

9th Final	Jubilee Week	Key Week	10th		Jubilee			Final Week
9 Jubilees	≈ 441 Years	Decree of Melchizedek		Author's Present				Day of Atonement at 10th Jubilee's End
		1st Week of 10th Jubilee						
63 Weeks	= 441 Years	Herald Cut Off						Melchizedek Returns
		441–448 years	449–455	456–462	463–469	470–476	477–483	484–490
62	63	64	65	66	67	68	69	70

Notice that the period in the author's past, the "Key Week," was a time of activity for both the Herald and Melchizedek. The Herald had been cut off (killed) in the very week when Melchizedek was said to make his decree. And the most prominent completed function of the two protagonists was identical. Both had heralded God's good news. The *Melchizedek Book* even used the same biblical portion—Isaiah 61:1–4—to characterize both messengers. These correlations of time and function suggest a surprising thought: our author identified the Herald with Melchizedek.[18]

If this inference is correct, and if, as we have already concluded, Judah was the Herald of the *Melchizedek Book,* then Judah was Melchizedek. We can therefore equate beliefs about Melchizedek's actions with beliefs about Judah, the first messiah. Everything Judah's followers believed about the angel they called Melchizedek, they believed about Judah. Judah was that angel. He was coming again, and the chronological scheme of the *Melchizedek Book* shows that believers even knew when: in about forty years (arrived at by subtracting year 448, the end of the period of activity, from year 490, the end of the tenth jubilee).

At that time Judah would release believers from the debt of all their sins, apparently rendering them sinless as they entered millennial bliss. He would atone for all those predestined to belong to him. Judah would judge the wicked angels and cast down Satan their king, so ending the long reign of wickedness on earth. Under the name of Melchizedek he would institute the Kingdom of God.

Notice, finally, how well the Hymn of the Exalted One correlates with the *Melchizedek Book.* For if it is true that the Hymn of the Exalted One cast Judah as the highest angel in heaven; and if Judah was, as seems evident, the Herald of the *Melchizedek Book,* then to take the next step and identify Judah with Melchizedek is almost required, since Melchizedek was the highest angel in heaven. This series of identifications would scarcely have been avoidable for believers who were reading both works.

JUDAH'S DEATH DROVE his followers back to the scriptures, where he had taught them to find themselves.

You will remember from chapter 6 that Judah's own chronology, based on Daniel 9:27, held that the End would come within seven years of the Pharisee takeover. So he had taught his crisis cult. The agonized followers somehow had to reconcile that teaching with their messiah's unexpected demise. To do so they chose a well-trodden crisis-cult path. They returned to the original source of the teaching to reconfigure its elements. They reinterpreted. They decided that what was wrong was not the prophecy of the End, only their previous understanding of it.

How to reconfigure the elements was precisely what Judah's death taught them. For they found predicted in Daniel 9:24–27 the death of an Anointed One, a messiah. We do not know how Judah himself had understood those words, but the moment his followers read them anew, they realized that Judah's death was not the cruel climax of a cunningly devised fable. According to Daniel, the messiah was to be "cut off." They ended up making this statement a part of the *Melchizedek Book,* calling Judah the Herald.[19] Judah's murder had been prophesied long ago! Daniel had foreseen the event just as had Zechariah, but Daniel added information by placing Judah's death in a chronological sequence of events.

Making a virtue out of a necessity, Judah's death became for the group a foundational and positive event. The Daniel passage that gave it meaning came to structure the group's entire understanding of prophecy and fulfillment and where they stood in time. Judah's death seen in Daniel's context became the bedrock for the group's most fundamental postmortem doctrinal development: the teaching of the forty years.

We have observed that the ideology of a final forty years of wickedness leading up to the End was widespread in the writings of Judah's movement. The *Melchizedek Book* allows us to retrace the process by which this number emerged. Judah's followers reconfigured Judah's teaching of the "seven years," now interpreting him as speaking of the period until his own death. Accordingly, they removed a week from the tenth jubilee (the "Key Week" in figure 1). This move left the group with forty-two years (forty-nine minus seven).

That number harmonized well with the chronologies of two other conceptual building blocks: the typology of the wilderness wandering, or Exile, and Judah's affirmation that he had arisen to address the millennial generation. A biblical generation counted as forty years, hence the time for the millennial generation. The biblical time span given for Israel's wilderness wandering was likewise, as we have seen, forty years. That all these matters fit together so neatly must have confirmed for Judah's believers that their reinterpretation was on the right track.[20]

Judah's death became, then, the basis for his follower's precise statement of when the end would come. It was therefore essential to the dynamic of their message. Paul and the early Christians preached "Christ crucified," and Judah's death was not the focus of his believers' message in that way. Still, it was there, the hidden linchpin of the idea that was more and more central to their message as time passed: the Year of the End would arrive in 34 B.C.E.

And finally, the *Melchizedek Book* suggests how Judah's movement dealt with the most problematic of his prophecies, the prediction that he would rule in Jerusalem.

They adopted two strategies, both common to crisis cults faced with disconfirmed prophecies. The first was projection. What Judah had prophesied he would do, he would indeed do—only later. The movement projected Judah's rule, and others of his prophecies such as the conquest of the Gentiles, into the future. After the forty years, at the end of the tenth jubilee, he would return as Melchizedek and establish God's Kingdom.

The other strategy was to spiritualize Judah's words. Even now, the group maintained, Judah was indeed a king. He reigned in heaven, the most godlike of all creatures; thus his name, Melchizedek, "King of Righteousness" (Hebrew *malki-tsedeq*). This name was chosen in part because it resonated with Judah's frequent title, "Teacher of Righteousness" (Hebrew *moreh-tsedeq*).

Judah's prophecies were now explained, what might have seemed false proved true. The greatest crisis the followers had yet faced, the death of their founder, they had managed to survive. Soon enough, however, they would face a crisis greater still, and this one of their own making.

THE RISE AND FALL OF
A JUDAEAN CRISIS CULT

Kenelm Burridge concluded his book *Mambu* with a keen observation. "Once it is accepted," he wrote, "that the charismatic role is to sustain the myth-dream, not completely fulfill it, much light is shed on the fact that it is so often *after* a charismatic figure has failed in his political or organizational role that he becomes of real significance."[21] Judah had indeed failed in his political role. If that had been the end of the story, we would never have known of the first messiah's existence. Moreover, he would have had no impact on the subsequent history of the Jewish people and, through them, the Western world. In its first translation into flesh, the messianic idea would have ended an abortion.

But Judah's failure did not mark the end of his movement, and so the first life ever lived as a messiah became of real significance. Like any charismatic, Judah could have significance only if followers were willing to ascribe to him significance, willing to pass on his revelations about himself and what God now required. If we are to understand fully the phenomenon of the first messiah, then, we must consider what became of his movement in the years that followed.

For it was because of these followers that Judah's ideas penetrated the myth-dream of Israel.

U PON JUDAH'S DEATH, his followers had two options. They could choose, as sociologists put it, to "routinize the charisma" of their founder, or they could conclude that they had been deceived and cease to exist as a group. The first choice was the one they made, of course, but it was not easy.

As if to pour salt in wounds already deep with the first messiah's demise, the acolytes discovered among his private things his hymns. They were able to read in his ninth hymn what their leader thought of their chances without him:

> *By my hand You have opened up its wellspring with all its channels. [You have planted i]t facing the true measuring line; the planting of its trees aligns with the plumb line of the sun . . . becoming glorious branches. When I extend my hand and dig out its channels, its roots stretch forth even into flinty rock and [it anchors] its trunk in the earth. Even in a season of heat it remains strong.*

> *But were I to withdraw my hand, it would become like a bus[h in the wastelands], its trunk as nettles in a salt flat. Its channels would nourish only thorns and thistles, briars and weeds. [The trees] on the banks would become trees yielding bad fruit. In the heat its leaves would wither, unrenewed by [gushing] rain.*[22]

Judah wrote here of his role in bringing the Tree to maturity. Growth was possible only through him: *When I extend my hand and dig out its channels, its roots stretch forth even into flinty rock.* If he were to cease his revelatory nurturing, Judah believed, the Tree would wither and die: *But were I to withdraw my hand, it would become like a bush in the wastelands, its trunk as nettles in a salt flat.* Now that Judah was no longer with them, his followers read, their own viability was dubious.

They could not grow. They could not become the Israel of the prophecies, the remnant rulers of the land, proclaiming God's true law given by his ultimate prophet. This, his followers would realize, was the first messiah's judgment of what they could be apart from him: nothing. Without him, they were like one-handed applause.

The group not only had to find a way to survive, they had to do it in the face of their inspired founder's statement that they could not. A more crushing psychological burden upon any nascent crisis cult is hard to imagine. Yet, amazingly, they did survive. The small group of men and their families left behind must have counted among them at least one remarkable individual.

This person had to be able to shoulder the burden of Judah's final words and begin to explain the apparent disconfirmation of the prophecies. And at the same time, he had to lead the group as they strove to routinize Judah's charisma. As Max Weber wrote, "The pure type of charismatic rulership is in a very specific sense unstable, and all its modifications have basically one and the same cause: the desire to transform charisma and charismatic blessing from a unique, transitory gift of grace of extraordinary times and persons into a permanent possession of everyday life."[23] The great leader was gone. Now his followers had to lay hold of his essence and somehow make it their own.

"If it wants to transform itself into a perennial institution, the first problem [for a crisis cult] is that of finding a successor to the prophet. . . . This problem inescapably channels charisma into the direction of legal regulation and tradition."[24] So added Weber in further defining the notion of routinization. Legal regulation, codification of tradition, and the designation of a successor: these are precisely what we find in the earliest identifiable document produced by Judah's followers.

SOON AFTER JUDAH had died, the tiny movement set down in writing a manifesto for their continued existence. In it they named a successor to the first messiah, a man who, while never claiming to be his equal, would continue central aspects of Judah's role. And the collective began to take on Judah's charisma.

This manifesto can be retrieved by literary criticism of a work variously called the *Manual of Discipline* or *Community Rule*. At the heart of this work's earliest kernel lies a section that we may call the Original Manifesto.[25] It comprises four paragraphs set off by their parallel grammatical structure and reads as follows:

> *The Society of the Yahad consists of twelve men and three priests, blameless with respect to all that has been revealed from all the Law.*
>
> *They are to work truth, righteousness, justice, lovingkindness, and humility with one another.*
>
> *They are to preserve faith in the land with self-control and a contrite spirit.*
>
> *They are to atone for sin by working justice and suffering affliction.*
>
> *They are to conduct themselves with all people with the support of the truth and the dictates proper to the age.*

. . .

These men having come together in Israel, the Society of the Yahad is hereby constituted in truth.

It is an eternal Tree, a holy temple for Israel and a foundation of the Holy of Holies for Aaron.

They are true witnesses for justice, chosen by God's will to atone for the land.

They are to recompense the wicked their due.

. . .

These men having been established in the doctrine of the Yahad for two years, they are to keep themselves separate—the temple stands among the Society of the Men of the Yahad.

No biblical doctrine concealed from Israel but discovered by the Interpreter is to be hidden from these men out of fear that they may backslide.

. . .

These men having come together in Israel, they are to keep themselves separate from the habitation of perverse people.

They are to go to "the wilderness, to prepare there the Way of the Truth" (Isaiah 40:6)—that is, the study of the Law that God commanded through Moses.[26]

The Manifesto was a foundation document, a charter for Judah's followers as a group. They called themselves the *Society of the Yahad* (*Yahad* being a Hebrew word for "unity"). The full phrase (Hebrew *atsat ha-yahad*) was their official, "legal" name, used in the most formal contexts, though they would apply many other appellations to themselves in years to come.[27] Indeed, one of those others, the Many, was Judah's own name for his followers, as known from his hymns.

The Manifesto affirmed that only fifteen men remained of the fifty to one hundred who had originally followed Judah into the Land of Damascus. All of the others had either apostatized, died under attack by Hyrcanus, or been tracked down and killed by bandit hunters. Three of the fifteen were priests, twelve laymen. This small group—numbering perhaps sixty including women and children—specifically identified themselves as the *eternal Tree,* adopting the apocalyptic phrase Judah had coined in his ninth hymn.[28] Their faith was strong despite their weak numbers, and they fully believed what Judah had said of his followers' future role in judgment: *They are to recompense the wicked their due.*

They also believed that they were to *atone for sin by working justice and suffering affliction.* This statement signified their assumption of Judah's charisma: they would fill up what remained of the sufferings of the Suffering Servant. They would do what Judah had done. They spoke of *having been established in the doctrine of the Yahad for two years.* This was the period of their tutelage under Judah in exile (reinforcing our earlier conclusion of Judah's death shortly into "the forty years"). In future years this two-year span would become the time that new recruits would have to prove themselves before attaining full membership.

Twice the Manifesto alluded to the Society's severed relationship with the Jerusalem Temple. The group called themselves a *holy temple for Israel* and claimed that *the temple stands among the Society.*[29] These statements were a development of Judah's First Commandment: *You shall not enter the Temple to kindle God's altar in vain.* Judah had conceived of his commandment as a temporary, emergency measure, for he expected to reestablish the proper laws shortly. He imagined that he and his followers would soon be sacrificing again. But with his death, the Society had to evolve a longer-term view.

They resolved to have nothing more to do with the Temple until they received their inheritance. For the duration of the present age, they refused to sacrifice. The First Commandment had become permanent. Yet, since the Society believed they were *chosen by God's will to atone for the land,* and since they had mystically become "the Temple," they and the land would still enjoy the benefits of God's cleansing, normally obtained through sacrifice. From their perspective, the Jerusalem Temple was now inoperative, obsolete until the climax of the Latter Days. In the meantime, as Paul would urge the Christians in Rome to do, Judah's followers had become living sacrifices. And the group resolved to live apart from unbelievers: *they are to keep themselves separate from the habitation of perverse people.*

The Society called its new leader the Interpreter (Hebrew *doresh*), and he was to be first and foremost a scholar expert in the scriptures. Doubtless the Interpreter was one of the three priests among the survivors,

for the interpretation of the Bible was traditionally a priestly role. In desig-
nating the leader who would take up Judah's mantle, the Manifesto implied
a certain resentment, even criticism, of the first messiah. The new leader
was forbidden to conceal from the others whatever secret doctrines he might
uncover in the Bible. The implication, of course, is that Judah had done
just that. Probably this secrecy and suspicion had been part of Judah's reaction to the apostasy, for the Interpreter is charged never to hide the truth
out of fear that they may backslide.

SOMETIME AFTER the first followers composed the Original Manifesto, most of the original group returned from exile to settle once again
in Judaea. With their founder dead and their numbers small, they were now
politically insignificant and nonthreatening. The Jerusalem establishment
made no move to stop their repatriation. Judah's movement limped along in
these first years after his death, trying its best simply to survive—and then,
beginning about 63 B.C.E. and continuing for three decades, it suddenly exploded in growth. This was the time of the upstroke. The reason: war.

War with Rome broke out in 65 B.C.E. and shortly cost the Jewish
nation its independence. The disastrous loss of national autonomy left
many searching for a convincing explanation, and more than any other
group in their society, Judah's followers could offer one. Judah, they claimed,
had predicted this war, had warned that it was inevitable because the nation had abandoned God's covenant. The fact of the war proved the truth,
not only of Judah's statements about the war itself, but also of every other
aspect of the first messiah's teaching. History had proved him a true
prophet. Therefore, to be counted among the righteous remnant and to
avoid the destruction otherwise fated, better listen to Judah's teachings and
join his followers.

The movement presented this argument in the *Damascus Docu-
ment,* in a loose sense the declaration of the Gospel of the Teacher. Like the
Christian Gospels, it combined the words and teaching of the charismatic
founder with interpretation and shaping added by later believers. It was the
fate of their own generation that the *Damascus Document* claimed Judah
had announced aforetime—that generation whose pride had perished in
the Roman conquest.

Historical analogies abound for successful crisis-cult prophecies becoming the springboard for subsequent growth. Consider, for example, the

case of the dispensational premillennialists and World War I. As Timothy Weber remarked in his classic study, *Living in the Shadow of the Second Coming,* "No event in the fifty years after 1875 did more for the morale of American premillennialists than World War I. There at last was indisputable vindication of their dire predictions about the inevitable decline of the age."[30]

The premillennialists were persuaded that Jesus Christ would return to establish a thousand-year reign they knew from the book of Revelation as "the millennium." At the time of World War I this was still a relatively new idea among American Christians, having no significant support before William Miller arose to proclaim it about 1840.

On the opposite side were ranged liberal Christians, who argued either that the millennium was not a literal concept or that the millennium was a child of the church and would be brought to birth by the church's efforts. The foundation of liberal Christianity's position was the doctrine of the innate goodness of humankind, a notion that many contemporaries felt World War I gassed and left for dead in the trenches. Hence the premillennialists, like Judah's crisis cult, found in the fact of a war general support for their ideas. But both actually found a good deal more than general support.

For in both cases, prophecies made before the war lent a daunting power to their postwar declarations. Opponents could not easily counter arguments for which there apparently existed tangible, empirical proof.

Premillennialists had long studied the prophecies of the Old Testament for help in piecing together an elaborate scenario of what would happen in the "end times." They particularly relied upon the book of Daniel. Well before the war, many had come to agree on the following tableau, which their publications daily trumpeted to a skeptical world.

In the last days a final Gentile power would arise; it would be a revival of ancient Rome, comprising a ten-nation confederacy led by a powerful king who in coming to power had crushed three of his confederates. This king, the Antichrist, would be the focal figure in the events of the End. The Antichrist would enter into a treaty with Israel, which must itself first be regathered from the four corners of the globe and settled in Palestine. Rome reborn would negotiate with Israel reestablished. Their pact would be for mutual defense, permitting the Jews to rebuild their ancient Temple and reinstitute the sacrificial system. Yet three years after signing the treaty, premillennialists foresaw, the Antichrist would repudiate it, suspend all sacrifices, enter the Temple, and declare himself divine.

Aiding the Antichrist in all his machinations was to be a false prophet called the Beast. He and the Antichrist would wage a pogrom for three and one-half years against all who refused the Antichrist worship.

But certain spheres of influence would lie beyond the Antichrist's grasp. A northern confederacy of powers under Russia was one. They would team up with a southern "king," Egypt, to attack the Jewish state. So ferocious would be the counterattack of the Antichrist that it would trigger a preemptive response from yet another power, the "kings of the east"— China particularly—who would march an army of two hundred million men to confront the Antichrist in the valley of the ancient city of Megiddo. Armageddon would be at hand.

Though ostensibly a political conflict, the war would escalate into an all-out attack on true Christians. Just when things looked their bleakest, Jesus Christ would return, overthrow the armies of both sides, and destroy Antichrist, the Beast, and all nonbelievers. The Kingdom would at last begin. It would endure for one thousand literal years, after which would come the final judgment and the creation of a new heaven and new earth.

Most premillennialists, in keeping with their doctrine of strict biblical literalism, insisted that the new Roman empire must stay roughly within the bounds of the original. But the national boundaries of 1914 Europe did not conform at all to the shape of things that must come. Drastic changes must be in the offing, the premillennialists were convinced, for to their thinking the end was imminent.

So with scriptures in hand, premillennialists propounded a number of prophecies about what the world would look like when World War I ended. Their projections:

> Since Germany had not been a member of the original empire and did not seem to figure prominently in the prophetic future, except as part of the northern confederacy that would oppose the new Rome, it would probably lose the war, suffer national humiliation, and give up some of its western territory, which had originally belonged to Rome. The Austro-Hungarian Empire would have to be broken up so that some of its Slavic provinces north of the Danube would be free to fall under the influence of Russia and its northern confederation. Russia, though now closely allied with powers formerly within the Roman Empire, would end that association with the West and eventually develop as an independent power with

influence over other nations in northern and eastern Europe. The Ottoman Empire, whether as a result of the war or some later series of events, would relinquish control over Palestine or at least allow the regathering of the Jews there. Ireland would gain its independence from Great Britain.[31]

A glance at a map of the region before and after the war will convince you: the premillennialists came extremely close to drawing the future. And, as they loved to point out, they did it with nothing but a Bible. Their predictions were not based on prolonged study of politics or of social or military history. They derived from a peculiar reading of the prophets of Israel. As Weber observed, "The war earned the premillennialists the best reception they had [ever] received."[32]

The number of premillennialists rose dramatically. Their view of the Bible had been "proven" correct, whereas the Panglossian optimism of the liberals had been shattered by events. That growing numbers should align themselves with the side that had won was only natural. "It was obvious that as soon as the liberals began attacking it openly, premillennialism had arrived."[33]

History is replete with other examples of the power of accurate prophecy to propel political and social groups to success. Consider another: in the Florence of the 1490s, Savonarola helped to overthrow the power of Lorenzo de Medici and his faction by correctly predicting Lorenzo's death in 1492 and the invasion of the French two years later.

In similar fashion, the number of Judah's followers mushroomed in the aftermath of the war with Rome, a war they had predicted, a prediction that had been proven true.

IF THEN JUDAH'S movement grew rapidly because of the war, is there any way to quantify that growth? Just how large did the movement become? Where did it direct its appeal?

One way to approach these questions is through paleographic analysis of the writings Judah's movement produced. Scholars dispute the extent to which this method of dating by handwriting analysis is accurate, but whatever the precise dates, the script sequencing (the *rate of change* as the scripts developed) reveals a manuscript production that began very small and remained static for a while, then increased by leaps and bounds in an almost geometric progression.[34] More than half the copies were produced in a single script phase that equates approximately with the years 45–35 B.C.E.[35] This is a striking result. What does this pattern mean?

As the apostle Paul was fond of saying, much in every way.

The Dead Sea Scroll deposits appear to be a random cross-section of what their final readers possessed. That is to say, these readers saved what they had, and they had what they did by the accidents of history, operating more or less uniformly over time. That randomness is useful. We can reasonably (though not, of course, certainly) extrapolate from it that the number of texts belonging to any given script phase reflects what was needed by Judah's Society at that time.

Texts imply readers. More texts imply more readers. Texts are the tools of movements such as Judah's. The very rapid increase of textual production during the last two script phases of the first century B.C.E. implies a snowballing membership. Judah's crisis cult evidently peaked in the years 45–35 B.C.E.

We have no precise way of establishing how many readers the group's texts discovered in the caves served. Study of both the texts and the caves indicates, however, that only the tip of the original iceberg survived. Not all of the group's manuscripts were put in the caves; of those that were, not all endured the vermin and elements. Probably no more than 20 percent of the scrolls Judah's followers produced survived to our century. For each one that survived, at least four did not. Add to this reasoning the fact that reading and study in ancient times were mostly communal activities; ten people seems a reasonable guess for the minimum number of believers that each text, on average, served.[36] If so, then the number of surviving scrolls equates with no more than 2 percent of the membership in the Society in any given script phase.

If this rough-and-ready reasoning is at all on target, the following are the numbers of believers implied (each generation's texts were used by the next before coming to us): 75–65 B.C.E.: five surviving texts = 250 believers; 65–55 B.C.E.: nine surviving texts (five old, four new) = 450 believers; 55–45 B.C.E.: thirty-two surviving texts (nine old, twenty-three new) = 1,600 believers; 45–35 B.C.E.: eighty-one surviving texts (thirty-two old, forty-nine new) = 4,050 believers.

Judah's Society grew very, very rapidly. The numbers are startling— and yet, in view of analogies, reasonable. Measured by the percentage of growth, the texts indicate a growth rate of 417 percent for the first decade (most of which probably came during the final two years); 180 percent for the second decade; 355 percent for the third, and 253 percent for the fourth.

Early Christianity grew more slowly, according to a recent estimate by the sociologist of religion Rodney Stark, but the absolute numbers of the two Jewish sects are comparable. From a group of about 1,400 Christians in 50 C.E., the movement grew over five decades to become 7,530. A dynamic modern comparison with the Society is the Mormon Church, which has sustained a growth rate of 43 percent per decade for a full century.[37] Judah's crisis cult apparently grew faster than either of these movements, especially in its third decade, when the gravity of the Jewish situation following the war with Rome began to sink in.

Why? The crisis of the time was more acute, and the answer for it— thanks to the physical Roman presence—more broadly compelling.

The rapidity of the Society's growth tells us something about how it grew and to whom it made its appeal. A basic principle of social movements requiring conversion such as Judah's is that "they grow much faster when they spread through preexisting social networks."[38] The Society could never have grown as it did by appealing only to isolated individuals. As Stark has written:

> Typically people do not *seek* a faith; they *encounter* one through their ties to other people who already accept this faith. In the end, accepting a new religion is a part of conforming to the expectations and examples of one's family and friends. . . .
>
> Religious movements can grow because their members continue to form new relationships with outsiders. . . . [Yet] movements can also recruit by spreading through preexisting social networks, as converts bring in their families and friends. This pattern has the potential for much faster growth than the one-by-one conversion of social isolates. The best example of this is provided by the Mormons. Although they often get an isolated recruit on the basis of attachments built by missionaries, the primary source of Mormon converts is along network lines. The average convert was preceded into the church by many friends and relatives. . . .
>
> Network growth requires that missionaries from a new faith *already have, or easily can form,* strong attachments to such networks.[39]

What was the network for Judah's movement? First and foremost it was the friends and extended families of the original sixty people who belonged to the Society when Judah died. But two other groups would have strong ties with Judah's members: the precursors still living in Jerusalem, and the priesthood more generally.

When Judah's Society returned to Judaea, their appeal for the precursor movement was, because of the war, far stronger than Judah's own ten years earlier. Remember, the precursors were not very different from Judah's followers to begin with; the added impetus of Judah's proven prophecies would be sufficient to sway many to join the New Covenant. The message of the *Damascus Document*—being complimentary of the precursors' motives, yet critical of their methods—was well tailored to induce that response.

The priests outside the precursor group were a diverse lot, ranging from Hellenized, indifferent aristocrats to wild-eyed revolutionaries. Many of the more conservative priests were doubtless sympathetic to Judah's ideas, at least with regard to Temple law. Judah's was, after all, a priest-centered movement, a backlash against the Pharisees who now claimed for themselves ancient priestly prerogatives. By its nature it would appeal to priests.

It was this preexisting network of ties to the Jerusalem precursors and the priests of Israel that waited, dry tinder for the Gospel of the Teacher.

THE *DAMASCUS DOCUMENT* preserves rules regarding the procedure for becoming a member of the Society. Reading between the lines, we can see network growth in action:

> *This is the rule during all the era of wickedness for any who repents of his wicked ways: On the day he speaks to the Overseer of the Many, they shall register him by the oath of the covenant that Moses made with Israel, the covenant to return to the Law of Moses with a whole heart, and to return with a whole spirit to that which is found therein to do during the era . . . Let no one tell him the laws prior to the time they stand before the Overseer, lest the Overseer be fooled by him during the examination. Thus, when he imposes upon him the oath to return to the Law of Moses with a whole heart and with a whole soul, they are innocent with respect to him if he proves false.*[40]

The regulations presupposed that the prospective initiate enjoyed a prior relationship with one or more members of the Society who brought the new person to the Overseer. The Overseer had to decide whether the man could join and what rank to assign him. Therefore, it was crucial that no initiate have an unfair advantage for the Overseer's examination—no crib sheet of questions with their proper responses. The present member stood alongside the person he was sponsoring and was silent as the Overseer conducted the examination: *Let no one tell him the laws prior to the time they stand before the Overseer, lest the Overseer be fooled by him during the examination.*

The fact that rules against unfairly helping prospective members had to be legislated proves that people were doing just that. Since they could hardly help someone to cheat whom they did not know, this passage requires the understanding of at least loose preexisting ties. But it suggests more. Only family ties or close friendship explain a desire to obtain a higher position than he deserved for a new recruit.

And there was another aspect to network growth. When the man was sworn to membership, the Society often gained more than a single member. The man's wife and minor children would become members when he did. As the years passed and his sons came of age, they were no longer automatically a part of the Many. They now had to take upon themselves the same oath their father had, as the *Damascus Document* requires: *Whoever enters the covenant for all Israel, this is a perpetual law: any of his sons who reach the age to be included in the registrants, they shall impose the covenant oath upon him.*[41]

Life together for those who joined the Society focused upon meals and biblical study. At other times the members were scattered to their various means of livelihood, but when it came time to eat they would gather, for their peculiar purity regulations made it difficult for them to eat with anyone not living by the same laws. For this reason a principal method of communal discipline was separation from the common meals for a given time, varying according to the severity of the offense.

The Society studied the Bible together every day, relating what they read there to Judah's hymns and other aids to interpretation. Over time such study, even by uneducated rustics, must have produced a membership more intimately familiar with the books of scripture than virtually any other body of Jews.[42] This procedure created an almost literal "priesthood of all believers." The *Community Rule* describes this daily life:

*By these rules they are to govern themselves wherever they dwell,
in accordance with each legal finding that bears upon communal
life. Inferiors must obey their ranking superiors as regards work and
wealth. They shall eat, pray and deliberate communally. Wherever
ten men belonging to the Society of the Yahad are gathered, a
priest must always be present. The men shall sit before the priest
by rank, and in that manner their opinions will be sought on any
matter.*

*When the table has been set for eating or the new wine readied for
drinking, it is the priest who shall stretch out his hand first, blessing
the first portion of the bread or the new wine. In any place where is
gathered the ten-man quorum, someone must always be engaged in
study of the Law, day and night, continually, each one taking his turn.
The Many will be diligent together for the first third of every night of
the year, reading aloud from the Book, interpreting Scripture, and
praying together.*[43]

Thus the Society lived as brothers. The first messiah's movement
now numbered in the thousands, scattered throughout the land as a major
social force. In some form many of their ideas about Judah must have become common knowledge, and interest in him undoubtedly escalated as
time went on.

For the doctrine of the forty years pointed to the year 34 B.C.E.—or
close to it—as the Year of the End.

THOUSANDS AWAITED 34 B.C.E. with taut expectancy. Analogy suggests that membership tipped sharply upward as the year drew nearer
and nearer. Such is commonly the case with crisis cults who urge a specific
date for the end of the world; as the nineteenth-century Millerites explained, "preaching 'the time' raised audiences and brought 'results.' "[44]

Surviving texts of the Society tell us nothing of their growing mood
of expectancy. We can only imagine the rush of emotions among believers,
and the probable hostility among outsiders, as the year 34 B.C.E. dawned.
As the year progressed and the hopeful expectancy was tinged with greater
and greater measures of anxiety—when would Judah come?—the movement's writers were, so far as our evidence indicates, silent.

And then the year passed. We can scarcely intuit the soul-shattering disappointment that the believers must have experienced when the year had reached its end and yet the End had not reached them. For decades the Society had been pointing toward this year. Its understanding of the biblical prophets, much of its structure of belief, its reconfiguring of Judah and his failed prophecies to give them new life: all rested on this foundational prophecy. The End shall come when the forty years are complete.

Yet the End had not come.

The explanation that the Society offered for this failed apocalypse appears in the *Commentary on Habakkuk.* It is the last roughly datable entry in the group's writings, set down shortly after the passing of the Year of the End. The words are as follows:

> *"For a prophecy testifies of a specific period; it speaks of that time and does not deceive." (Habakkuk 2:3a)*
>
> *This means that the final period will extend, even beyond all that the prophets have spoken, for the mysteries of God are wondrous.*
>
> *"If it tarries, be patient, for it will surely come and not be late." (Habakkuk 2:3b)*
>
> *This refers to the Men of Truth, Performers of the Law whose hands will not grow weary of doing the truth when the final period is extended, for all the periods of God will come as established for them, just as He has decreed for them in His mysterious wisdom.*[45]

To the thousands of Judah's followers, this was the explanation offered by the movement's leadership: the final period was to be extended. The author admitted the disconfirmation of the group's prophecy. He further admitted that there was no way to account for that failure but the mysteries of God. Yet these mysteries were precisely what the group had claimed all along to understand. To concede now that they really did not understand them was to undermine their entire claim to legitimacy. Did they, or did they not, have special knowledge of God's truth?

The Society's response to the failure of the End to arrive was strikingly similar to that of the Millerites at the time of the Great Disappointment. Referring to the very same verse adduced by Judah's movement, Habakkuk 2:3, Miller and his fellow leaders declared: "We now find ourselves occupying a time, beyond which we can extend none of the prophetic periods, according to our chronology and date of their commencement. . . . We admit that it is proved that we do not know the definite time."[46]

The Millerites found the same verse, and they offered more or less the same explanation: their prediction had failed, but they did not know why. They never suggested a better explanation. History records the fate of the Millerites. After the Great Disappointment they disappeared almost overnight.

Faced with their greatest crisis ever, Judah's followers offered a response that history has shown to be potentially fatal. The *Commentary*'s explanation would not have been effective in combating the sense of being lost and adrift that millenarian groups experience when their predictions fail. The sheer inadequacy of the explanation forces upon us the question: Did the Society recover from this blow?

Or was this indeed the end for the movement, though not the end they had been expecting?

TO FIND OUT, we must return to the manuscripts of Judah's movement and call the ancient scribes to the witness stand. We must ask them two very pointed questions, beginning with this one: "What historical events, people, and processes do you know, and from what distance in time?"

The purpose of this question is to uncover historical allusions. Any scribal text containing an allusion must have been composed after the person, event, or process to which it alludes. Thus allusions are an excellent clue for determining when a literary work was written.

When this approach is brought to bear on the works of Judah's followers, it turns up twenty-nine possible allusions.[47] Of these, the vast majority are to events that fell in the first century B.C.E.—nearly 80 percent (twenty-three of twenty-nine). The texts mention just a handful of second-century B.C.E. people and happenings, and these they saw from a first-century B.C.E. perspective. Also, the allusions evidence the interest of the writers in the war with Rome, together with the events running up to it and those of the aftermath. Eighteen of the references are to this period (62 percent of the total identifiable events).[48] The war and attendant Roman invasion were the engine of the Society's message. That these things should occupy many of the writers is natural and understandable.

When we question the ancient scribes, then, their answer is clear: the overwhelming majority of datable Society writings were first-century B.C.E. compositions. Indeed, the texts give no indication by their allusions that any of the writings preceded the first century B.C.E., which is, of course, just what we should expect for a group born in 76 B.C.E. More startling is what we find when we move forward in time.

The writings of Judah's followers contain *not a single identifiable allusion to any event of the first century C.E.* That silence means that not even one writing of Judah's movement can be shown to have originated after the turn of the eras—after, in fact, the failure of the End in 34 B.C.E. The silence is ominous. Vital crisis cults continually reconfigure earlier ideas to fit the new circumstances brought about by prophetic disconfirmation. Reinterpretation is their lifeblood. When that blood no longer flows, one must suspect that the heart no longer beats.

Judah's Society had suffered a backbreaking disconfirmation in the failure of its prophesied Year of the End to arrive as scheduled. Had the group survived this failure, we should expect to find writings identifiably composed after 34 B.C.E. We should find in those writings at the least reinterpretation and probably substantial numbers of historical allusions in the context of that revised perspective. We find nothing.

With the scribes still on the witness stand, we must ask them the second question: "When did you copy your books?"

This question is not merely a rephrasing of the first one. The aim of the first question was to find out when *new* books were composed. This second question aims to discover when *old,* worn-out books were recopied. The scribal reply to the question comes from analysis of the handwriting, the script sequencing we discussed earlier when estimating the rate of growth for Judah's movement. The assumption is that the vitality of Judah's Society at any given time would make itself apparent through its recopying of writings held to be important.

When we pursue this approach we discover that nearly 90 percent of all the Society's books were copied in the first century B.C.E. As noted earlier, 52 percent of them originate in a single script period that likely represents approximately the years 45–35 B.C.E.[49] For the years 75–35 B.C.E., the profile of manuscript production follows the pattern expected for a very dynamic movement, the number increasing exponentially from one generation to the next. But then production falls off a cliff. A growing or even stable movement should have continued to produce more and more copies to serve its membership. That is not what we find.

The scribes testify instead to the rise *then the rapid fall* of a crisis cult.

Judah's followers failed to conserve the heritage of the movement's past once the curtain rose on the Christian era. In a scribal culture, to neglect to "reprint" any book by renewed copying is to consign it to oblivion. People do not act that way with writings that provide meat for their faith—unless, of course, there are no people.

As one scholar has put it, "The key to converting an effervescent apocalypticism into an established, complex religious system includes, above all, *an elongation of the eschatological timetable.* As long as a group sustains short term, specific predictions of the end, it remains volatile."[50] Did Judah's Society take this tack? Did the believers reconfigure the doctrine of the forty years after 34 B.C.E., dulling their sharp-edged expectations in favor of an open-ended wait on the millennium?

If so, we would expect to find them writing new texts in the first century C.E. We do not. And if they settled in for a long winter's nap, their charged, angry adolescence given way to a quietistic senescence, we nevertheless should find them recopying older writings in that same period. We do not. This striking silence is reminiscent of the Sherlock Holmes story "Silver Blaze."

Watson asks the famous detective, "Is there any other point to which you wish to draw my attention?"

"To the curious incident of the dog in the nighttime."

"The dog did nothing in the nighttime."

"That was the curious incident."

Silence when there should not have been silence. Three separate trails of evidence: the inadequate explanation for the disconfirmation of a foundational prophecy; the failure to write new books; and the failure to copy old ones; taken together, these argue that the Society died in the first century B.C.E. At least, we have no textual evidence that the movement survived and strong reason to think that it did not.[51]

With the shock of the End's falsification, the membership presumably suffered a precipitous, almost overnight decline, much as did that of Millerism. Some members drifted back into normal society, others joined this or that sect of the day. A core of diehards doubtless remained, impossible to persuade of any truth but Judah's. These diehards continued secure in the faith of the *Commentary on Habakkuk:* though the prophets be deceived, God had a mysterious plan. All his periods would yet come as he had promised. But that message of perplexity would attract few outsiders. The diehards lived out their lives, and the specter of the first messiah gradually faded to black as, one by one, the believers perished.

With the advent of a generation that had never known the upstroke, the Society passed from this world, though it did not die before etching Judah into the myth-dream. The final extinction must have occurred around the turn of the eras, if not a decade earlier. Given the nature of things, one cannot rule out the possibility that a few people continued Judah's teaching, perhaps even for decades, a trickle in a dry riverbed. If so, they wrote no new texts that we possess and can have been neither a large group nor a vital one.

THIS HAS BEEN the story of a Jerusalem wisdom teacher, Judah, priestly prophet, member of the elite, and a leader of the political coalition that supported King Alexander. When Alexander died in 76 B.C.E. and his wife and successor, Queen Alexandra, anointed the Pharisee perspective on Temple laws, Judah led a crisis-cult reaction that was in many ways similar to other crisis cults. Yet Judah's was different from earlier movements in a crucial way. Not content merely to be a prophet, a mouthpiece for God's new laws, Judah would be their centerpiece. With that move of paranormal audacity, he became the first messiah known to history.

This has been the story of that first messiah's conflict with the Jerusalem authorities, of his trial on charges of false prophecy, of his subsequent exile to the Wilderness of Damascus, of his life in the twilight world of banditry, of his betrayal by some of his own followers. Judah's death (execution?) and the response of remaining believers, his apotheosis to a throne at the right hand of God, the rise of his Society to numbers and influence as a result of fulfilled prophecy, and their death by the same prophetic sword by which they had lived: all of this has been his story.

Yet in the background has lingered another figure, sometimes mentioned, often implied, and doubtless always in the reader's mind. He has been in the background long enough. Let him come to the fore.

What does the story of the first messiah mean for our views of Jesus, the other messiah?

CHAPTER 10

THE OTHER MESSIAH

The Baptist appears, and cries: "Repent, for the Kingdom of Heaven is at hand." Soon after that comes Jesus, and in the knowledge that he is the coming Son of Man lays hold of the wheel of the world to set it moving on that last revolution which is to bring all ordinary history to a close. It refuses to turn, and he throws himself upon it.

Albert Schweitzer, *The Quest of the Historical Jesus*

History does not consist only in differences, in the unique and novel—whatever will not happen twice. . . . How could anyone believe in a history confined exclusively to the unique occurrence?

Fernand Braudel, *On History*

W HEN WE BRING the Jesus we meet in the Gospels to the fore and place him against the backdrop of the first messiah and the history of Judah's movement, the parallels between the two men blaze forth in sharp relief.

A TALE OF TWO SAVIORS

As Jesus declared himself a prophet, and more than a prophet, so had Judah.

As Jesus struck contemporaries with his authoritative teaching and rare gifts of expression, so had Judah.

As Jesus proclaimed a completed Law of Moses, perfected by his own direct revelations from God, so had Judah.

As Jesus spoke of charity, the poor, and love of one's fellows, forbade divorce, and proclaimed the imminent coming of the Kingdom of God, so had Judah.

As Jesus was hailed by followers as He Who Is to Come and worked attendant wonders, so had Judah.

As Jesus' message and claims were rejected by most of his fellow Jews, so it had been for Judah.

As Jesus came into conflict with the ruling powers, the Pharisees, and the high priestly families, so had Judah.

As Jesus was tried before the council and sentenced to die, so had been Judah.

As Jesus pronounced judgment upon Jerusalem and predicted that for rejecting him it would be destroyed by the Romans, so had Judah.

As Jesus founded a vital and long-lasting movement before leaving this world, so had Judah.

As the Christian church grew into an institution composed of "overseers" (bishops), priests, and laity, so it had been with Judah's followers.

As Jesus' followers argued that he was the Suffering Servant, the Messiah, the Good Shepherd, and other figures foretold by scripture, so the followers of Judah had argued.

As Jesus' sufferings were proclaimed a divine healing for all believers—an atonement—so it had been with Judah.

As growing numbers came to believe that Jesus had been glorified and now sat at the right hand of God, so it had been with Judah.

As early Christians anticipated the imminent return of Jesus to judge the quick and the dead, redeem Israel, and initiate a millennium wherein believers would rule the world, so it had been with Judah's followers.[1]

And in all of these things, Judah was first, anticipating the far more famous prophet from Galilee by a full century. How can this correspondence be explained?

Some of the elements are pure coincidence. They derive from the fact that both men were the leaders of crisis cults. For certain things, as we have seen, typically happen in the course of a crisis cult's internal development and as it interacts with the larger society. Parallels of this sort are thin gruel for historical understanding.

But other elements are not coincidental at all. These elements were connected to the myth-dream of Israel, which Judah had fed, molded, and changed and which came to Jesus in that changed form, ready for him to tap. Like all myth-dreams, the myth-dream of Israel was a not-quite-conscious set of shared beliefs and assumptions about ideal reality. Like all myth-dreams, that of the Jews was dynamic rather than static. It changed over time as it was fed by charismatic prophets. Ineffable for most people, for prophets the myth-dream represented a lode that they might mine, a mine whose product they could engineer into a vehicle for partisan hopes and social protest. They could speak it aloud, try to make it happen.

The myth-dream is what renders critical parallels between Judah and Jesus more than sizzle and smoke.

For when Judah made claims about himself while giving voice to the ancient hopes of his people and those claims were accepted and acceptance became widespread as his movement grew, seeds were planted. Judah's movement was dynamic and widely distributed throughout Judaea and, perhaps, other Jewish centers of population, including Galilee. The things that Judah did and said about himself and God, the things that his followers believed of him—these were no secrets. It did not happen in a corner. Much of it centered in Jerusalem, the intellectual, cultural, and religious center of all Jewry.

Judah gave flesh to what before him had been only an idea, and a fairly new one at that: the idea of a messiah. And though Judah did not live much longer after realizing who he was, nevertheless the life lived by Judah solidified a way of thinking messianically. The wet concrete of Judah's original notions hardened and set in the following decades as his followers proclaimed the Gospel of the Teacher.

Judah's biblical notions, his collocation of central portions of the scriptures, became part of the myth-dream. In this way Judah changed his world and, through Jesus, ours. When, later, Jesus claimed for himself that he was the New Moses, the Servant, the Good Shepherd, and other scriptural figures all rolled into one—and despite the denials of many modern scholars, he probably did make those claims—he drew the imagery ready-made from the myth-dream of 30 C.E. Judah had fed the myth-dream that package in 75 B.C.E., and his followers had given the notions some permanence.

For Jesus to evoke those figures was natural, and he could do it with no thought of Judah. These had simply become expected roles for the One.

In the same way, Melanesians called Yali the Black King, though it was a name he never chose for himself. The title and role had earlier been Mambu's. When Yali arose they fell to him, his mantle by the mechanism of the myth-dream.

So let us put sizzle and smoke and sensationalism aside and state a simple fact: viewed as religious systems, early Christianity and the first messiah's movement were remarkably similar. Both movements were entered by adult conversion. Both movements regarded themselves as the fulfillment of Israel's ancient prophecies. Both were salvationist, holding that only members would be part of the Kingdom; outsiders would be damned. Both were apocalyptic movements, believing that—as Jesus is quoted by Mark's Gospel—"The kingdom of God is at the door." And the focus of each was the charismatic messiah in whom one had to believe, come with a message from God whose truth had to be acknowledged. Without that faith the Kingdom was forfeit.

Consider what the *Melchizedek Book* and the Hymn of the Exalted One, taken together, declared of Judah, the first messiah. After a ministry of prophetic proclamation on earth, he had died and was now in heaven. There he resided at the right hand of God. Within a generation, he would return with a legion of angels, overthrow evil, forgive the sins of believers, and atone for them personally. He would then establish the Kingdom of God.

Apart from the name of the central figure, that drama might well have come directly from the Gospels. Judah was the savior before Jesus.

True, the messages of Judah and Jesus were very different. Yet the specific content of the messages is, from a systematic perspective, secondary. What matters is the hardware of the movements, so to speak, not the software. And the hardware was virtually identical. We know of no other form of ancient Judaism nearly as similar to Christianity as Judah's movement was. In that sense one might describe the Society as "proto-Christianity."

Crisis cults, as we have seen, are common historical phenomena, attested all over the world and down through time. Yet the Teacher's movement is the best parallel to the Jesus movement in all of world history. Both arose at roughly the same time, in the same place, among the same people, and within the same cultural milieu. How then can we affirm the recent judgment by two prominent New Testament specialists, Tom Wright and Stephen Neill, who have said, "We shall not expect to find in the Scrolls direct light on the New Testament, on the ideas of John the Baptist or Jesus, or on the views and practices of the early Church"?[2]

Moreover, in the *Thanksgiving Hymns* we have in our hands an even more profound potential insight into Jesus and earliest Christianity.

JUDAH AND THE HISTORICAL JESUS

The authors of the Christian Gospels wrote to bear witness to their faith in Jesus as messiah. They wrote to convince readers of the truth of this faith. They were not interested in an "objective," academic study of Jesus' life, and the narratives they produced were not history as modern historians write it, though they are in some ways comparable to ancient biographies, such as Plutarch's *Parallel Lives of the Greeks and Romans*. When, at the tail end of the eighteenth century, biblical scholars began to apply the methods of historical inquiry lately developed in the study of classical Greek and Roman texts to the Gospels—thereby removing them from the realm of the sacred untouchable and subjecting them to a skeptical scrutiny previously undreamed of—the process was unsettling to many of the faithful.

The results proved no less unsettling. For if one begins with secular methods, one gets secular results, and with them—by definition—a natural, not supernatural Jesus. The faith element is abstracted, and it is left up to the reader of such studies to reinsert it if desired. When the German theologian David Strauss published his *Life of Jesus* in 1835, a milestone in the application of the new approaches to the Gospels, he was greeted with international horror and condemnation. As Albert Schweitzer later wrote with his typical eloquence, "The theologians declared Strauss bankrupt, and felt themselves rich because they had made sure of not being ruined by a similar unimaginative honesty."[3]

Despite Strauss's ruination, the "quest for the historical Jesus" has continued, waxing and waning until our own day, now ending, now beginning again as skepticism, then optimism about the possibility of finding this Jesus predominates. According to the reckoning one follows, we are presently in either the Second or the Third Quest.[4] And despite the continued misgivings of many of the faithful about the propriety of such research, interest in the historical Jesus has spilled over from the world of scholarship into broader culture.

For example, in December 1994 *Life* magazine devoted a cover story to Jesus, as had *Newsweek* seven months earlier. The April 8, 1996, issues of the three major American news weeklies—*Time, Newsweek,* and *U.S. News and World Report*—simultaneously ran cover stories on the modern, scholarly study of Jesus. The verdicts of the Jesus Seminar, a group that meets to consider the historicity of the words and deeds reported in the Gospels, are regularly reported in the media.

Because historians ask different questions than the ancient writers were concerned to answer, the quest for the historical Jesus will continue. Indeed, quite apart from the goals of the quest, the need for such research arises from a desire to understand the Gospels themselves as literary works.

When the Gospels are read "vertically" (straight through from Matthew to John), they seem to present one coherent story. But when they are read "horizontally" as historians do it—comparing topics and sayings from Gospel to Gospel—the dominant impression is of the differences.[5] Consider figure 2, which schematizes a single portion of the Gospel of Luke, chosen more or less randomly, compared with the parallel portions of Matthew and Mark.[6]

Even a cursory reading of figure 2 spotlights the sort of questions raised by a horizontal reading of the Gospels. Did Jesus tell the twelve to wear sandals on their mission (Mark) or not to wear sandals (Matthew), or did he say nothing about sandals (Luke)? Were they to take a staff (Mark) or not (Matthew and Luke)? More generally, what exactly did Jesus say? Matthew renders as direct quotation statements that Mark presents as narrative, and Luke is somewhere in between. Do we then possess the so-called *ipsissima verba Iesu,* the actual words of Jesus? If so, where are they to be found, Matthew, Mark, or Luke? Or do the words come forth only after a melding of these sources, and perhaps John? The questions are many. They multiply considerably as one folds into the consideration other portions of the Gospels.

Historians have often been pessimistic about the Gospels as reliable purveyors of the sort of truth modern history seeks. The noted ancient historian Robin Lane Fox has concluded,

> The Gospels' disagreements begin at the most basic level: they
> do not even agree about the day on which things happened.
> The synoptic Gospels [Matthew, Mark, and Luke] believe that
> the Last Supper took place on the day of Passover, whereas the

Figure 2: Luke 9:1–6 and Gospel Parallels

MATTHEW	MARK	LUKE
And Jesus went about all the	And he went about among	
cities and villages, teaching in their	the villages teaching.	
synagogues and preaching the		
gospel of the kingdom, and healing		
every disease and every infirmity.		
And he called to him his twelve	And he called to him the twelve, and began	And he called the twelve together
disciples	to send them out two by two	
and gave them authority	and gave them authority	and gave them power and authority
over unclean spirits, to cast them	over the unclean spirits.	over all demons
out, and to heal every disease and		and to cure diseases,
every infirmity.		
"And preach as you go, saying, 'The		and he sent them out to preach the
kingdom of heaven is at hand.' Heal		kingdom of God
the sick, raise the dead,		and to heal.
cleanse lepers, cast out demons.		
You received without paying, give without	He	
pay. Take no gold,	charged them to take nothing	And he said to them, "Take nothing
nor silver, nor copper in your belts,	for their journey except a staff; no bread,	for your journey, no staff,
no bag for your journey,	no bag, no money in their belts; but	nor bag, nor bread, nor money;
nor	to wear sandals and not	and do not
two tunics, nor sandals, nor a	put on two tunics.	have two tunics.
staff; for the laborer deserves his	And he said	

continued

Figure 2, continued

MATTHEW	MARK	LUKE
food. And whatever town or village you	to them, "Where you enter a house,	And whatever house you enter,
enter, find out who is worthy in it,		
and stay with him until you depart.	stay there until you leave the place.	stay there, and from there depart.
And if any one will not receive you or	And if any place will not receive you and	And wherever they do not receive you,
listen to your words, shake off	they refuse to hear you, when you	when you
the dust from your feet as you	leave	leave that town
leave that house	shake off the dust that is on	shake off the dust from
or town."	your feet for a testimony against them."	your feet as a testimony against them."
	So they went out and preached that men	And they departed and went through
	should repent. And they cast out many	the villages, preaching the gospel
	demons, and anointed with oil many that	
	were sick and healed them.	and healing everywhere.

fourth Gospel [John] . . . puts the Supper on the day before. This conflict should put us on our guard: the exact day of Jesus's Crucifixion was a basic fact, but the Gospels do not agree on it.[7]

One need not be as skeptical of the narratives as is Fox to see that the Jesus of history will not emerge simply through reading the Gospels. One must compare, question and probe, and call upon sources outside the canonical Gospels for perspective. As the data thus culled is sifted and studied, some portrait of the historical Jesus will come into focus.

Indeed, scholars have found reason to sketch of Jesus an entire gallery of portraits, bewildering at first for its sheer irreconcilable diversity. A walk down the gallery will bring you to the aphoristic sage of the Jesus Seminar; the itinerant Cynic philosopher of John Dominic Crossan, Burton

Mack, and F. Gerald Downing; the man of the Spirit, Galilean holy man of Marcus Borg and Geza Vermes; the apocalyptic prophet of the Last Days of E. P. Sanders and Maurice Casey; the prophet of social change of Richard Horsley and Gerd Thiessen; and yet other Jesuses rendered by such scholars as John Meier, James Dunn, Marinus de Jonge, and N. T. Wright.[8] Which portrait, if any, is the true likeness?

The *Thanksgiving Hymns* may help us pick the real historical Jesus out of the lineup.

B ETWEEN 100 B.C.E. and 70 C.E. many prophets and messiahs arose among the Jews. The roster includes Judas the Galilean, the shepherd Athronges, Simon the Perean, a Samaritan messiah in the days of Pontius Pilate, Theudas, "the Egyptian," Menahem ben Hezekiah, John the Baptist, and, of course, Jesus of Nazareth. Others are mentioned in the sources as existing, but with the last of their followers likewise perished their names. Not one of these prophets wrote anything (at least, anything that has survived), Jesus included.

Judah was different. Precisely in that difference lies his greatest significance for us today. He wrote of his feelings and reactions to the Pharisee takeover, of his own ideas about who he was, of what would happen when shortly the Kingdom dawned. Within the limits natural to written transmission of ideas, careful study can lead us to know something of Judah's mind. And it was the *mind of a prophet like Jesus.*

Research into the historical Jesus has often circled back to the question, "What was his messianic self-understanding?"[9] In ordinary terms, who did Jesus think he was? A recent book by J. C. O'Neill took that very question for its title. "Did the historical Jesus really regard himself as the Son of God?" asked N. T. Wright in his 1992 book *Who Was Jesus?*[10]

The question is fundamental, and the historian's view of the problem of Jesus' self-understanding affects how he or she will read the Gospels and other pertinent documents fundamentally. Statements and deeds there recorded will be judged historical or not according to how well they fit what a scholar thinks Jesus *could* have said or done. This procedure is defensible, for history is a gray realm, with few sunlit corners or pitch-black vertices. Certain knowledge of the past is almost as elusive as certain knowledge of the future. The gray judgment of probability is usually the essence for the historian.

To decide what is probable, historians often have recourse to analogy. Analogy is a plumb line of historical research, guiding the scholar's judgment on what is straight and what is crooked in records of the past. Since classical antiquity, historians have recognized the value of analogy— of searching out, as did Thucydides, and "clearly examining both past events and those that will, in all human likelihood, recur in much the same or similar manner."[11] The constant of human nature is what makes analogy such a powerful tool for research into the past.

Much depends upon judging the mind of Jesus, upon weighing his possible ideas about himself. This is a primary sieve through which the data must strain. Those that pass through can then be fit into the puzzle of the Jesus of history. But we do not have direct access to Jesus' mind. He left no record of his thoughts. He wrote no autobiography. Because of the centrality of analogy to the historical enterprise, though, we can seek the next best thing: access to the mind of someone who was, in essential ways, like Jesus—the more like Jesus, the better. This boon is exactly what we received when, in 1947, the first messiah's writings began to issue forth from the caves of the Judean desert. In the crucial sense of messianic consciousness, Judah was like Jesus. But the boon was not recognized for what it was.

The situation calls to mind the story of a young man who begged his father for a new car as a high school graduation gift. When the day of his graduation arrived, instead of a set of keys the father handed him a book, telling him, "Here is everything you'll need to begin to make your way in life." Disgusted, the young man threw the book in a corner of his room, never even opening it. Only years later, on the day his father died, did he again seek out the volume. Turning its now yellowing pages with trembling hands, he found pressed between two of them a check, large enough to buy his car.

So it has been with Judah's hymns: scholars have not recognized what they had. The gift has sat unopened. But if we open it and read and consider Judah's words, as we have done above, we are transported, ushered into the presence of a Jewish messiah roughly contemporary with Jesus— and we are ushered there directly. These are not his thoughts as disciples more or less accurately recalled them years later. They are not his thoughts as tradition sifted them, keeping only what later times found congenial. Pure and simple, these are his thoughts.

So in the case of Judah we have what is urgently needed yet is lacking for Jesus: his actual words, the diary of an ancient Jewish crisis-cult prophet, telling us how he viewed himself, giving us his messianic self-understanding. In Judah we have an analogical key to the previously locked mind of the Nazarene.

And when we turn the key, what do we find?

W E   F I N D   W H A T   I would call a "scripture prophet." The "scripture prophet" stands in contradistinction to another type, the "free prophet," who claims to receive divine revelation yet without extensive interaction with his culture's sacred, written tradition. The free prophet's self-understanding is thus "unbound," able to develop in any conceivable direction. Mambu and Yali were such men, and so was Jim Jones of the People's Temple, and many others down through the ages.

In contrast, the scripture prophet derives his self-understanding in large measure via prolonged meditation on earlier written revelation. Because of the force of this written tradition, the scripture prophet is "bound." The tradition channels the directions in which his self-concept may grow. Judah was this type of prophet, and analogy suggests that Jesus was, too. Possessing similar psyches (the sort that would lead a person to become a prophet in the first place), they came to their self-understandings through an identical process and using the same materials, essentially the Bible.

It was through contemplating the Bible that they came to know who they were. They were akin to Norman Cohn's medieval European prophets, of whom he said—recall—"Whenever the career of one of them can be traced, it turns out that he was obsessed with eschatological phantasies [*sic*] long *before* it occurred to him, in the midst of some great social upheaval, to [found a crisis cult]."[12]

Judah and Jesus had long been familiar with the defining biblical passages before they realized what the words truly meant.

Scripture prophets often have notably capacious memories. They combine these capacities with unusual associative abilities. And those belonging to the tradition of the myth-dream of Israel share something else in common. In their search for meaning, they discern "someone else" in the Bible: an exalted being, a presence, of stature second only to God.

Scripture prophets read the Bible and discern the Voice. They reflect, for example, on Psalm 110:1: "The Lord (Hebrew YHWH) says to my Lord (Hebrew *Adonai*), 'Sit at my right hand until I put your enemies under your feet.'" Here they reason that since God is YHWH, the *Adonai* of this passage must be someone else, even though *Adonai* is elsewhere in the Bible a second name for God. That reasoning opens up the possibility that in other biblical passages, things said about *Adonai* refer not to God, but to the Voice.

With their unusual capacities, scripture prophets are able to hold much of the Bible active, combustible in their minds. Their constant meditations on its meaning lead them to compare and interweave many collateral biblical portions. This method of association was the way all ancient Jews read the Bible; it was the way the Greeks read Homer. Association is a natural process of the human mind. Scripture prophets just do it better than anyone else.

Thus, to continue our example: Psalm 110:2 reads, "The Lord [YHWH] sends out from Zion your mighty scepter. Rule in the midst of your foes." The prophet already knows from verse 1 that *your* refers to *Adonai,* the Voice. The term *scepter* leads by association to another passage inhabited by an exalted presence, Isaiah 11:4, "He shall strike the earth with the *scepter* of his mouth, and with the breath of his lips he shall kill the wicked." In turn, this passage leads by verbal association to Isaiah 9:5–7, a third portion describing an exalted being—and so the process continues, each new passage furnishing additional information about the Voice. As we have seen, Judah made the identification of these Isaiah passages explicit in his hymns. He was pursuing the Voice.

By interweaving, scripture prophets read out from the Bible a consistent drama of past, present, and future that is so subtle, and yet so comprehensively explanatory, that its discovery strikes their followers as beyond human capacity. This process of interweaving is what we have observed in tracking Judah's hymns to their sources. Judah was not quoting and alluding to scripture just for poetic purposes or to show off his erudition. He was resignifying the portions he chose. He gave them new meaning, a meaning made full in himself.

All scripture prophets resignify, for scripture prophets *recognize themselves as the Voice.* With this knowledge in hand, they begin to resignify passages of the Bible. In Psalm 110 they see themselves as *Adonai.* This is how Judah arrived at his view of himself, and it is probably how Jesus did as well. To find oneself in a single passage is to find oneself in many, for the initial discovery acts as a sort of trip wire.

Once the momentous first step has been taken, sirens blare. Like the steps of a march, the other motifs of the Voice follow—though naturally in a cadence varying from prophet to prophet—by process of association:

passage compared with passage, meaning with meaning, step by step, each scripture prophet almost ineluctably being led to the same congeries of biblical portions. This is the reason that, as J. J. M. Roberts has observed, "passages selected as messianic proof texts remain remarkably consistent for both Jewish and Christian interpreters."[13]

Once the Voice has been recognized and one begins to pursue it through the text, these are the places the associative human mind will naturally go.

W E   H A V E   S E E N by close analysis of his hymns that Judah combined an uncanny ability to synthesize the holy, written tradition of Israel with the psyche of a prophet. This was an understanding the Society had of him when the *Commentary on Habakkuk* was set down. Recall this passage that we considered in the last chapter:

> God told Habakkuk to write down what is going to happen to the generation to come; but when that period would be complete He did not make known to him. When it [Habakkuk 2:2] says, "so that with ease someone can read it," this refers to the Teacher of Righteousness, to whom God made known all the mysterious revelations of His servants the prophets.[14]

Judah was believed able to explain the full meaning of the ancient prophecies, unknown even to their original spokesmen. In this ability was rooted much of his attraction.

There have been many scripture prophets down through the ages. Karl Schmid, god-man of the secret flagellants of Thuringia, was one. Other scripture prophets of the Middle Ages include Tanchelm of Antwerp (c. 1125) and John of Leyden (1530s). Still others have arisen nearer to our own day. Because they are modern, we possess much greater documentation for them than we do for any ancient analogue. Since that documentation allows us to discover something of how their minds operated, two are worth a brief look. One was David Koresh; the other was the so-called Messiah of the Cave, Moses Guibbory.

In the early 1920s Guibbory left his native Russia and emigrated via Turkey to Palestine. He took up residence in the Cave of the Sanhedrin on the north side of Jerusalem. There for several years he met with a messianic sect he founded that later crossed the Atlantic and grew to become notable

in 1950s America, numbering in California alone several thousand followers. Guibbory was the talk of Jerusalem, a small town in those days, and late
in 1927 the famous writer Arthur Koestler was a skeptical visitor to his cave.
Koestler described the meeting in his autobiography, *Arrow in the Blue*:

> I climbed down the shaft into a small, damp burial chamber steeped
> in a foul smell and muddy twilight; and there was the prophet. He
> was short, and thus able to stand almost upright in the low cave; he
> had black, tangled hair which fell in locks onto his shoulders and
> around his rotting shirt; a bloodless face, and large, gentle eyes. He
> seemed to take my visit for granted. . . .
>
> He said, "I know you want proofs. That is simple. Think of the
> earthquake (there had been that year one of the worst earthquakes
> in Palestine's history). Four hundred dead! I did it. It was simple.
> Like this . . ." He picked up two stones which were the only furnish-
> ings of the cave, and hit them against each other in a sudden fury.
> "That is how I made the earthquake."[15]

To Koestler, Guibbory proved only that he was a madman. Yet we
have seen earlier when evaluating such matters that perspective is everything and that, from a clinical perspective, crisis-cult leaders are seldom
mentally ill. Recall the questions of the Oxford clinical psychiatrist, Anthony
Storr: "Can people be regarded as psychotic merely because they hold eccentric ideas about the universe and their own significance as prophets or
teachers? What are the boundaries between sanity and madness? What
does labelling someone psychotic really mean?"[16]

The biblical prophets Ezekiel and Isaiah, to take just two examples,
were not outwardly different from Guibbory and his stones. Ezekiel lay on
the ground, first on one side, then on the other, "besieging" a brick for over a
year to make a prophetic point (Ezekiel 4). Isaiah roamed naked through
Jerusalem for three years as a sign to the nation of impending exile (Isaiah
20). Were these actions any less "mad" than Guibbory's? We are comfortable with the actions of the biblical prophets because they stand within our
culture's Judaeo-Christian heritage. Were others to do what they did, what
would we think of them?

Guibbory understood himself to be Jehovah the Last (in a sense, an
incarnation of God) and also the Lord of All the Earth, the Shepherd, the
New Moses, and so forth—all images drawn from prophetic texts of the

Bible. He was a premier example of the scripture prophet, not least because he left behind a two thousand-page Hebrew book, *The Bible in the Hands of Its Creators*. Beginning with Genesis and going through to the Bible's last page, Guibbory tried to demonstrate the true meaning of scripture. He discovered the Voice and maintained that all such parts of the Bible referred to him.

On June 28, 1932, in the presence of seven witnesses, Guibbory anointed a Swedish-born American Jew, David Horowitz, as the "Messiah, Son of David." Horowitz would later go on to a long and distinguished career. He was a United Nations correspondent for fifty years beginning with the inception of the U.N. and became a confidant of Dag Hammarskjöld, U Thant, and Abba Eban. He was instrumental in behind-the-scenes efforts to establish and recognize the state of Israel in 1948, personally securing needed votes from three South American countries. In 1977 Menachem Begin bestowed upon him a Defender of Israel Medal, and in 1991 Yitzhak Shamir presented Horowitz with a Defender of Jerusalem Award.[17]

Doubtless few of the world leaders among whom Horowitz circulated were aware of his 1932 anointing, which he always maintained was genuine, or imagined that after a life full of accomplishment he still looked back upon that youthful time with Guibbory as the high point of his life, when he was privileged to "study at the feet of 'the Declarer of the Generations from the Beginning—Shilo.'"[18]

In his 1943 book, *Thirty-Three Candles,* Horowitz described the charismatic relation between himself and Moses Guibbory. He for two years (1932–34) had been involved with Guibbory in the writing of *The Bible in the Hands of Its Creators,* which he called "nothing less grandiose than the writing of a new law for Israel—the final completion by Moses the second of the unfinished task begun at Mount Sinai more than 3,500 years ago by Moses the first."[19] Using no tools of scholarship, neither dictionaries nor concordances, merely flipping occasionally the pages of a small Hebrew Bible, Guibbory dictated to Horowitz for ten to twelve hours a day, weaving passage together with passage, comparing portion with portion in an astounding display of memory and virtuosity. As Horowitz would often say years later, "No one can do this on their own; it's impossible."[20]

What really went on was a dissecting of the Bible in a manner hitherto unknown to man. The Cave-dweller [Guibbory] had gained his knowledge of these facts while he was still in the Cave. The time had now come for the execution of the work. For me it was a wonderful adventure. Without worry of a livelihood, it afforded me an opportunity to give all my time to study of the Bible from its original source—and at the feet of a true teacher. As we journeyed through the Bible, many wonderful things evolved—things I had never seen before; yet they were there in the Hebrew. . . . For me it had been a wonderful "journey"—marvelous things revealed themselves in the Law, in the prophets, and in the Psalms—things I had never dreamt about. In Isaiah, Jeremiah, Ezekiel an entire new world opened up—especially in Isaiah, the dean of the major prophets! . . . The things that [Guibbory] ferreted out amazed me.

Horowitz had long been intimately familiar with the Bible, but not with the Bible Guibbory showed him. Guibbory demonstrated a hallmark of the scripture prophet, the ability to uncover hidden truths in his culture's sacred, written tradition.

The scripture prophet's charisma is not so much a matter of elocution or manner. He often lacks the overwhelming personality common to free prophets. His charisma arises from being convincing, combining an unmatched *ability to explain* with the fact that he *knows*. And much of the explanation focuses on his own person, and on the correspondence between the logic of the text and observable reality outside it.

David Koresh is a second, well-documented scripture prophet of modern times. As with Guibbory, many of Koresh's followers (some with graduate degrees in theology, others with doctorates in physics) were attracted by his ability to explain the sacred texts as they had never heard anyone else do. In the years since Waco, virtually all of them have told interviewers, "He showed me the Seven Seals," a reference to Koresh's elucidation of obscure portions of the book of Revelation central to Seventh-Day Adventist religion.

Koresh focused especially on texts from Isaiah, the Psalms, and the twelve Minor Prophets, and he drew out all the motifs of the Voice: the Servant, the New Moses, the Messiah, the Shepherd, the Chosen One, the Herald (Isaiah 61), and so on. In all of these portions he found prophecies of his own person; he was fond of calling himself "the Christ of Christ." Like Judah, Koresh also discovered in the scriptures prophecies of universal opposition figures, a notion that led him directly to the Waco tragedy.

In the final weeks before that incident, James Tabor, a respected New Testament scholar with expertise in the study of modern millenarian movements, communicated with Koresh through the FBI and tried to avert the misunderstandings and possible loss of life to which the preliminary confrontations were already pointing. Though he is today a sophisticated professor of religion at the University of North Carolina, Tabor was raised in a fundamentalist church. He grew up a devoted student of the biblical texts, studying them with ferocious intensity from the time he was fourteen. He came to know biblical content extremely well, especially the Hebrew Prophets. Even when working on his Ph.D. at the prestigious University of Chicago, Tabor encountered no one—not even his professors—who could match his mastery of biblical texts.[21]

Yet when Tabor had the opportunity to study Koresh's biblical commentaries, listen to Koresh's tapes, and speak with the Waco messiah's informed disciples, he was astounded. Here was someone who left him in the starting gate when it came to the Bible. Operating from memory alone and in answer to an unanticipated question, Koresh was able to draw a single word from Revelation, a second from Zechariah, and a third from Psalms and bring them together to make a point. His knowledge of the biblical text was photographic. Tabor was astonished at the quality of Koresh's mind. Within the boundaries of the world that he created for others, Tabor concluded, Koresh was a genius.

As do all scripture prophets, Koresh freely merged biblical texts to resignify and create new meaning. As had Judah, Schmid, Guibbory, and many other scripture prophets, Koresh recognized himself as the Voice. And he used his phenomenal ability to manipulate written texts to explain what no one else had ever been able to explain to his followers and so draw them to himself. The comprehensive ability to *explain* because he *knew*, because the text came to life in him—this was the essence of Koresh's charisma. It was the basis for his crisis cult.

ACCORDING TO THE Gospel of Mark, the earliest of the Gospels, Jesus, too, excited wonderment because he offered new and profound understandings of the scriptures and because he *knew*.

Thus Mark 1:22, "The people were amazed at his teaching, because he taught them as one who had authority, not as the teachers of the law." Mark 1:27 says, "The people were all so amazed that they asked each other,

'What is this? A new teaching—and with authority!'" Taken at face value, the Jesus tradition enshrined in the New Testament supports this understanding of the Christian messiah explicitly:

> Now on that same day two of [the disciples] were going to a village called Emmaus, about seven miles from Jerusalem, and talking with each other about all these things that had happened. While they were talking and discussing, Jesus himself came near and went with them. . . . Then he said to them, "Oh, how foolish you are, and how slow of heart to believe all that the prophets have declared! Was it not necessary that the Messiah should suffer these things and then enter into his glory?" Then beginning with Moses and all the prophets, he interpreted to them all the things about himself in the scriptures. . . . [Later] they said to each other, "Were not our hearts burning within us while he was talking to us on the road, while he was opening the scriptures to us?"[22]

According to this passage, Jesus *knew,* and his followers fed off his certainty and ability to explain. It created for them, as Guibbory later did for Horowitz, the feeling that God was present, as real as in the days of Isaiah and Jeremiah. Their hearts burned.

Yet scholarship on the historical Jesus has seldom taken this passage at face value. Instead, this and allied Gospel passages have been relegated to the post-Easter period in the growth of the Jesus tradition. Weighing probabilities as always, many scholars have doubted that Jesus was the sort of person here depicted. They have been skeptical that he found himself in Old Testament texts, suggesting instead that such "this is that" identifications arose only in the wake of the crucifixion, as believers struggled to make sense of their leader's seemingly inexplicable end and turned to find answers in the sacred tradition. They, not Jesus, were responsible for the claims made in this last passage.

One might read the evidence that way. Certainly significant interpretation did occur in the early years of the Church. During that period believers more and more came to terms with who Jesus had been, what his life and teaching had meant, and what these things must continue to mean for them.

Yet as we now understand him through his hymns, the analogy of Judah argues against modern scholarship. If Judah could demonstrably make the sort of arguments and interpretive identifications that the Gospels attribute to Jesus, then why not Jesus?

As a historian, I consider it eminently reasonable to think that Jesus did make at least some of the claims tied up with the Voice that the Gospels say he did. Consider the last question Jesus ever asked according to Mark's Gospel:

> While Jesus was teaching in the Temple, he said, "How can the scribes say that the Messiah is the son of David? David himself, by the Holy Spirit, declared 'The Lord said to my Lord, "Sit at my right hand, until I put your enemies under your feet"' (Psalm 110:1). David himself calls him Lord; so how can he be his son?" And the large crowd was listening to him with delight. (Mark 12:35–37)[23]

In contrast to what a significant number of his contemporaries believed, Jesus argued that the messiah was more than just a war leader. Even the messiah, he suggested, would be no greater than his father David—and so David would never call him "Lord"—if he were merely David's warrior descendent. Thus the messiah motif was not all there was to the Voice, and the One to Come was not merely David's son. To have such thoughts, Jesus must have been drawing together a number of relevant passages, pursuing the Voice through the text. But scholars are skeptical.

Nevertheless, the suggestion that Jesus thought in this way, the manner of the scripture prophet, becomes even more reasonable when one considers that the Dead Sea Scrolls offer new evidence that Jesus hit one of the Voice's trip wires. This trip wire has only in the last five years come to light, appearing in a hitherto unknown scroll that describes the resurrection in the time of the messiah.

HE SHALL RAISE THE DEAD

Known technically as 4Q521 and more popularly as *Redemption and Resurrection,* the scroll in question dates, according to the paleography, to the early first century B.C.E. The relevant portions read as follows:

> *[For the hea]vens and the earth shall obey his Messiah, [and nothing w]hich is in them shall turn away from the commandments of the*

holy ones. Strengthen yourselves in his service, you who seek the Lord.

Will you not find the Lord in this, all who await him with hope in your hearts? Surely the Lord seeks the pious, and calls the righteous by name. Over the poor his spirit hovers, and in his strength he renews the faithful. He will glorify the pious upon the throne of his eternal kingdom, setting prisoners free, opening the eyes of the blind, raising up those who are bo[wed down.] . . . For he shall heal the wounded, resurrect the dead, and preach glad tidings to the poor . . .[24]

This writing appears to be a sort of admonition, though the fragmentary state in which it is preserved precludes any firm decision as to genre. An unknown speaker instructs his audience on various matters concerning their relationship to God. In particular, the speaker addresses the question, "What will it be like on the Day of the Lord?" He describes that time by drawing on many different biblical portions, especially Psalm 146 and Isaiah 40 and 61.

After the first general statements about the messiah and God's service, the author focuses on the actions of God in that day. He speaks of how God will glorify the pious, renew the faithful, and attend to the poor. He describes the blind receiving back their sight and the broken and stooped standing straight and tall again. Then the easily legible portions of the text break off. When confident reading once more becomes possible in the last line, it is no longer clear who is the agent of the actions being recounted: *he shall heal the wounded, resurrect the dead, and preach glad tidings to the poor.*

Is the agent God, who has been acting just before the textual break, or is it the messiah, so loftily described as commanding heaven and earth? Favoring the second possibility is the fact that the Hebrew verb *bisser,* "preach glad tidings," never appears in biblical Hebrew as an action God performs. This is an action of human beings, including the Herald (a motif of the Voice). But whichever conclusion one reaches on the problem, no large gap interposes between the two options. Presumably any actions the messiah does are thought possible only because God's power is working in him, and if the actions are God's, they are in any case happening at a time when the messiah is manifest.

Yet if this last line of the text is problematic, it is also remarkable, for it contains perhaps the closest, most direct parallel to a New Testament text ever discovered in the scrolls.

We read in Matthew and Luke that after John the Baptist had been imprisoned by Herod Antipas, he sent several disciples to inquire of Jesus, "Are you the Coming One, or do we look for another?" Jesus couched his answer in terms of certain signs (italics mark key words): "Go and report to John what you have seen and heard: the blind receive sight, the lame walk, the lepers are cleansed, and the deaf hear, *the dead are raised up, the poor have glad tidings preached to them*" (Matthew 11:4–5; Luke 7:22–23).

Notice that the language of *Redemption and Resurrection*'s last line is almost identical to the italicized portion of Matthew and Luke. The Christian "signs of the messiah" were foreshadowed in the older Jewish writing found buried in the bat dung of the Judaean caves.

The fact that the phrasing of the two Gospels, Matthew and Luke, agree almost verbatim at this point indicates that the passage from the Gospels originated in a very early Christian tradition known by scholars as "Q" (from German *Quelle,* "source"). Q is a hypothetical collection of the sayings of Jesus thought to have been compiled in the middle of the first century, before the writing of the synoptic Gospels (Matthew, Mark, and Luke). The Q hypothesis accounts for the many virtually identical sayings in Matthew and Luke, since both used it as one of their sources.

The wording of Matthew and Luke here resonates with Isaiah 61:1–4. These same verses of Isaiah also appear in another strand of the Gospel traditions, Luke 4:18–21. In this latter passage, as in the Matthew-Luke parallel on which we are focusing, Jesus refers to himself as fulfilling Isaiah's words. The resulting correspondence between the passages is important because scholars questing for the historical Jesus place great emphasis on the criterion of "multiple attestation." Their reasoning is that one can be more confident that Jesus really did say something attributed to him, rather than the early church putting the words in his mouth, if the saying appears in more than one place—not just in parallels between the Gospels, but in entirely different literary contexts. Because the words we are considering meet the criterion of multiple attestation, most scholars would agree that they are authentic words from Jesus.[25]

In the entire Hebrew Bible nothing at all is said about a messiah raising the dead. Yet the reference to the messiah raising the dead, linked to preaching glad tidings for the poor, appears in both Luke and Matthew (quoting from Q). The two phrases are presented as signs of the messiah: *the dead are raised up, the poor have glad tidings preached to them*—precisely as in *Redemption and Resurrection.* Thus, operating independently of the Hebrew Bible, both the scroll and the Gospels connect three critical elements: the raising of the dead, the preaching of glad tidings to the poor, and the time of the messiah.

This conjunction between the Qumran scroll and the Jesus tradition of the New Testament cannot be mere coincidence. Instead, it requires the understanding that there existed within Palestinian Judaism of Jesus' day certain expectations of what anyone claiming to be a messiah must do. These expectations were evidently widespread, since no genetic link existed between *Redemption and Resurrection* and early Christianity. Divergent movements shared these ideas. Given the first-century B.C.E. date of *Redemption and Resurrection*, we must suppose that these signs became invested in the myth-dream of Israel well before Jesus rose up to claim them of himself.

If this chain of reasoning is correct, then as Jesus gave his reply to John's disciples he was consciously, intentionally embracing a set of expectations that the myth-dream associated with one motif of the Voice, that of messiah. With a reply much more forceful than banal assent to the Baptist's question, Jesus declared that he was the One. Every Jew who heard what he said would have recognized the reply for what it was. Jesus—and by the common criteria of the quest, this was the *historical* Jesus—thereby stumbled over a prominent trip wire of the Voice.

If analogy is a guide, then Jesus must have made further associations. All scripture prophets do; none known to history has stopped with a single motif such as Jesus' reply claimed for himself. And because of Judah and his movement, many of these motifs were already interwoven in the myth-dream of Jesus' day. Doubtless the Galilean was led to motif after motif in the holy texts. He found himself in them. He knew himself to be the Voice, just as Judah had one hundred years before.

If Judah could make the claim in his hymns to be the Voice, then why not Jesus? Why not the other messiah? These claims need not have followed the cross as inventions of the early believers. Analogy suggests that they came first, as teachings of the charismatic founder. If Judah, why not Jesus?

Indeed, that is the broad significance of the story of the first messiah for an understanding of the Christian messiah. If Judah, why not Jesus? In general, the analogy with the first messiah argues that much of what the Gospels tell us about Jesus—the claims he made as the founder of a crisis cult, the reactions of followers, the rejection by the greater society, early belief in his heavenly ascension, and much else—happened along the lines the Gospels present. And the specific analogy of the first messiah is supported by a more universal one, for the fact is that the Gospels present a story typical of crisis cults. Not to speak of specific points and particular details, the story the Gospels present is plausible.

The analogy of Judah urges an acceptance of substantially more material in the Gospels as historical than has commonly been recognized by scholars in quest of the Jesus of history.

We may return to our portrait gallery to ask whether it is now possible to pick out the true image of Jesus. But when we look it over again, we get a surprise: he is not there. None of the pictures looks quite right. Rather, drawing the analogy with Judah, along with recognizing a larger core of historical material within the Gospels, argues for hanging a new portrait. It is not entirely different from older renderings. What have previously been separate portrayals of the historical Jesus—that of wise man or sage, and that of apocalyptic prophet—ought to be merged. Many Gospel data support this merged portrait, but historians have previously dismissed some as unhistorical or have separated them into distinct, incompatible piles. These piles may now be tossed together. For we know from Judah's hymns that he was both wisdom teacher and prophet of the apocalypse.

If Judah, why not Jesus?

C. S. LEWIS RECALLED in his autobiography, *Surprised by Joy*, how shaken he once was by a statement made to him by a hard-boiled atheist with whom in his pre-Christian days Lewis enjoyed occasional philosophical discussions. "Rum thing, all that stuff about the Dying God. Rum thing. It almost looks as if it had really happened once." Coming from a man Lewis described as "a cynic of cynics, the toughest of the tough," this assessment cut him to the bone. The man's words assailed the defenses Lewis had erected, as he said, to protect himself from the "hound of heaven."

What then of Judah and the *Thanksgiving Hymns*? Does recognizing Judah's self-identity and the significance of his hymns somehow mean, when applied to Jesus and the Gospels, that it all "really happened once"? Not necessarily. What the analogy of Judah suggests for the historical Jesus is not that he was who he claimed to be, for the historian cannot decide that issue. Rather, the analogy suggests that we reconsider what much scholarship has denied: that the Jesus of history *did* make those claims, just as the Gospels say. Whether the claims were true or not is a different question.

The sequence of events given by the Gospel of Mark in its first chapter is highly plausible as the beginning of the story of a charismatic crisis-cult leader. The perspective on the meaning of the events is of course that of later believers, so the language in which the story is cast is the language of faith. Still, making allowance for that language, with a little imagination we can flesh out the sequence from Jesus' perspective.

One day while Jesus was working in his carpenter shop in Nazareth, visitors came with breathless news of great happenings elsewhere. "A new prophet has been raised up of God," the men said. "His name is John, and they call him the Baptist." Struck by their lightning-bolt statement, Jesus turned upon the men. "Tell me of him!" He demanded ferociously, frightening them with his intensity. For several hours the men regaled Jesus with their stories of John and his message: "The time is fulfilled; the Kingdom of God is at hand. Repent, and believe." "The people are streaming to him," the men finished, "they come from everywhere, but especially from Jerusalem. The authorities are starting to take notice."

When the men left, Jesus' heart was on fire. Sweat poured down his forehead and into his eyes. The Kingdom at hand! For so long he had studied the scriptures, pondered the prophecies, sought to penetrate the hidden mysteries of God. And now a prophet had come who knew the answers!

Of late, Jesus' family had noticed a change in him. The apocalyptic notions that had long fascinated him seemed now to have taken hold of Jesus down to his core. He was no longer satisfied, it seemed, to be what he had been, what he was. He was restless, always distracted. When they entered the shop, they usually found him gazing into the distance. Thus Mary and his brothers and sisters were upset but hardly surprised when Jesus left with muttered explanation the next morning. They had known what he would do as soon as they got wind of the visitors' tale.

Jesus made his way to John and joined the hordes swirling about him near the Jordan River. He listened to the fiery preacher and soon joined the multitudes in being baptized at the prophet's hand. John took notice of the intense but clearly brilliant Galilean and drew him closer to himself. Soon Jesus was a member of John's inner circle of disciples. Jesus listened to everything the prophet said and questioned John endlessly about the scriptures.

While much of what John said seemed to make sense, Jesus could not shake the feeling that something was missing from the picture that

John presented. Jesus continued to ponder the prophecies, continued to puzzle over them and endlessly turn them over in his mind. Of one thing he was convinced: John was right—the Kingdom was at the door.

Then one day what John's closest associates had feared, and what many others had expected would happen, took place. The Baptist was arrested by agents of Herod and imprisoned in the great fortress of Machaerus. Jesus, who as John's intimate disciple had himself been baptizing farther north on the Jordan, was shaken, nearly broken by Herod's act. "The fox!" he thought. "Herod does not realize what he is risking."

Jesus did not know what to do next. What now of the Kingdom? In despair, he made his way to the east, pushing farther and farther into the Wilderness of Judaea. Despite the heat, he drank little and ate less. When night fell and it was cool enough to move, he wandered aimlessly. By day Jesus huddled in the shade of this or that large stone, praying, seeking a God who seemed to have grown silent; and Jesus pondered, always pondered the scriptures he had stored in his mind.

His memory had always been more retentive than most, and when he closed his eyes Jesus could almost read the holy texts on his eyelids. He knew them, knew them so well—but what did they mean? Sometimes he felt that he almost understood, that the meaning was there to grasp, and he reached for it. But just as he was about to close his hands, the understanding would always vanish, like the desert illusions Jesus was seeing more and more often on the horizon. He needed to eat, to sleep, but he could not. Jesus grew weak, then weaker still.

One day he could no longer rouse himself to move from the shade of his stone. The world seemed to spin. Jesus closed his eyes and turned into himself: he found the prophecies, the mysteries—a jumble as usual. But today they seemed closer somehow. He reached for them, began to close his hands upon them. They did not move. Jesus pounced. There! He had them! Jesus slumped into a waking unconsciousness.

Hours later he came out of it, his mind still and preternaturally alert. Something was different about him. He sought for a moment to discover what it was. And then it became clear—it was all so clear. The prophecies, the mysteries, the meaning—he had it. Jesus *knew*. He knew now, for the first time, how it all fit together. He knew how the Kingdom must come. He knew what must be done. Most of all, he knew who he was.

Jesus arose, suddenly strong, and turned his face toward Jerusalem.

NOTES

CHAPTER 1

1. Irving Wallace, David Wallechinsky, and Amy Wallace, "They Wanted to Buy Lyndon Johnson," *Los Angeles Times*, April 22, 1984.

2. The literature on cargo cult is immense. For an excellent recent introduction in brief, see Lamont Lindstrom, *Cargo Cult: Strange Stories of Desire from Melanesia and Beyond* (Honolulu: Univ. of Hawaii Press, 1993). Another work very useful for background is Peter Worsley, *The Trumpet Shall Sound: A Study of "Cargo" Cults in Melanesia*, 2d augmented ed. (New York: Schocken Books, 1968). On 104–8 Worsley discusses Mambu, and I have incorporated some of his comments in the description below. In the main, however, I have relied upon Kenelm Burridge, *Mambu: A Melanesian Millennium* (London: Methuen, 1960; Princeton: Princeton Univ. Press, 1995). For Yali, below, I have surveyed Burridge and the more detailed treatment in Peter Lawrence, *Road Belong Cargo: A Study of the Cargo Movement in the Southern Madang District, New Guinea*, 2d ed. (Prospect Heights, IL: Waveland Press, 1989), 116–221.

3. The classic account of the events I describe below was written by an eyewitness to many of them, an amateur ethnographer who was sympathetic to the Native American cause. I refer to George Mooney, *The Ghost-Dance Religion and the Sioux Outbreak of 1890,* abridged by Anthony F. C. Wallace (1896; Chicago: Univ. of Chicago Press, 1965).

4. Mooney, *Ghost-Dance Religion,* 74.

5. Mooney, *Ghost-Dance Religion,* 138.

6. Recollections of Wovoka are from the account by Porcupine of the Cheyenne, in Mooney, *Ghost-Dance Religion,* 39. On Tavibo's movement, known as the "Ghost Dance of 1870," see A. H. Gayton, "The Ghost Dance of 1870 in South-Central California," *Univ. of California Publications in American Archaeology and Ethnology* 28 (1930): 57–82; and Leslie Spier, "The Ghost Dance of 1870 Among the Klamath of Oregon," *Univ. of Washington Publications in Anthropology* 2 (1927): 39–56. Some scholars doubt that Tavibo was Wovoka's father, arguing that confusion has identified the prophet of 1870 with Wovoka's father, a lesser medicine man. Be that as it may, doubtless Wovoka was familiar with the doctrine of this earlier movement, which did originate in his own home valley.

7. This is the version of the doctrine contained in a report by J. M. Lee, who received the statement in the autumn of 1890 from a Paiute, Captain Dick. See Mooney, *Ghost-Dance Religion,* 26.

8. Mooney, *Ghost-Dance Religion,* 39.

9. Mooney, *Ghost-Dance Religion,* 102.

10. For this discussion of Konrad Schmid and self-flagellation, I rely on Norman Cohn, *The Pursuit of the Millennium,* rev. ed. (New York: Oxford Univ. Press, 1970), esp. 127–47.

11. Cohn, *Pursuit,* 127.

12. Henry of Herford, cited in Cohn, *Pursuit,* 141.

13. Though I cite sources for specific points in the pages that follow, this discussion of Millerism is generally based on Francis D. Nichol, *The Midnight Cry* (Washington, DC: Review and Herald Publishing Association, 1944); the various essays in Ronald L. Numbers and Jonathan M. Butler, eds., *The Disappointed: Millerism and Millenarianism in the Nineteenth Century* (Knoxville: Univ. of Tennessee Press, 1993); and George R. Knight, *Millennial Fever and the End of the World: A Study of Millerite Adventism* (Boise, ID: Pacific Press Publishing Association, 1993).

14. So said an approximately contemporary historian, R. M. Devers, in his *American Progress: Or The Great Events of the Greatest Century* (Chicago: Hugh Heron, 1883), 307.

15. Knight, *Millennial Fever,* 163.

16. "Remembrance of Former Days," *The Advent Review and Sabbath Herald* (May 7, 1901), reprinted in Nichol, *Midnight Cry,* 291.

17. Whitney R. Cross, *The Burned-over District* (Ithaca, NY: Cornell Univ. Press, 1950), 308.

18. Cross, *Burned-over District,* 321; Eric Anderson, "The Millerite Use of Prophecy: A Case Study of a 'Striking Fulfillment,'" in *The Disappointed,* ed. Numbers and Butler, 79–91.

19. Reprinted in Nichol, *Midnight Cry,* 262. The same statement also appeared in *The Advent Herald* of November 13, 1844.

20. Knight has shown that three basic trajectories emerged from the comparative handful of Millerites who did not apostatize after the Great Disappointment. One group, the "Albany Adventists," rejected Miller's date as wrong, without biblical warrant. According to this view, what had happened on October 22, 1844, was just as it seemed: nothing. They went on to deny Miller's principles of biblical interpretation and the prophecies of Daniel and Revelation. With these developments they ceased to be Millerites.

Over the next years the Albany Adventists splintered into many small sects who found their raison d'être in issues other than the Second Coming. One such was whether or not the wicked dead would be resurrected. Most of these sects died out in the next decades, and none of the survivors flourished.

A second group, the "Spiritualists," held that Christ indeed had come on October 22. But he had not come in the clouds of heaven. Rather, he had come in heaven as the bridegroom to the Ancient of Days and there had received the kingdom. Others said that he had come into human hearts. The Spiritualists abandoned Miller's principles of literal interpretation of the Scriptures and began to find spiritual meaning everywhere, soon arriving at doctrines far removed both from Protestant orthodoxy, as it then existed, and from Millerism. It was to these splinter groups that

Shakerism had a real appeal. By the end of the nineteenth century, all of these groups had ceased to exist. Most were already gone by the late 1860s.

A third, small group of about two hundred—who would later develop into the Seventh-Day Adventists—affirmed both the fulfillment of prophecy on October 22 and Miller's literal interpretation of the biblical prophecies more generally. In order to establish the reality of Christ's coming on October 22, however, they found it necessary to reinterpret Miller's idea. They claimed that he had the date right but had misidentified the event that was to happen on that date. Christ was never supposed to come to earth then.

Instead, Daniel's "cleansing the sanctuary" meant that Christ had moved from the outer sanctuary to the inner sanctum of the heavenly temple. There, as a prelude to the imminent end of the world, he had begun to investigate the sins of believers. In subsequent years new prophets arose among this group, principally Ellen White, and they developed doctrines foreign to Millerism. Prominent here was the celebration of the sabbath on Saturday. Indeed, White urged that the failure of the 1844 return was caused by believers' abandonment of the proper sabbath. Observance of the proper day would yet help bring Christ in the flesh.

Miller himself lived long enough to repudiate both the new prophetic visions and seventh-day sabbatarianism. This group was not really a continuation of Millerism (their modern arguments to the contrary notwithstanding). Seventh-Day Adventism was a new movement with its own prophets. Millerism functioned for them as a precursor group. And of all the offshoots of Millerism, this group alone enjoyed vitality. From the measly two hundred believers immediately after the Great Disappointment, it grew to thirty-five hundred at their incorporation as a church in 1863, then to more than seven hundred thousand members in the United States and seven million worldwide by the early 1990s. It was from a splinter group of a splinter group of the Seventh-Day Adventists that David Koresh came forth.

Within a few years of the Great Disappointment, Millerism as a vital movement was dead. Its leadership was never able to offer any adequate explanation for the empirical disproof of a foundational prophecy. William Miller later came to say of October 22 that it was not "a fulfillment of prophecy in any sense."

21. Gershom Scholem, *Sabbatai Sevi: The Mystical Messiah* (Princeton: Princeton Univ. Press, 1973), 2. For the discussion of Sabbatai, below, I follow the analysis presented in this classic work. I have also found several of the essays in Scholem's *The Messianic Idea in Judaism* (New York: Schocken Books, 1971) very helpful.

22. Scholem, *Sabbatai Sevi*, 149.

23. Descriptions are from Abraham Cuenque and Israel Hazzan in Scholem, *Sabbatai Sevi*, 189, 190.

24. This quotation and the one preceding are from Scholem, *Sabbatai Sevi*, 132.

25. Scholem, *Sabbatai Sevi*, 272–74.

26. See "The Crypto-Jewish Sect of the Dönmeh (Sabbatians) in Turkey," in Scholem, *Messianic Idea*, 142–66.

27. Historically the seminal article for the study of crisis cults—also known as "revitalization movements" and "nativistic movements," among other labels—has

been Anthony F. C. Wallace, "Revitalization Movements," *American Anthropologist* 58 (1956): 264–81. Many subsequent studies have refined Wallace's ideas, and earlier ones adumbrated them. In addition to Wallace and various studies specifically mentioned in this chapter's notes, I have relied upon K. Burridge, *New Heaven New Earth* (New York: Schocken Books, 1969); D. Emmet, "Prophets and Their Societies," *Journal of the Royal Anthropological Institute* 86 (1956): 13–23; Frances Hill, "Nationalist Millenarians and Millenarian Nationalists," *American Behavioral Scientist* 16 (1972): 269–88; E. J. Hobsbawm, *Primitive Rebels* (New York: Frederick A. Praeger, 1963); V. Lanternari, *The Religions of the Oppressed* (New York: Alfred A. Knopf, 1963); Ralph Linton, "Nativistic Movements," *American Anthropologist* 45 (1943): 230–43; M. I. Pereira de Queiroz, "Messianic Myths and Movements," *Diogenes* 90 (1975): 78–99; M. W. Smith, "Toward a Classification of Cult Movements," *Man* 59 (1959): 8–12, 25–28; Y. Talmon, "Millenarism," *International Encyclopedia of the Social Sciences,* ed. D. Sills (1968); Y. Talmon, "Pursuit of the Millennium: The Relation Between Religious and Social Change," *Archives européenes de sociologie* 3 (1962): 125–48; and B. Wilson, "Millennialism in Comparative Perspective," *Comparative Studies in Society and History* 6 (1963–64): 93–114. Virtually all of the essays in S. Thrupp, ed., *Millennial Dreams in Action* (The Hague: Mouton, 1962), are helpful.

28. On radical changes leading to crisis cults, see Michael Barkun, *Disaster and the Millennium* (New Haven: Yale Univ. Press, 1974), 6. Under the rubric of "perceived disaster" I place the concept of "relative deprivation," often suggested as a cause contributing to the development of a crisis cult. For the notion, see David F. Aberle, "A Note on Relative Deprivation Theory as Applied to Millenarian and other Cult Movements," in Thrupp, *Millennial Dreams,* 209–14. Although no earlier writer has systematically investigated the phenomena of the Dead Sea Scrolls in terms of the crisis cult model, a tentative first step was taken by J. Duhaime, "Relative Deprivation in New Religious Movements and the Qumran Community," *Revue de Qumran* 16 (1993): 265–76. For an application of the model to an early Christian community, see R. Jewett, *The Thessalonian Correspondence: Pauline Rhetoric and Millenarian Piety* (Philadelphia: Fortress, 1986), 161–78.

29. Max Weber, *On Charisma and Institution Building: Selected Papers,* ed. S. N. Eisenstadt (Chicago: Univ. of Chicago Press, 1968), 253–61. I have compressed the quotation. Weber has been criticized for his overemphasis on "ideal types" and his focus on personality rather than on larger social structures. These are valid criticisms, but they do not empty Weber's model of its usefulness. As we will see, it clearly fits the data of the *Thanksgiving Hymns* with respect to social change. For the criticism, see Worsley, *The Trumpet Shall Sound,* 266–72; Edward Shils, *The Constitution of Society* (Chicago: Univ. of Chicago Press, 1972), 119–42, and Rodney Hutton, *Charisma and Authority in Israelite Society* (Minneapolis: Fortress Press, 1994).

30. I follow here Sture Ahlberg, *Messianic Movements* (Stockholm: Almqvist & Wiksell International, 1986), 8–11. Note also Norman Cohn, "Medieval Millenarism," in Thrupp, *Millennial Dreams,* 42: "It is the prophet who carries out this adap-

tation of traditional lore and who becomes the bearer of the resulting ideology. If in addition the prophet possesses a suitable personality and is able to convey an impression of absolute conviction, he is likely in certain situations of emotional tension to become the nucleus of a millenarian movement."

31. Reported in Anthony Storr, *Feet of Clay* (New York: Free Press, 1996), 97, emphasis his.

32. Charles Lindholm, *Charisma* (Cambridge, MA: Blackwell, 1990), 110. For much of this discussion on charisma I am indebted to Lindholm's book, the most recent and fullest study of the phenomenon.

33. Lindholm, *Charisma,* 149, describes Jim Jones as an "empathetic mirror." On the appeal of crisis cults to lower classes, see William Sims Bainbridge, *The Sociology of Religious Movements* (New York: Routledge, 1996), 47: "Among the best-established principles of the sociology of religion is the proposition that people who join radical religious movements tend to come from deprived groups, such as the poor and downtrodden."

34. Percy Schramm, *Hitler: The Man and the Military Leader* (Chicago: Quadrangle, 1971), 35, cited in Lindholm, *Charisma,* 102–3.

35. Burridge, *Mambu,* 148.

36. This is by definition so, though the flash of insight need not be religious in origin. The phenomenon is much the same in the political arena, wherein "the leader who becomes charismatic is the one who can inadvertently or deliberately tap the reservoir of relevant myths in his culture." Thus Ann Ruth Willner, *The Spellbinders: Charismatic Political Leadership* (New Haven: Yale Univ. Press, 1984), 62.

37. For insight into how this process takes place, see, for example, Peter Berger and Thomas Luckmann, *The Social Construction of Reality: A Treatise in the Sociology of Knowledge* (Garden City, NY: Doubleday, 1966).

38. Burridge, *Mambu,* 28–29.

39. I borrow the terminology from Richard Landes, *Relics, Apocalypse and the Deceits of History* (Cambridge: Harvard Univ. Press, 1995).

40. "Jesus standing before Pilate" is the observation of Fokke Sierksma, review of Lanternari, *Religions of the Oppressed,* in *Current Anthropology* 6 (1965): 455–56. On the various rebellions, see Michael Adas, *Prophets of Rebellion: Millenarian Protest Movements Against the European Colonial Order* (Chapel Hill: Univ. of North Carolina Press, 1979). On David Koresh, see James D. Tabor and Eugene V. Gallagher, *Why Waco?* (Berkeley and Los Angeles: Univ. of California Press, 1995).

41. Note Joseph Zygmunt, "When Prophecies Fail," *American Behavioral Scientist* 16 (1972): 245–68. I do not embrace the argument for "cognitive dissonance" put forth in the famous book by Leon Festinger, Henry Riecken, and Stanley Schachter, *When Prophecy Fails* (Minneapolis: Univ. of Minnesota Press, 1956). This book, based on the authors' study of a small crisis cult that believed in the imminent arrival of flying saucers to take believers to another world, held by its theory of cognitive dissonance that disconfirmation would not result in disbelief. Rather, members would seek to alleviate the stress of unfulfilled predictions by redoubling efforts to spread

their message. The fact that they could convince others of the truth of their beliefs despite the disconfirmation would reassure them that their views must be true. Otherwise, how could they persuade anyone else of them? But several subsequent studies of this proposition have never found the predicted outcome; see, for example, Robert W. Balch et al., "Fifteen Years of Failed Prophecy," in *Millennium, Messiahs, and Mayhem,* ed. Thomas Robbins and Susan J. Palmer (New York: Routledge, 1997), 73–90. Even the original study has been criticized as flawed, corrupted by the sociologists' own process of observing the cult. Recent leading sociologists of religion therefore deny the notion of cognitive dissonance as put forth by Festinger et al. See Rodney Stark, *The Rise of Christianity: A Sociologist Reconsiders History* (Princeton: Princeton Univ. Press, 1996), 220, and Bainbridge, *Religious Movements,* 137–38.

CHAPTER 2

1. On silence in the Temple cultus, see Israel Knohl, "Between Voice and Silence: The Relationship Between Prayer and Temple Cult," *Journal of Biblical Literature* 115 (1996): 17–30, and literature cited there.

2. For the purposes of this narrative I am taking Josephus, *Ant.* 13.372–73, as describing the same occasion as the Babylonian Talmud, Sukk. 48b; cf. Yom. 26b.

3. The phrase "covenant of repentance" appears in CD Manuscript B at 19:16. The phrase does not appear in the equivalent portion of Manuscript A.

4. For the redactional arguments favoring the identification of these laws from CD 6:11–7:4 as Judah's own, see the discussion of the *Damascus Document* in chap. 8, below.

5. Regarding the significance of the calendar, note the words of Ralph Linton, "Nativistic Movements," *American Anthropologist* 45 (1943): 231: "What really happens in all nativistic movements is that certain current or remembered elements of culture are selected for emphasis and given symbolic value. The more distinctive such elements are with respect to other cultures with which the society is in contact, the greater their potential value as symbols of the society's unique character."

6. *New York Times Book Review* of August 18, 1996, 35.

7. The best summary of scholarship on the *Thanksgiving Hymns* is now Michael C. Douglas, "Power and Praise in the Hodayot: A Literary Critical Study of 1QH 9:1–18:14" (Ph.D. diss., University of Chicago, 1998), 15–84. Jeremias brought together the work of a number of predecessors who had discussed the hymns but combined them in a new way for an effective argument.

8. In the pages that follow I rely on Douglas's literary criticism in "Power and Praise" for determining where the authentic Teacher Hymns are to be found and for the demonstration that they are indeed authentic. I shall not rehearse his demonstration here. Beyond Douglas's dissertation, further discussion of the problem of the Teacher Hymns will appear in a forthcoming commentary on the *Thanksgiving Hymns* that Douglas and I are coauthoring.

The Community Hymns represent columns 1–8 and 20:8–column 28 of the reconstructed scroll. Douglas's literary-critical conclusions find empirical support in two of the more fragmentary copies of the *Hymns*. These copies apparently never included any Community Hymns, comprising only Teacher Hymns. They therefore seem to represent two copies of Douglas's postulated first edition that have survived.

9. Gert Jeremias, *Der Lehrer der Gerechtigkeit* (Göttingen: Vandenhoeck & Ruprecht, 1963), 176, my translation.

10. I shall try to demonstrate this point below; note especially the discussions in chaps. 7 and 10.

11. Though this is true, the hymns may also evidence some reworking. One finds interpretations of biblical portions divided among hymns; that is, one hymn explicates or alludes to one aspect of the biblical passage, then later another hymn alludes to a different aspect of that same passage. It is therefore clear that Judah already knew a unified exegesis of the relevant biblical passages before he cited any of them in his hymns. He was not devising new understandings as time went on but merely revealing those understandings piecemeal. There are two ways to understand this situation, not necessarily mutually exclusive. Either Judah reworked the hymns near the end of his life to make them univocal, or, as seems more likely, he already had an exegesis of these passages long before the crisis arose. The effect of the crisis was to make him insert himself into this exegesis—find himself in the biblical passages where earlier he had seen only anonymous prophesied figures. This is a common phenomenon for charismatics; compare Konrad Schmid in chap. 1 and Moses Guibbory and David Koresh in chap. 10.

12. *Ant.* 13.408. Here and in the pages below I cite Josephus according to the *Loeb Classical Library*, trans. H. St. J. Thackeray, Ralph Marcus, and Louis H. Feldman, though I occasionally modify their renderings.

13. 1QH 10:6–22. The numbering and reconstruction of the columns follow the work of É. Puech, "Quelques aspects de la restauration du Rouleau des Hymnes (1QH)," *Journal of Jewish Studies* 39 (1988): 38–55, with slight adjustments that Douglas and I will defend in our forthcoming commentary. Also, here and in the following hymns I have incorporated a number of new readings that I will discuss in the forthcoming work. I have not tried to render the hymns poetically, choosing rather to seek to convey the religiopolitical aspects and nuances with a straightforward prose style.

14. Bruce Lincoln, *Discourse and the Construction of Society* (Oxford: Oxford Univ. Press, 1989), 3.

15. Victor Turner, *Dreams, Fields, and Metaphors: Symbolic Action in Human Society* (Ithaca: Cornell Univ. Press, 1974), 41.

16. Turner, *Dreams, Fields, and Metaphors,* 41.

17. Translations of *Ben Sira* follow P. W. Skehan and A. A. Di Lella, *The Wisdom of Ben Sira* (New York: Doubleday, 1987), with occasional slight variations.

18. For a helpful discussion of retainers in the social world of ancient Judaism, see Anthony Saldarini, *Pharisees, Scribes and Sadducees in Palestinian Society* (Wilmington, DE: Michael Glazier, 1988).

19. Stephen Neill and Tom Wright, *The Interpretation of the New Testament, 1861–1986,* 2d ed. (New York: Oxford Univ. Press, 1988), 327, emphasis theirs.

Against the common but mistaken claim that prophecy had ceased among the Jews—a claim usually dependent on rabbinic literature, which was hostile to the priestly prophetic perspective—see the measured discussion of David Aune, *Prophecy in Early Christianity and the Ancient Mediterranean World* (Grand Rapids: Eerdmans, 1983), 103–6. Aune unhesitatingly deems the Teacher of Righteousness a prophet.

20. It has been suggested by a number of scholars that 4Q417, the work in which the phrase *wondrous mysteries* appears, was the *Sepher he-Hagu* referenced in CD and 1QSa. I find the notion attractive, but it is unclear at this time whether 4Q417 preceded Judah or was a work of his later movement. In the latter case, the phrase *wondrous mysteries* was perhaps Judah's own invention, but 4Q417 and 1QH 9 would still be useful for explicating his probable meaning.

21. For this discussion I am indebted to the excellent brief summary of wisdom literature given by Edward Cook in our joint work (with Martin Abegg), *The Dead Sea Scrolls: A New Translation* (San Francisco: HarperSanFrancisco, 1996), 174–75.

22. Torlief Elgvin, in "The Reconstruction of Sapiential Work A," *Revue de Qumran* 16 (1995): 559, argues that the seven copies are 1Q26, 4Q415, 4Q416, 4Q417, 4Q418a, 4Q418b, 4Q423. The comparison with the Sermon on the Mount is Cook's from Wise, Abegg, Cook, *Dead Sea Scrolls*, 379. The following quotations from the *Secret of the Way Things Are* follow largely Cook, 379–90 of that work. It should be noted that Cook included not only the manuscripts that Elgvin calls Sapiential Work A, but also 4Q410, 4Q412–13, and 4Q419–21 under his rubric. Elgvin is the official editor of the scrolls in question and has devoted considerable time to their sorting, so his notions must be respected, but the questions involved are complex and we shall have to see what consensus develops on Elgvin's views.

23. 4Q417 Frag. 2 Col. 1:12b–18. For the Hebrew text, see B. Z. Wacholder and M. Abegg, *A Preliminary Edition of the Unpublished Dead Sea Scrolls* (Washington, DC: Biblical Archaeology Society, 1992): 2:66. Note also Daniel J. Harrington, *Wisdom Texts from Qumran* (New York: Routledge, 1996), 53.

24. *Ant.* 1.69–71.

25. The example from Tertullian is found in *On Baptism* 17.5. For useful comments and analysis of the phenomenon of pseudepigraphy, see D. G. Meade, *Pseudonymity and Canon* (Grand Rapids: Eerdmans, 1986). For a perspective critical of Meade's, see G. Lüdemann, *Heretics: The Other Side of Early Christianity* (Louisville: Westminster John Knox, 1996), 104–47.

26. I make no claim for the truth or falsity of the pseudepigraph theory of the pastoral Epistles. It is a fact that most scholars embrace the idea, but good ones have denied it. The question lies outside my area of expertise. I merely refer to the theory as a useful example of my point regarding Judah and his disciple.

27. 1QH 9:8–42.

28. Astrology was also an important source of prophecy in the Renaissance period. Note the comments of Donald Weinstein, "The Savonarola Movement in Florence," in *Millennial Dreams in Action*, ed. S. Thrupp (The Hague: Mouton, 1962), 197.

29. *Ben Sira* 38:24–25.

30. *Ben Sira* 39:1–8.

31. Note *War* 1.648–50 and the parallels in *Antiquities* for further evidence of wisdom teachers attached to the Temple in the general period. Josephus calls such a person *exegetes* (= Hebrew *melits?*). He chose the word advisedly, with an eye to the milieu of his Greek-speaking readers. In the Greco-Roman world an *exegetes* was an interpreter or expounder of sacred lore. Such people were often attached to temples. In Athens, where we are best informed of their role, the *exegetai* (plural) were official figures who interpreted the sacred and ancestral laws. Their office served as an adjunct to written legislation. On such figures, see especially Felix Jacoby, *Atthis: The Local Chronicles of Ancient Athens* (Oxford: Clarendon Press, 1949), 1–70.

32. Intellectuals have often filled this role in other societies as well. Note the words of Lewis Coser, *The Functions of Social Conflict* (New York: Free Press, 1956), 116: "Intellectuals have been of central importance in 'objectifying' social movements, in transforming them from interest groups into ideological movements."

33. Only here in the Bible do the words *open* and *fount* occur together, making it highly probable that this passage lies behind Judah's words.

CHAPTER 3

1. *Ant.* 13.410.

2. 1QH 10:23–33.

3. 1QH 10:34–11:7.

4. I have translated the Hebrew *avodah* as "Temple service" because that is the best rendering for the circumstances of the hymn. It is not an original suggestion; see J. Licht, *The Thanksgiving Scroll from the Judaean Desert Scrolls* (Jerusalem: Mossad Bialik, 1957), 62 n. 27 (Hebrew). The note there is in reference to 1QH 9:30, but Licht draws attention also to the present passage. For other passages in the scrolls where the word bears the meaning of "ritual act" or "Temple service," note Y. Yadin, *The Scroll of the War of the Sons of Light Against the Sons of Darkness* (Oxford: Oxford Univ. Press, 1962), 267, note on 1QM 3:15, *hatruah lekol avodatam;* and Avi Solomon, "The Prohibition Against Tevul Yom and Defilement of the Daily Whole Offering in the Jerusalem Temple in CD 11:21–12:1: A New Understanding," *Dead Sea Discoveries* 4 (1997): 18, on *ha-avodah* in CD 11:23.

5. On the council and political realities in Judah's time, note James S. McLaren, *Power and Politics in Palestine: The Jews and the Governing of their Land, 100 B.C.–A.D. 70* (Sheffield: JSOT Press, 1991), esp. 54–79.

6. 4Q171 iv 7–9. I follow the reconstruction of the text suggested by Elisha Qimron and John Strugnell, *Discoveries in the Judaean Desert X: Qumran Cave 4 V: Miqsat Ma'ase Ha-Torah* (Oxford: Clarendon Press, 1994), 120.

7. 4QMMT C 7–8. Here and in what follows I refer to the edition by Qimron and Strugnell, *Miqsat Ma'ase Ha-Torah.*

8. 4QMMT B 69–70. In the Java War of 1825–1830 the leader of the revolt against Dutch authorities, the prince Dipanagara, similarly asserted his legitimacy through religious letters to his adversaries. See Michael Adas, *Prophets of Rebellion: Millenarian Protest Movements Against the European Colonial Order* (Chapel Hill: Univ. of North Carolina Press, 1979), 143.

9. This story of Shimeon appears twice in the Palestinian Talmud, yBerakhot VII 11b and yNazir V 54b. It also appears in Genesis Rabbah at Parasha 91 4, and there are some differences between the stories. I have translated the Genesis Rabbah version, adding certain explications with a view to the others. On Shimeon and Jannaeus, see Joshua Efron, *Studies on the Hasmonean Period* (Leiden: Brill, 1987), 143–218.

10. bTaan 23a. Leviticus Rabbah 35:10 also tells the story, and, unlike the Babylonian Talmud, it includes Shelamzion's name.

11. CD 1:1–15. To my knowledge, the suggestion that the Man of the Lie was Shimeon ben Shetah was first made by F. F. Bruce, *Second Thoughts on the Dead Sea Scrolls*, 2d ed. (London: Paternoster, 1956; Grand Rapids: Eerdmans, 1964), 104.

12. 4Q176 iv 8–9.

13. The quotations are from *Ant.* 13.323.

14. For the reasons behind this statement, see the section "Bruta Facta" in chap. 4.

15. 4QMMT C 12–16.

16. 4QMMT C 20–22, with suggested restorations.

17. 4QMMT C 28–32.

18. On the legal aspects of the conflict of visions, especially helpful are Y. Sussman, "The History of the Halakha and the Dead Sea Scrolls," app. 1, in Qimron and Strugnell, *Miqsat Ma'ase Ha-Torah,* 179–200 (a fuller version of the article with additional documentation appeared in Hebrew in *Tarbiz* 59 [1989–90]: 11–76); and Daniel R. Schwartz, "Law and Truth: On Qumran-Sadducean and Rabbinic Views of Law," in *The Dead Sea Scrolls: Forty Years of Research,* ed. D. Dimant and U. Rappaport (Leiden: Brill, 1992), 229–40, though neither formulates the issue the way I suggest doing. I draw attention to the recent words of A. I. Baumgarten, "The Zadokite Priests at Qumran: A Reconsideration," *Dead Sea Discoveries* 4 (1997): 153–54:

> The history of the Qumran community is proving to be far more complex than previously imagined. Legal traditions, widely proclaimed recently in the aftermath of the impact of 4QMMT as the key to understanding Qumran sectarianism, are not as all-illumining as thought. Difficulties in this approach arose almost immediately, as the individual legal rulings of the Qumran group do not seem to form a coherent whole. Even more important than individual rulings, on which members of a group may have some measure of disagreement . . . is *legal authority, the right to establish normative practice"* [emphasis his].

I think Baumgarten is precisely correct. The conflict of visions was about who was to have this right: the priests, or the upstart Pharisees.

19. *Against Apion* 1.60–61.

20. The quote is from *War* 2.161. For a compelling demonstration that Josephus was not a Pharisee—contrary to long-cherished notions of scholarship—see Steve Mason, *Flavius Josephus on the Pharisees* (Leiden: Brill, 1991), 325–41.

21. Thomas Sowell, *A Conflict of Visions: Ideological Origins of Political Struggles* (New York: William Morrow, 1987), 16–17.

22. CD 1:15–18, following essentially the translation of Edward Cook in Michael Wise, Martin Abegg, Edward Cook, *The Dead Sea Scrolls: A New Translation* (San Francisco: HarperSanFrancisco, 1996), 52.

CHAPTER 4

1. The location of the council chamber or Bouleuterion is clear from *War* 5.144. It stood in the region where the first wall of Jerusalem joined the west wall of the Temple area, so in or above the Tyropoeon valley and outside the Temple. For the present narrative the assumption is that Judah was imprisoned in the Maccabean palace.

2. Of course, it is also true that in his hymns Judah at times incorporated biblical language simply because he was so immersed in that literature that the language came to him effortlessly. In trying to decide his intent in any given case, I have relied upon the criterion of coherence. Where the biblical portion seems to lend itself to Judah's situation, I have judged the reference purposeful. Where this resonance did not seem to be present, I have considered the quotation or allusion to be merely stylistic. It must be admitted that the boundary between these types of usage is not always clearly defined.

3. CD 8:12, 19:25.

4. This duality underlies a passage of the *Damascus Document* that has seldom been understood rightly. I would translate it as follows: "Any man whom the spirits of Belial rule so that he preaches apostasy shall be judged in accordance with the law of the necromancer and the medium. But anyone he leads astray so as to profane the Sabbath or the festivals should not be executed; rather, his confinement becomes a human responsibility. If then he should be healed of it [the evil spirit], then they must observe him for seven years [to assure proper behavior]. Afterward, he may re-enter the congregation" (CD 12:2–6). For brief discussion, see my forthcoming article on "Healing" in the *Encyclopedia of the Dead Sea Scrolls*.

5. For these last two paragraphs see Robert Wilson, *Prophecy and Society in Ancient Israel* (Philadelphia: Fortress Press, 1980), 210–11 and 249–50. Note also the apropos comments of I. M. Lewis, *Ecstatic Religion,* 2d ed. (New York: Routledge, 1989), 152–53:

> In [a] competitive situation where authentic enthusiasm is a scarce commodity, and where many feel themselves called but few are actually chosen, it is obviously essential to be able to discriminate between genuine and spurious inspiration. It is also necessary to have a foolproof means of discrediting those established shamans who are considered to abuse their power. . . . Thus, if the same ostensible symptoms, or behaviour, can be seen, either as an intimation of divine election, or as a dangerous intrusion of demonic power, this will provide an adequate basis for acknowledging the claims of some aspirants while rejecting those of others.

6. For Theudas, see Josephus, *Ant.* 20.97–99; for "the Egyptian," *War* 2.261–63 and *Ant.* 20.169–72. For the other movements, see *Ant.* 20.167–68 and *Ant.* 18.85–87. For secondary literature, note especially P. W. Barnett, "The Jewish Sign

Prophets—A.D. 40–70—Their Intentions and Origin," *New Testament Studies* 27 (1981): 679–97, esp. 682–83.

7. Despite the claims of many excellent scholars that the Servant passages were never connected, either by himself or by followers, to the Teacher of Righteousness. Cf., for example, Joseph Fitzmyer, *Responses to 101 Questions on the Dead Sea Scrolls* (New York: Paulist Press, 1992), 116–17. Though his earlier writings were generally more dilute, by his eighth and ninth hymns Judah came to speak of himself as the Servant of the Lord in concentrated fashion. He made allusion after allusion to the passages of Isaiah that modern scholars designate Servant Songs, and others to portions that might easily be so construed.

Consider the figure below and the passages of Isaiah that Judah imported into these two hymns and thereby wrote large as prophecies of himself:

Figure 1: The Servant in Isaiah and in Judah's Hymns Eight and Nine

ISAIAH	JUDAH'S HYMNS EIGHT AND NINE
Those who *prosecuted you* shall be as nothing and perish (Isa. 41:11) Those *who wage war against you* shall be as nothing at all (Isa. 41:12)	Those *who waged war against me* and who *prosecuted me* shall be scattered like chaff before the wind
Here is My Servant *whom I uphold*, My Chosen, in whom My soul delights; *I have put My spirit upon him* (Isa. 42:1)	I thank You, O Lord, for You have *upheld me* by Your might and *have poured out Your holy spirit within me*
YHWH called me before I was born, *while I was inside my mother's womb* he named me (Isa. 49:1)	Surely You knew me before my father begot me; You set me apart from the *womb. I was yet inside my mother* and You lavished kindness upon me
I have given you the *covenant* of the people, the light of the nations (Isa. 42:6) I have kept you and given you the *covenant* of the people, to establish the land, to apportion the desolate heritages (Isa. 49:8) The Lord YHWH has given me a *tongue of teachings* (Isa. 50:4a)	You have reinforced me in Your *covenant* and emboldened my *tongue* according to Your *teachings*
That I may know how *to sustain the weary with a word* (Isa. 50:4b)	Though You ceaselessly empower my *tongue*, I am unable to lift my voice, unable to proclaim the *teachings* that revive the stumbling spirit, unable *to sustain the weary with a word*
For he grew up before Him like a young plant, and like a *Root* out of *dry land* (Isa. 53:2)	I thank You, O Lord, for You set me at the source of streams in a *dry land*
He was despised and *forsaken* by men, a man of *suffering* and acquainted with *sickness* (Isa. 53:3) We accounted him *afflicted* (Isa. 53:4)	I sojourn with *sickness* and my heart is *stricken* with *afflictions*. I am like a man *forsaken*

8. The scholarly literature on the Servant passages of Isaiah is immense. For the capsule summary of the passages here, I am particularly indebted to the sensitive exposition by Henri Blocher, *Songs of the Servant* (London: IVP, 1975). I have also relied upon his summary of the New Testament uses of the concept.

9. 1QH 10:20–21, *You placed insight in my heart whereby to open the fount of knowledge for all the initiated.*

10. Understanding the Hebrew as from *kwn*, not *tkn*. Compare Ezek. 38:7.

11. A possible objection against the proposed translation/understanding might be raised here, focusing on the Hebrew particle *et*. I take this use in the Isaiah Scroll to be an example of the particle's nominative function—or more precisely, that is how I think readers in Judah's day understood this text. For a good brief discussion of nominative use, see Bruce Waltke and Michael O'Connor, *An Introduction to Biblical Hebrew Syntax* (Winona Lake, IN: Eisenbrauns, 1990), §10.3.2, and bibliography.

12. CD 1:11.

13. As a matter of fact, this version of Isaiah better fits the continuation. It may have been the original text. So one must allow for the possibility that Judah knew, not the *Great Isaiah Scroll,* but merely a text like it. That seems a needless complication, however, for it postulates a vanished text to explain something that a text we actually have can do just as well. The only witness to this reading is 1QIsaᵃ.

14. It can also be shown that sometimes Judah quoted Isaiah in a form identical to that of the traditional text, in preference to a different reading in 1QIsaᵃ. Depending on the situation he either used the text form that best suited his point or made his choice indiscriminately.

The other disagreements between the *Great Isaiah Scroll* and the Isaiah we know: (1) In the second hymn, at 1QH 10:25, *m'tkh grw* leads to Isa. 54:17; where in that verse the MT (traditional text) reads *hn, m'wty,* and *gr,* 1QIsaᵃ reads *hnh, m'ty,* and *ygr.* The Isaiah Scroll reading thus leads directly to the interpretation of the hymn, and may be translated: "Behold, one can attack you only ('ps, cf. Numbers 22:35) by my command; who can (otherwise) attack you, (who) fall upon you?"

(2) In the same hymn, at 1QH 10:30, *ybq'w* leads to Isa. 59:5, where, however, the MT reads *bq'w;* 1QIsaᵃ contains the exact reading of the hymn, *ybq'w.*

(3) In the fourth hymn, at 1QH 11:18, *wytgrshw glym* leads to Isa. 57:20. Here the MT reads *ygrshw,* while 1QIsaᵃ reads *ytgrshw.* Of this difference between 1QIsaᵃ and the MT, E. Y. Kutscher wrote, "The Qal [of this root] is found in the Bible only here, the Hithpael is not found at all . . . hence, the substitution is surprising. . . . A really satisfactory solution [for the question of why the substitution occurred] has not been arrived at." So his *The Language and Linguistic Background of the Isaiah Scroll (1QIsaᵃ)* (Leiden: Brill, 1974), 359.

(4) In the seventh hymn, at 1QH 13:30, *lk'yb 'nwsh* leads to Isa. 17:11. Here the MT reads *k'b,* whereas 1QIsaᵃ reads *k'yb,* the exact reading of the hymn. The spelling *k'yb* never occurs in the MT.

(5) In the eighth hymn, at 1QH 15:20–21, *lhsis mt' wlgdl ntsr* leads to Isa. 60:21. Here the MT contains the phrase *ntsr mt'w* [usually emended to *mt'y*] *m'sh ydy,* rendered something like "the shoot I have planted, the work of my hands." 1QIsaᵃ

witnesses instead *ntsr mt'y yhyh m'sy ydyw.* Two readings are different and an additional word has been inserted. I suggest the portion was understood to say, "Then will all your people be righteous, and they will inherit the land forever. The Shoot of My Tree will be the work of his hands, by which he will receive glory." Thus in this version the Shoot or *ntsr* (which the Teacher Hymns interpret to mean the Teacher's followers, as will become clear; see chap. 6) is the work of someone in addition to God. This version would generate the claim of 1QH 15, the MT would not. See further chap. 9, below.

(6) In the ninth hymn, at 1QH 16:14, the universally accepted reading (with an emendation) is *lbz'y nhrwt.* This reading leads to Isa. 18:2, 7, where the MT has *bz'w nhrym.* The reading of 1QIsaᵃ is identical with the hymn: *bz'y.* Kutscher commented on the reading of the Isaiah Scroll: "The *yod* is clear, but it is difficult to fathom what the scribe had in mind" (*Isaiah Scroll,* 231). Whatever the meaning, in his hymn—where the passage is difficult and its sense is disputed—Judah manifestly held to a different interpretation of the word than one finds in modern translations of Isa. 18.

(7) More weakly pointing to the use of 1QIsaᵃ is 1QH 13:26, which should be read *wylwzw* (Niphal, not Hiphil) *'ly.* The informing passage was Isa. 30:12, where, however, the MT reads *nlwz.* 1QIsaᵃ has instead *wtlwz,* which leads more readily to the phrase in the hymn.

(8) Another less certain use is 1QH 15:23, *'wlwl bhyq.* This use apparently relied on Isa. 40:11. There the MT includes the word *tl'ym,* "lambs." In contrast, 1QIsaᵃ reads *tlym,* apparently an Aramaism for "youths." This creates a parallelism that would more strongly encourage Judah to interpret this biblical text of himself and so make the hymn's statement. It should be noted that pIsaᵉ i–ii 2–3 relates this biblical text to the Moreh Ha-Sedeq.

(9) A third less certain usage appears in the fourth hymn, at 1QH 11:20–21. There the two words *m'sy* and *rwhy* appear in parallel, apparently deriving from a reading of Isa. 41:29. The last word of that verse in the MT is *nskyhm,* "their idols." The equivalent portion of 1QIsaᵃ reads instead *nsykyhmh,* "their rulers." This reading would better support the apparent use of Isaiah in the hymn, since the context is describing the destruction of Judah's foes, which included the rulers of Jerusalem.

The readings of 1QH discussed in 1, 3, and 4 appear not only as indicated, but elsewhere in the Teacher Hymns as well. Thus the total number of probable and possible connections between 1QH and 1QIsaᵃ is more than ten.

15.   For an excellent discussion of the evidence for Jewish trials in this period, see Raymond Brown, *The Death of the Messiah* (New York: Doubleday, 1994), 1:328–97. For the first portion of Shimeon ben Shetah's statement, I have transplanted some of the wording used in a later trial before Hyrcanus, that of Herod the Great. The charge that Josephus reports, that Herod was not sufficiently humble as shown by his dress, strikes me as believable also in Judah's case. I do not think that a man who believed he was God's prophet would go to court and become a simpering suppliant. For Herod's trial, see *Ant.* 14.172–73.

16.   Generally this Hebrew word, *tokhahat,* has been rendered something like "re-

buke" or "chastisement" by translators of this scroll. For example, note the oft-cited work of Maurya Horgan, *Pesharim: Qumran Interpretations of Biblical Books* (Washington, DC: Catholic Biblical Association of America, 1979), 15, or the well-known translation by Geza Vermes, *The Complete Dead Sea Scrolls in English,* 5th ed. (London: Penguin Books, 1997), 481. Such renderings cluster on the weak side of this term's semantic range. They have arisen and have been perpetuated in scholarship on the scrolls because the political aspects of the scrolls, their message, and setting have been overlooked. A better translation is "judgment," which becomes, in a political setting, "trial." This rendering captures the forensic overtones present in many of the twenty-three biblical uses of *tokhahat* and the fifty-five uses of its verbal root, *ykh.* Note especially Gen. 20:16, 31:37; Isa. 2:4, 11:3, 11:4, 29:21; Hos. 4:4; Mic. 4:3, 6:2; Job 9:33, 13:3, 13:6, 13:15, 15:3, 16:21, 22:4, 23:7, 32:12, 40:2; and 1 Chron. 12:17. Furthermore, the forensic element is clearly to be seen in the use of *tokhahat* in the passage of the *Commentary on Habakkuk* immediately prior to ours, *1QpHab* 5:4.

17. At least once earlier in the literature on the scrolls the possibility that Judah was impugned as a false prophet has been raised. Shemaryahu Talmon, "The Calendar of the Covenanters of the Judaean Desert," in *The World of Qumran from Within: Collected Essays* (Leiden: Brill, 1989), 148, argued on the basis of the Mishnah and tractate Sanhedrin that Judah was a "rebellious elder," liable for strangulation, and in note 2 on that page he pointed out that Judah may have suffered "the slur of being a false prophet." But Talmon did not follow up his observations to say whether Judah was actually charged with these crimes as opposed to being liable to such charges, and he made no historical argument based on these observations. Neither did he connect Judah's exile to the charges.

18. 4Q375 1 i 4–9. For the *editio princeps,* edited by John Strugnell, see M. Broshi et al., *Discoveries in the Judaean Desert 19: Qumran Cave 4. XIV Parabiblical Texts, Part 2,* (Oxford: Clarendon Press, 1995), 113.

19. My reasoning here is as follows. One stanchion of the priestly power had been priests' monopolistic stranglehold on the scriptures. Only a modest percentage of people besides priests could read. Few but priests could write much more than their names. Writing, in fact, was a particular trade, like metalworking or tanning. The connection of writing with the priesthood was a phenomenon general to the entire ancient Near East and extended back into the third millennium B.C.E. when writing first developed. Recent scholarship suggests that in Greco-Roman times only about 15 percent of the Judaean populace could read; see W. V. Harris, *Ancient Literacy* (Cambridge: Harvard Univ. Press, 1989), 328–30. Again, many fewer could write. Since, then, it was mainly the priests who were able to read and copy the scriptures, naturally it was they who interpreted their meaning. "Written" often meant "priestly," and written culture was overwhelmingly the province of priests.

When the Pharisaic movement began to stir they faced this problem. How could they hope to compete for prestige with priestly interpreters of the nation's laws? Simply producing alternative written legislation was a hopeless strategy. Why would anyone prefer newfangled Pharisaic legislation when they could instead rely on the age-old priestly ordinances? In the ancient world attitudes were the opposite of our own: older meant better. In the mind of the ordinary Jew, the association of written laws and the priesthood extended so far back into the mists of time that direct assault on that association was unlikely to succeed. So the Pharisees bypassed literacy, the priestly foundation of power, and developed a different approach. Their authority became not written documents, but an oral law. And this orality played well with the ordinary illiterate peasant, whose own life was oriented to oral rather than written transmission of ideas.

Josephus wrote of this development in a famous portion of his *Antiquities* that has seldom been understood: "At this juncture I wish to explain that the Pharisees passed on to the people certain ordinances from a succession of Fathers, which are not written down in the laws of Moses. For this reason those of the Sadducean faction reject them: they argue that one must have regard only for those ordinances that are written down, and not observe those from the tradition of the Fathers" (*Ant.* 13.297–98, my translation).

Josephus was as time bound as any of us, of course. He wrote of the Pharisees as he knew them: the Pharisees of 70 C.E. Consequently, in reading this passage one finds the priestly Sadducean faction on the defensive, whereas the Pharisees are proactive. Yet in the period when the Pharisees first arose the opposite would have been true. In 150 B.C.E. the established way of interpreting the biblical laws was through written ordinances, and the Pharisees were neither dictating policy nor passing binding ordinances on the people. One might further get the impression from what Josephus says that the Sadducees accepted only what was *written down in the laws of Moses.* Some scholars do read the passage that way. Accordingly, they understand the phrase *for this reason* to point backward, to what Josephus has just said. But while this interpretation of the words is grammatically possible, it makes Josephus say something that was not true and that could not work. A myriad of examples could be mustered to illustrate the difficulties that result. For the sake of brevity I will offer just one.

Lev. 27:32 reads, "All tithes of herd and flock, every tenth one that passes under the shepherd's staff, shall be holy to the Lord." This law of Moses requires the people of Israel to tithe their cattle, goats, and sheep and give that tithe to the Lord. The earthly recipients were the Temple priests. After the animal had been sacrificed and certain portions offered on the altar, most of the meat and all of the valuable hide would belong to them. Yet Deut. 14:23 says something different: "In the presence of the Lord your God . . . you shall eat the tithe of your grain, your wine, and your oil, as well as the firstlings of your herd and flock." This law of Moses does not require the people to donate the animals to the priests. Instead, after a portion has been sacrificed, they themselves get the meat. Read straightforwardly, these two laws clash. What, then, is *written down in the law of Moses?* Many of the biblical laws similarly turn out to be complicated, incomplete, or even contradictory when it comes to actually doing what they say. No group—not the Pharisees or the Sadducees or any other Jewish faction—could hold simply to what *was written down in the laws of Moses.* When performing the laws, interpretation, explication, and reconciliation of apparent contradictions would prove necessary at every turn, as Victor Tcherikover long ago pointed out in *Hellenistic Civilization and the Jews* (1959; New York: Atheneum, 1982), 83–84.

Since it is manifestly Josephus' intention to describe the way people actually tried to live, it seems preferable to read him that way when he described the Pharisaic approach. Presumably the passage is balanced, in that he described the priestly side of things with equal accuracy. The phrase *for this reason* must then point forward, to the words that follow. If this logic is correct, then Josephus is making two statements about the Pharisees, one explicit and one tacit. He states explicitly that the Pharisees held to certain ordinances they had received from *a succession of Fathers.* Josephus also suggests tacitly that these ordinances were not passed down in writing. That means they were orally transmitted, like the later rabbinic dictates. Moreover, Josephus is saying that the Sadducean faction rejected these ordinances simply for this reason: they were not written down.

In reality that was but one among a cadre of reasons for the Sadducean rejection, and probably it was not even the captain of the troop. The Sadducees would object to the ordinances if for no other reason than that they originated within a rival group. But the reason they *gave*—their politically religious argument—hinged on method of transmission. Another implication that emerges, therefore, is that these priestly factions possessed written ordinances that were not a part of *the laws of Moses* as we understand that term today. Precisely such is what we find evidenced among the Dead Sea Scrolls. The scrolls include dozens of written interpretations of the biblical laws. With respect to what Josephus says about written laws of Moses, it is striking that at least eleven of the extrabiblical texts claim Moses as their author, including 4Q375. Were these claims believed, by some people at least? Almost certainly. If so, then for such groups the corpus of the laws of Moses was larger than we think. I suggest that it is to these kinds of written interpretations of the biblical laws that the Sadducees and, presumably, other priestly groups attached themselves.

These *ordinances that are written down* among the Dead Sea Scrolls derived from Judah's followers and one or more precursor groups as well as one or more movements later than Judah's. These are the laws and this is the method that the Pharisees circumvented by recourse to word of mouth. They might even claim that their oral laws were just as old as the written priestly ones and thus garner the crown of age and Mosaic authority for their ordinances. The succession of Fathers could go straight back to Sinai. That was the strategy of the later rabbis. Who could prove otherwise? As we might say, there was no paper trail. Popularity with the people proved the brilliance of their strategy.

20. 1QpHab 11:4–8. For the translation of *beth* as "place," compare Neh. 2:3, Prov. 8:2, and Job 8:17.

21. *War* 1.114.

22. On the Hellenization of Jews, see the classic studies by Martin Hengel: *Judaism and Hellenism* (Philadelphia: Fortress Press, 1974); *Jews, Greeks and Barbarians* (Philadelphia: Fortress Press, 1980); and *The "Hellenization" of Judaea in the First Century After Christ* (Philadelphia: Trinity Press International, 1989). On tithe

and tax, see Shimon Applebaum, *Judaea in Hellenistic and Roman Times* (Leiden: Brill, 1989), 21–22 and n. 55.

23. 11QTemple 64; see J. Baumgarten, "Hanging and Treason in Qumran and Roman Law," *Eretz Israel* 16 (1982): 7–16 (English section).

24. For Roman exile, note John Crook, *Law and Life of Rome* (Ithaca: Cornell Univ. Press, 1967), 272–73 and the *Oxford Classical Dictionary,* 2d ed., s.v.v. *"exsil-ium"* and *"relegatio."* For both Greek and Roman practices, see the *Oxford Classical Dictionary,* 3d ed., s.v. "exile."

25. E.g., Thucydides 1.115.4, 6.7.1, and 6.7.3.

26. *War* 1.108–9.

27. Not all Jewish exile was permanent. Note *Ant.* 13.409 of the Pharisees in the reign of Alexandra: "They recalled exiles and freed prisoners and, to put it simply, differed not a bit from absolute rulers." Even a penalty of permanent exile need not actually be permanent, of course; with a shuffling of those in power, an expatriate might be repatriated. Note also *War* 1.195–99: "About this time Antigonus, son of Aristobulus, waited upon Caesar and . . . accused Hyrcanus and Antipater. They had, he said, in utter defiance of justice, banished him and his brothers and sisters from their native land altogether." This passage shows that twenty years after Judah's trial, Hyrcanus was continuing to use exile to punish elite opponents.

28. Anthony Storr, *Feet of Clay* (New York: Free Press, 1996), xiv.

29. 1QH 12:7–31a. The statement of 12:31b reads like a response added by later followers: "What being of mere flesh has done such as this, and what vessel of mere clay has so multiplied wonders?" One is reminded of Mark 4:39–41: "He woke up and rebuked the wind, and said to the sea, 'Peace! Be still!' Then the wind ceased, and there was a dead calm. He said to them, 'Why are you afraid? Have you still no faith?' And they were filled with great awe and said to one another, 'Who then is this, that even the wind and sea obey him?' "

CHAPTER 5

1. William James, *The Varieties of Religious Experience* (1902; New York: Penguin Books, 1982), 388.

2. Unlike the hymns that precede or those that immediately follow, hymn 4 lacks any chronological or sociological indicator that might serve as a peg for a relative dating. Equally absent is literary-critical evidence to suggest that the chronological arrangement generally evident throughout the hymns was at any point abandoned. By default, therefore, I conclude—very tentatively—that this hymn was indeed composed after hymn 3 and before hymn 5. The event to which it responds may actually have happened before any of the hymns were written; on the basis of parallels, that would be the expectation psychologically.

3. 1QH 11:6–21. Precisely where the hymn begins is not certain; line 6 is where the sense begins to be clear.

4. Judah used the *Hiphil* of the verb *'wr,* which here has a transitive meaning. In the Hebrew Bible the *Hiphil* of this verb is almost always intransitive, an "internal

Hiphil." The only biblical use parallel to Judah's is Eccles. 8:1, which speaks of the "wise man," who alone knows the "true import of a matter" *(pesher davar)*. This verse is also the only biblical use of the latter phrase. Note that this entire line reappears in hymn 5.

    5. *Ant.* 3.79–83.

    6. Ben Sira—or perhaps only his grandson—embraced a notion akin to that of Josephus. At 45:2 Ben Sira wrote of Moses, "And He named him 'Ish Elohim' and made him strong with fearful powers." In biblical Hebrew *Ish Elohim* is not mysterious. The phrase is one typical designation for a prophet; it is used of Elijah, for example, and would ordinarily be translated "man of God." But when, sometime in the years 132–117 B.C.E., Ben Sira's grandson translated his book from Hebrew into Greek, he produced an interpretive rendering: "God made him equal in glory to the angels, and made him strong with fearful powers."

    The grandson read *Elohim* as a term for *angel,* a meaning the word rarely has in the Bible but more frequently has assumed in postbiblical Hebrew. Whether he correctly took Ben Sira's point we cannot know; in any case, his own is more important. To say that Moses was equal in glory to the angels was to refer to his shining skin. The angels shone as a mirrored reflection of God's glory. Moses, too, reflected that divine effluent, and that was why he appeared brilliant. For Ben Sira's grandson, then, Moses had been to heaven and there assumed an angelic appearance. Only by entering the divine presence was this transformation possible.

    Note that 45:2 is damaged in the Hebrew manuscript of Ben Sira that is its witness. For the probable restoration of *ish* or *be-ish,* see W. O. E. Osterley, *The Wisdom of Jesus the Son of Sirach or Ecclesiasticus* (Cambridge: Cambridge Univ. Press, 1912), 204, who follows R. Smend, *Die Weisheit des Jesus Sirach* (Berlin: G. Reimer, 1906). For the Hebrew text I have used Israel Lévi, *The Hebrew Text of the Book of Ecclesiasticus* (Leiden: Brill, 1969).

    7. The phrase *enduring dawn* Judah derived from Hos. 6:3. This was the verse that, together with Hos. 10:12, gave rise to his name, "Teacher of Righteousness." The latter half of 6:3 was evidently applied to Judah—and not, as in modern translations, to God, the subject of the first half. The portion reads, "And he will come like spring rains to us, as spring rains that water (Heb. *yoreh*) the earth." In fact, it seems Judah made this application himself, for in 1QH 16:16 he used it to describe his own role *(keyoreh geshem)*. Thus "Teacher of Righteousness" also meant "He who rains righteousness" and might have been a title Judah used of himself. This case illustrates the fact that a complex biblical exegesis underlies Judah's writings but is often only revealed piecemeal, dribbled out over several hymns. Such is reasonable if the hymns were intended, not as public vehicles for his teaching, but as private meditations, which is how I view them.

    All through his hymns Judah used water imagery of his enemies and of the judgment that would come upon them. In the later movement, too, water imagery was used of the enemies. The Man of the Lie was called "He who baptizes with untruth" *(metif kazav)*—Judah's evil doppelgänger. Cf. CD 4:19–20, 8:13, and 1QpHab 10:9.

8. 4Q403 1 i 39–45. I have slightly adapted my translation from Michael Wise, Martin Abegg, Edward Cook, *The Dead Sea Scrolls: A New Translation* (San Francisco: HarperSanFrancisco, 1996), 371–72. For the *editio princeps,* see Carol Newsom, *Songs of the Sabbath Sacrifice: A Critical Edition* (Atlanta: Scholars Press, 1985), 209–10 and comments.

9. I have here modified my colleague Martin Abegg's translation as it appears in Wise, Abegg, Cook, *Dead Sea Scrolls,* 356–57. For the preliminary scholarly publication, see B. Z. Wacholder and M. Abegg, *A Preliminary Edition of the Unpublished Dead Sea Scrolls, Fascicle Two* (Washington, DC: Biblical Archaeology Society, 1992), 38.

10. *Sir.* 33:15, "Consider all of God's creation: everything comes in pairs, the one corresponding to the other." I have rendered the Hebrew text from J. Marcus, *Ben Sira—The Fifth Manuscript* (Philadelphia: Dropsie College for Hebrew and Cognate Learning, 1931), 17. In a note *ad loc,* Marcus calls attention to the *Testament of Asher* 1:4, part of the *Testaments of the Twelve Patriarchs,* some of which had its ultimate origin in the early second century B.C.E. It reads, "Therefore all things are by twos, one over against the other."

11. James, *Religious Experience,* 251–53. These "sensible" experiences must be distinguished from the use of light as a literary element in allegorical descriptions of a sudden realization or new apprehension. With regard to Paul, I see no particular reason to associate his photism with his heavenly journey.

12. For a good discussion, see Alan F. Segal, "Heavenly Ascent in Hellenistic Judaism, Early Christianity and Their Environment," *Aufstieg und Niedergang der Römischen Welt* 23, no. 2 (1980): 1333–94.

13. See my "To Know the Times and the Seasons: A Study of the Aramaic Chronograph 4Q559," *Journal for the Study of the Pseudepigrapha* 15 (1997): 3–51.

14. Enochic literature includes *1 Enoch* (4Q201–2, 204–12) and the *Book of Giants* (1Q23, 2Q26, 4Q203, 530–32, and 6Q8). One might well include 4Q227, "Enoch and the Watchers." For a translation and suggested arrangement of the fragments of the *Book of Giants,* see Cook's reconstruction in Wise, Abegg, Cook, *Dead Sea Scrolls,* 246–50; for 4Q227, see 264 in the same work.

Whether the New Testament book of Jude is a product of Jesus' brother of the same name is a vexed issue, but I am persuaded by the arguments of Richard Bauckham, *Jude and the Relatives of Jesus in the Early Church* (Edinburgh: T & T Clark), esp. 171–78. Jude 14–15 contains the quotation of *1 Enoch* 1:9. Bauckham finds in Jude many other uses of, and allusions to, *1 Enoch.*

15. I cite portions of the translation of M. A. Knibb, 14:8–24, in H. F. D. Sparks, ed., *The Apocryphal Old Testament* (Oxford: Clarendon Press, 1984), 201–3.

16. The quote is from Segal, "Heavenly Ascent," 1359. Note I. M. Lewis, *Ecstatic Religion,* 2d ed. (New York: Routledge, 1989), 30: "The circumstances which encourage the ecstatic response are precisely those where men feel themselves constantly threatened by exacting pressures which they do not know how to combat or control, except through those heroic flights of ecstasy by which they seek to demonstrate that they are the equals of the gods."

17.   For the early dating of the work, note J. Becker, *Untersuchungen zur Entstehungsgeschichte der Testamente der zwölf Patriarchen* (Leiden: Brill, 1970), 376; E. J. Bickerman, "The Date of the Testaments of the Twelve Patriarchs," *Studies in Jewish and Christian History* (Leiden: Brill, 1980): 1–23; J. T. Milik, "Le Testament de Lévi en araméen: Fragments de la grotte 4 de Qumran," *RB* 62 (1955): 399; and J. T. Milik, *The Books of Enoch* (Oxford: Oxford Univ. Press, 1976), 24.

The Dead Sea Scroll copies are 1Q21, 4Q213–14, 4Q540–41. The latter two may not belong to the *Aramaic Levi*. Also, precisely how many different manuscripts are grouped under the designations of 4Q213–14 remains unclear because of uncertainty about how many different scribal hands they represent. See M. E. Stone and J. C. Greenfield, "Aramaic Levi Document," in James VanderKam et al., *Discoveries in the Judaean Desert XXII: Qumran Cave 4: XVII Parabiblical Texts, Part 3* (Oxford: Clarendon Press, 1996), 1–72, and E. Puech, "Fragments d'un apocryphe de Lévi et le personnage eschatologique: 4QTestLévi^{c-d}(?) et 4QAja," in *Proceedings of the International Congress on the Dead Sea Scrolls, Madrid, 18–21 March 1991,* ed. J. Trebolle Barrera and L. Vegas Montaner (Leiden: Brill, 1992), 449–501.

18.   The translation is Edward Cook's from Wise, Abegg, Cook, *The Dead Sea Scrolls,* 252. To arrive at his rendering, Cook combines a Qumran manuscript, 4Q213, with a later Greek translation of the *Aramaic Levi,* the Mount Athos fragment.

19.   *Testament of Levi* 2:3, 5–10, cited according to the translation of H. W. Hollander and M. de Jonge, *The Testaments of the Twelve Patriarchs* (Leiden: Brill, 1985), 132.

20.   James Tabor, *Things Unutterable* (New York: Univ. Press of America, 1986), 81. Tabor's second chapter, "The Heavenly Journey in Antiquity," is a valuable adjunct to Segal's article cited above. See also Tabor's article "Heaven, Ascent to," in the *Anchor Bible Dictionary,* eds. D. N. Freedman, et al. (New York: Doubleday & Co., 1992) 3:91–4.

21.   Tabor, *Things Unutterable,* 82.

22.   Marcus Borg, *Meeting Jesus Again for the First Time* (San Francisco: HarperSanFrancisco, 1994), 32.

23.   Borg, *Meeting Jesus,* 33.

24.   Borg, *Meeting Jesus,* 35.

25.   Anthony Storr, *Feet of Clay* (New York: Free Press, 1996), 152.

26.   Storr, *Feet of Clay,* 171, emphasis mine. In Storr's book these two sentences appear in the reverse order.

27.   Tabor makes this observation in *Things Unutterable,* 57 and 69.

28.   Lewis, *Ecstatic Religion,* 33.

29.   Lewis, *Ecstatic Religion,* 60.

30.   Mircea Eliade, *Shamanism: Archaic Techniques of Ecstasy* (Princeton: Princeton Univ. Press, 1964), 33–66.

31.   Mircea Eliade, *Rites and Symbols of Initiation: The Mysteries of Birth and Rebirth* (New York: Harper Torchbooks, 1958), 91.

32.   Eliade, *Rites,* 90.

33. Reports of Tukano Indian shamans are found in Lewis, *Ecstatic Religion,* 52. The quote is from Eliade, *Rites,* 36.

34. 1QH 11:13.

35. I have translated from 1QIsaᵃ, which has some significant differences from the traditional text. For reasons set forth in the last chapter, I believe this was the primary text of Isaiah that Judah was using.

36. 1QH15:22. Note also 15:23–24, *They are like children who play in the embrace of their foster father.* Judah arrived at the birth imagery of Isa. 9 in part by analogy to passages about the Servant that mention birth or babies. Such passages include Isa. 49:1, "YHWH has called me from the womb, called me by name from inside my mother" (his mother being himself). Another portion is Isa. 53:2, "He grew up before Him like a suckling." Judah wove all these passages together in a particular way. As a result, he saw Isa. 9:6–7 as describing the Servant in his moment of self-recognition. This was a mystical, not a literal birth.

37. The suffix was the reflex of *el gibbor.*

38. 1QH 15:20–21 for hymn 8; 16:10–11 for hymn 9.

39. Judah understood the use of *netser* in Isa. 60:21 as referring to his followers and—in the different text form of 1QIsaᵃ—saw himself there also. In his ninth hymn, however, Judah made it clear that the roots are not only himself, but the precursor group. See chap. 8 below.

40. 1QH 15:8–9.

41. We see how immensely clever Judah could be—punning, alluding to scripture, and creating new meaning all at once. Not for nothing had Judah risen to his erstwhile prominence in Jerusalem. His was among the most formidable minds of his generation.

The hymn's next lines are metaphorical descriptions of the prophesied judgment, loosely inspired by Ezekiel's image of a storm but quickly becoming more horrific. Water was a recurring motif in Judah's hymns and wild seas a favorite way to portray the destruction of judgment. The seas would wash over his enemies (*surely all their wisdom shall be swallowed up*). Sucked under the surface of the boiling water, the Pharisees and their followers would descend as in a whirlpool to the abyss. The earth would open and engulf them, and they would find themselves in Hell (*the gates of Sheol will swing open to receive all these handiworks of wickedness*).

Much that Judah said was cast as metaphors, but the reference to Hell was literal. For him and virtually all Jews of his day, it was as real as a third-degree burn. In line with their developing cosmology, most people located Hell beneath the surface of the earth. Judah fervently wished that his enemies would take up residence there immediately. Whether it happened immediately or not, though, he knew with the certain knowing of the charismatic leader that Hell was their eventual destination. And they deserved no less, for they had perverted the truth of God and refused his chosen one.

42. I might have said more precisely that with his fourth and fifth hymns Judah has written enough for his messianic notions to emerge clearly. The question of development is problematic because of the reworking of his hymns. I therefore present

only one possible rationalization of the evidence, but it is plausible since it accords more generally with the model of millennial movements and their leaders.

43. One might make the argument, as some scholars do, that the idea of messianism was born, not in the second century B.C.E., but in the early postexilic period, in the time of Zerubbabel, Haggai, and Zechariah. There is perhaps some truth to this position. Prophecies of Haggai and Zechariah that centered on Zerubbabel and hopes that he would restore the Davidic monarchy might be defined as messianic, if by that term one means only a limited notion, "the restoration of the Davidic line"; see John Collins, *The Scepter and the Star* (New York: Doubleday, 1995), 30.

The hope of these prophets was merely for the reestablishment of the pre-exilic situation of king, priest, and Temple. They sought a return to the *status quo ante*. They conceived of no ideal age. That the entire world would come under Israel's dominion, that people might live to antediluvian ages, that evil would cease—such things they did not dream (Collins's interpretation of Hag. 2:21–24 is overdrawn; no "ideal era" is being described, merely a window of opportunity for Israel while the great nations are in turmoil). In any case, whatever hopes were held for Zerubbabel, he did not claim to communicate with God or broker the divine message to his people.

It therefore seems better to consider these Persian period prophets and their hopes "protomessianic." They thought in terms of contemporary kings and priests, not an eschatological age of salvation. Their concepts were in line with the use of *mashiah* ("messiah") in the Hebrew Bible: "In the original context not one of the thirty-nine occurrences . . . refers to an expected figure of the future whose coming will coincide with the inauguration of an era of salvation"; see J. J. M. Roberts, "The Old Testament's Contribution to Messianic Expectations," in *The Messiah: Developments in Earliest Judaism and Christianity,* ed. J. H. Charlesworth (Minneapolis: Fortress Press, 1992), 39. Protomessianism later became messianism, just as protoapocalypticism issued in apocalypticism; see P. D. Hanson, "Messiahs and Messianic Figures in Proto-Apocalypticism," in *The Messiah,* ed. Charlesworth, 67–75. Apocalyptic and messianism were connected. Messianism required apocalyptic because of its need for linear and telic concepts of time, as many scholars have observed; cf., for example, R. J. Zwi Werblowsky, "Messiah and Messianic Movements," *The New Encyclopedia Brittanica,* 1982 ed., and the words of Gershom Scholem, "When the Messianic idea appears as a living force in the world of Judaism . . . it always occurs in the closest connection with apocalypticism"; see *The Messianic Idea in Judaism* (New York: Schocken Books, 1971), 4.

44. Scholem, *Messianic Idea,* 35.

45. M. I. Pereira de Queiroz, "Messianic Myths and Movements," *Diogenes* 90 (1975): 78.

46. James Charlesworth, "From Messianology to Christology: Problems and Prospects," in *The Messiah,* ed. Charlesworth, 4. The volume is very useful for anyone seeking a rapid conspectus on the topic of the title. Equally useful is J. Neusner et al., eds., *Judaisms and Their Messiahs at the Turn of the Christian Era* (New York: Cambridge Univ. Press, 1987). In the preface of the latter work Neusner defined *messiah* in the Jewish context as "a man who at the end of history, at the eschaton, will

bring salvation to the Israel conceived by the social group addressed by the way of life and world view of that Judaism" (ix).

47. J. Barton, *Oracles of God: Perceptions of Ancient Prophecy in Israel After the Exile* (Oxford: Oxford Univ. Press, 1990).

48. In the interests of objectivity I have adapted this list from the summary of Jonathan A. Goldstein, "How the Authors of 1 and 2 Maccabees Treated the 'Messianic' Promises," in *Judaisms and Their Messiahs,* ed. Neusner et al., 69.

49. Moreover, if he were the Root of Isa. 11, then Judah must also be the person described by verse 10 of that chapter: "On that day the Root of Jesse shall stand as a banner *(nes)* to the nations." As Isa. 11:10 is the only instance in the Bible of the word *banner* referring to a person, it seems certain that Judah had it in mind when he wrote in the first hymn, *You have set me as a banner to the chosen righteous.* Judging by context, Judah read of the figure in Isa. 11 and saw himself.

50. 1QH 15:24–25. On one level the *house* designated the remnant, Judah's followers, the faithful of Israel installed in power. Judah drew his words from Isa. 22:21, a coded promise that authority would be stripped from a man who abused it and transferred to another: "I [God] will clothe him with your robe and fasten your sash around him and hand *your rule* over to him. He will be a father to those who live in Jerusalem and to the *House of Judah.*" The elderly priest read Isaiah as predicting that he was to supplant the unfaithful Jerusalem rulers, especially Hyrcanus. For his hymn he therefore adjusted Isaiah's word *memsheltekha* ("your rule") and made it *memshalti* ("my rule," = "I shall rule"). For Judah it was neither prodigy nor coincidence that Isaiah spoke plainly of the *House of Judah,* actually calling him by name.

Yet there was another level of scriptural resonance in Judah's prophecy *I shall rule over my house.* We can uncover this second level by tracking back to its origins something else Judah said. The expatriate priest wrote elsewhere in the eighth hymn, *Indeed You, my God, have chosen me and made me a father to the pious—a guardian, as it were, to the men who are a sign of things to come.* This statement lifted a pregnant phrase from the third chapter of the biblical book of Zechariah. With its context, the portion reads (italics as usual):

> Thus says YHWH of Hosts: If you will walk in My ways, and if you will observe what I require, then you shall rule My *house* and have charge of My Temple courts. I will give you the right of access among those who are standing here. Now listen, Joshua: You are the high priest, and your colleagues who sit before you—they are indeed *the men who are a sign of things to come!* I am certainly going to bring My servant, the Branch. (Zech. 3:7–8)

In Judah's hymn, Zechariah's *the men who are a sign of things to come* (Hebrew *anshe mofet*) became his own followers. Through this entrée we perceive how Judah read the biblical prophet: *the things to come* evidently meant *the Branch,* another name for the Shoot, the flowering of Judah's movement. Judah's present group was but the foretaste of a much greater following soon to come.

In the *Joshua* of the scripture Judah recognized a cipher for himself, the man before whom sat these personal portents. So Judah will have inferred that the divine promise, *You shall rule my house and have charge of My Temple courts,* applied to him. He took it seriously. He, *Joshua,* was the true high priest.

This was the fuller meaning, the second level of his statement *I shall rule over my house.* Judah, driven from the Temple by his Pharisee enemies, and from the city by a high priest who danced to their tune and wanted to dance on his grave, knew that one day he would return to Jerusalem. There he would take power over the Temple, the house his enemies had defiled.

51. Note especially Lam. 2:17, and less politically 1 Sam. 2:1; Ps. 75:10, 89:17, 92:10, 148:14; and 1 Chron. 25:5.

52. 1QH 14:28–32.

53. 1QH 14:33–36.

54. 1QH 14:37.

55. Note the judgment of the famous rabbinic scholar Saul Lieberman: "Jewish Palestine of the first century swarmed with different sects. Every sect probably had its divisions and subdivisions"; see his "The Discipline in the So-Called Dead Sea Manual of Discipline," *Journal of Biblical Literature* 71 (1951): 206.

56. Charlesworth, "Messianology," 13. Strangely, after making this point, Charlesworth pursues his study using the following criterion: "The discussion of Jewish messianology over the past one hundred years has been vitiated by loose criteria and the inclusion of passages that are now widely recognized as nonmessianic. To avoid this dilemma, only documents that actually contain the noun 'Messiah' or 'Christ' will be included" (17). Thus, reacting against overly loose criteria of the past, Charlesworth devises one overly strict and so defines out of his study much of the genuine evidence for messianic ideas.

57. John Collins, "Messianism in the Maccabean Period," in *Judaisms and Their Messiahs,* ed. Neusner et al., 98. The only evidence for the hope of restoring the Davidic line that Collins could point to was 4Q504, the oldest copy of the Dead Sea Scroll known as "The Words of the Heavenly Luminaries." To my mind the extremely early paleographic date suggested by the scroll's original editor—150 B.C.E.—is unlikely to be correct. In any event, as Collins notes, the work gives voice only to a "traditional expectation" of the restoration someday of the Davidic monarchy. By my definition this is not a messianic idea per se, for the restoration could well be imagined as taking place only after the millennium dawns (cf. the messiah of 4 Ezra). It does not necessarily require the Davidic figure to act as messianic agent of the kingdom.

58. The translation is that of Cook in Wise, Abegg, Cook, *Dead Sea Scrolls,* 256.

59. Jonas Greenfield and Michael Stone, "Remarks on the Aramaic Testament of Levi from the Geniza," *Revue Biblique* 86 (1979): 223–24. Note also their comments and examples on 219, where they say, "In *[Aramaic Levi]* royal terminology is consistently applied to Levi, suggesting that Judah's role in *[Testament of Levi,* in *Testaments of the Twelve Patriarchs]* may have been introduced by editorial activity."

60. For matters of textual dislocation and the identification of the high priest, see P. W. Skehan and A. A. Di Lella, *The Wisdom of Ben Sira* (New York: Doubleday, 1987), 548–50.

61. In the Christian reworking of *Aramaic Levi* that became part of the *Testaments of the Twelve Patriarchs,* the eighteenth chapter of Levi's *Testament* invoked a great high priest yet to come. This was a priestly messiah. Of this Latter Day figure it was said, "Then will the Lord raise up a new priest, to whom all the words of the Lord will be revealed; and he will execute true judgement on earth for many days, and his star will arise in heaven, as a king" (translation by M. de Jonge in *Apocryphal Old Testament,* ed. Sparks, 536). Although we must be careful in drawing conclusions from this later version about the contents of the earlier *Aramaic Levi,* in this case there is little doubt that the words are "pre-Christian in essential points"; so G. Nickelsburg, "Salvation Without and with a Messiah: Developing Beliefs in Writings Ascribed to Enoch," in *Judaisms and Their Messiahs,* ed. Neusner et al., 63. Nickelsburg refers to his further comments in the book coauthored with Michael Stone, *Faith and Piety in Early Judaism* (Philadelphia: Fortress, 1983), 199 nn. 2–3. Since Nickelsburg wrote, the publication of 4Q541, an Aramaic work that obviously has some relationship to Test. Levi 17, has strengthened considerably the case for a second-century B.C.E. provenance of the messianic wording. For the specifics of the publication, see Puech in n. 18 above. Like *Aramaic Levi* itself, these words probably go back to the time when the messianic idea first was born, with the priest as king, and with the Latter Day messiah as priest.

A similar date and social context apparently lie behind the following statements of the *Testament of Reuben,* like Levi's *Testament* now found in the *Testaments of the Twelve Patriarchs.* Reuben is about to die when he breathes these famous last words (*Test. Reuben* 6:5–12, translation by de Jonge in *Apocryphal Old Testament,* ed. Sparks, 520):

> *For to Levi the Lord gave the sovereignty . . . For this reason I command you to listen to Levi, for he will know the law of the Lord and interpret His precepts and offer sacrifice for all Israel until the coming of the anointed high priest of whom the Lord spoke . . . And approach Levi with humility, . . . for he shall bless Israel and Judah, because the Lord has chosen him to rule as king over all the peoples. And accord his sons their proper reverence for they will die in wars on our behalf . . . and he [Levi] will be among you an eternal king.*

The author of the likely Hebrew or Aramaic source for this portion of the *Testament of Reuben* was a priest of the early second century B.C.E. He imagined that the ruler of the Latter Days—*the anointed high priest of whom the Lord spoke*—would, like himself, be of the tribe of Levi, a priest. When he appeared, he would follow in the footsteps of his ancestor Levi and function as king.

62. Werblowsky, "Messiah and Messianic Movements," *New Encyclopedia Brittanica,* 1982 ed.

63. I exclude biblical passages later read as containing such ideas. Scholars do not regard these as messianic in their original social context. They were read as such beginning only in the second century. Even very conservative theologians largely concede this point. Note, for example, George Eldon Ladd, *A Theology of the New Testament* (Grand Rapids: Eerdmans, 1974), 136: "In fact, the simple term 'the Messiah' does not occur in the Old Testament at all."

64. That is, *1 Enoch* 1–36 and 72–105. On the White Bull of the Animal Apocalypse, see Nickelsburg, "Salvation," 55–56.

65. Collins, "Messianism," 106.

66. The problem is that we know about them primarily from Josephus. The Jewish historian was concerned to minimize messianic pretension for his Roman audience, in order to assure them that the Jews were not violent and could be expected to cooperate. Had he been straightforward about just how powerful the messianic idea was among his people, his histories would have had the opposite of their intended effect.

67. Tacitus, *Hist.* 5.9. For Josephus, see *War* 2.57.

68. *War* 7.29.

69. Charlesworth, "Messianology," 35. Note also Norman Cohn, "Medieval Millenarism," in *Millennial Dreams in Action,* ed. S. Thrupp (The Hague: Mouton, 1962), 32: "The oldest form of millenarism of which much is known is the messianic hope of the Jews."

70. Collins, *The Scepter and the Star,* 13.

71. Charlesworth, "Messianology," 27.

CHAPTER 6

1. The complaint he made in his fifth hymn—*all my allies and kinsmen have distanced themselves from me*—was exaggerated by Judah's sense of persecution; certainly some of his allies did remain loyal and left with him. These allies may not, however, have been his peers, the "reprovers" of his first hymn.

2. That Judah (or conceivably, one of his followers) probably brought a copy of the Minor Prophets, or at least of Habakkuk, can be deduced from the following considerations. In his fifth hymn, at 1QH 12:13–14, Judah quoted Hab. 2:15 in a variant form, unknown from any witness to the text but one. The one witness to the text that accords with Judah's quotation is the *Commentary on Habakkuk,* which regularly quotes the biblical lemma in the process of interpretation. The telltale variant occurs in 1QpHab 11:3. What presumably happened was that the pesharist interpreted Habakkuk based on a copy of the book he knew, which failed to survive antiquity.

He and Judah therefore knew the same version of Habakkuk, never quoted or referred to anywhere else. It seems reasonable to suppose that Judah's copy of the book—he owned a copy of Isaiah, and doubtless others; why not the Twelve?—passed on to his followers after his death. This was the copy the pesharist used to compose his work.

3. 1QH 13:7–21.

4. Scroll scholars commonly assert that he went to the site on the shores of the Dead Sea, Qumran, near the caves where the scrolls were later discovered. There they suppose Judah founded a sort of monastery where, among other things, the Dead Sea Scrolls were written and copied.

The primary argument in favor of this conclusion is simply proximity. The caves are near the site. Since they believe that Judah's later followers inhabited this site in the first century C.E. and hid the scrolls in the nearby caves in a time of danger, it seems to many scholars logical to assert that they had lived there from the beginning. Indeed, some consider it so logical that the assertion needs no defense. James Charlesworth is an example: "Khirbet Qumran [the technical name for the site]—in my judgment—is *obviously* the place in the wilderness of Judaea in which the Righteous Teacher settled with the priests who followed him into the wilderness" (emphasis mine); see his "Morphological and Philological Observations: Preparing the Critical Text and Translation of the *Serek Ha-Yahad,*" in *Methods of Investigation of the Dead Sea Scrolls and the Khirbet Qumran Site,* ed. M. O. Wise et al. (New York: New York Academy of Sciences, 1994), 281. Charlesworth is by no means alone in his views; note, for example, the fuller argument in the standard work by F. M. Cross, *The Ancient Library of Qumran and Modern Biblical Studies,* rev. ed. (Grand Rapids, MI: Baker, 1980), 81 n. 46. Cross ends by ruling out the possibility of any view other than his own: "The problems . . . are insurmountable, I think, if 'Damascus' is *not* taken as referring to the desert retreat in the wilderness of Qumran" (emphasis mine). Like Cross, scholars who take this approach interpret the Damascus of the *Damascus Document* figuratively, as a cipher for Qumran.

Yet beyond the sixth hymn and the "northern evidence" argued below, Judah's own words do not favor the common interpretation. He wrote in his fifth hymn, *I have been exiled from my country like a bird driven from its nest.* Judah plainly stated that he was no longer in his country (Hebrew *artsi*). The borders of that country in his time are no mystery. Alexandra had inherited the realm unchanged from Alexander, and Josephus provides an explicit statement of the borders in that king's reign. Alexander had extended Jewish power throughout Idumea on the south, as far as Seleucia on Lake Merom in the north, and along the sea coast from the Egyptian frontier north to Mount Carmel on the west. On the east, all the territory east of the Jordan from Lake Merom to the Dead Sea lay within his rule (thus Josephus, *Ant.* 12.395–97).

A glance at any historical geography will show that Qumran lay well within these boundaries. Alexandra controlled territory extending some twenty miles east of the Dead Sea. Qumran was on the west side of the sea. A person living at that site was nowhere near Judaea's border, much less outside of it. (And the same applies in the mid–second century B.C.E., the time when the "Essene hypothesis" generally locates Judah.) In fact, there is no reason to believe that Judah was ever at Qumran.

In my view many scholars have made three fundamental mistakes. In no particular order, these are: (1) They have not recognized the political character of Judah's exile and therefore have not realized its severe practical consequences; (2) they have not used the evidence of the Teacher Hymns; and (3) through neglecting to apply the model of millenarian movements to Judah and his group, they have misordered the literary evidence. The primary evidence must be the writings of the charismatic founder, not the "bureaucratic" products of later followers. Charlesworth, for example, mistakenly tries to solve the question of the "Damascus" exile by referring to the *Serek Ha-Yahad,* a work that demonstrably reached its final form only decades after Judah's hymns were composed.

5. CD 6:5, 6:19, 7:15, 7:19, 8:21, 19:34, and 20:12. The two quotations that follow are from 20:12 and 6:5, in that order.

6. This translation represents not what I think the biblical text says, but rather

what I believe the authors of the *Damascus Document* thought it meant. In ordinary usage, biblical Hebrew would have preposed a preposition (*el,* for instance) or added the locative *heh* to *Damascus* in order to represent the meaning here suggested. Still, the simple adverbial placement, akin to the Greek accusative of respect, is not unknown in biblical Hebrew. By late Second Temple times, the "*he* of direction lost its syntactical function"; so E. Qimron, *The Hebrew of the Dead Sea Scrolls* (Atlanta: Scholars Press, 1986), §340. Thus the reader of Judah's day would be free to interpret *Damascus* here in identical fashion, regardless of the presence or absence of this otiose syntactic marker.

7. CD 7:14–7:18a. This early gloss interrupted the flow of the text from 7:14a, continued in 7:21b: "and those who held fast were rescued to a land in the north" (7:14a). "These people escaped in the first time of Visitation" (7:21b). Later a second interpretive gloss was added as a corrective to the first. This second gloss appears in 7:18b–7:21a. Its purpose was to promulgate the "two messiah" ideology that developed only after an early form of the *Damascus Document* was already in circulation, as I shall try to show below. That the first pesher (commentary) stood alone in the text at one time, absent the second gloss, is clear because the quotation of Amos 5:26–27 includes only the elements that this first pesher interprets. That is, the first pesher meshes with the quotation, while the second one does not. The second interpretive gloss has to go back to an unquoted portion of Amos 5:26 to pick up the "star."

8. For similar expressions, note also 1 Sam. 9:4; 1 Sam 9:5; 2 Sam. 24:6; Jer. 50:28, 51:29, 52:9, 52:27, etc.

9. A brief history of the region and its rulers: the first king was the Seleucid dynast Demetrius III, the man the Pharisees called in for help in their civil war against Alexander Jannaeus. He ruled the region from 96/95 to 88/87 B.C.E. (One cannot escape the irony that Judah, implacable enemy of the Pharisees, should now wind up in exile in the domain of the Pharisees' ally.) After Demetrius died his brother, Antiochus XII, ruled for a single year.

Then Aretas III killed Antiochus in battle and established his own hegemony over Coele-Syria. It was he who was sovereign when Judah and his followers arrived about 74 B.C.E. After a dozen years under Aretas, Tigranes I overran the kingdom in the process of conquering all of Syria. Defeated in battle by the Roman Lucullus, Tigranes retreated to his homeland in 69 B.C.E., but the Romans did not take immediate possession when he left. Instead, they ceded Coele-Syria to sons of the Seleucid dynasty. Their reign lasted until the triumphal march of Pompey (who had replaced Lucullus as commander of Roman forces in the region) in 64 B.C.E. All of Syria, including the Damascus region, then became a Roman province.

10. The Original Manifesto of Judah's first followers can be reconstructed by comparing 1QS with various copies of the *Serekh* (Hebrew for "Order") from Cave Four. As reconstructed, it contained the sentence, "They are to go to 'the wilderness, to prepare there the Way of the Truth'—that is, the study of the Law that God commanded through Moses." I take the reference to the wilderness to be literal, though the point could be argued inasmuch as the defining "that is" (Hebrew *hy'*) is ambiguous: it refers either to going to the wilderness or to preparing the Way of Truth. To my mind the latter is more consonant with the following description, "study of the law."

For wilderness language as the texts now stand, note especially 1QS 8:13, 8:14, and 9:20, and 1QM (the *War Scroll*) 1:2 and 1:3. The *War Scroll,* though describing an apocalyptic war and not always to be taken literally, nevertheless speaks of its heroes as "those exiled to the wilderness" and those who "return from the Wilderness of the Peoples to camp in the Wilderness of Jerusalem."

11. The reading and restoration are suggested by Michael C. Douglas. He and I shall defend it in our forthcoming commentary on the *Thanksgiving Hymns.*

12. For "children of guilt" (Hebrew *bene ashmah*), note 1QH 14:33 and 15:13; for the "powerful" (Hebrew *adirim*), note 1QH 10:38; for the "warriors" (*gibborim*), compare 1QH 10:28.

13. It is also clear by his usage that Judah interpreted these verses as a reference to the destruction of the wicked in Israel, and not—as modern interpreters generally do—the destruction of the invading army.

14. The term *fisherman* then led Judah to incorporate Isa. 19:8, whose context suggests that Judah believed the invaders themselves would be destroyed thereafter. This idea would be consistent with his hymns as a whole. For more of Jeremiah's prophecies of disaster from the north, see Jer. 6:22–30, 10:22, 13:20–25, 15:11–14. Later in the book—e.g., 36:29—the unnamed enemy force becomes Babylon.

15. The Aristotle quote is from *Politics* 1253a 3–10. For exiles and their way of life in the ancient Eastern Mediterranean, note especially E. Balogh, *Political Refugees in Ancient Greece* (Johannesburg: Witwatersrand Univ. Press, 1943), 41–82; Paul McKechnie, *Outsiders in the Greek Cities in the Fourth Century* B.C. (New York: Routledge, 1989), 16–33, 79–100; and Joseph Roisman, "The Image of the Political Exile in Archaic Greece," *Ancient Society* 17 (1986): 23–32. Final quote is from Roisman, "Image," 24.

16. This is the thrust of the Laws of the *Damascus Document,* of which an early form guided Judah and the original group, known by that text as "The First Ones" (*rishonim*). The later followers knew these laws as "the first laws" (*ha-mishpatim ha-rishonim*). Note CD 4:6, 20:8, 20:31.

17. *War* 2.561 puts the number at ten thousand; *War* 7.368 gives the number at eighteen thousand. Whatever the true figure, many Jews lived in Damascus, and many died.

18. *Politics* 1256a 29-b 9.

19. McKechnie, *Outsiders,* 102–6.

20. This is probably an image of the Servant of the Lord; only in Isa. 49:2, a recognized Servant passage, does the Bible speak of God hiding the author ("He hid me. . . . He concealed me").

21. The language here may be another Servant reference. In Isa. 53:5 and 53:10 the term *crush* (Hebrew *piel, dikke*) appears of the Servant ("He was crushed for our iniquities. . . . It was the will of YHWH to crush him").

22. Thucydides 1.5–9. Quotations are from 1.5 and 1.6, respectively, using the translation of Rex Warner, *Thucydides History of the Peloponnesian War,* rev. ed. (Baltimore: Penguin Books, 1972).

23. For the following discussion of banditry, I rely particularly on two recent, detailed studies of the phenomenon in antiquity: Benjamin Isaac, "Bandits in Judaea

and Arabia," *Harvard Studies in Classical Philology* 88 (1984): 171–203, and Brent D. Shaw, "Bandits in the Roman Empire," *Past and Present* 105 (1984): 3–52. I have also drawn material from Ramsay MacMullen, *Enemies of the Roman Order* (New York: Routledge, 1966), 192–241 and 255–68. A useful theoretical discussion is E. J. Hobsbawm, *Primitive Rebels* (New York: Frederick A. Praeger, 1959), 13–29. Though it is questionable whether social banditry as Hobsbawm romantically conceived it is anything but a very rare phenomenon (see Shaw's critique, "Bandits," 4), his observations for the most part pertain to banditry in general and are therefore helpful.

The order of Antoninus Pius is found in *Berliner griechische Urkunden,* Aegyptischen Urkunden aus den königlichen Museen zu Berlin, 9 vols. (Berlin: Königliche Museen zu Berlin, 1892–1937), no. 372.

24. *Ant.* 15.119–120, translation by Ralph Marcus, modified.

25. Brent D. Shaw, "Tyrants, Bandits and Kings: Personal Power in Josephus," *Journal of Jewish Studies* 44 (1993): 199.

26. CD 12:6–8.

27. The reading in the Cairo Genizah copy of the *Damascus Document* is *havur,* but 4Q267 9 iii 3 preserves the original *hever.* See Joseph Baumgarten, *Discoveries in the Judaean Desert XVIII. Qumran Cave 4: XIII The Damascus Document (4Q266–273)* (Oxford: Clarendon Press, 1996), 107. The full phrase "the Council of the Jews" seldom appears because of the common numismatic practice of abbreviation by suspension. For a helpful, nontechnical conspectus of the coins, see David Hendrin, *Guide to Biblical Coins* (New York: Amphora Books, 1987), 40–54. The standard technical work is Yaakov Meshorer, *Ancient Jewish Coinage I and II* (New York: Amphora Books, 1982).

28. 1QS 9:23–24, from Michael Wise, Martin Abegg, Edward Cook, *The Dead Sea Scrolls: A New Translation* (San Francisco: HarperSanFrancisco, 1996), 140. The first phrase has usually been translated along the lines of Geza Vermes, *The Complete Dead Sea Scrolls in English,* 5th ed. (London: Penguin Books, 1997), 111: "He shall perform the will of God in all his deeds." The difference depends upon the vocalization of the underlying Hebrew. Is it to be read as Vermes has done, *mishlah kapayim,* or as I have done, *mishloah kapayim?* Neither expression occurs in biblical Hebrew, but the roughly equivalent syntagm *shalah yad* is well attested. Variants of Vermes's *mishlah yad* occur six times (Deut. 12:7, 12:18, etc.; it is a Deuteronomic expression) and have the meaning he suggests.

The vocalization I have preferred occurs but once, in Isa. 11:14: "They will swoop down on the slopes of Philistia to the west; together they will plunder the people to the east. They will lay hands on *(mishloah yad)* Edom and Moab, and the Ammonites will be subject to them." This biblical portion describes violence against Gentiles that includes plundering, i.e., brigandage. Which vocalization did the ancient writers/copyists of the *Serekh* intend? We cannot be certain, but there is one clue. The orthography of a Cave Four copy of the text, 4QS^f, is unequivocal; it reads *mishloah.* So at least some ancient readers of this text read here an allusion to Isa. 11:14. Since they were much closer and more attuned to the original social milieu than are we, I think we do well to follow their lead.

29. *War* 1.204.

30. For recent discussion, see Peter Richardson, *Herod: King of the Jews and Friend of the Romans* (Columbia: Univ. of South Carolina Press, 1996), 109–11.

31. *Ant.* 20.5; *War* 2.228.

32. Denis Baly, *The Geography of the Bible* (London: Lutterworth Press, 1964), 222–23.

33. Cited in Isaac, "Bandits," 176 n. 19. For aerial photographs and further details of the region, see Le R. P. A. Poidebard, "Reconaissance aérienne au Ledja et au Safa (Mai 1927)," *Syria* 9 (1928): 114–23, with plates.

34. Strabo 16.2.756, describing a time just a decade after Judah, when Pompey led his army into the territory of Damascus and tried to clean up the bandits.

35. *Ant.* 15.344–47.

36. William Miller, "Rules of Interpretation," in *Views of the Prophecies and Prophetic Chronology, Selected from Manuscripts of William Miller, with a Memoir of His Life,* ed. Joshua Himes (Boston: Joshua V. Himes, 1842), 21.

37. For analysis of the Lindsey phenomenon, see Stephen D. O'Leary, *Arguing the Apocalypse: A Theory of Millennial Rhetoric* (New York: Oxford Univ. Press, 1994), 134–71.

38. For Josephus on Tigranes, see *Ant.* 13.419–21. The quote is from Richard D. Sullivan, *Near Eastern Royalty and Rome, 100–30 B.C.* (Toronto: Univ. of Toronto Press, 1990), 79. Pages 96–105 are a concise and valuable treatment of Tigranes. See also David Magie, *Roman Rule in Asia Minor to the End of the Third Century After Christ* (Princeton: Princeton Univ. Press, 1950) 1:295–96.

39. *Ant.* 10.267.

40. I owe this observation to Michael Douglas. Note especially the relation between Dan. 9:27 and the wordplay in 1QH 12:29–30. The only use of *gbr* in the *Hiphil* in biblical Hebrew other than Dan. 9:27 is Ps. 12:5, and this passage does not fit Judah's meaning at all.

41. Recall the ubiquitous use of flood and water imagery as metaphors for judgment throughout Judah's hymns.

42. *Ant.* 14.48.

43. Of the authors I have read, only A. Dupont-Sommer, *The Dead Sea Scrolls: A Preliminary Survey* (Oxford: Basil Blackwell, 1952), 56, was on the right track, in my view. He has been ignored, for his reading of the passage does not fit the "Essene hypothesis" as it has been developed. The passage is CD 8:4–12. The translation is that of Cook in Wise, Abegg, Cook, *Dead Sea Scrolls,* 58–59, very slightly modified.

44. 4QpNah 3–4 i 1–3. I have followed the translation of Cook in Wise, Abegg, Cook, *Dead Sea Scrolls,* 217, with some modifications.

45. This is the point of the argument made, for example, in the *Damascus Document.*

CHAPTER 7

1. A second scribe inserted a superlinear correction: "Blessed are You, O Lord." Ordinarily this incipit characterizes the Community Hymns.

2. 1QH 13:22–15:7.

3. Substantial passages in 1QS address the problem of defection and insincere membership. Even more particularly focused on this issue were CD and the *Commentary on Psalms*, 4QpPs[a], both of which devote significant space to apostasy. They return to the problem again and again.

4. William Sims Bainbridge, *The Sociology of Religious Movements* (New York: Routledge, 1996), 145. Although Judah's movement had begun as a political faction, it was now moving in the direction of a sect. It would later become a sect proper. I shall discuss this point more fully below.

5. Bainbridge, *Religious Movements,* 235.

6. CD 20:3–4, translation by Edward Cook in Michael Wise, Martin Abegg, Edward Cook, *The Dead Sea Scrolls: A New Translation* (San Francisco: HarperSanFrancisco, 1996), 59.

7. CD 19:33–35, 20:8–13. Translation according to Cook in Wise, Abegg, Cook, *Dead Sea Scrolls,* 59–60, with slight modifications.

8. As usual, I translate to bring out what I believe was Judah's understanding of the passage. His understanding is not necessarily that of modern scholars.

9. 1QH 15:23. As explained in chap. 4, n. 14, I believe Judah referred specifically to 1QIsa[a] at this point. 4QpIsa[e] 1–2 2–3 directly relates Isa. 40:11 to the Teacher of Righteousness, showing that followers recognized the allusion here.

10. I borrow the term *Voice* for the mysterious figure of this and other biblical passages from my colleague James Tabor. The form of the *Damascus Document* linking Zechariah's "oppressed of the sheep" to Judah's movement is CD 19:8–9, the so-called "B Version" of the *Damascus Document.* I shall argue below that this version is earlier than the "A Version." The Teacher is connected to the Shepherd in 4QpIsa[e] 1–2 2–3 (n. 9 above) and 4QpIsa[c] frag. 21 6–8. In the latter case line 6 is almost totally destroyed, but it preserves the word *Teacher* (*moreh*). After a short lacuna (enough for just a few words), the author cites Zech. 11:11. Maurya Horgan, *Pesharim: Qumran Interpretations of Biblical Books* (Washington, DC: Catholic Biblical Association of America, 1979), comments, "The apparent allusion to Zech 11:11 must be considered as part of the interpretation rather than as a separate lemma, since it is followed immediately by the citation of Isa 30:1–5" (118). The citation of Zech. 11:11, with its reference to the poor, probably means that in the very broken lines of pIsa above line 6, there was some reference to Isa. 29:19. This possibility seems likely, also, because pIsa 21 2–3 relate to Isa. 29:17. In any case, the *Commentary* evidently relates the "poor" to the sheep of Zechariah, and the Shepherd to the Teacher, just as in CD B Version. The reference in pIsa 21 4 to "by the sword" (*baherev*) may also tie in with CD 19 and the smiting of the Shepherd.

11. The writing r῾ym is ordinarily understood as "shepherds." The defective spelling of this *Qal* participle in the biblical text opened the door for Judah's probable reading, a reading that doubtless developed only after the apostasy of his peers. In other words, this is a particularly clear example of importing meaning into the text, something that happens continuously in all groups that maintain a living relationship with a set of holy writings. The reverse possibility—that Judah took the term in

Zechariah to mean "shepherds" and so himself meant "shepherds" by *r'ym* in 1QH 13:25—is virtually ruled out by orthography. In some eighty relevant instances of *Qal* participles in 1QH, the spelling is always *plene,* never defective. Note the allusion to this Teacher Hymn usage in CD 20:10, *reeyhem.*

12. Brent D. Shaw, "Tyrants, Bandits and Kings: Personal Power in Josephus," *Journal of Jewish Studies* 44 (1993): 196–97.

13. Ezek. 40:1–2, excerpted. The Hebrew phrase *bemarot elohim* I have rendered "by means of angelic visions" to try and capture the way Judah and others of the late second century B.C.E. may have read it. Modern scholars think it means something like "in visions of God" (so, for example, the New Revised Standard Version).

14. 1Q32, 2Q24, 4Q554–55, 5Q15, and 11Q18. For convenient perusal of the Aramaic as transcribed, see the preliminary work by R. Eisenman and M. Wise, *The Dead Sea Scrolls Uncovered* (Shaftesbury, Dorset: Element, 1992), 39–46; K. Beyer, *Die aramäischen Texte vom Toten Meer* (Göttingen: Vandenhoeck & Ruprecht, 1985), 214–22; K. Beyer, *Die aramäischen Texte vom Toten Meer: Ergänzungsband* (Göttingen: Vandenhoeck & Ruprecht, 1994), 95–104, and F. García-Martínez, "The Last Surviving Columns of 11QNJ," in *The Scriptures and the Scrolls,* ed. F. García-Martínez (Leiden: Brill, 1992), 178–92.

I have drawn some of what I say here, and the translation of the portions of the *Vision* I give, from Edward Cook's work in Wise, Abegg, Cook, *Dead Sea Scrolls,* 180–84. I have slightly modified Cook's work to make it dovetail with the terms I use in the narrative.

15. See my *A Critical Study of the Temple Scroll from Qumran Cave 11* (Chicago: Oriental Institute, 1990), 64–83. In this earlier book I suggested that the Teacher of Righteousness redacted or composed the Temple Scroll. I still believe that its ideas are intimately connected with his own peculiar legal contributions as those emerge from a redactional analysis of the *Damascus Document* (see below). The Hebrew style of the *Temple Scroll*'s redactional seams, however, varies so much from Judah's hymns and is so comparatively inelegant that I can no longer see him as the actual redactor.

16. J. Licht, "An Ideal Town Plan from Qumran—The Description of the New Jerusalem," *Israel Exploration Journal* 29 (1979): 45–59; and M. Chyutin, "The New Jerusalem: Ideal City," *Dead Sea Discoveries* 1 (1994): 71–97.

17. Norman Cohn, *The Pursuit of the Millennium,* rev. ed. (New York: Oxford Univ. Press, 1970), 284–85.

18. James D. Tabor and Eugene V. Gallagher, *Why Waco?* (Berkeley and Los Angeles: Univ. of California Press, 1995), 59. The details I here relate about Koresh come from this same study, 58–59.

19. E. J. Hobsbawm, *Primitive Rebels* (New York: Frederick A. Praeger, 1963), 13–29. That Judah should single out the presence of the families for mention seems to indicate that they were not normally together. This inference, if true, constitutes further support for the suggestion that Judah and his band subsisted for a time by banditry.

20. *Jubilees* 34:18–19, translation by R. H. Charles and Chaim Rabin in *The Apocryphal Old Testament,* ed. H. F. D. Sparks (Oxford: Clarendon Press, 1984), 106, slightly modified.

21. The Samaritans and Falashas both refused to sleep; some Karaite leaders required that one stand continuously as well. The broad variety of medieval Jewish groups who could not have influenced one another yet followed these customs suggests that the customs had great antiquity. They may therefore go back to common practices of the Second Temple and may antedate the rise of the Pharisaic approach. For details, see the discussion by Wieder, note 23 below.

22. Mishnah *Taanit* 4.8.

23. Naphtali Wieder, *The Judean Scrolls and Karaism* (London: Horovitz, 1962), 172. Pages 163–73 of Wieder's book constitute the study to which I refer; I have here followed the lines he laid down.

24. If it is correct to use the equivalencies established by 4Q321, Mishmarot B^a. In year 1, 7/15 solar equates with 7/19 luni-solar; in year 2, the equivalence is 7/15 = 7/29; in year 3, 7/15 solar equates with 8/10 luni-solar.

25. Note *Jubilees* 50:13: making war on the Sabbath was defined as a capital offense. Note also the implications of *First Maccabees* 2:32–41.

26. CD 19:33–34, 20:14–15, respectively.

27. The foregoing is my reading of the evidence. It makes sense of the facts so far as they go. As is often true with Judah's story, they do not go as far as we would like. The sources can be read more than one way. Or perhaps I should say, they *have been* read more than one way but—if I am correct—never properly.

The case of the attack on the Day of Atonement affords perhaps a clearer example than any other of how the ancients read Judah's writings. It demonstrates that Judah's followers knew his hymns to be his and believed these writings recorded Judah's reactions to historical events. Absent compelling reasons to the contrary, we ought to follow their example and read his hymns as did the ancients. After all, Judah's followers were at home in the society that produced these texts. We are not. They knew the cultural norms, the regnant rules of reading. We do not. We must learn them.

The sources for the attack teach us. What is equally important for the historian's task, they shine a light on the processes that produced some of the most important of the Dead Sea Scrolls.

The "sources" for the attack on Judah are four in number. One is his own seventh hymn; a second is the *Commentary on Habakkuk*. Neither of these is surprising, though the first has gone unrecognized. The *Commentary* is the more helpful source, for it is the more explicit. A less expected source, perhaps, is the text of the prophet Habakkuk itself, which affected the *Commentary's* understanding; entirely unexpected is that the biblical book of Lamentations strongly colored—a skeptical historian might say defined—the *Commentary's* narrative.

Habakkuk and the attendant portion of the *Commentary* read as follows. Underlines highlight the Hebrew words of the biblical verse that are explicitly cited for interpretation by the *Commentary*:

> *"Woe to the one who gets his friend drunk, pouring out <u>his anger</u>, making him drink just to get a look at their <u>festivals</u>"* (Hab. 2:15).

> *Its true import concerns the Wicked Priest, who pursued the Teacher of Righteousness to destroy him in the heat of <u>his anger</u> at his place of exile. At*

the time of the <u>festival</u>, the repose of the Day of Atonement, he appeared to them to destroy them and bring them to ruin—on the fast day, the Sabbath intended for their repose. (1QpHab 11:2–8. The translation follows Cook in Wise, Abegg, Cook, Dead Sea Scrolls, 121–22, with slight modifications.)

That so few of the words of Hab. 2:15 appear as part of the interpretation is puzzling. In their absence one wonders why what is said, is said. Why did the author choose this word, not that? Why say one thing and not another? Was the interpretive process entirely arbitrary? The biblical text exercised few apparent constraints. How did the author of the *Commentary* come to believe that Hab. 2:15 concerned the Teacher? He interpreted few other verses of Habakkuk that way. Why this one? Why did he insert such specific words as *exile, repose, pursue*? And why define the *festival* of Habakkuk as the Day of Atonement? The Jews of his time knew many other festivals.

Maybe the author had no particular reason for most of these choices. Perhaps he knew only that an attack had occurred on the Day of Atonement, which he now referred to because of Habakkuk's convenient mention of *festival*. Scholars have often taken such a line. But consider the words of Judah's hymn and where they lead. The first two *mems* of the crucial reading "from our fa[mi]lies" (Heb. *mimi[sh]pahot*) are read in 1QH frag. 29. All that remains is to restore the *shin*, a suggestion made (apparently) independently by É. Puech, *La croyance des Esséniens en la vie future: immortalité, résurrection, vie éternelle?* (Paris: J. Gabalda, 1993), 2:350, and M. Abegg in an unpublished reconstruction of the Thanksgiving Hymns:

> *They <u>overtook</u> me <u>at the pass</u>, where there was no place to escape, and it was impossible to separate from our families. They played the lyre against which I had contended, and mingled music with their mockery, ruin and destruction. Chest pains seized me, and agonies like the birth pangs of a woman in labor; my heart was pounding wildly within my chest. I was dressed for mourning, and my tongue clove to the roof of my mouth. For they had surrounded me with plans of destruction, and their intention appeared bitterly clear to me. (Judah's hymn)*

> *Judah has gone into exile on account of suffering and on account of numerous things in the Temple service. She dwells among the Gentiles, and finds no repose. All her pursuers <u>overtook</u> her <u>at the pass</u>. (Lam. 1:3)*

Judah used two uncommon Hebrew words here, and these two words lead right to Lam. 1:3 (underlines). This is the only place they ever occur together. Judah had this biblical passage in mind.

When the later author of the *Commentary on Habakkuk* came to consider Hab. 2:15, he read that verse through the lens of Judah's discourse and—strikingly—also integrated Judah's biblical source. This fact is obvious the moment the passages are set side by side. Observe how many defining terms of the *Commentary* derive from Lamentations (underlines):

> *Its true import concerns the Wicked Priest, who <u>pursued</u> the Teacher of Righteousness to destroy him in the heat of his anger at his place of <u>exile</u>. At the time of the festival, the <u>repose</u> of the Day of Atonement, he appeared to*

them to destroy them and bring them to ruin—on the fast day, the Sabbath intended for their <u>repose</u>.

Judah has gone into <u>exile</u> on account of suffering and on account of numerous things in the Temple service. She dwells among the Gentiles, and finds no <u>repose</u>. All her <u>pursuers</u> overtook her at the pass.

The processes by which this part of the *Commentary* was composed now evident, we realize that the author was simultaneously interpreting *all* of his sources. He did key his explication of the attack on the Day of Atonement to Habakkuk's mention of *festival,* but once that attachment was made, the greater input came, not from Habakkuk, but from Judah's hymn and its biblical source, Lamentations. Both of those sources supplied the author with specific vocabulary that shaped the way he described the attack.

From a recognition of these processes two conclusions emerge: first, that Judah's hymns were indeed read historically; and second, that Judah's later followers read his hymns with a full appreciation of the biblical sources behind them. The germinal influence that Judah's hymns had upon these followers all through their history also stands clear, for the *Commentary on Habakkuk* was written some forty years after Judah's death. Study sessions must have focused on the founder's writings, having as their goal the fullest possible understanding of all that had happened to him, together with all that he had both said and implied.

Yet recognizing the *Commentary's* method also raises a vexatious issue for the historian. How, exactly, did the author of the *Commentary* know that Judah had been attacked on the Day of Atonement?

To this question two answers stand at either extreme, defining the range of the reliability spectrum: either oral tradition attached to Judah's hymns (and possibly Habakkuk also) informed him that the messiah had been attacked; or, he "discovered" the fact through his own reading of Judah's words.

My analysis leans toward the first option, but what about the second? The author might have read Judah's words *They overtook me at the pass, where there was no place to escape,* and mistakenly might have taken them as concrete when Judah intended them as metaphors. (Judah undeniably used considerable metaphor in this hymn.) The author would falsely deduce that an attack occurred, when Judah actually meant to say that he felt surrounded by foes, just as he said elsewhere in the hymn using other metaphors. The same could apply to Judah's *For they had surrounded me with plans of destruction, and their intention appeared bitterly clear to me.*

The author could then glean from Judah's words *I was dressed for mourning* that the attack took place on a day when Judah would be so arrayed—perhaps the Day of Atonement. With this understanding Judah's mention of the lyre and music would take on special force. When the author traced Judah's words back to their biblical source, the association with the Day of Atonement would be fortified by Lamentations's wording, *finds no repose.* He would understand that the attack happened at a time when repose was desired or even required: logically, a Sabbath or festival. And the military interpretation of Judah's phrases would find support in Lamentations's term *pursuers.*

Pursuing such reasoning, the *Commentary*'s author might invent out of whole cloth an episode that never happened. Is that what he did? This question has grave implications for historical understanding of all that the *Commentary on Habakkuk* says, as well as the other biblical commentaries of Judah's group that seem to allude to historical events.

A more moderate perspective—recognizing the influence of biblical resonance without rejecting the basic historicity of the events—seems more defensible than claiming wholesale invention. Consider: at a bare minimum, Judah's hymns reflect an escalating social struggle arising from disagreement about aspects of Jewish law. The attack on Judah accords with all that we can infer of the Jerusalem conflict. And Josephus tells us of Alexandra and her times and how such conflicts were handled. Judah's hymns in turn describe a particular instance of just such handling (exile). The broad parameters of Judah's story fit the historical period too well to be mere fabrication.

After all, something gave birth to his movement, and so one can reason from the effect to the cause. The group's own explanations, and those of their founder, are reasonable. They also fit the cross-cultural patterns associated with the human dynamics of crisis cults. Thus they meet the historical test of analogy. To reject the events as untrue merely because they are related in language derived from literary sources would be to overreact. We may conclude that the attack really happened.

Yet we must take account of the processes that produced the *Commentary* and the language it used to describe the attack. These processes certainly had the potential to distort any facts with which they began. For this reason—though it is credible that it may have—we cannot be entirely certain that the attack occurred on the Day of Atonement. I believe it did. Given the calendar difference, timing the attack that way would be brilliant strategy. And if there was an attack, it must have happened on some day; the timing would always be a military consideration.

But objectively speaking, we remain ignorant about how the author of the *Commentary* "knew" the occasion of the battle. He may have received it by tradition, but we know little of how the group passed down their traditions or how those traditions may have changed in the telling. The earliest source for the attack, and so the primary one, is Judah's hymn. The more explicit picture in the *Commentary* is consonant with Judah's own words, but it is not demanded by them. Judah's hymn, we may say, was understood to speak of this event, and it is reasonable to conclude that he really did intend to describe an attack. To say that much is not the same as finding in his words a definite reference to the Day of Atonement. We cannot be sure how the prophet meant oblique expressions such as *I was dressed for mourning*.

For anyone seeking to understand the past, discovering what to question in a source long believed is almost as good as discovering a new source. In the case of the attack on the Day of Atonement, we gain both.

28.   The only biblical passages where *neelam (niphal of alam)* appears, and that clearly resonate with Judah's situation, are the two I quote. In general, it may be said that the term is a part of prophetic vocabulary. It describes prophets who, for one reason or another having to do with their mission, are silent: Ezek. 24:27 and 33:22 and

Dan. 10:15. Note more generally Ps. 31:18, 39:2, and 39:9 (recalling that the Psalms were also understood prophetically by Judah and his movement). These eight constitute the totality of occurrences of this verbal form in the Masoretic Text.

29. The Original Manifesto adopted by Judah's followers after his death, and now found in the Discipline Scroll, included the provision: "No biblical doctrine concealed from Israel but discovered by the Interpreter is to be hidden from these men out of fear that they may backslide." The Interpreter (Hebrew *doresh*) was an office modeled after Judah, the original and preeminent biblical interpreter for the movement. I infer from this provision that Judah had kept things from his followers, explaining that they might desert, implying that they could not be trusted with the most precious secrets. Such a policy most likely arose from Judah's experience with desertion, the topic of the seventh discourse. Hence I associate this probable action of Judah's with this period in his story.

CHAPTER 8

1. Michael Adas, *Prophets of Rebellion: Millenarian Protest Movements Against the European Colonial Order* (Chapel Hill: Univ. of North Carolina Press, 1979), 119.

2. 1QH 15:8–27.

3. 1QH 16:4–17:36. Like hymn 7, the ninth hymn is more of a discourse.

4. So LXX; the MT reads "thick boughs." Presumably Judah knew a Hebrew text like that behind the LXX.

5. CD 1:1–11. I have adapted the translation of Edward Cook in Michael Wise, Martin Abegg, Edward Cook, *The Dead Sea Scrolls: A New Translation* (San Francisco: HarperSanFrancisco, 1996), 51–52.

6. For a fuller discussion of the numbers of the *Damascus Document,* see chap. 9 below.

7. This and the parallel descriptions in the other sermons of the *Damascus Document,* which present the precursors as only approximately correct (see below), are important elements of the evidence that shows that the Admonition is not an older, reworked document. Unlike the Laws of the *Damascus Document,* at least some of which antedate Judah, the Admonition did not exist before his time. It is a reflection on Judah's significance that seeks in part to reinterpret his message.

8. CD 5:20–6:11. Again I follow, with slight changes, Cook in Wise, Abegg, Cook, *Dead Sea Scrolls,* 56. Some of the changes I make in accordance with Cave Four copies of the *Damascus Document,* 4Q266 and 4Q267, which have a few different readings. For these texts, see Joseph Baumgarten, *Discoveries in the Judaean Desert XVIII. Qumran Cave 4: XIII The Damascus Document (4Q266–273)* (Oxford: Clarendon Press, 1996), esp. 41.

9. This honor may underlie one of the laws of the *Damascus Document* that did not survive in the sheets of the Cairo *Damascus Document.* It appears at 4Q270 7 i 14–15 (Baumgarten, *Qumran Cave 4: XIII The Damascus Document,* 163), and can be translated (with reference to the penal code of 1QS): "Anyone who murmurs

against the Fathers shall be expelled from the Congregation, never to return; but if he murmurs against the Mothers, then he shall only be punished by ten days of reduced rations. For the Mothers lack the fullest honor (? meaning of the term uncertain) among the Congregation." Baumgarten himself has suggested that the Fathers and Mothers were occupants of a previously unknown office in the movement's organization, and that is possible. It seems to me more likely that the terms refer to the generation of the founders, the original few faithful who stayed with Judah, now all dead. Their names were known and had once been written down in a list (later removed and no longer extant in any copy we possess) that appeared in the *Damascus Document* (cf. CD 4:3–6). This sort of reverence for the founders is common in crisis cults.

10. Which is precisely the redactional reason for believing that these were Judah's laws, and why I called them his in the second chapter.

11. CD 3:12–20, according to Cook in Wise, Abegg, Cook, *Dead Sea Scrolls*, 54, with modifications.

12. *Jubilees* 1:10 = 4Q216 ii 7–10. 4Q216 has been published in exemplary fashion by James VanderKam and J. T. Milik in H. Attridge et al., *Discoveries in the Judaean Desert XIII: Qumran Cave 4: VIII Parabiblical Texts, Part 1* (Oxford: Clarendon Press, 1994). Trying to spare the general reader as much confusion as possible, I have not indicated the restorations. They are virtually certain thanks to complete copies preserved in Ethiopic.

13. E.g., Lev. 20:21; Ezek. 18:6; Lev. 12:2, 15:19, 20, 24, 25; Num. 19:9, 13, etc.

14. CD claims that during the years of Belial's being loosed among Israel, many were caught up in one or the other of the "three nets of Belial" (CD 4:15–19). The word used for *net (metsudah)* is uncommon and not the most obvious way to describe doctrine, but it is the very word Judah used in his fifth hymn of the teaching of his enemies (1QH 12:14). The teaching about the three nets may well go back to the Teacher, who will then have taught that it was wrong to remarry (or at least have two wives simultaneously) and that niece marriage was wrong; he would also have introduced new ideas about the proper observance of the prohibition against intercourse with a woman during her menstruation, and about keeping the Temple pure through correct methods of quarantine for impure persons *(havdalah)* (CD 4:20–5:8). Significantly, the Temple Scroll also touches on these areas directly.

15. This portion is even more directly parallel to CD 1 than is first apparent. The statement that *God atoned for their iniquity* is doubtless to be linked to Isa. 59:16 (1QIsaᵃ version), since Isa. 59:10 is the passage from which the language *they became as blind men, like those groping for the way* comes. The whole of Isa. 59 was central both to the *Damascus Document* and Judah's hymns. Isa. 59:16a in the *Great Isaiah Scroll* version is distinctly different from the traditional text. Where the MT reads, "And He saw that there was no man . . . ," 1QIsaᵃ reads instead, "And YHWH saw and knew their iniquity, for there was no man of law *(ish mishpat)*. . . ." The differences are crucial; the *Isaiah Scroll* version would explain the CD connection: God saw the group's iniquity, attributed it to the lack of a teacher of the true law, and so raised one up (CD 1), that is, built the group a faithful House (CD 3). Thus CD 3 incorporates the "iniquity" of Isa. 59:16, CD 1 the "man of law."

16. It seems likely that the precursors were among the priestly coalition that supported Aristobulus II in the civil war against Hyrcanus II in 67–63 B.C.E., just as—with Judah's participation—they had earlier supported Alexander Jannaeus. Josephus makes clear the continuity of the priestly faction from Alexander to Aristobulus.

17. For Judah's followers' usage, I have in mind the earliest form of the Manifesto, found in 1QS 8.

18. For the age-thirty requirement, see 1QS* 1:13–14; cf. also 1QM 7:1–3 for different, higher age requirements. Recall that we are only approximating. Regarding the "forty years" of Judah's ministry, I will argue this point below and so do not here.

19. Whatever the Enoch groups had been as social movements, Judah's following either repudiated or had forgotten them. They traced no direct continuity between the Enoch circles and the Staff's groping group, even though the Staff's movement, like their own, treasured the Enoch writings. What the Staff created, they believed, was new under the sun. Numerous scholars have shown that *Jubilees*—somehow connected to the precursor movement—knew and quoted various Enoch writings, including the *Apocalypse of Weeks*.

20. *Ant.* 13.293–97. On the date when Hyrcanus I shifted to the Sadducean coalition, note the comments by David Rokeah, "The Temple Scroll, Philo, Josephus, and the Talmud," *Journal of Theological Studies* 34 (1983): 517.

21. Isa. 53:3, 53:2.

22. 1QH 12:25.

23. *1 Enoch* 48:7 and 62:7–8, respectively. I have slightly modified the translation by M. A. Knibb in *The Apocryphal Old Testament*, ed. H. F. D. Sparks (Oxford: Clarendon Press, 1984), 229 and 244. I am impressed by the mention in the *Similitudes* of the Parthians, who invaded Judaea in the course of the struggles between Herod and Antigonus, 40–37 B.C.E. The date could be somewhat later, as scholars have most recently argued, and my suggestion is not important to my general argument.

The reverence of the mighty is a Servant theme: "Kings will shut their mouths because of him" (Isa. 52:15). The Son of Man of the *Similitudes* was to be the Servant; in this regard and in many others this figure of the Enochic work resonates with Judah's claims for himself. It seems possible that the authors of the Similitudes knew of Judah and his movement and, rejecting them, nevertheless drank deeply of Judah's contribution to the myth-dream in describing their own apocalyptic redeemer figure.

24. The Ezra passage is 4 Ezra 13:52, following the Ethiopic rather than Syriac version for the last phrase of the verse. I have modified the translation of Bruce Metzger in *The Old Testament Pseudepigrapha*, ed. James Charlesworth (Garden City, NY: Doubleday, 1983), 1:553. Justin Martyr's comment is found in *Dialogue with Trypho* 8.4.

25. For example, J. C. O'Neill, *Who Did Jesus Think He Was?* (Leiden: Brill, 1995), 42–54.

26. 1QpHab vii 17–viii 3. See the helpful comments in William Brownlee, *The Midrash Pesher of Habakkuk* (Missoula, MT: Scholars Press, 1979), 125–30, and Bilhah Nitzan, *Megillat Pesher Havaqquq* (Jerusalem: Bialik Institute, 1986), esp.

175–76 (Hebrew). The Christian scholars whose views I characterize below can be met in Brownlee. For the meaning of the Hebrew of the pesher, I find Nitzan persuasive, provided she means by the ambiguous gloss on *emunatam* on 176—"they received his *torah* and conducted themselves by it" (my translation)—that the Teacher's disciples received his *teaching* and not merely his law, *stricto sensu* (Hebrew *torah* can mean either).

27. Brownlee, *Pesher of Habakkuk*, 128–29. Regarding the *Commentary* quote, it does not actually say *heemin be* but phrases the concept with the cognate substantival expression, *emunah be*.

28. Gen. 15:6, 14:31 (note here Moses as an object of faith as well as God; without Moses true belief in God is impossible), Num. 14:11, 20:12, etc.—a total of ten occurrences.

29. Stephen Neill and Tom Wright, *The Interpretation of the New Testament, 1861–1986,* 2d ed. (New York: Oxford Univ. Press, 1988), 233.

30. CD 4:10–13, 19:34–20:1, and 20:13–16, respectively. I have modified the translation of Cook in Wise, Abegg, Cook, *Dead Sea Scrolls,* 54–55, 59–60.

31. Cf. Gen. 49:29; Judg. 2:10; 2 Kings 22:20; and 2 Chron. 34:28. CD speaks only of "gathering" *(heasef)* without the customary "to his fathers" (Hebrew *el abotaw*). Some have suggested therefore that it means something other than the Teacher's death. But note the niceties of the biblical usage of *asaf* in the *Niphal*: when the verb refers to a "coming together, a gathering," the subject is plural because it takes more than one to gather (Judg. 9:6; Neh. 8:1; Isa. 49:5; etc.). When the verb describes an individual who gathers an object, that object is always made explicit (Gen. 29:22; Num. 11:24; 2 Sam. 6:1; etc.). Ordinarily this usage of the verb requires the *Qal*, at least as the Hebrew Bible is pointed by the Masoretes. In the CD passages the subject is singular and no object is given; thus the meaning of the *Niphal* is that it was the Teacher himself who was "gathered."

32. See the discussion in chap. 9, n. 10.

33. Philip Davies, *The Damascus Covenant: An Interpretation of the "Damascus Document"* (Sheffield: JSOT Press, 1983), 66–67 and 128, and H. W. Huppenbauer, "Zur Eschatologie der Damaskusschrift," *Revue de Qumran* 4 (1963–64): 567–73.

34. 4QpPs[a] 1–10 ii 7–9. The force of the definite article has sometimes been overlooked, as for example in Maurya Horgan, *Pesharim: Qumran Interpretations of Biblical Books* (Washington, DC: Catholic Biblical Association of America, 1979), 196.

35. Cf. also Josh. 5:4 and Deut. 2:14, which use much of the same phraseology.

36. CD 19:5–10. I have here modified the translation of Cook in Wise, Abegg, Cook, *Dead Sea Scrolls,* 58. The translation of Zech. 13:7 *tsoarim* follows the sense required by its equation with *aniyim* of Zech. 11:11. Ordinarily in biblical Hebrew the word is rendered "small, insignificant," but this passage shows that a meaning "oppressed, persecuted" was known to the Jews of Judah's day. In that respect it is instructive that similar meanings are found in rabbinic Hebrew (see Marcus Jastrow, *Sepher Millim* reprint [New York: Judaica Press, 1982], s.v.) and especially in Aramaic, where the best guide may be Syriac, since that literature preserves the largest

Aramaic lexicon. The *Pael* of *tsaar* in Syriac largely overlaps the semantic range of the *Piel* of *anah* in biblical and postbiblical Hebrew.

This is the "B Version" of the *Damascus Document,* which I shall argue in a note in chap. 9 below was the original, the "A Version" being secondary.

37. Note that this was also the way that another Jewish messianic movement, earliest Christianity, read Zech. 13:7. Mark 14:27 applies the verse to Jesus' death, which, as here, is then by implication something that God has planned.

38. Gershom Scholem, *Sabbatai Sevi: The Mystical Messiah* (Princeton: Princeton Univ. Press, 1973), 918–19.

39. Quotation from Scholem, *Sabbatai Sevi,* 919. For Sabbatai's last days and developing reactions to his death, principally the doctrine of "occultation," see 821–929 of this same volume.

CHAPTER 9

1. Edson's statement can be found most conveniently in Ronald L. Numbers and Jonathan M. Butler, eds., *The Disappointed: Millerism and Millenarianism in the Nineteenth Century* (Knoxville: Univ. of Tennessee Press, 1993), 215.

2. The diligent study of Judah's writings emerges as fact particularly from a point that we have touched on earlier: at the hands of Judah's later followers, his hymns received a historical interpretation. Some of this interpretation found its way into the group's biblical commentaries. It is possible to isolate a half dozen examples. The following two are especially striking.

In his first hymn, Judah had written as follows (underlines for key words): *You have set me as a banner to the chosen righteous, a prophet given knowledge* [Hebrew *melits daat*] *of wondrous mysteries . . . All their thoughts are so many schemes of Belial.*

Through the relatively uncommon word *schemes* these statements included an allusion to Ps. 37:7. When one or more followers later produced the *Commentary on Psalms,* they recognized the allusion and glossed 37:7 with reference to Judah's hymn:

> *"[Be] silent before* [YHWH] *and wait for Him, and do not be jealous of the successful man who carries out schemes." (Ps. 37:7)*

> *[The true import] concerns the Man of the Lie who led many people astray with deceitful statements, because they had chosen accommodation but did not listen to the prophet given knowledge [melits daat], so that they will perish by sword, famine and pestilence.*

The followers perceived this portion of the psalms through the prism of Judah's hymn, as shown by the quotation of Judah's self-description: *the prophet given knowledge (melits daat).* This phrase occurs nowhere else in known Hebrew literature: not in the Bible, not outside it, only in Judah's hymn—and in the *Commentary.*

What had been a general "they" hatching *schemes* in Judah's hymn became in the *Commentary* a specific reference to the *Man of the Lie.* This move was made because of the followers' belief, probably accurate, that Judah had Shimeon ben Shetah in mind (among others) when he decried Belial's influence.

The group's interpretive process was complex, but part of the repertoire used to unlock meaning was a deliberate attention to the life of the founder.

The second example of this phenomenon involves Judah's second hymn. Judah had written: <u>*Surely* You *decree* the direction of my life</u> [Hebrew *mitsaday*]!

The Hebrew *mitsaday*, literally "my steps," can only refer to Ps. 37:23, where the literal phrase "from YHWH are the steps of a man" (*mitsadey gever*) appears. When the author of the *Commentary on Psalms* came to this point in Ps. 37, here is what he set down:

> "<u>*Surely the direction of a man's life*</u> *is established by* YHWH *when he delights in His way. If he stumbles, he will not fall, for* Y[HWH *holds his hand."*] (Ps. 37:23–24)

> *The true import concerns the Priest, the Teacher of [Righteousness, whom] God chose as a pillar; f[or] He established him to build for Him the Congregation [of His Chosen Ones in truth.] And he made His [wa]y straight by the truth.*

Reading the *Commentary* and questioning its topics and methods, one searches in vain for a contextual reason why this portion of Ps. 37 should have been held to apply to Judah, the Teacher. The group might rather have applied this portion to themselves, for example, claiming it as a promise. They took that line with similar language in the Psalm. But that is not what they did here, and the reason was Judah's hymnic usage.

Judah had quoted the Psalm, as his later followers knew, for as they read his hymns they traced, consciously or unconsciously, the scriptural connections. The point cannot be overstressed: theirs was an intertwining interpretation—Judah's hymns clarified the Bible, and the Bible, his hymns.

3. Columns 1–8 are the only columns of 1QH whose language betrays a knowledge of the existence of the group in its developed form, the Yahad. The clearest intersection occurs in column 6:20–34. Literary dependence shows that the author of this portion knew an early form of the *Community Rule*.

In addition to literary-critical reasons for seeing 1QH as comprised of three units, Michael Douglas has shown in his dissertation that the orthography of each unit is distinctive, implying that for 1QH the scribe copied—or copied a *Vorlage* that had copied, etc.—from three different scrolls: one containing columns 1–8, one the Book of Judah, and one comprising 20:7 and following. See Douglas, "Power and Praise in the Hodayot: A Literary Critical Study of 1QH 9:1–18:14" (Ph.D. diss., Univ. of Chicago, 1998).

4. The two other copies of the *Thanksgiving Hymns* are 4Q427 and 4Q431. The *editio princeps* of the relevant portions of 4Q431 was published by Esther Eshel under the rubric of 4Q471b. Subsequently, Hartmut Stegemann has suggested that the fragments of 4Q471b actually belong with those acknowledged to be a copy of the *Thanksgiving Hymns*, 4Q431. This suggestion seems to be correct. The edition of Eshel, very unsatisfactory because of its incorrect reconstruction of the fragments

and a number of mistaken readings, appeared in "4Q471b: A Self-Glorification Hymn," *Revue de Qumran* 17 (1996):175–203. The *editio princeps* of the relevant portions of 4Q427 was published by Eileen Schuller, "A Hymn from a Cave Four Hodayot Manuscript: 4Q427 7 i+ii," *Journal of Biblical Literature* 112 (1993): 605–28.

The other, shorter, version is 4Q491 frag. 11 i–xii. The original editor, Maurice Baillet, mistakenly believed that this fragment belonged to a copy of the War Scroll. See his *Discoveries in the Judaean Desert VII: Qumrân Grotte 4 III (4Q482–4Q520)* (Oxford: Clarendon Press, 1982), 26–29 and plate V. Extreme caution must be exercised in making judgments using the published plate, as masking has obscured the joins between fragments. Baillet made a number of errors in his reconstruction, some of which I pointed out in a paper delivered on November 24, 1996, at the Qumran Section of that year's annual meeting of the Society of Biblical Literature. A revised form of that paper, dealing with the problems of this hymn in all its versions, is forthcoming.

5. The translation is of the reconstructed 1QH 26:2–10, with lacunae filled in where possible from the other witnesses. Brackets indicate only reconstructions attested in none of the witnesses.

6. 1QH 15:26.

7. 1QH 12:26–27. For the idea of becoming angels after death among Christians, note the *Martyrdom of Polycarp* 2:3, "With the eyes of their heart they looked up to the good things which are preserved for those who have endured . . . shown by the Lord to them who were no longer men but angels." Translation by Kirsopp Lake in Loeb Classical Library, *The Apostolic Fathers*, vol. 2; see also his notes *ad loc.*

8. 1QH 14:15–17.

9. From time to time it has been suggested that the *Damascus Document* may have referred to Judah with its expression, "the Messiah of Aaron and Israel" (*meshiah aharon weyisrael*); CD 13:1, 19:9, and 19:35–20:1 (latter two in Version B). That is not impossible, but to my mind 19:35–20:1 makes the equation difficult given the phrase, "from the day when the Teacher of the Yahad was gathered until there shall arise the Messiah of Aaron and Israel." Here was a clear opportunity to make the equation explicit, and the author(s) did not do it. Moreover, the natural inference from the expression is that these are two different individuals, the second coming on the scene only after the first has passed from the stage of history. The author(s) did nothing to dispel that natural inference.

It does seem that after Judah's death a "messiah" so designated (whether Judah or another) was expected by the writers of CD and that this expectation underwent development, perhaps with the coming of the Zadokites made evident by comparison with various forms of the *Community Rule*. One may suggest that the Zadokites brought a traditional doctrine, also known from second century B.C.E. priestly texts, whereby *two* distinct anointed figures were expected. Yet there is evidence for the priority of the "one messiah" notion in the redaction history of the *Damascus Document*.

My reasoning is the following. The use of *berito* in CD 19:13–14 (B Version) looks back both to the Teacher's statement in his hymn (13:25, *bae beriti*) and to Zech. 11:10, where the Shepherd speaks of having a covenant (*beriti*). This term *berito* appears in CD 8:1 in the A Version, where its presence demonstrates the priority of the "Zechariah recension" now extant only in Version B. For the suffix on *berito* makes sense in the Zechariah recension. This recension is using the masculine singular suffix in response to the underlying passages of Zechariah. Although the A version retains the word in 8:1, in that recension—which has replaced the Zechariah quotation with other materials—the suffix has neither explicit referent in the text that can be read, nor implicit referent in the underlying biblical quotations. In other words, *it no longer makes sense,* showing that A cannot have been the original version of the text.

When next one observes that the material replacing the Zechariah complex in Version A speaks of two eschatological figures in place of that complex's single "Messiah of Aaron and Israel," and when one considers that sectarian texts that—judging by their extremely high valuation of the Sons of Zadok—postdate the coming of the Zadokites (e.g., 1QS, 1QS^a, 1QS^b, 4Q174) also speak of two eschatological figures, the conclusion seems reasonable that the Zadokites were connected to this doctrine. Thus my inference that the earliest followers of Judah looked to the coming of a single messiah other than Judah and that the later sectarian texts preserve a change connected with the Zadokite intrusion.

As to the relation Judah was later thought to have to the two Zadokite messiahs, we have no textual evidence.

10.   11Q13 ii 2–25. The translation is mine from Michael Wise, Martin Abegg, Edward Cook, *The Dead Sea Scrolls: A New Translation* (San Francisco: HarperSanFrancisco, 1996), 456–57, with minor adjustments. The most important studies, especially for establishing the reading of the text, include the *editio princeps* by A. S. van der Woude, "Melchisedek als himmlische Erlösergestalt in den neugefundenen eschatologischen Midrashim aus Qumran Höhle XI," *Oudtestamentisch Studiën* 14 (1965): 354–73; M. de Jonge and A. S. van der Woude, "11Q Melchizedek and the New Testament," *New Testament Studies* 12 (1965): 301–26; J. T. Milik, "Milki-sedeq et Milki-resa," *Journal of Jewish Studies* 23 (1972): 96–109, 124–26; P. J. Kobelski, *Melchizedek and Melchiresa* (Washington, DC: Catholic Biblical Association of America, 1981); and É. Puech, "Notes sur le manuscrit de XIMelkisedeq," *Revue de Qumran* 12 (1985–87): 483–513.

11.   I hope to defend this assertion in some detail in a forthcoming study.

12.   Michael Douglas, "Melchizedek's *Mebasser:* Who Was That Masked Man?" (paper presented at the annual meeting of the Society of Biblical Literature, Chicago, 1994), emphasis his; I thank him for his generous permission to cite his research.

13.   1QpHab 7:1–5. Translation adapted from Cook in Wise, Abegg, Cook, *Dead Sea Scrolls,* 119.

14.   CD 1:11–12. Isa. 61:1–4 is, in the judgment of many modern scholars, an Oracle of the Servant. The ancients agreed, including the *Great Isaiah Scroll.* The interpretation of the *Great Isaiah Scroll* was recognized by E. Y. Kutscher, *The Language and Linguistic Background of the Isaiah Scroll (1QIsa^a)* (Leiden: Brill, 1974), 262, who opined regarding the scribal insertion of *mshhty* at 52:14, "This seems to be an expression of the scribe's conception of the [Servant of the Lord] as the anointed Messiah."

Note that Isa. 61:3 constituted a link in one of Judah's interpretive chains, since it mentions the Tree (his followers) and thus informed his eighth and ninth hymns.

15. The ambiguous Hebrew may also be translated *he proclaimed to them the ju-bilee*, a past event. The sequence of tenses is obscured by the lacuna in ii 5, so that *wqr'* in line 6 may represent the simple perfect or the converted perfect.

16. In addition to the example given of Isa. 61:2, compare Ps. 82:1: "God has taken his place in the divine council; in the midst of the divine beings he holds judgment" (the Bible); and "A godlike being has taken his place in the divine council; in the midst of the divine beings he holds judgment" (*Melchizedek Book,* reading *elohim* as angelic). Also Ps. 7:7–8: "Return to it on high; YHWH will judge the peoples" (the Bible); and "Return to it on high; A divine being [Hebrew *el*] will judge the peoples" (*Melchizedek Book*).

17. Alan F. Segal, *Paul the Convert* (New Haven: Yale Univ. Press, 1990), 62, emphasis mine. Segal does not note the equations of Melchizedek with the names *El* and *Yahweh* in 11Q13; cf. *Paul*, 42–43.

18. Of course, one might imagine different ways in which the author intended this identification. Perhaps Melchizedek was active in heaven, the Herald on earth, the latter mirroring the former as a dim, earthly reflection of heavenly reality. But the relation between Melchizedek and the Herald was probably intended to be more intimate than one of model and mime. Particularly forceful on this score, as J. C. O'Neill has observed, was the author's use of Ps. 7:8: <u>*Return*</u> *to it on high; A divine being will judge the peoples*. The "it" of the Hebrew "return to it" is a reference to the "council" (*edah*) mentioned in the unquoted first half of this biblical verse. The whole of Ps. 7:8 reads, "A council of the peoples surrounds you; return to it on high." *Council* was a linking word between Ps. 7:8 and Ps. 82:1 (which, note, the Melchizedek author adduced just before Ps. 7). O'Neill pointed out that the command to return to God's council logically required an earlier departure from it. Melchizedek was assuming no new position. He was returning to his former standing. But returning from where? From earth, presumably, where he had functioned as the Herald. See J. C. O'Neill, *Who Did Jesus Think He Was?* (Leiden: Brill, 1995), 71–72.

After I had thought for a long time about the relationship between the Herald and Melchizedek in this text and had arrived at the conclusion that they were identical, my attention was drawn to O'Neill's arguments. The route by which he has arrived at his conclusion is very different from mine, and in general I do not agree with much of his chapter on "The Teacher of Righteousness." Yet it is encouraging to find that another scholar has arrived at a very similar position independently. Note also Jean Carmignac, "Le document de Qumrân sur Melkisédeq," *Revue de Qumran* 7 (1970): 363–69.

19. Scholars have generally restored the relevant broken portions of 11QMelch using not Dan. 9:26, but instead Dan. 9:25. I have been convinced by the arguments of Michael Douglas, "11Q Melchizedek and a Dying Eschatological Figure" (paper read at the meetings of the Society of Biblical Literature in Washington DC, 1993) that 9:26 is a much better restoration. I shall briefly summarize Douglas's arguments here (for permission to do so, I thank him). The first argument Douglas offers is that

of space. Three lines in 11QMelch can be restored positively from margin to margin. These lines (3, 10, and 11) suggest that the lines of this manuscript were generally between 55 and 66 letters long, with 58 to 64 being average. The usual restoration of Dan. 9:25 results in a line of 58 letters, which would seem good, except for Douglas's second argument, that of form.

His study of Qumran midrashic or pesharistic texts shows that they use two basic citation formulas, one based on *amar* and the other on *katuv*. The restoration in question is an *amar* type of citation, yet these do not use the preposition *al* preferred by the *katuv* type and restored by scholars urging Dan 9:25. *Amar* citations place the biblical quotation immediately after the citation formula *asher amar*, without the preposition *al*. Indeed, an exact parallel to 11QMelch *weha-mevasser huah meshiah ha-ruah asher amar daniel* is CD 6:7–8, *weha-mehoqeq hu doresh ha-torah asher amar yeshaya* (followed immediately by the biblical quotation). CD 4:19–20 is another exact parallel. Therefore one must subtract from the usual restoration the word *alaw*, which reduces the line to just 54 letters in length. While not impossibly short, the restoration of 9:25 is not as good as that of 9:26 on the criteria of form and space.

The decisive argument Douglas brings against 9:25 and in favor of 9:26 concerns the temporal framework. It is clear on any reading of 11QMelch that the critical period being discussed falls within the tenth jubilee. Moreover, the "messiah" of Daniel who is identified by the text with both the prophet of Isa. 61:1 and the Herald of Isa. 52:7 must be present in week 64 (or later) of Daniel's 70 weeks. Otherwise, he is outside the parameters of 11QMelch's chronology. Douglas further notes that the ancient versions read the content of Dan. 9:25 as reflecting *two* time periods, [7 + 62] + 1 = 69 +1, with one messiah. The Masoretic and modern interpretations see the weeks as referring to *three* time periods, 7 + 62 + 1, and two messiahs. Douglas then argues,

> If 11QMelch saw three time periods . . . in Dan 9:25–26, he could not have referred to the messiah prince of Dan 9:25 because this figure is present in the first and not the tenth jubilee. There is no way we can alter or transpose the order of Daniel's weeks (7, 62 and 1) so that the first enumeration of seven weeks belongs to the end of the list. Therefore, if the author adopted this tripartite interpretation, he must have referred to the messiah of Dan 9:26 who is "cut off" after 62 weeks. . . . The other conclusion that follows from the correlation of Daniel's 70 weeks and 11QMelch's ten jubilees is that if the author read Daniel so as to refer to two time periods . . . then the *meshiah nagid* of Dan 9:25 who arrives in week 69 is the same figure as the *meshiah* of Dan 9:26 who is cut off after week 69, [7 + 62].

In short, the basic point Douglas makes here is that "the restoration proposed by Milik et al.—'until the messiah prince, seven weeks'—must be rejected because there is *no way it can place the anointed figure in the tenth jubilee*" (emphasis mine).

Restoring Dan. 9:26, on the other hand, has several advantages. It results in a line length of 63 letters, the same as line 10. It follows 11QMelch's clear preference for starting a quotation at the beginning of the biblical unit of meaning, i.e., the beginning of the "verse" (six times in eight instances). It also ends the quotation with the climatic theme word, *meshiah*. Most important, it places the anointed figure in the sixty-fourth week. So this restoration fits the formal, spatial, and temporal criteria perfectly.

To all of Douglas's points I add my own argument in favor of 9:26: the echo of *aharey* in 11QMelch's twisted language describing Melchizedek's coming, virtually inexplicable if the author were not thinking of 9:26. Thus it is the more likely that he actually cited 9:26 a bit later, in the context of the herald.

In the wake of these arguments for Dan. 9:26, the burden of proof must now shift to those who favor restoring Dan. 9:25. It should be noted in passing that even before Douglas's study, Puech had expressed doubts about 9:25 in his full-scale study of 11QMelch: "The citation of Dan. 9:25 in the lacuna is not certain inasmuch as there is the matter of another anointed figure in Dan. 9:26 who is cut off after 62 year-weeks, to be sure, in the context of a decreed war" ("Notes sur le manuscrit," 509).

20. The Melchizedek text is not the only source among the group's writings providing evidence of Daniel's chronology. Many scholars have pointed out that the numbers of the *Damascus Document* also imply a total of 490 years or seventy week-years. The figures actually stated in the text are 390 years from Nebuchadnezzar to the rise of the precursors; twenty years of precursor blindness until the coming of the Teacher; and forty years of wickedness. These total 450 years. If to that sum one adds forty more years representing Judah's mature leadership in Jerusalem and his exile (a reasonable number, though probably higher than the reality; apocalyptic calculations are always flexible enough to accommodate approximations), Daniel's 490 years are the result.

The followers started with the 490 years and subtracted to arrive at most of the other elements in their equation. The final forty years, the number furnished by Judah's death, embraced the wicked present. The twenty blind years was an actual, historical datum: the time from the founding of the precursors by the Staff until Judah came to leadership. Judah's ministry counted as one generation. The remaining 390 years were just that, a remainder, a nondescript number that the group attached to Nebuchadnezzar by default. In an age when historical documentation was exceedingly sparse, neither they nor anyone else really knew how long ago Nebuchadnezzar had lived.

All extant Jewish chronologies of the late Second Temple period, and early Christianity, calculated the time of the "Persian period" on the basis of Daniel. No one could say how long that period had been, since the Bible gave no definite numbers and the Bible was the only record they had of it. Thus the Persian period could, if necessary, be counted as very short; a leading rabbinic chronology put together after the fall of the Temple in 70 C.E. (*Seder Olam Rabbah*) counted it as a mere forty years—after subtracting various things from Daniel's 490, this was the remainder.

21. Kenelm Burridge, *Mambu: A Melanesian Millennium* (London: Methuen, 1960; Princeton: Princeton Univ. Press, 1995), 269–70; emphasis his.

22. 1QH 16:21–26.

23. Max Weber, *Economy and Society* (2 vols.; Berkeley: Univ. of California Press, 1968), 1121.

24. M. Weber, *Economy and Society*, 1123.

25. One copy of the *Community Rule* was among the first seven scrolls discovered in Cave One in 1947. Altogether, at least thirteen copies have turned up among the scroll caches (1QS, 4Q255–264a, and 5Q11). The number of copies says something about the work's importance to the movement, and yet the copies are not identical. Some differ dramatically from others, and there are basically three recensions, or versions. The *Community Rule* underwent development over the years that it was in use, variations being introduced as circumstances changed, as new ideas gained prominence, or simply because a copyist had a notion he wished to insert. Still, by comparing the different copies it is possible to isolate many of the changes and sometimes even to estimate when they may have happened and why.

The Original Manifesto underlies 1QS 8:1–16 and equivalent portions of 4Q258 and 4Q259. For the literary criticism of the period before the Cave Four copies became available, see J. Murphy-O'Connor, "La genèse littéraire de la Règle de la Communauté," *Revue Biblique* 76 (1969): 528–49, and J. Pouilly, *La règle de la communauté de Qumrân: Son évolution littéraire* (Paris: Gabalda, 1976). Murphy-O'Connor and Pouilly succeeded in isolating something close to what I believe were the boundaries for the document, but they mistakenly believed that the Manifesto was for a group not yet existent. In fact the Manifesto, their Guide for the Maskil (1QS 9:12–10:8), and an early form of 1QS 5:1–7:25, their Laws of Life, all date to the period immediately after the Teacher's death. See the next note for my scribally based argument for the Manifesto's isolation.

26. At first glance one is struck by the number of erasures, rewrites, and adjustments—both of individual words and of spacing—in 1QS 8:4–16. No other part of 1QS evidences this much correction and adjustment. What lies behind this scribal activity?

What appears to have happened is the following. As was usual, the scribe responsible for 1QS planned his work column by column, sheet by sheet, apportioning the space at various junctures in the scroll according to what he planned to inscribe there. When working on column 8, he left a large blank—two lines wide—between the last word of 8:7, *gemulam,* and the first word of the next section he planned to write, *behakhin* in 8:10. He had left a similar large gap in column 7.

Subsequently, he decided to add additional material after 8:7. He made this decision, it would seem, because he was comparing more than one exemplar of the *Manual of Discipline* and had now come into possession of materials he had earlier lacked. The words that he decided to add are extant, in slightly variant form, in both 4Q258 and 4Q259, which are, on the whole, earlier versions of the *Manual of Discipline* than is 1QS. Apparently the main *Vorlage* of 1QS was even shorter than those short versions of the *Manual of Discipline,* at least at this point. The text or texts that the scribe had now got for comparison were similar, but not identical, to 4Q258 and 259.

To make the changes, the scribe left a small blank subsequent to the original end of the section, then set off a line and a half combining key words from Isa. 28:16 with a quotation from the eighth Teacher Hymn (1QH 15:11). Sometime later, in a third step, additional comparison or rethinking led him to add still one more word, not extant in the other witnesses *(yesodoteyhu)*—this time between the lines. Leaving some space after the end of the newly added quotation/exegesis, the scribe now wrote a portion beginning with the words *meon qodesh qodashim.* He did not extend this phrase and the subsequent words to the left margin, however. This peculiar situation—contrary to his practice everywhere else in the scroll—argues that there is some special purpose to the placement of these words. I suggest that they were an alternate reading for 8:5–7, *yesod qodesh qodashim leAharon . . . gemulam.* The placement was to align them just below the words for which they were an alternate. Thus, 1QS 8:8b–10a (including the long interlinear portion that extends to the end of 8:10) were not originally part of 1QS and are merely an alternate form of 1QS 8:5b–7.

There was additional scribal reworking at the end of line 10. In adding the new materials, the scribe was forced to write small letters between lines 9 and 10 in order to make it all fit. He therefore had to erase an earlier superlinear inscription, *betammim derekh,* then to erase *yibadelu,* which had been on line 10, insert the words *betammim derekh* on the line in place of *yibadelu* (in somewhat smaller than ordinary writing), and transfer *yibadelu* to a superlinear position above the next line.

An awareness of all this scribal activity, together with a comparison with 4Q258 and 4Q259, makes it possible to recover an early, short version of the text for 1QS 8:1–16. For lines 8:4–10, the uncorrected, unexpanded wording of 1QS is the shortest—and presumably therefore the earliest—form of this material. Lines 8:11–16 can be pared down in straightforward manner using the two Cave Four texts. The resulting text of 8:1–16 would seem to be the earliest form recoverable of the Original Manfesto of the *Yahad.*

In the process of arriving at this text, one gets a glimpse of one way in which the *Manual of Discipline* grew. Growth was not always due to changes in the group or widespread new developments of ideas; it happened simply because this or that text happened to be available to a particular scribe for comparison. Doubtless the scribes were often themselves *Maskilim* (on which see below). The copies of the *Manual of Discipline* were books they were copying out for themselves from available *Vorlagen,* seeking books and availing themselves of whatever opportunities might arise, much in the manner of other scholars in the Greco-Roman world of whom the Greek papyri speak.

27. The original short form of the Laws for Life (equivalent to 1QS 5–7, now best attested by 4Q258) preserves an early name for the group not found in the longer Laws of 1QS, "the council of the men of the Yahad" *(atsat anshe ha-yahad).* Since this term is essentially that of the Manifesto (and may actually appear in 4Q259 1 iii 1–2), it may be surmised that the Manifesto is describing the entire early community and not, as some scholars have thought, an elite council within its membership. A literal translation of 8:1, read in the indicative mood just as the rules of Hebrew grammar would normally require, is therefore preferable. There is no longer any reason to suppose that this statement is idealizing or modal, as has often been suggested, for example, by James Charlesworth: "there *are to be* twelve (lay)men and three priests," *The Dead Sea Scrolls: Hebrew, Aramaic and Greek Texts with English Translations:*

Volume 1, Rule of the Community and Related Documents (Tübingen: J. B. Mohr, 1994), 35, emphasis mine.

28. 1QH 16:6.

29. Such appears to be the correct reading of 4Q259 ad loc, as suggested by Elisha Qimron in Charlesworth, *Dead Sea Scrolls,* 86.

30. Timothy P. Weber, *Living in the Shadow of the Second Coming: American Premillennialism, 1875–1925* (New York: Oxford, 1979), 105. For the following discussion of American premillennialists I rely upon chap. 5 of this book.

31. T. Weber, *Second Coming,* 109–10.

32. T. Weber, *Second Coming,* 115.

33. T. Weber, *Second Coming,* 119.

34. For the purposes of the argument, the following are the manuscripts that I consider certainly sectarian and the dates proposed by their official editors. References for the manuscripts in question are scattered throughout the professional literature; specialists can consult the relevant *editiones principes* for specific details; I have felt it unnecessary to present them in cumbersome fashion here.

SERIES NUMBER	NAME	Q-NUMBER	PROPOSED DATE
1.	Community Rule (Serek Ha-Yahad, 1QSa, 1QSb)	1Q28–1Q28b	100–75 B.C.E.
2.	Serek a	4Q255	100 B.C.E.
3.	Serek b	4Q256	30–1 B.C.E.
4.	Serek c	4Q257	30–1 B.C.E.
5.	Serek d	4Q258	100–75 B.C.E.
6.	Serek e	4Q259	50–25 B.C.E.
7.	Serek f	4Q260	30–1 B.C.E.
8.	Serek g	4Q261	50–1 B.C.E.
9.	Serek h	4Q262	1–50 C.E.
10.	Serek i	4Q263	30–1 B.C.E.
11.	Serek j	4Q264	50–25 B.C.E.
12.	Serek z	4Q264a	No date proposed
13.	Serek	5Q11	25–50 C.E. (? "tardive")
14.	Damascus Document	4Q266	100–50 B.C.E.
15.	Damascus Document	4Q267	30–1 B.C.E.
16.	Damascus Document	4Q268	30 B.C.E.–20 C.E.
17.	Damascus Document	4Q269	30 B.C.E.–1 C.E.
18.	Damascus Document	4Q270	1–50 C.E.
19.	Damascus Document	4Q271	50–25 B.C.E.
20.	Damascus Document	4Q272	30–1 B.C.E.
21.	Damascus Document	4Q273	25–1 B.C.E.
22.	Damascus Document	5Q12	50–1 B.C.E.
23.	Damascus Document	6Q15	100–1 B.C.E.

SERIES NUMBER	NAME	Q-NUMBER	PROPOSED DATE
24.	War Scroll	1Q33	30–1 B.C.E.
25.	War Scroll	4Q491	50–1 B.C.E.
26.	War Scroll	4Q492	30–1 B.C.E.
27.	War Scroll	4Q493	100–50 B.C.E.
28.	War Scroll	4Q494	30–1 B.C.E.
29.	War Scroll	4Q495	30–1 B.C.E.
30.	War Scroll	4Q496	50 B.C.E.
31.	Miqsat Maase Ha-Torah (MMT)	4Q394	30–1 B.C.E.
32.	MMT	4Q395	30–1 B.C.E.
33.	MMT	4Q396	30 B.C.E.–20 C.E.
34.	MMT	4Q397	30–1 B.C.E.
35.	MMT	4Q398	30–1 B.C.E.
36.	MMT	4Q399	20–50 C.E.
37.	Songs of the Sabbath Sacrifice	4Q400	75–50 B.C.E
38.	Songs of the Sabbath Sacrifice	4Q401	25 B.C.E.
39.	Songs of the Sabbath Sacrifice	4Q402	25 B.C.E.
40.	Songs of the Sabbath Sacrifice	4Q403	25–1 B.C.E.
41.	Songs of the Sabbath Sacrifice	4Q404	25 B.C.E.
42.	Songs of the Sabbath Sacrifice	4Q405	50 B.C.E.
43.	Songs of the Sabbath Sacrifice	4Q406	No date proposed
44.	Songs of the Sabbath Sacrifice.	4Q407	50 B.C.E
45.	Songs of the Sabbath Sacrifice	11Q17	20–50 C.E.
46.	Thanksgiving Hymns (Hodayot)	1Q35	30–1 B.C.E.
47.	Hodayot copy b	1Q35b	30–1 B.C.E.
48.	Hodayot a	4Q427	75–25 B.C.E.
49.	Hodayot b	4Q428	80 B.C.E.
50.	Hodayot c	4Q429	75–25 B.C.E.
51.	Hodayot d	4Q430	30–1 B.C.E.
52.	Hodayot e	4Q431	30–1 B.C.E.
53.	Hodayot f	4Q432	30–1 B.C.E.
54.	Commentary on Isaiah A	4Q161	30–1 B.C.E.
55.	Commentary on Isaiah B	4Q162	50–25 B.C.E.
56.	Commentary on Isaiah C	4Q163	50 B.C.E.
57.	Commentary on Isaiah D	4Q164	30–1 B.C.E.

SERIES NUMBER	NAME	Q-NUMBER	PROPOSED DATE
58.	Commentary on Isaiah E	4Q165	30–1 B.C.E.
59.	Commentary on Hosea A	4Q166	30–1 B.C.E.
60.	Commentary on Hosea B	4Q167	30–1 B.C.E.
61.	Commentary on Micah (?)	4Q168	30–1 B.C.E.
62.	Commentary on Nahum	4Q169	50–35 B.C.E.
63.	Commentary on Zephaniah	4Q170	No date proposed
64.	Commentary on Psalms A	4Q171	30–1 B.C.E.
65.	Commentary on Psalms B	4Q173	50–25 B.C.E.
66.	Commentary on Habakkuk	1QpHab	30–1 B.C.E.
67.	Commentary on Micah	1Q14	No date proposed
68.	Commentary on Zephaniah	1Q15	No date proposed
69.	Commentary on Psalms	1Q16	No date proposed
70.	Commentary on Isaiah	3Q4	30–1 B.C.E. ("Herodian")
71.	Florilegium	4Q174	30–1 B.C.E.
72.	Testimonium	4Q175	125–100 B.C.E.
73.	Tanhumim	4Q176	50–25 B.C.E.
74.	Catena A	4Q177	30–1 B.C.E.
75.	Ages of Creation	4Q180	50 C.E.
76.	Ages of Creation	4Q181	30–1 B.C.E.
77.	Catena B	4Q182	30–1 B.C.E.
78.	Historical Work	4Q183	30–1 B.C.E.
79.	Melchizedek	11Q13	50–25 B.C.E.
80.	Serek and Damascus Medley	4Q265	No date proposed
81.	Prayer of Michael	4Q471b	20–50 C.E.
82.	War Scroll (*sic*)	4Q471	30 B.C.E.–70 C.E. ("Herodian")
83.	Serek Ha-Milhamah	4Q285	50–20 B.C.E.
84.	Berakhot (*sic*)	11Q14	50 B.C.E.
85.	Decrees	4Q477	30 B.C.E.–20 C.E.
86.	Ritual of Purification	4Q512	100 B.C.E.
87.	Berakhot a	4Q286	1–20 C.E. ("Early first century")
88.	Berakhot b	4Q287	1–20 C.E.
89.	Berakhot c	4Q288	1–20 C.E.
90.	Berakhot d	4Q289	1–20 C.E.
91.	Berakhot e	4Q290	1–20 C.E.
92.	Berakhot f	4Q280	50 B.C.E.
93.	Songs of the Sage a	4Q510	25–1 B.C.E.
94.	Songs of the Sage b	4Q511	1 B.C.E. ("Herodian, turn of the eras")
95.	Liturgical text	1Q30–31	No date proposed

SERIES NUMBER	NAME	Q-NUMBER	PROPOSED DATE
96.	Commentary on Genesis A	4Q252	30–1 B.C.E. ("Herodian")
97.	Ways of Righteousness A	4Q420	No date proposed
98.	Ways of Righteousness B	4Q421	No date proposed
99.	Men of People Who Err	4Q306	No date proposed
100.	Words of Sage to Sons of Dawn	4Q298	No date proposed
101.	Temple Scroll a	11Q19	1 B.C.E. ("Turn of the eras")
102.	Temple Scroll b	11Q20	1 B.C.E. ("Turn of the eras")
103.	Tohorot a	4Q274	30–1 B.C.E.
104.	Tohorot g	4Q284a	40 B.C.E.
105.	Horoscope	4Q186	No date proposed
106.	Otot	4Q319	50–25 B.C.E.
107.	Liturgy of Baptism	4Q414	No date proposed

Note that Devorah Dimant, "The Qumran Manuscripts: Contents and Significance," in *Time to Prepare the Way in the Wilderness,* ed. D. Dimant and L. Schiffman (Leiden: Brill, 1995), 23–58, has recently tried to isolate sectarian works among the scrolls. She concludes that about a third of the nonbiblical works are products of the "Qumran community," a group she thinks lived at the site of Qumran. She goes wrong, in my view—and so arrives at a higher estimate than mine—by including as "sectarian" many works that do not manifest the elements that definitely align a given writing with the central works of 1QS, the *Damascus Document,* etc. For example, she includes 4Q471a simply because "its polemical character suggests a classification with [the Qumran community's] works." Did no other Second Temple Jewish group engage in polemics, then? She includes hymnic writings such as *Barki Nafshi,* which has no specifically sectarian character that she can point out. She likewise includes many miscellaneous poetic fragments whose sentiments would be acceptable to many Jews of the time and have no identifiable sectarian features: 4Q369, 1Q36–40, 3Q6, etc. She includes a fair number of writings that I would view as products of the precursor movement or related circles: 4Q504–6, Sapiential Work A and B, the *Book of Mysteries* (4Q299–301, 1Q27), etc. Thus, though Dimant should be credited with helping to develop a methodology for distinguishing among the nonbiblical scrolls from Qumran, she has failed to prosecute her own methodology in a consistent way, and she includes many texts for reasons outside her defining criteria for "sectarian."

35. I hope to argue this suggestion in a future publication. By the years 45–35 B.C.E. I refer to what the conventional schema designates the final quadrant of the first century B.C.E., the time designated Late Hasmonean–Early Herodian. I believe the scripts changed more rapidly in the first century B.C.E. than the once-per-generation rate conventionally maintained.

36. For example, the *Community Rule* specified quorums of ten men for biblical study: *Wherever ten men belonging to the Society of the Yahad are gathered, a priest must always be present.* 1QS 6:3–4, translation mine from Wise, Abegg, Cook, *Dead Sea Scrolls*, 133.

37. On the growth of Christianity, see Rodney Stark, *The Rise of Christianity: A Sociologist Reconsiders History* (Princeton: Princeton Univ. Press, 1996), 4–12. On the growth of the Mormon Church, see Rodney Stark, "The Rise of a New World Faith," *Review of Religious Research* 26 (1984): 18–27, and "Modernization and Mormon Growth," in *A Sociological Analysis of Mormonism*, ed. M. Cornwall, T. B. Heaton, and L. Young (Champaign: Univ. of Illinois Press, 1994), 1–23.

38. Stark, *Rise of Christianity*, 55.

39. Stark, *Rise of Christianity*, 56–57, emphasis his. Compare William Sims Bainbridge, *The Sociology of Religious Movements* (New York: Routledge, 1996), 168:

> Religious conversion is only partly a matter of faith; it is also a process of affiliation with a social group, and the history of a sect or other religious movements is greatly controlled by the rates of conversion and defection of individual members. . . . Processes of social bonding alone may be responsible for success or failure of religious movements. Research on voluntary organizations in general, including nonreligious as well as religious groups, confirms the importance of social bonds both in holding an individual in a group and drawing him or her out, perhaps to join a competing group.

40. CD 15:6–13. With slight variation I follow Cook in Wise, Abegg, Cook, *Dead Sea Scrolls*, 65.

41. CD 15:5–6. With slight variation I follow Cook in Wise, Abegg, Cook, *Dead Sea Scrolls*, 65.

42. This is a point made to me by Hartmut Stegemann in Göttingen in July 1997, while we enjoyed a very pleasant evening meal together.

43. 1QS 6:1–8, according to my translation in Wise, Abegg, Cook, *Dead Sea Scrolls*, 133–34.

44. Jonathan Butler, "From Millerism to Seventh-day Adventism: 'Boundlessness to Consolidation,'" *Church History* 55 (1986): 55.

45. 1QpHab 7:6–13. I have substantially reworked here the translation of Cook in Wise, Abegg, Cook, *Dead Sea Scrolls*, 119.

46. Reprinted in Francis D. Nichol, *The Midnight Cry* (Washington, DC: Review and Herald Publishing Association, 1944), 262. The same statement also appeared in *The Advent Herald* of November 13, 1844.

47. These allusions, whether to event, person, or process, and their dates or date ranges, together with source, are the following: the high priesthood of Onias III, 174 B.C.E. (all subsequent dates are B.C.E.), 4Q245; the taking of Jerusalem by Antiochus IV Epiphanes, 170/69, *Commentary on Nahum*; the high priesthood of Jonathan Maccabee, 161–143/42, 4Q245; the high priesthood of Simon Maccabee, 143/42–135/34, 4Q245; one or more events involving John Hyrcanus I (Yohanan), 135/34–104, 4Q324[b]; John Hyrcanus as false prophet, 135/34–104, 4Q339 (uncer-

tain); the reign of Alexander Jannaeus, 103–76, 4Q448; one or more events of his reign, 4Q523 (uncertain); the invasion of Demetrius III at Pharisee invitation, 88, *Commentary on Nahum;* the crucifixion of Pharisee supporters of Demetrius by Alexander, 88, *Commentary on Nahum* and *Commentary on Hosea*[b] (for 4QpHos[b] 2 1–7, see Menahem Kister, "Biblical Phrases and Hidden Biblical Interpretations and *Pesharim,*" in *The Dead Sea Scrolls: Forty Years of Research,* ed. D. Dimant and U. Rappaport [Leiden: Brill, 1992], 30–31 and discussion); an event involving Alexandra, 76–67, 4Q322; a second event involving her, 4Q324[b]; the shift of power over Temple activities from Alexander's faction to the Pharisees, 76, *Damascus Document* and 4QMMT; the rebellion of Hyrcanus II against Aristobulus II, 67, 4Q322; the flight of Hyrcanus II to the Nabateans, 67, 4Q322; the civil war between these two brothers and their supporters, 67–63, 4Q183 (see here Kister, "Biblical Phrases," 37 n. 27 and references. Kister makes the point that this *pesher* seems to locate the origin of the group near to the time of the civil war it describes and suggests that war may have been in the time of Jannaeus); an action against Aristobulus, 4Q323 (uncertain); the coming of the Roman general Pompey, 65, *Damascus Document;* the taking of Jerusalem by the Romans, 63, *Commentary on Nahum;* the defeat of Aristobulus and his faction, 63, *Commentary on Nahum;* the exile of Aristobulus, his family, and followers to Rome, 63, *Commentary on Nahum;* a murder or massacre involving the Roman general Aemilius Scaurus, 63–62, 4Q324[b]; a second murder or massacre involving him, 63–62, 4Q324[b]; the exaction of tribute by the Romans, 63, *Commentary on Habakkuk;* the establishment of Roman soldiers in Jerusalem after the war, 63–55, *Commentary on Nahum;* the rule of the Jews by a succession of Roman governors living in Syria, 63–40, *Commentary on Habakkuk;* Hyrcanus II's rebuilding of the walls of Jerusalem, 47, *Commentary on Habakkuk;* his being taken prisoner by the Parthians, 40, *Commentary on Psalms* and *Commentary on Habakkuk;* and the plunder of Jerusalem by the Roman army under Sosius, 37, *Commentary on Habakkuk.*

48. I include the events of 88 B.C.E. in this number because they were used to argue against Pharisee actions at the time of the civil war in 67–63 B.C.E.

49. Of 107 identifiable manuscripts produced by the Society, the official editors have suggested paleographic dates for ninety-four. Fifty-two percent of these manuscripts date to the Late Hasmonean–Early Herodian script phase. See note 34 above.

50. Butler, "Millerism," 58–59, emphasis mine.

51. The relatively few copies of the society's writings that were produced in the first century C.E. can be explained as the work of carriers, people who for one reason or another found the works valuable but who were not related to the original movement.

CHAPTER 10

1. Here I have adapted, with appropriate adjustments, the thrust of the comparison made by A. Dupont-Sommer in *The Dead Sea Scrolls: A Preliminary Survey* (Oxford: Basil Blackwell, 1952), 99.

2. Stephen Neill and Tom Wright, *The Interpretation of the New Testament, 1861–1986*, 2d ed. (New York: Oxford Univ. Press, 1988), 329.

3. Albert Schweitzer, *The Quest of the Historical Jesus: A Critical Study of Its Progress from Reimarus to Wrede* (New York: Macmillan, 1968), 76.

4. For an incisive conspectus, see William R. Teleford, "Major Trends and Interpretive Issues in the Study of Jesus," in *Studying the Historical Jesus: Evaluations of the State of Current Research*, ed. B. Chilton and C. Evans (Leiden: Brill, 1994), 33–74.

5. I borrow the terminology of "vertical" and "horizontal" from John Dominic Crossan in his many writings.

6. Kurt Aland, ed., *Synopsis of the Four Gospels* (Stuttgart: Württembergische Bibelanstalt, 1976), 131–32.

7. Robin Lane Fox, *The Unauthorized Version* (London: Viking Penguin, 1991; New York: Random House, 1993), 294.

8. Central publications of the Jesus Seminar include Robert Funk, Bernard Scott, and J. R. Butts, eds., *The Parables of Jesus: Red Letter Edition* (Sonoma, CA: Polebridge, 1988); and Robert Funk and Roy Hoover, eds., *The Five Gospels: The Search for the Authentic Words of Jesus* (New York: Macmillan, 1993). John Dominic Crossan's central work is *The Historical Jesus: The Life of a Mediterranean Jewish Peasant* (San Francisco: HarperSanFrancisco, 1991); for Burton Mack, see *A Man of Innocence: Mark and Christian Origins* (Philadelphia: Fortress, 1988); for F. Gerald Downing, *Christ and the Cynics: Jesus and Other Radical Preachers in First Century Tradition* (Sheffield: Sheffield Academic Press, 1988). Marcus Borg's primary writings include *Conflict, Holiness, and Politics in the Teachings of Jesus* (Lewiston, NY: Mellen, 1984) and *Jesus: A New Vision* (San Francisco: HarperSanFrancisco, 1987). Geza Vermes has made his principal contribution in *Jesus the Jew: A Historian's Reading of the Gospel*, 2d ed. (New York: Macmillan, 1983), *Jesus and the World of Judaism* (Philadelphia: Fortress, 1984), and *The Religion of Jesus the Jew* (Minneapolis: Augsburg Fortress, 1993). E. P. Sanders has written *Jesus and Judaism* (Philadelphia: Fortress, 1985) and *The Historical Figure of Jesus* (London: Penguin, 1993), while Maurice Casey is author of *From Jewish Prophet to Gentile God: The Origins and Development of New Testament Christology* (Louisville, KY: Westminster/John Knox, 1991). For Richard Horsley, see his *Jesus and the Spiral of Violence* (San Francisco: HarperSanFrancisco, 1987) and *Sociology and the Jesus Movement* (New York: Crossroad, 1989); Gerd Thiessen has written several important books, including *Sociology of Early Palestinian Christianity* (Philadelphia: Fortress, 1978). John Meier is the author of a mammoth work in progress, *A Marginal Jew*, 2 vols. (New York: Doubleday, 1991–). James Dunn's works include *Jesus and the Spirit* (Philadelphia: Westminster, 1975). Marinus de Jonge has penned *Jesus, the Servant Messiah* (New Haven: Yale Univ. Press, 1991), and N. T. Wright is producing *The New Testament and the People of God*, 2 vols. (Minneapolis: Fortress, 1992–). For the capsule descriptions, I follow the witty summaries of Ben Witherington III, *The Jesus Quest* (Downers Grove, IL: IVP, 1995).

9. F. Dreyfus, *Jésus savait-il qu'il était Dieu?* (Paris: Cerf, 1984); R. E. Brown,

"Did Jesus Know He Was God?" *Biblical Theology Bulletin* 15 (1985): 74–79; G. Rochais, "Jésus savait-il qu'il était Dieu? Réflexions critiques à propos d'un livre récent," *Studies in Religion/Sciences religieuses* 14 (1985): 85–106; B. F. Meyer, *The Aims of Jesus* (London: SCM, 1979); R. Leivestad, "Jesus-Messias-Menschensohn: Die jüdischen Heilandserwartungen zur Zeit der ersten römischen Kaiser und die Frage nach dem messianischen Selbstbewusstsein Jesu," *Anstieg und Niedergang der römischen Welt* 2.25.1 (1982): 220–64; O. Betz, "Die Frage nach dem messianischen Bewusstsein Jesu," *Novum Testamentum* 6 (1963): 20–48. The question of Jesus' self-understanding is central also to Sanders's argument about Jesus' action in the Temple, in *Historical Figure*.

10. The question in so many words actually appears on the back of the cover, but it is integral to the content of much of the material between the covers.

11. Thucydides 1.22.4.

12. Norman Cohn, *The Pursuit of the Millennium,* rev. ed. (New York: Oxford Univ. Press, 1970), 284, emphasis his.

13. J. J. M. Roberts, "The Old Testament's Contribution to Messianic Expectations," in *The Messiah: Developments in Earliest Judaism and Christianity,* ed. J. H. Charlesworth (Minneapolis: Fortress Press, 1992), 41.

14. Michael Wise, Martin Abegg, Edward Cook, *The Dead Sea Scrolls: A New Translation* (San Francisco: HarperSanFrancisco, 1996), 119, following Cook's translation.

15. Arthur Koestler, *Arrow in the Blue* (New York: Macmillan, 1952), 195–98. The quotations are from 196–97.

16. Anthony Storr, *Feet of Clay* (New York: Free Press, 1996), 152.

17. For profiles of Horowitz, see the *Jerusalem Post* for Wednesday, November 6, 1996 (Features), and Francis X. Clines's column "On Sunday" in the *New York Times* of Sunday, August 14, 1994. See also David M. Eichhorn, ed., *Conversion to Judaism: A History and Analysis* (New York: Ktav, 1965), 163–64. I thank James Tabor for bringing these materials to my attention.

18. The phrase was addressed to Guibbory in a letter from Horowitz dated November 1, 1981. The letter is evidence of his feelings nearly forty years after he and Guibbory had gone their separate ways.

19. David Horowitz, *Thirty-Three Candles* (New York: World Union Press, 1949), 156.

20. The comment was made by Horowitz to James Tabor on more than one occasion. Tabor informed me of it in an interview on April 10, 1998. The subsequent quotations are from Horowitz, *Thirty-Three Candles,* 158–62.

21. For these paragraphs on Koresh I rely upon several lengthy interviews with James Tabor that took place on February 27, 1996; March 1, 1998; and April 10, 1998.

22. Luke 24:13–14, 25–27, 32.

23. I thank James Tabor for focusing my attention on this example.

24. The translation of 4Q521 Frag. 2 + Frag. 4 Col. 2:1–13 follows, with modifications, Abegg in Wise, Abegg, Cook, *Dead Sea Scrolls,* 421. For the *editio princeps,* see É. Puech, "4Q Apocalypse Messianique (4Q521)," *Revue de Qumran* 15 (1992):

475–522. Further on this text, see my joint articles with James Tabor, "The Messiah at Qumran," *Biblical Archaeology Review* 18, no. 6 (1992): 60–65, and "4Q521 'On Resurrection' and the Synoptic Gospel Tradition: A Preliminary Study," *Journal for the Study of the Pseudepigrapha* 10 (1992): 151–63.

25.   This is a point that Tabor and I made in "Messiah at Qumran," 65, but it is more sharply focused in Graham Stanton, *Gospel Truth?: New Light on Jesus and the Gospels* (Valley Forge, PA: Trinity Press International, 1995), 187.

INDEX